D1199277

SHURLEY ENGLISH

07-15
2013 Edition
Level 3 Student Textbook

ISBN 978-1-58561-242-0
ISBN 978-1-58561-240-6 (Book A)
ISBN 978-1-58561-241-3 (Book B)

Copyright © 2013 by Shurley Instructional Materials, Inc.
No part of this book may be reproduced or transmitted in any form or by any means,
electronic or mechanical, including photocopying, recording, or by any information
storage or retrieval system, without written permission from the Publisher.

Printed in the United States of America by RR Donnelley, Roanoke, VA.

For additional information or to place an order, write to: Shurley Instructional Materials, Inc.
366 SIM Drive
Cabot, AR 72023

1 2   15 13

Table of
Contents

Table of Contents

CHAPTER 1

CHAPTER 2

Table of Contents

CHAPTER 3

CHAPTER 4

Table of Contents

CHAPTER 5

CHAPTER 6

Lesson 1

Lesson 2

Lesson 3

Lesson 4

Lesson 5

Lesson 6

Lesson 7

CHAPTER 7

Lesson 1

Lesson 2

Lesson 3

Lesson 4

Table of Contents

CHAPTER 9

Table of Contents

CHAPTER 12

CHAPTER 12 (cont'd)

Table of Contents

Table of Contents

CHAPTER 18

CHAPTER 19

CHAPTER 19 (cont'd)

Lesson 6

Lesson 7

CHAPTER 20

Lesson 1

Lesson 2

Lesson 3

Lesson 4

Lesson 5

Lesson 6

Lesson 7

Lesson 8

Lesson 9

Quick Reference

Unit Studies

Start
Book B

Jingle Time

Listening and Speaking

Jingle 21   The Direct Object Jingle

A **direct object** is a NOUN
Or a PRO,
Is a noun or a pro,
Is a noun or a pro.
A **direct object**
Completes the meaning,
Completes the meaning
Of the sentence.

A **direct object** follows the verb,
Follows the *verb-transitive*.

To find a direct object,
Ask **WHAT** or **WHOM**
Ask **WHAT** or **WHOM**
After the verb.

What?   Whom?

Grammar Time

Direct Object, Verb-transitive, and Pattern 2

You have studied one sentence pattern so far. Look at the core of a Pattern 1 sentence.

→ **Pattern 1 core:** one noun and a verb (**SN V**)

Today, you will learn another sentence pattern, Pattern 2, which has **two nouns** and a **verb** (**noun-verb-noun**) for its core. To understand Pattern 2, you must first understand its core parts, the **subject noun**, **transitive verb**, and **direct object**: (**SN V-t DO**)

SN   V-t   A DO
Nana made a cake.

Direct Object, Verb-transitive, and Pattern 2

Direct Object

1. A **direct object** is a noun or pronoun in the predicate that receives the action of the verb.

2. The direct object does not mean the same thing as the subject noun.

3. To find the direct object, ask *what* or *whom* AFTER the verb.

4. A **direct object** is labeled with the abbreviation **DO**.

   ➡ Example: **SN   V-t   A   DO**
   　　　　　Nana made a cake.

   ➡ **Nana made what? cake - direct object**

Transitive Verbs

1. If there is a direct object in the sentence, the verb is a transitive verb.

2. A **transitive verb** is an action verb that transfers action from the subject to the direct object.

3. A **transitive verb** is labeled with the abbreviation **V-t**, which stands for **verb-transitive**.

Pattern 2

1. Sentence Patterns identify the order of the core parts of sentences. The second pattern, **Pattern 2**, has *three* core parts: a Subject Noun (**SN**), a Verb-transitive (**V-t**), and a Direct Object (**DO**).

2. **Pattern 2** is identified by its core parts: **SN V-t DO P2** (*Subject Noun, Verb-transitive, Direct Object, Pattern 2*).

CONTINUED ON NEXT PAGE

Lesson 1

Adding Direct Objects and Verb-transitive to the Question and Answer Flow

Sample Sentence: **Nana made a cake.**

1. Who made a cake?
   Nana – Subject Noun .... (Write **SN** above *Nana.*)

2. What is being said about *Nana*?
   Nana made – Verb .... (Write **V** above *made.*)

3. Nana made what? **cake – verify the noun**
   Note: This check is to make sure the second noun
   does not mean the same thing as the subject noun.

4. Does *cake* mean the same thing as *Nana*? **No**

5. **Cake – Direct Object** .... (Write **DO** above *cake.*)

6. **Made – Verb-transitive** .... (Write **-t** above *made.*)
   Note: The main verb is labeled with a **V** until the direct object has been identified.
   Then, add a "t" to the main verb to identify it as transitive. Always get the core,
   SN V-t DO, before you classify the rest of the sentence.

7. **A – Article Adjective** .... (Write **A** above *a.*)

8. **Subject Noun, Verb-transitive, Direct Object, Pattern 2**
   (Write **SN V-t DO P2** in the blank.)

9. **Skill Check!**

   ➥ **Verb-transitive – check again**
   (This check is to make sure the "**t**" is added to the verb.)

   ➥ No prepositional phrases

   ➥ **Period, statement, declarative sentence**
   (Write **D** at the end of the sentence.)

   ➥ Go back to the verb.
   Divide the complete subject from the complete predicate.

   ➥ Is this sentence in a natural or inverted order? **Natural – no change**

```
                    SN    V-t  A  DO
 SN V-t         Nana / made  a cake.  D
 DO P2
```

Discussion Questions:

1. What is a noun called that receives the action of the verb and does not mean the same thing as the subject?

2. Where is the direct object located?

3. What kind of verb transfers action from the subject to the direct object?

4. What are the core parts of a Pattern 2 sentence?

5. What are the pattern labels in a Pattern 2 sentence?

Review: Sentence Patterns

→ **Pattern 1** is **SN V**. It has a **noun-verb** (**N V**) core.

→ **Pattern 2** is **SN V-t DO**. It has a **noun-verb-noun** (**N V N**) core.

The location of a noun determines its job in a sentence. Only certain noun jobs form the pattern parts of a sentence. A noun that is an object of the preposition is not part of a sentence pattern.

Classifying Sentences

Classify the Introductory Sentences with your teacher, using the Question and Answer Flow. Classifying these sentences will help you learn direct objects and transitive verbs.

Introductory Sentences   ORAL PARTICIPATION

1. _____ Two eagles built a nest.

2. _____ Two beautiful eagles built a large nest high above the river.

3. _____ Mom and Travis met Dad at the airport.

Noun Check
Adding Direct Objects

Now that you have classified the Introductory Sentences, it is time to do a Noun Check. During a Noun Check, you identify nouns doing different noun jobs. Today, you will add the **direct object** to the Noun Check. Now, recite the Noun Check with your teacher.

Noun Check Introductory Sentences

Circle the nouns in the sentences.

Sentence 1: Two (eagles) built a (nest.)

> Subject Noun **eagles**, *yes, it is a noun;*
> Direct Object **nest**, *yes, it is a noun.*

Sentence 2: Two beautiful (eagles) built a large (nest) high above the (river.)

> Subject Noun **eagles**, *yes, it is a noun;*
> Direct Object **nest**, *yes, it is a noun;*
> Object of the Preposition **river**, *yes, it is a noun.*

Sentence 3: (Mom) and (Travis) met (Dad) at the (airport.)

> Compound Subject Noun **Mom**, *yes, it is a noun;*
> Compound Subject Noun **Travis**, *yes, it is a noun;*
> Direct Object **Dad**, *yes, it is a noun;*
> Object of the Preposition **airport**, *yes, it is a noun.*

Are there any Possessive Nouns in the sentences? **No**

Bringing It All Together
The Noun Chart Adding Direct Objects

The Noun Chart below adds the direct object and reviews the other information about nouns that you have learned. Discuss the Noun Chart below with your teacher.

Reference 140

Noun Chart

Directions: Use Sentence 3 to complete the table below.

3. **SN V-t**
   DO P2   Mom and Travis / met Dad **(**at the airport**).**   **D**

            CSN   C   CSN   V-t   DO   P   A   OP

LIST THE NOUNS USED	NOUN JOB	SINGULAR or PLURAL	COMMON or PROPER	SIMPLE SUBJECT	SIMPLE PREDICATE
Mom	CSN	S	P	Mom, Travis	met
Travis	CSN	S	P		
Dad	DO	S	P		
airport	OP	S	C		

Guided Practice

Directions: Classify these sentences on notebook paper.

1. _____ Sam watched TV after dinner.

2. _____ Kate baked brownies for dessert.

3. _____ Rake the leaves today.

Directions: Use the sentences above to answer the following questions.

1. What are the subjects?

2. What are the direct objects?

3. What are the transitive verbs?

JOURNAL WRITING **20**

Write an entry in your notebook journal or digital journal. Before you begin your journal entry, write one or two sentences with a direct object. Then, try to include at least one sentence with a direct object in your entry.

Listening and Speaking

Practice Jingle 21 in the Jingle Section. **PAGE Q10**

Classifying Sentences

Classify the Practice Sentences with your teacher, using the Question and Answer Flow.

Practice Sentences   ORAL PARTICIPATION

1. _____ Yesterday, we planted our vegetable garden.

2. _____ After the storm, our neighborhood had trash and tree limbs everywhere!

3. _____ April showers bring May flowers.

Word Study

Sentence 3 is a common **adage**, or traditional saying. Adages are one way people have passed wisdom from one generation to the next. In this case, the wisdom preserved is that sometimes bad things cause good things to happen: a gloomy, rainy April will lead to a cheerful and colorful May!

Noun Check

Now that you have classified the Practice Sentences, it is time to do a Noun Check. A Noun Check helps you identify information about each noun in a sentence. Recite the Noun Check with your teacher.

Noun Check

☐ 1. **Identify the nouns in a Noun Check.**
(Say the job and the noun. Circle each noun.)

☐ 2. **Identify the nouns as singular or plural.**
(Write **S** or **P** above the noun.)

☐ 3. **Identify the nouns as common or proper.**
(Write **C** or **P** above the noun.)

Skill Time

Simple Verb Tenses

Nouns and verbs have many jobs. Throughout the year, you have been learning about different jobs of nouns. Now, you will learn some of the different jobs of verbs.

Simple Verb Tenses

Verbs can tell time. Within every verb is a little piece of information called its **tense**. The **tense** of a verb tells you when the action of the verb takes place. The word **tense** means **time**. There are three simple verb tenses that show when an action takes place: *present* tense, *past* tense, and *future* tense.

1. **Present Tense:** A verb in the present tense shows action that is happening now. Present-tense verbs can be singular or plural to agree with the subject.

   • **(He talks. They talk.)**

2. **Past Tense:** A verb in the past tense shows action that has already happened. Many verbs in the past tense end with *–ed*.

   • **(We talked.)**

3. **Future Tense:** A verb in the future tense shows action that will happen later. Verbs in the future tense use the helping verbs *will* or *shall*.

   • **(They will talk.)**

> **Student Note:**
> The helping verb will is the form most often used to make verbs future tense, but you can also use the helping verb shall to make the simple future tense.

Directions: Identify the tense of the verb by checking the correct box.

VERB	SIMPLE PRESENT	SIMPLE PAST	SIMPLE FUTURE
1. stop	✓		
2. will eat			✓
3. talked		✓	
4. listen	✓		
5. shall sing			✓
6. studied		✓	

Guided Practice

Directions: Identify the tense of the verb by checking the correct box.

VERB	SIMPLE PRESENT	SIMPLE PAST	SIMPLE FUTURE
1. dance			
2. will run			
3. skated			
4. push			
5. shall see			
6. rained			

Writing Tip...

Use the simple verb tenses correctly in your writing.

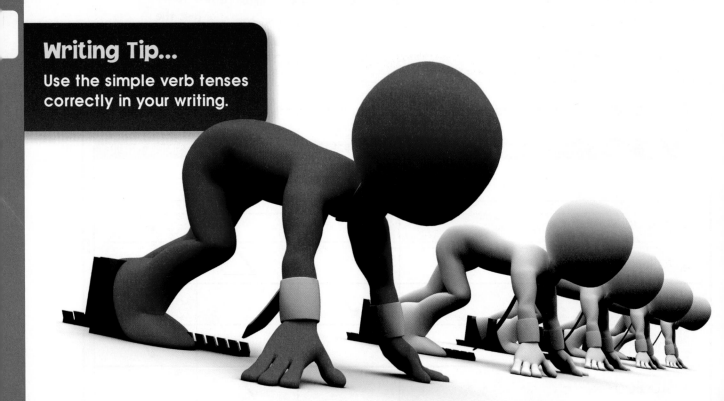

Lesson 2

Classroom Practice 46

Name: _____ Date: _____

GRAMMAR:

Exercise 1: Classify each sentence.

1. _____ Kelly bought a new computer for college.

2. _____ Yeah! Our teacher allowed fifteen extra minutes for recess!

Exercise 2: Use **Sentence 2** above to complete the table below.

LIST THE NOUNS USED	NOUN JOB	SINGULAR or PLURAL	COMMON or PROPER	SIMPLE SUBJECT	SIMPLE PREDICATE

SKILLS:

Exercise 3: Identify the tense of the verb by checking the correct box.

VERB	SIMPLE PRESENT	SIMPLE PAST	SIMPLE FUTURE
1. work			
2. will play			
3. ate			
4. spelled			
5. shall give			
6. start			
7. began			
8. try			
9. will fall			
10. turn			

Listening and Speaking

Practice Jingle 21 in the Jingle Section. **PAGE Q10**

Classifying Sentences

Classify the Practice Sentences with your teacher, using the Question and Answer Flow.

Practice Sentences ORAL PARTICIPATION

1. _____ Oh, no! My crazy dog is chasing the neighbor's cat around our yard!

2. _____ Did Carson share his book report with the class yesterday?

3. _____ In two weeks, Jesse's mom will begin a new job at the bank.

Noun Check

Now that you have classified the Practice Sentences, it is time to do a Noun Check. A Noun Check helps you identify information about each noun in a sentence. Recite the Noun Check with your teacher.

Noun Check

☐ 1. **Identify the nouns in a Noun Check.**
(Say the job and the noun. Circle each noun.)

☐ 2. **Identify the nouns as singular or plural.**
(Write **S** or **P** above the noun.)

☐ 3. **Identify the nouns as common or proper.**
(Write **C** or **P** above the noun.)

Review: Parts of Speech

REMINDER: How a word is used in a sentence determines its part of speech. What are the eight parts of speech?

What are the labels for the eight parts of speech?

Skill Time

Review: Simple Verb Tenses

The word **tense** means **time**. The three simple verb tenses show that an action takes place in the present, past, or future.

1. A verb in the simple **present** tense shows that an action is happening now.
2. A verb in the simple **past** tense shows that an action has already happened.
3. A verb in the simple **future** tense shows that an action will happen later.

Reference 142

Regular and Irregular Verbs

Verbs are divided into two groups: **regular** and **irregular**.

1. **Regular Verbs:** A main verb is regular if it is made past tense by adding an *–ed* ending:

   ## talk ⟹ talked

2. **Irregular Verbs:** A main verb is irregular if it is made past tense by making a spelling change:

   ## sing ⟹ sang

To decide if a verb is regular or irregular, do these things:

- Look only at the main verb.
- Decide if the past tense is made by adding an *–ed* or by making a spelling change.
- Compare the present- and past-tense forms to verify your decision.

Directions: Compare the present and past tense of the main verb. Determine how the past tense is made to help you decide whether it is regular or irregular. Then, write **R** for Regular or **I** for Irregular.

VERBS	PRESENT TENSE FORM	PAST TENSE FORM	MADE PAST TENSE BY	R or I
1. run	**run**	**ran**	spelling change	**I**
2. will stop	**stop**	**stopped**	adding –ed	**R**
3. ate	**eat**	**ate**	spelling change	**I**

Guided Practice

Directions: Check the correct box to identify the tense of the verb. Then, write the present and past tense of the main verb. Write **R** for Regular or **I** for Irregular.

VERBS	SIMPLE PRESENT	SIMPLE PAST	SIMPLE FUTURE	PRESENT-PAST TENSE FORMS OF THE MAIN VERB	R or I
1. will blow			✓	**blow/blew**	**I**
2. help					
3. looked					
4. come					
5. drank					

Writing Tip...

Use regular and irregular verbs correctly in your writing.

Name: _____ Date: _____

GRAMMAR:

Exercise 1: Classify each sentence.

1. _____ Today, Carlos and Anna rode their bikes around the block.

2. _____ Mom had turkey sandwiches and fresh fruit for lunch.

Exercise 2: Use **Sentence 2** above to complete the table below.

LIST THE NOUNS USED	NOUN JOB	SINGULAR or PLURAL	COMMON or PROPER	SIMPLE SUBJECT	SIMPLE PREDICATE

SKILLS:

Exercise 3: Identify the tense of the verb by checking the correct box.
Then, write the past tense of the main verb. Write **R** for Regular or **I** for Irregular.

VERBS	SIMPLE PRESENT	SIMPLE PAST	SIMPLE FUTURE	PAST TENSE FORMS OF THE MAIN VERB	R or I
1. help					
2. rode					
3. will blow					
4. looked					
5. will open					
6. come					
7. will run					
8. tried					
9. saw					
10. will sit					

Jingle Time

Listening and Speaking

Practice Jingle 21 in the Jingle Section. **PAGE Q10**

♪ Jingle 22 — The Object Pronoun Jingle

There are seven
Object pronouns
That are easy as can be.
OBJECT PRONOUNS!

Me and **Us**,
Him and **Her**,
It and **Them** and **You**.
Those are the object pronouns!

Object Pronouns

So far, you have learned about two kinds of pronouns, the subject pronoun and the possessive pronoun. Today, you will learn a third kind of pronoun, the **object pronoun**.

Reference 143

Object Pronouns

1. An **object pronoun** is a pronoun that is used in any noun job that has the word *object* in it. You have studied two objects: **object of the preposition** and **direct object**.

2. Only certain pronouns can be used as object pronouns: *me*, *us*, *him*, *her*, *it*, *them*, and *you*. Use the Object Pronoun Jingle to remember these object pronouns.

3. Object pronouns do not have a special label of their own. An **object pronoun** is labeled with the abbreviation of the job it does in the sentence: **OP** or **DO**.

   ➡ Examples:

                                                            OP

   Nana made a birthday cake for him.

                  DO

   Dad took us to the zoo.

Adding Object Pronouns to the Question and Answer Flow

Sample Sentence: ▸ **Dad took us to the zoo.**

1. Who took us to the zoo?
Dad - Subject Noun .... (Write **SN** above *Dad.*)

2. What is being said about *Dad*?
Dad took - Verb .... (Write **V** above *took.*)

3. Dad took whom? **us - verify the pronoun**

4. Does the pronoun *us* mean the same thing as *Dad*? **No**

5. **Us - Direct Object** .... (Write **DO** above *us.*)
Note: The **object pronoun** us is labeled **DO** as the **direct object** of the sentence.

6. **Took - Verb-transitive** .... (Write **-t** above *took.*)

7. **To - Preposition** .... (Write **P** above *to.*)

8. To what? **zoo - Object of the Preposition** .... (Write **OP** above *zoo.*)

9. **The - Article Adjective** .... (Write **A** above *the.*)

10. **Subject Noun, Verb-transitive, Direct Object, Pattern 2**
(Write **SN V-t DO P2** in the blank.)

11. **Skill Check!**

➡ **Verb-transitive - check again**

➡ **(To the zoo) - Prepositional Phrase**

➡ **Period, statement, declarative sentence**
(Write **D** at the end of the sentence.)

➡ Go back to the verb.
Divide the complete subject from the complete predicate.

➡ Is this sentence in a natural or inverted order? **Natural - no change**

```
              SN    V-t   DO  P    A    OP
 SN V-t    Dad /took  us (to  the  zoo). D
 DO P2
```

Classifying Sentences

Classify the Introductory Sentences with your teacher, using the Question and Answer Flow. Classifying these sentences will help you learn object pronouns.

Introductory Sentences

ORAL PARTICIPATION

1. _____ You will find me at the pool.

2. _____ You will find Edward and me at the community pool today.

3. _____ Did the jury make a quick decision about the case?

Pronoun Cases

You have already learned about subject, possessive, and object pronouns through the pronoun jingles. Now, you will learn that these pronouns are grouped into **pronoun cases**.

The case of a pronoun shows whether it is being used as a subject, an object, or a possessive. Personal pronouns are grouped into three cases: *subjective* for subject pronouns, *objective* for object pronouns, and *possessive* for possessive pronouns.

Usually, the pronouns in the subjective and objective cases are the ones that give us the most trouble. Learning about pronoun cases will help you know how to use pronouns correctly.

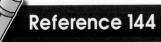

Reference 144

Pronoun Cases

The pronouns in the example below all refer to the same person, but they have three different forms because of their different uses in the sentence.

I carried my toothbrush with me.

Subjective Case   Possessive Case   Objective Case

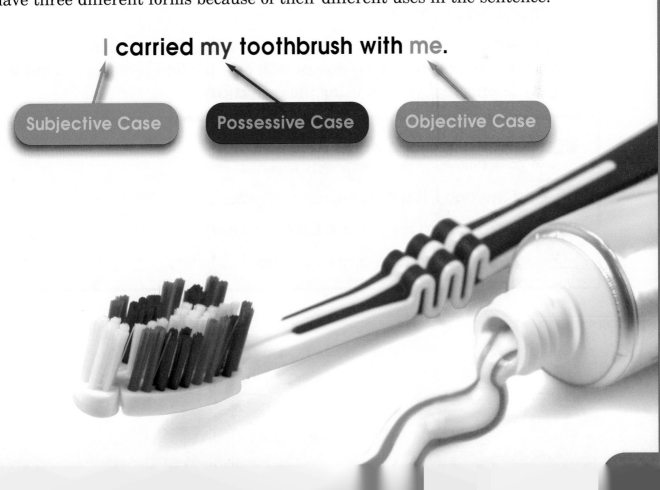

Pronoun Cases

1. Subjective Case Pronouns

Pronouns that are used as **subjects** are in the subjective case.

➡ SP: **He went to work.**

> **Subjective Case:**
>
> **I, we, he, she, it, they,** and **you**

2. Objective Case Pronouns

Pronouns that are used as **objects** of the prepositions and direct objects are in the objective case.

➡ OP: **The principal talked to** me **after class.**

➡ DO: **Mom took** me **to the zoo.**

> **Objective Case:**
>
> **me, us, him, her, it, them,** and **you**

3. Possessive Case Pronouns

Pronouns that are used to **show ownership** are in the possessive case.

➡ PPA: **Luke walked to** his **office.**

> **Possessive Case:**
>
> **my, our, his, her, its, their,** and **your**

Compound Pronouns

Many people often confuse subject pronouns and object pronouns when they are compound. Reading the sentence with only the first pronoun is a quick way to determine if you are using the correct case.

Directions: Write **S** for subjective, **O** for objective, or **P** for possessive in the blank. Underline the correct answer in parentheses.

S 1. (**She and I**, **Her and me**) drove home.

O 2. Dora looked for (**he and I**, **him and me**).

O 3. Lucy phoned (**she and I**, **her and me**) today.

GRAMMAR AVE.
SKILL ST.

Guided Practice

Directions: Write **S** for subjective, **O** for objective, or **P** for possessive in the blank. Underline the correct answer in parentheses.

__S__ 1. (**They**, **Them**) rode to town on the bus.

____ 2. Justin whispered to Fred and (**I, me**).

____ 3. The big dog looked straight at (**we, us**).

____ 4. We slept in (**us, our**) new tent.

Case Check

After you have classified the Introductory Sentences, you will do a **Case Check**. During a Case Check, you will say the pronoun, identify its job, and then tell its case. **Subject** pronouns are in the subjective case, **possessive** pronouns are in the possessive case, and **object** pronouns are in the objective case.

Object pronouns are easy to identify. Any pronoun that uses the letter **O** as part of its classified label is in the objective case because the **O** stands for *object*: **DO** for **direct object** and **OP** for **object of the preposition**. Now, recite the Case Check with your teacher.

Case Check Introductory Sentences

Sentence 1: You will find me at the pool.

you: subject pronoun, *subjective case*

me: direct object pronoun, *objective case*

Sentence 2: You will find Edward and me at the community pool today.

you: subject pronoun, *subjective case*

me: compound direct object pronoun, *objective case*

Sentence 3: Did the jury make a quick decision about the case?

None

Cases for Compound Pronouns

Many people often confuse subject pronouns and object pronouns when they are compound. In sentences with pronouns as compound subjects or as compound objects, you must pay careful attention to whether the pronouns are acting as the subject of the sentence or as an object.

It is important to use compound subject pronouns and compound object pronouns in the correct places. The **subject pronouns** (*I, we, he, she, it,* and *they*) should only be used as the subject of a sentence. The object pronouns (*me, us, him, her, it,* and *them*) should only be used as the object in a sentence. The pronoun *you* can be used as a subject or as an object.

CORRECT He and I went to the lake.
→ He went to the lake.
→ I went to the lake.

INCORRECT Him and me went to the lake.
→ Him went to the lake.
→ Me went to the lake.

CORRECT Jack went to town with him and me.
→ Jack went to town with him.
→ Jack went to town with me.

INCORRECT Jack went to town with he and I.
→ Jack went to town with he.
→ Jack went to town with I.

Student Tip...

A handy trick for determining whether a compound pronoun should be an object pronoun or a subject pronoun is to cover the conjunction and the other compound part with your finger. Then, read the sentence with just the pronoun. The correct pronoun will sound much more natural than the incorrect one.

ACTIVITY — Using Compound Pronouns Correctly

With a partner, recite the incorrect sample and then the correct sample for each set. Listen to each one very carefully. Listening to compound pronouns and knowing how they are used in the sentence will help you select the correct case.

Next, write a sentence using a compound subject or compound object pronoun correctly. Then, break the compound pronouns into single pronouns in separate sentences, like the examples.

Noun Check
Identifying Direct Objects as Pronouns

Now, it is time to do a Noun Check. During a Noun Check, you identify nouns in different noun jobs. You must decide whether the direct object is a noun or a pronoun. If it is a noun, it will be circled. If it is a pronoun, it will not be circled. Now, recite the Noun Check with your teacher.

Noun Check Introductory Sentences

Circle the nouns in the sentences.

Sentence 1: You will find me at the (pool.)

Subject Noun **you**, *no, it is a pronoun;*

Direct Object **me**, *no, it is a pronoun;*

Object of the Preposition **pool**, *yes, it is a noun.*

Sentence 2: You will find (Edward) and me at the community (pool) today.

Subject Noun **you**, *no, it is a pronoun;*

Compound Direct Object **Edward**, *yes, it is a noun;*

Compound Direct Object **me**, *no, it is a pronoun;*

Object of the Preposition **pool**, *yes, it is a noun.*

Sentence 3: Did the (jury) make a quick (decision) about the (case)?

Subject Noun **jury**, *yes, it is a noun;*

Direct Object **decision**, *yes, it is a noun;*

Object of the Preposition **case**, *yes, it is a noun.*

Are there any Possessive Nouns in the sentences? **No**

Skill Time

Review: Simple Verb Tenses

The word **tense** means *time*. The three simple verb tenses show that an action takes place in the present, past, or future.

1. A verb in the simple **present** tense shows that an action is happening now.

2. A verb in the simple **past** tense shows that an action has already happened.

3. A verb in the simple **future** tense shows that an action will happen later.

Review of Regular and Irregular Verbs

Verbs are divided into two groups: **regular** and **irregular**.

A verb is **regular** if it is made past tense by adding an *–ed* ending to the main verb.

A verb is **irregular** if it is made past tense by making a spelling change.

Verb Chants

In a Verb Chant, you will recite each form of the verbs in the chart below, one after the other in a lively manner. This will help you learn the forms of some common regular and irregular verbs. Recite the Verb Charts with your teacher.

Verb Chart for Regular Verbs

COLUMN 1 PRESENT TENSE	COLUMN 2 PAST TENSE	COLUMN 3 HV PLUS AN -ED MAIN VERB	COLUMN 4 HV PLUS AN -ING MAIN VERB
help	helped	(has, have, had) helped	(am, is, are, was, were) helping
jog	jogged	(has, have, had) jogged	(am, is, are, was, were) jogging

Verb Chart for Irregular Verbs

COLUMN 1 PRESENT TENSE	COLUMN 2 PAST TENSE	COLUMN 3 HV PLUS AN -ED MAIN VERB		COLUMN 4 HV PLUS AN -ING MAIN VERB	
become	became	(has, have, had)	become	(am, is, are, was, were)	becoming
begin	began	(has, have, had)	begun	(am, is, are, was, were)	beginning
blow	blew	(has, have, had)	blown	(am, is, are, was, were)	blowing
break	broke	(has, have, had)	broken	(am, is, are, was, were)	breaking
bring	brought	(has, have, had)	brought	(am, is, are, was, were)	bringing
buy	bought	(has, have, had)	bought	(am, is, are, was, were)	buying
choose	chose	(has, have, had)	chosen	(am, is, are, was, were)	choosing
come	came	(has, have, had)	come	(am, is, are, was, were)	coming

End Lesson 4

Name: _____ Date: _____

GRAMMAR:

Exercise 1: Classify each sentence.

1. _____ Marcus and I saw her yesterday at the ballpark.

2. _____ Ouch! The thorns on that rosebush scratched the

   top of my hand!

Exercise 2: Write **S** for subjective, **O** for objective, or **P** for possessive in the blank.
Underline the correct answer in parentheses.

____ 1. Will you save a seat for Shane and (**me, I**)?

____ 2. I played video games with (**my, me**) brother.

____ 3. Jesse and (**me, I**) sat on the top row.

____ 4. Will you help Zach and (**me, I**) with math?

SKILLS:

Exercise 3: Write the four parts of the verbs **save** and **throw**.

COLUMN 1 PRESENT TENSE	COLUMN 2 PAST TENSE	COLUMN 3 HV PLUS AN *-ED* MAIN VERB	COLUMN 4 HV PLUS AN *-ING* MAIN VERB

Exercise 4: Identify the tense of the verb by checking the correct box.
Then, write the past tense of the main verb. Write **R** for Regular or **I** for Irregular.

VERBS	SIMPLE PRESENT	SIMPLE PAST	SIMPLE FUTURE	PAST TENSE FORMS OF THE MAIN VERB	R or I
1. will become					
2. save					
3. climbed					
4. will drive					
5. throw					

Listening and Speaking

Practice Jingles 21 and 22 in the Jingle Section. **PAGE Q10**

Mixed Patterns

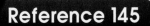
Reference 145

Mixed Patterns 1–2

So far, you have classified Pattern 1 and Pattern 2 sentences separately.
Today, you will practice classifying a mix of Pattern 1 and Pattern 2
sentences. Study the two sentence patterns shown. As you classify the
sentences, pay close attention to the core parts of each sentence.
This will help you decide which pattern to choose.

→ **Pattern 1 is SN V.**
  It has a **noun-verb (N V)** core.

  ➡ Example:

           A   SN   V   P A   Adj   OP

$\dfrac{\text{SN V}}{\text{P1}}$ The boys / played **(**on the baseball field**)**. **D**

→ **Pattern 2 is SN V-t DO.**
  It has a **noun-verb-noun (N V N)** core.

  ➡ Example:

           A   SN   V-t   DO

$\dfrac{\text{SN V-t}}{\text{DO P2}}$ The boys / played baseball. **D**

Classifying Mixed Patterns 1-2

Classify the Introductory Sentences with your teacher, using the Question and Answer Flow.

Introductory Sentences   ORAL PARTICIPATION

1. _____ Yesterday, we painted our house.

2. _____ They took us to the parade.

3. _____ The leaves swayed gently in the breeze.

4. _____ Tony raked and burned the leaves for us.

Checks and Chants

Now that you have classified the Introductory Sentences, recite the Case Check, Noun Check, and Verb Chant with your teacher. These checks help you analyze nouns, pronouns, and verbs and understand how they are used in sentences.

Case Check Introductory Sentences

Sentence 1: Yesterday, we painted our house.

we: subject pronoun, *subjective case*

our: possessive pronoun, *possessive case*

Sentence 2: They took us to the parade.

they: subject pronoun, *subjective case*

us: direct object pronoun, *objective case*

Sentence 3: The leaves swayed gently in the breeze.

None

Sentence 4: Tony raked and burned the leaves for us.

us: object of the preposition pronoun, *objective case*

REMINDER: Any pronoun that uses the letter **O** as part of its classified label is in the objective case because the **O** stands for *object*: **DO** for direct *object* and **OP** for *object* of the preposition.

Noun Check

Do a Noun Check with the sentences just classified.

☐ 1. **Identify the nouns in a Noun Check.**
(Say the job and the noun. Circle each noun.)

☐ 2. **Identify the nouns as singular or plural.**
(Write **S** or **P** above the noun.)

☐ 3. **Identify the nouns as common or proper.**
(Write **C** or **P** above the noun.)

Verb Chant

Recite the Verb Chant with your teacher.

Verb Chart for Regular Verbs

COLUMN 1 PRESENT TENSE	COLUMN 2 PAST TENSE	COLUMN 3 HV PLUS AN -ED MAIN VERB		COLUMN 4 HV PLUS AN -ING MAIN VERB	
look	looked	(has, have, had)	looked	(am, is, are, was, were)	looking
open	opened	(has, have, had)	opened	(am, is, are, was, were)	opening

Verb Chart for Irregular Verbs

COLUMN 1 PRESENT TENSE	COLUMN 2 PAST TENSE	COLUMN 3 HV PLUS AN -ED MAIN VERB		COLUMN 4 HV PLUS AN -ING MAIN VERB	
cut	cut	(has, have, had,)	cut	(am, is, are, was, were,)	cutting
do	did	(has, have, had)	done	(am, is, are, was, were)	doing
drink	drank	(has, have, had)	drunk	(am, is, are, was, were)	drinking
drive	drove	(has, have, had)	driven	(am, is, are, was, were)	driving
eat	ate	(has, have, had)	eaten	(am, is, are, was, were)	eating
fall	fell	(has, have, had)	fallen	(am, is, are, was, were)	falling
fly	flew	(has, have, had)	flown	(am, is, are, was, were)	flying
freeze	froze	(has, have, had)	frozen	(am, is, are, was, were)	freezing

Skill Time

Review: Simple Verb Tenses

The word **tense** means *time*. The three simple verb tenses show that an action takes place in the present, past, or future.

1. A verb in the simple **present** tense shows that an action is happening now.

2. A verb in the simple **past** tense shows that an action has already happened.

3. A verb in the simple **future** tense shows that an action will happen later.

Review of Regular and Irregular Verbs

Verbs are divided into two groups: **regular** and **irregular**.

A verb is **regular** if it is made past tense by adding an –*ed* ending to the main verb.

A verb is **irregular** if it is made past tense by making a spelling change.

Subject-Verb Agreement for Regular and Irregular Verbs

Regular and irregular verbs in present tense must follow the subject-verb agreement rules:

1. Adding **–s** to verbs makes them singular—*s* means *singular*.
   With a singular subject, use a singular verb (add **–s** to the end).
   He talks. She talks. It talks. Paula talks.   The nurse talks.
   He sings. She sings. Paula sings.   The nurse sings.

2. Not adding **–s** to verbs makes them plural.
   With a plural subject, use a plural verb (don't add **–s** to the end).
   They talk. We talk. Paula and Pam talk.   The nurses talk.
   They sing. We sing. Paula and Pam sing.   The nurses sing.

EXCEPTIONS: Do not add **–s** if the subject is *I* or *you*.
   I talk. You talk. I sing. You sing.

Verb Chart for Regular Verbs

COLUMN 1 PRESENT TENSE	COLUMN 2 PAST TENSE	COLUMN 3 HV PLUS AN -ED MAIN VERB		COLUMN 4 HV PLUS AN -ING MAIN VERB	
help	helped	(**has**, have, had)	helped	(am, **is**, are, was, were)	helping
jog	jogged	(**has**, have, had)	jogged	(am, **is**, are, was, were)	jogging
look	looked	(**has**, have, had)	looked	(am, **is**, are, was, were)	looking
open	opened	(**has**, have, had)	opened	(am, **is**, are, was, were)	opening
play	played	(**has**, have, had)	played	(am, **is**, are, was, were)	playing
spell	spelled	(**has**, have, had)	spelled	(am, **is**, are, was, were)	spelling
start	started	(**has**, have, had)	started	(am, **is**, are, was, were)	starting
try	tried	(**has**, have, had)	tried	(am, **is**, are, was, were)	trying
turn	turned	(**has**, have, had)	turned	(am, **is**, are, was, were)	turning
work	worked	(**has**, have, had)	worked	(am, **is**, are, was, were)	working

The room **was freezing** after I **opened** the door.

Verb Chart for Irregular Verbs

COLUMN 1 PRESENT TENSE	COLUMN 2 PAST TENSE	COLUMN 3 HV PLUS AN -ED MAIN VERB		COLUMN 4 HV PLUS AN -ING MAIN VERB	
become	became	(**has**, have, had)	become	(am, **is**, are, was, were)	becoming
begin	began	(**has**, have, had)	begun	(am, **is**, are, was, were)	beginning
blow	blew	(**has**, have, had)	blown	(am, **is**, are, was, were)	blowing
break	broke	(**has**, have, had)	broken	(am, **is**, are, was, were)	breaking
bring	brought	(**has**, have, had)	brought	(am, **is**, are, was, were)	bringing
buy	bought	(**has**, have, had)	bought	(am, **is**, are, was, were)	buying
choose	chose	(**has**, have, had)	chosen	(am, **is**, are, was, were)	choosing
come	came	(**has**, have, had)	come	(am, **is**, are, was, were)	coming
cut	cut	(**has**, have, had)	cut	(am, **is**, are, was, were)	cutting
do	did	(**has**, have, had)	done	(am, **is**, are, was, were)	doing
drink	drank	(**has**, have, had)	drunk	(am, **is**, are, was, were)	drinking
drive	drove	(**has**, have, had)	driven	(am, **is**, are, was, were)	driving
eat	ate	(**has**, have, had)	eaten	(am, **is**, are, was, were)	eating
fall	fell	(**has**, have, had)	fallen	(am, **is**, are, was, were)	falling
fly	flew	(**has**, have, had)	flown	(am, **is**, are, was, were)	flying
freeze	froze	(**has**, have, had)	frozen	(am, **is**, are, was, were)	freezing
get	got	(**has**, have, had)	gotten	(am, **is**, are, was, were)	getting
give	gave	(**has**, have, had)	given	(am, **is**, are, was, were)	giving
go	went	(**has**, have, had)	gone	(am, **is**, are, was, were)	going
grow	grew	(**has**, have, had)	grown	(am, **is**, are, was, were)	growing
know	knew	(**has**, have, had)	known	(am, **is**, are, was, were)	knowing
lay	laid	(**has**, have, had)	laid	(am, **is**, are, was, were)	laying
lie	lay	(**has**, have, had)	lain	(am, **is**, are, was, were)	lying
lose	lost	(**has**, have, had)	lost	(am, **is**, are, was, were)	losing
make	made	(**has**, have, had)	made	(am, **is**, are, was, were)	making
ride	rode	(**has**, have, had)	ridden	(am, **is**, are, was, were)	riding
ring	rang	(**has**, have, had)	rung	(am, **is**, are, was, were)	ringing
rise	rose	(**has**, have, had)	risen	(am, **is**, are, was, were)	rising
run	ran	(**has**, have, had)	run	(am, **is**, are, was, were)	running
say	said	(**has**, have, had)	said	(am, **is**, are, was, were)	saying
see	saw	(**has**, have, had)	seen	(am, **is**, are, was, were)	seeing
sell	sold	(**has**, have, had)	sold	(am, **is**, are, was, were)	selling
sing	sang	(**has**, have, had)	sung	(am, **is**, are, was, were)	singing
sink	sank	(**has**, have, had)	sunk	(am, **is**, are, was, were)	sinking
set	set	(**has**, have, had)	set	(am, **is**, are, was, were)	setting
shoot	shot	(**has**, have, had)	shot	(am, **is**, are, was, were)	shooting
sit	sat	(**has**, have, had)	sat	(am, **is**, are, was, were)	sitting
speak	spoke	(**has**, have, had)	spoken	(am, **is**, are, was, were)	speaking
swim	swam	(**has**, have, had)	swum	(am, **is**, are, was, were)	swimming
take	took	(**has**, have, had)	taken	(am, **is**, are, was, were)	taking
teach	taught	(**has**, have, had)	taught	(am, **is**, are, was, were)	teaching
tell	told	(**has**, have, had)	told	(am, **is**, are, was, were)	telling
throw	threw	(**has**, have, had)	thrown	(am, **is**, are, was, were)	throwing
wear	wore	(**has**, have, had)	worn	(am, **is**, are, was, were)	wearing
write	wrote	(**has**, have, had)	written	(am, **is**, are, was, were)	writing

Name: _____ Date:_____

GRAMMAR:

Exercise 1: Classify each sentence.

1. _____ Several large ripe red tomatoes fell off the vines in the garden.

2. _____ After the party, we searched our house for Amanda's lost bracelet.

Exercise 2: Write **S** for subjective, **O** for objective, or **P** for possessive in the blank. Underline the correct answer in parentheses.

_____ 1. (**They, Them**) are playful kittens.

_____ 2. We saw (**he and she, him and her**) tonight.

_____ 3. Jackie gave the tickets to Cindy and (**I, me**).

_____ 4. We bought (**us, our**) house in March.

SKILLS:

Exercise 3: Write the four parts of the verbs **snow** and **take**.

COLUMN 1 PRESENT TENSE	COLUMN 2 PAST TENSE	COLUMN 3 HV PLUS AN -ED MAIN VERB	COLUMN 4 HV PLUS AN -ING MAIN VERB

Exercise 4: Identify the tense of the verb by checking the correct box. Then, write the past tense of the main verb. Write **R** for Regular or **I** for Irregular.

VERBS	SIMPLE PRESENT	SIMPLE PAST	SIMPLE FUTURE	PAST TENSE FORMS OF THE MAIN VERB	R or I
1. will snow					
2. take					
3. explained					
4. break					
5. began					

Listening and Speaking

Practice Jingles 21 and 22 in the Jingle Section. **PAGE Q10**

Classifying Mixed Patterns 1-2

Classify the Practice Sentences with your teacher, using the Question and Answer Flow.

Practice Sentences   ORAL PARTICIPATION

1. _____ We stopped at the pizza place for lunch.

2. _____ We ate pizza for lunch today.

3. _____ Will you make a cake for us?

4. _____ Will you stop at the bakery for a cake?

Reference 148

Identifying Pattern Numbers Only for Patterns 1-2

When classifying mixed patterns, you must concentrate on the core of each sentence. Since the core is the pattern of the sentence, classify only the main parts (**SN V**) and (**SN V-t DO**) without classifying all the other words in the sentence. Classify the core parts, determine the pattern, and write only the pattern number in the blank. With practice, you will be able to identify the pattern by sight.

Directions: Write the correct pattern number in each blank.
(**P1 = SN V, P2 = SN V-t DO**)

P2 1. Sarah made cookies for us.

P1 2. The small turtle crawled away.

P1 3. Rosemary walked around the track.

P2 4. We rode the bus to school today.

Guided Practice

Directions: Write the correct pattern number in each blank.
(**P1 = SN V, P2 = SN V-t DO**)

P2 1. I put my homework in my backpack.

_____ 2. I will write a note to your teacher.

_____ 3. Our canoe floated down the river.

_____ 4. The puppies played in the backyard.

_____ 5. My uncle trained my horse.

_____ 6. Mom made pancakes for us.

Checks and Chants

Now that you have classified the Practice Sentences, recite the Case Check, Noun Check, and Verb Chant with your teacher.

Case Check Practice Sentences

Sentence 1: |We| stopped at the pizza place for lunch.

we: subject pronoun, *subjective case*

Sentence 2: |We| ate pizza for lunch today.

we: subject pronoun, *subjective case*

Sentence 3: Will |you| make a cake for |us|?

you: subject pronoun, *subjective case*

us: object of the preposition pronoun, *objective case*

Sentence 4: Will |you| stop at the bakery for a cake?

you: subject pronoun, *subjective case*

Writing Tip...
Make sure you are using the correct case for each pronoun in your writing.

Noun Check
Do a Noun Check with the sentences just classified.

☐ 1. **Identify the nouns in a Noun Check.**
(Say the job and the noun. Circle each noun.)

☐ 2. **Identify the nouns as singular or plural.**
(Write **S** or **P** above the noun.)

☐ 3. **Identify the nouns as common or proper.**
(Write **C** or **P** above the noun.)

Verb Chant

Recite the Verb Chant with your teacher.

Verb Chart for Regular Verbs

COLUMN 1 PRESENT TENSE	COLUMN 2 PAST TENSE	COLUMN 3 HV PLUS AN -ED MAIN VERB		COLUMN 4 HV PLUS AN -ING MAIN VERB	
play	played	(has, have, had)	played	(am, is, are, was, were)	playing
spell	spelled	(has, have, had)	spelled	(am, is, are, was, were)	spelling

Verb Chart for Irregular Verbs

COLUMN 1 PRESENT TENSE	COLUMN 2 PAST TENSE	COLUMN 3 HV PLUS AN -ED MAIN VERB		COLUMN 4 HV PLUS AN -ING MAIN VERB	
get	got	(has, have, had)	gotten	(am, is, are, was, were)	getting
give	gave	(has, have, had)	given	(am, is, are, was, were)	giving
go	went	(has, have, had)	gone	(am, is, are, was, were)	going
grow	grew	(has, have, had)	grown	(am, is, are, was, were)	growing
know	knew	(has, have, had)	known	(am, is, are, was, were)	knowing
lose	lost	(has, have, had)	lost	(am, is, are, was, were)	losing
make	made	(has, have, had)	made	(am, is, are, was, were)	making
ride	rode	(has, have, had)	ridden	(am, is, are, was, were)	riding

Skill Time

Review: Simple Verb Tenses

The word **tense** means *time*. The three simple verb tenses show that an action takes place in the present, past, or future.

1. A verb in the simple **present** tense shows that an action is happening now.
2. A verb in the simple **past** tense shows that an action has already happened.
3. A verb in the simple **future** tense shows that an action will happen later.

Review of Regular and Irregular Verbs

Verbs are divided into two groups: **regular** and **irregular**.

A verb is **regular** if it is made past tense by adding an *–ed* ending to the main verb.

A verb is **irregular** if it is made past tense by making a spelling change.

Some Spelling Rules for Regular Verbs

1. When a regular verb ends with a **consonant** and **y**, change the **y** to **i** before adding **–ed**. (carr**y** ➡ carr**ied**)

2. When a regular verb ends with a **silent e**, drop the **e** before adding **–ed**. (smil**e** ➡ smil**ed**)

3. When a regular one-syllable verb ends with **one short vowel** and **one consonant**, double the consonant before adding **–ed**. (dr**op** ➡ dro**pped**)

4. Consult a dictionary if you are in doubt about the spelling of regular or irregular verb forms.

Lesson 6

Name: _____ Date:_____

GRAMMAR:

Exercise 1: Classify each sentence.

1. _____ Our friend invited us to a neighborhood picnic.

2. _____ A slippery fish on the seat of the canoe flipped

back into the water.

Exercise 2: Write the correct pattern number in each blank.
(P1 = SN V, P2 = SN V-t DO)

_____ 1. A wolf howled loudly.

_____ 2. Will you buy groceries today?

_____ 3. Did you hear the news?

_____ 4. The ladies baked for the holiday.

_____ 5. The ladies baked bread for us.

_____ 6. The monkey climbed the tree.

Exercise 3: Write **S** for subjective, **O** for objective, or **P** for possessive in the blank.
Underline the correct answer in parentheses.

_____ 1. (**They, Them**) are cute puppies.

_____ 2. The teacher talked to (**we, us**).

_____ 3. Will you ride with (**me, I**) to the store?

_____ 4. The family swam in (**their, them**) pool yesterday.

SKILLS:

Exercise 4: Write the four parts of the verbs **hop** and **tell**.

COLUMN 1 PRESENT TENSE	COLUMN 2 PAST TENSE	COLUMN 3 HV PLUS AN -ED MAIN VERB	COLUMN 4 HV PLUS AN -ING MAIN VERB

Exercise 5: Identify the tense of the verb by checking the correct box.
Then, write the past tense of the main verb. Write **R** for Regular or **I** for Irregular.

VERBS	SIMPLE PRESENT	SIMPLE PAST	SIMPLE FUTURE	PAST TENSE FORMS OF THE MAIN VERB	R or I
1. collected					
2. went					
3. fly					
4. will hop					
5. tells					

Chapter **12**

Word Time

Vocabulary and Analogy

Word 17 **abandon** (uh BAN duhn)

Definition: to leave behind or to forsake

Synonym: desert   **Antonym:** rescue

Sentence: Someone **abandoned** these poor little puppies!

Analogy **finger : hand :: toe : foot**

Relationship: Part-to-Whole

Thinking Process: Just as a **finger** is part of a whole **hand**, a **toe** is part of a whole **foot**. Therefore, this is a part-to-whole analogy.

ACTIVITY

Draw a picture or write a poem or story in your Vocabulary Notebook to help you remember the word abandon.

Picture Idea: Draw a rebus (picture puzzle) of the word **abandon**. Draw the following pictures in a straight line: a + picture of a band playing instruments + the word "done" in fancy letters. This rebus stands for **a + band + done = abandon**.

Spelling

Study this Spelling Rule to help you become a better speller.

Spelling Rule 6

Spelling with Silent Final **e**

Use a **silent final E** to make a short vowel **long** if the vowel is followed by a consonant or consonant blend (**CVCe**).

➥ Example: **cap ⟹ cape   past ⟹ paste**

English words don't end with **U** or **V**. If you see them, add a silent final **E**.

➥ Example: **true, blue, have, give**

English words don't end with the letter **J**. If you hear the ending **J** sound, use **-ge** or **-dge**. (Both **-ge** and **-dge** words end with a **silent final E**.)

➥ Example: **orange, edge**

Spelling Words For each word: **Recite**, **Spell**, and **Repeat**.

Recite note (A **CVC** pattern followed by **silent final e** makes the vowel long)

Spell n-o-t-e **Repeat** note

Recite fudge (an ending **j** sound, use **-ge** or **-dge**)

Spell f-u-d-g-e **Repeat** fudge

Recite give (if it ends in **u** or **v**, add **silent final e**)

Spell g-i-v-e **Repeat** give

1. **note**	3. **give**	5. **glue**
2. **fudge**	4. **range**	6. **kite**

Listening and Speaking

Practice Jingles 17 and 21–22 in the Jingle Section. **PAGES Q8, Q10**

Classifying Mixed Patterns 1-2

Classify the Practice Sentences with your teacher, using the
Question and Answer Flow.

Practice Sentences ORAL PARTICIPATION

1. _____ Remove the dish of hot potatoes from
   the oven very carefully.

2. _____ Mike and Chris are racing toward the
   ice-cream truck!

3. _____ Yesterday, we grilled steaks outside on
   our new barbecue grill.

4. _____ During the storm, the huge ocean waves
   crashed against the ship.

Word Study

Look at the word **steaks** in Sentence 3. The vowel pair in the middle of **steaks** (**–ea**) usually makes a **long e** sound. Using context clues, you can tell that the word must be pronounced with a long /**a**/ in the middle. You should know that the vowel pair **–ea** actually has three sounds in English: **ea** as in sn**ea**k, **ea** as in h**ea**d, and **ea** as in br**ea**k. In this case, the word steaks has a long /**a**/ sound in the middle. Together with a partner, create a chart, making three columns. Head each column with the examples provided: **ea** as in sn**ea**k, **ea** as in h**ea**d, and **ea** as in br**ea**k. Then, brainstorm and list examples under each **ea** vowel pair. Use a dictionary if needed.

The team headed east to eat a great steak.

Reference 149

Transitive and Intransitive Verbs

Verbs can be identified as transitive and intransitive. **Transitive verbs** are action verbs *with* a direct object. They are used in Pattern 2 sentences. **Intransitive verbs** are action verbs without a direct object. They are used in Pattern 1 sentences. Study the example below.

| **Transitive Verb** (action + **DO**) | **Intransitive Verb** (action + no **DO**) |

The children **played** basketball.   The children **played** in the park.

Directions: Identify the main verbs in the Practice Sentences as transitive or intransitive. Use **T** for transitive and **I** for intransitive.

1. Remove the dish of hot potatoes from the oven very carefully.
2. Mike and Chris are racing toward the ice-cream truck!
3. Yesterday, we grilled steaks outside on our new barbecue grill.
4. During the storm, the huge ocean waves crashed against the ship.

VERBS	T OR I	VERBS	T OR I
1. **remove**	T	3. **grilled**	T
2. **racing**	I	4. **crashed**	I

Lesson 7

Guided Practice

Exercise 1: Write the correct pattern number in each blank. (**P1 = SN V, P2 = SN V-t DO**)

P2 1. I left my coat at school.

_____ 2. Will you get some bread at the store?

_____ 3. Are you reading to the children?

_____ 4. The little kittens played with the string.

_____ 5. We found a cave in the forest.

_____ 6. They played volleyball on the beach.

Exercise 2: Write the main verbs in Exercise 1 and identify them with a **T** for transitive or an **I** for intransitive. Then, think of other sentences that use transitive and intransitive verbs.

VERBS	T OR I	VERBS	T OR I	VERBS	T OR I
1. left	**T**	3.		5.	
2.		4.		6.	

Noun Check and Verb Chart

Now that you have classified the Practice Sentences, it is time to do a Noun Check and a Verb Chant. A Noun Check helps you identify information about each noun in a sentence, and the Verb Chant reviews the main parts of verbs. Recite the Noun Check and Verb Chant with your teacher.

Noun Check

☐ 1. **Identify the nouns in a Noun Check.**
   (Say the job and the noun. Circle each noun.)

☐ 2. **Identify the nouns as singular or plural.**
   (Write **S** or **P** above the noun.)

☐ 3. **Identify the nouns as common or proper.**
   (Write **C** or **P** above the noun.)

Time

Review: Simple Verb Tenses

The word **tense** means *time*. The three simple verb tenses show that an action takes place in the present, past, or future.

1. A verb in the simple **present** tense shows that an action is happening now.

2. A verb in the simple **past** tense shows that an action has already happened.

3. A verb in the simple **future** tense shows that an action will happen later.

Review of Regular and Irregular Verbs

Verbs are divided into two groups: **regular** and **irregular**.

A verb is **regular** if it is made past tense by adding an *–ed* ending to the main verb.

A verb is **irregular** if it is made past tense by making a spelling change.

Name: _____ Date:_____

GRAMMAR:

Exercise 1: ▶ Classify each sentence.

1. _____ The neighbor's dog chased Matthew and me down the street!

2. _____ She drove very carefully through the heavy traffic.

Exercise 2: ▶ Write the correct pattern number in each blank.
(**P1 = SN V, P2 = SN V-t DO**)

_____ 1. My cat looked for the toy.

_____ 2. My cat chased the toy.

_____ 3. I played the drums in school.

_____ 4. Brad eats his cereal.

_____ 5. Are you doing your work?

_____ 6. Walk with us to school.

Exercise 3: ▶ Write the main verbs in Exercise 2 and identify them with a **T** for transitive or an **I** for intransitive.

VERBS	T OR I	VERBS	T OR I	VERBS	T OR I
1.		3.		5.	
2.		4.		6.	

End Lesson 7

SKILLS:

Exercise 4: Write **S** for subjective, **O** for objective, or **P** for possessive in the blank.
Underline the correct answer in parentheses.

____ 1. Did you call (**they, them**) at noon?

____ 2. (**You and I**), (**You and me**) are late.

Exercise 5: Write the four parts of the verbs **spell** and **buy**.

COLUMN 1 PRESENT TENSE	COLUMN 2 PAST TENSE	COLUMN 3 HV PLUS AN -ED MAIN VERB	COLUMN 4 HV PLUS AN -ING MAIN VERB

Exercise 6: Identify the tense of the verb by checking the correct box.
Then, write the past tense of the main verb. Write **R** for Regular or **I** for Irregular.

VERBS	SIMPLE PRESENT	SIMPLE PAST	SIMPLE FUTURE	PAST TENSE FORMS OF THE MAIN VERB	R or I
1. test					
2. knew					
3. speaks					
4. will spell					
5. buy					

Word Time

Vocabulary and Analogy

Word 18 ➤ **numeral** (NOOM uh ruhl)

Definition: a symbol that represents a number

Synonym: number   **Antonym:** None

Sentence: Can you read Roman **numerals**?

Etymology ➤ **Word History of numeral**

Latin Root: numerus (NOO muh ruhss)

Definition: number or quantity

Other words from the root: numerous, numerical

Analogy ➤ **numerous : humorous :: listened : glistened**

Relationship: Rhyming

Thinking Process: Just as **numerous** rhymes with **humorous**, **listened** rhymes with **glistened**. Therefore, this is a **rhyming** analogy.

ACTIVITY Draw a picture or write a poem or story in your Vocabulary Notebook to help you remember the word **numeral**.

Idea: Write as many Roman numerals as you can and put the Arabic number that stands for each one beside it. **Examples:**

Roman:	I	II	III	IV	V	VI	VII	VIII	IX	X
	↕	↕	↕	↕	↕	↕	↕	↕	↕	↕
Arabic:	1	2	3	4	5	6	7	8	9	10

Chapter 12

Review: Spelling

It's time to review what you've learned about spelling!

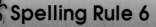

Spelling Rule 6

Spelling with Silent Final **e**

Use a **silent final E** to make a short vowel **long** if the vowel is followed by a consonant or consonant blend (**CVCe**).

➡ Example: **cap** ➥ **cape**   **past** ➥ **paste**

English words don't end with **U** or **V**. If you see them, add a silent final **E**.

➡ Example: **true, blue, have, give**

English words don't end with the letter **J**. If you hear the ending **J** sound, use **-ge** or **-dge**. (Both **-ge** and **-dge** words end with a **silent final E**.)

➡ Example: **orange, edge**

Spelling Words For each word: **Recite**, **Spell**, and **Repeat**.

Recite note (A CVC pattern followed by **silent final e** makes the vowel long)

 Spell n-o-t-e **Repeat** note

Recite fudge (an ending j sound, use **-ge** or **-dge**)

 Spell f-u-d-g-e **Repeat** fudge

Recite give (if it ends in **u** or **v**, add **silent final e**)

 Spell g-i-v-e **Repeat** give

1. **note**
2. **fudge**
3. **give**
4. **range**
5. **glue**
6. **kite**

Listening and Speaking

Practice Jingles 17 and 21–22 in the Jingle Section. **PAGES Q8, Q10**

Classifying Mixed Patterns 1-2

Classify the Practice Sentences with your teacher, using the Question and Answer Flow.

Practice Sentences   ORAL PARTICIPATION

1. _____ Are you going to your grandmother's house for the holidays?

2. _____ Julie and Dewayne play the drums in our school band.

3. _____ A tiny dog in the park bit Ryan on the foot!

4. _____ Beautiful, shade-loving plants lined the edge of our neighbor's yard.

Word Study

Did you notice that the adjectives describing plants in Sentence 4 are separated by a comma? The comma is necessary because the adjectives *beautiful* and *shade-loving* describe the same quality of plants. If the plants had been *big green plants* instead, no comma would be needed because *big* and *green* describe different qualities—size and color. When deciding whether to put a comma between adjectives describing the same noun, a handy rule of thumb is to read the sentence aloud, saying "and" between the adjectives. If it makes sense, use a comma. If it does not make sense, don't use a comma. For example, "beautiful and shade-loving plants" makes sense, but "big and green plants" does not.

Review: Parts of Speech

REMINDER: How a word is used in a sentence determines its part of speech. What are the eight parts of speech?

What are the labels for the eight parts of speech?

Writing Time

Blueprint for Building a Sentence

Today, you will learn how to add a Direct Object and Verb-transitive to your blueprint labels to write an original sentence.

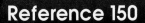

Reference 150

Designing a Sentence Blueprint,
Adding Direct Objects and Transitive Verbs

Design and build your sentence on Classroom Practice 52.

1. Use the core labels, **SN/SP**, **V-t**, and **DO**, only once and **in that order**.

2. The other labels, **Adj**, **Adv**, **A**, **P**, **OP**, **PPA**, **C**, **HV**, **I**, and **PNA**, can be used as many times as you wish, in any order you wish, as long as they make sense. (REMEMBER: Complete sense is one of the five parts of a complete sentence.)

3. **Instructions for the new labels, V-t and DO:** First, choose a verb that makes sense in your sentence. Write the verb under the **V-t** label. Then, think of a noun for the direct object by asking *what* or *whom* after the verb. Think of a different verb if you can't find a noun that makes sense. After the noun and verb fit, write the direct object noun under the **DO** label. NOTE: Sometimes, the direct object is a pronoun. If so, write it under the **DO** label.

4. Write the labels in the order you choose on the **Labels** line.

5. Write a word that makes sense for each label.

After writing your original sentence on Classroom Practice 52, use the revision strategies on page 532 to help you make revisions.

Use Revision Strategies to Revise Your Original Sentence

REMEMBER: Revising means looking for ways to improve your writing. As you revise your Original Sentence, write the abbreviation of the revision strategy you used under each word in your Revised Sentence.

1 Synonym (syn)   **2** Antonym (ant)   **3** Word Change (wc)

4 Added Word (add)   **5** Deleted Word (delete)   **6** No Change (nc)

When you have finished, your paper should resemble the example below.

Labels:	A	Adj	Adj	SN	V-t	A	Adj	DO
Original Sentence:	The		little	puppy	gave	a	loud	bark.
Revised Sentence:	The	frisky	little	puppy	gave	an	excited	yelp.
Revision Strategy:	(nc)	(add)	(nc)	(nc)	(nc)	(wc)	(wc)	(syn)

Student Tip...

1. Use your Vocabulary Words, Power Words, a thesaurus, and a dictionary to help you write your Original and Revised Sentences.

2. As you go through each word of your Original Sentence, think about the changes and improvements you want to make.

3. To help you improve your sentence, use your revision strategies.

4. As you revise your original sentence, keep this information in mind:

   • Antonyms and Word Changes will change your sentence's meaning.

   • Synonyms and No Changes will keep the meaning of the original sentence.

   • Added Words and Deleted Words can change the meaning of your sentence or keep it the same, depending on the words you choose to add or delete.

Name: _____

Date: _____

Exercise 1: Write your own blueprint labels. Use the labels to write an original sentence.
Then, revise your sentence, writing the abbreviation of the revision strategy under each word.

Labels:

Original Sentence:

Revised Sentence:

Revision Strategy:

Labels:

Original Sentence:

Revised Sentence:

Revision Strategy:

Exercise 2: Rewrite your revised sentence on the lines below. Use the checklist to check your sentence.

_____

Sentence Checklist: ☐ Capital letter ☐ Subject ☐ Verb ☐ Complete sense ☐ End mark

Lesson 8

Writing a *Mover* & **Shaker** Sentence in Your Journal:

Skip two lines below your last entry and write the date and chapter number. Then, skip one line and write a Mover & Shaker Sentence **with a repeated noun**. This is an amazing strategy that allows a writer to add more description with a distinctive flair. Repeat the noun at the end of a sentence; then, add more information about the repeated noun.

> **Simple Sentence:** A thief stole Sarah's diamond ring.
>
> *Mover* & **Shaker** **Sentence:** A thief stole Sarah's diamond ring, the ring that was one of a kind and very expensive!

Compare all of the Mover & Shaker Sentences you have written so far.

JOURNAL WRITING 21

Write an entry in your notebook journal or digital journal.
Use the spelling pattern in Spelling Rule 6 to help you spell words with a silent final **e** correctly.

Listening and Speaking

Practice Jingle 17 in the Jingle Section. **PAGE Q8**

Classifying Mixed Patterns 1-2

Classify the Practice Sentences with your teacher, using the
Question and Answer Flow.

Practice Sentences ORAL PARTICIPATION

1. _____ Yesterday, my little brother and sister took
   a very short nap.

2. _____ Are you and Diego going to the rodeo on
   Friday night?

3. _____ At the vegetable market, we bought corn,
   squash, and tomatoes.

4. _____ Ben and I made and sold several baskets
   and rugs.

Review: Transitive and Intransitive Verbs

Transitive verbs are action verbs with a direct object. They are used in Pattern 2 sentences. **Intransitive verbs** are action verbs without a direct object. They are used in Pattern 1 sentences. In the sentences that you just classified, which verbs are transitive? (*took, bought, made, sold*) Explain. (*They are action verbs with a direct object.*) Which verb is intransitive? (*going*) Explain. (*It is an action verb without a direct object.*)

Review: Regular and Irregular Verbs

Verbs are divided into two groups: **regular** and **irregular**.

A verb is regular if it is made past tense by adding an *–ed* ending to the main verb.

A verb is irregular if it is made past tense by making a spelling change.

Verb Chant

Recite the Verb Chant with your teacher.

Verb Chart for Regular Verbs

COLUMN 1 PRESENT TENSE	COLUMN 2 PAST TENSE	COLUMN 3 HV PLUS AN -ED MAIN VERB		COLUMN 4 HV PLUS AN -ING MAIN VERB	
start	started	(has, have, had)	started	(am, is, are, was, were)	starting
try	tried	(has, have, had)	tried	(am, is, are, was, were)	trying

Verb Chart for Irregular Verbs

COLUMN 1 PRESENT TENSE	COLUMN 2 PAST TENSE	COLUMN 3 HV PLUS AN -ED MAIN VERB		COLUMN 4 HV PLUS AN -ING MAIN VERB	
ring	rang	(has, have, had)	rung	(am, is, are, was, were)	ringing
rise	rose	(has, have, had)	risen	(am, is, are, was, were)	rising
run	ran	(has, have, had)	run	(am, is, are, was, were)	running
say	said	(has, have, had)	said	(am, is, are, was, were)	saying
see	saw	(has, have, had)	seen	(am, is, are, was, were)	seeing
sell	sold	(has, have, had)	sold	(am, is, are, was, were)	selling
sing	sang	(has, have, had)	sung	(am, is, are, was, were)	singing
sink	sank	(has, have, had)	sunk	(am, is, are, was, were)	sinking
swim	swam	(has, have, had)	swum	(am, is, are, was, were)	swimming
write	wrote	(has, have, had)	written	(am, is, are, was, were)	writing

Writing Time

Review: The Four Kinds of Sentences

Choose one of the following options:

1. Write a *declarative, exclamatory, interrogative,* and *imperative* sentence, using a different spelling word in each sentence. (*See Chapter 2 for a review of the four kinds of sentences.*)

2. Write a declarative sentence, using one of your spelling words. Then, change that sentence to the other three kinds of sentences (*exclamatory, interrogative,* and *imperative*).

3. Write a compound or complex declarative sentence, using at least one of your spelling words. (*See Chapter 7 for a review of compound and complex sentences.*)

For your sentences, use the spelling words from Rule 6:
note, fudge, give, range, glue, kite.

The Reading Club is a time to get into small groups and share a favorite book with others. Use the suggestions below to help you share your book.

◆ Give the title and author of the book. Show the book if you still have it.

◆ Describe a particular setting that is important to the story and tell where it is found in the book. Practice discussing how settings affect the plot of the story.

◆ Describe the main characters and tell something about them and discuss the specific evidence from the book that helps you focus your impressions about them.

◆ Tell what happens to the characters as the plot progresses. Be brief. Don't tell too much.

◆ Tell why you liked the book.

Write down the title and author of any book that you would like to read. Follow the Rules for Discussion and listen respectfully to other members of your group as different books are shared.

Name: _____ Date: _____

GRAMMAR:

Exercise 1: Classify each sentence.

1. _____ Dan and I bought apples, oranges, and bananas.

2. _____ Two beautiful swans glided gracefully around the pond.

Exercise 2: Write the correct pattern number in each blank.
(P1 = **SN V**, P2 = **SN V-t DO**)

_____ 1. Misty watches scary movies.

_____ 2. A mouse ran across our porch!

_____ 3. Bring your lunch tomorrow.

_____ 4. Wave to your brothers and sisters.

_____ 5. My sister took a very short nap.

_____ 6. Do you want a dessert?

Exercise 3: Write the main verbs in Exercise 2 and identify them with a **T** for transitive or an **I** for intransitive.

VERBS	T OR I	VERBS	T OR I	VERBS	T OR I
1.		3.		5.	
2.		4.		6.	

Exercise 4: Write **S** for subjective, **O** for objective, or **P** for possessive in the blank. Underline the correct answer in parentheses.

_____ 1. (**Him, His**) bike has a flat tire.

_____ 2. Albert rode to town with (**Robert and I, Robert and me**).

_____ 3. Oscar and (**me, I**) played in the park today.

_____ 4. The Smiths invited (**she and I, her and me**) to the picnic.

SKILLS:

Exercise 5: ▸ Write the four parts of the verbs **crawl** and **go**.

COLUMN 1 PRESENT TENSE	COLUMN 2 PAST TENSE	COLUMN 3 HV PLUS AN -ED MAIN VERB	COLUMN 4 HV PLUS AN -ING MAIN VERB

Exercise 6: ▸ Identify the tense of the verb by checking the correct box.
Then, write the past tense of the main verb. Write **R** for Regular or **I** for Irregular.

VERBS	SIMPLE PRESENT	SIMPLE PAST	SIMPLE FUTURE	PAST TENSE FORMS OF THE MAIN VERB	R or I
1. will review					
2. wear					
3. painted					
4. will crawl					
5. goes					

Exercise 7: ▸ Fill in the circle beside each correct answer.

1. Antonym for: **abandon**   ○ desert   ○ rescue

2. Definition: a symbol for a number   ○ numeral   ○ protest

3. We will not _____ this puppy.   ○ numeral   ○ abandon

WRITING:

Exercise 8: ▸ Write one of the four types of sentences (*declarative, exclamatory, interrogative,* or *imperative*), using the vocabulary word **numeral**.

_____

_____

Oral Review Time

With your teacher, read the questions below. Do you know all the answers? Listen carefully for answers you do not know. After the review, you will have a chapter test.

1. What do you call a noun that receives the action of a verb?

2. What kind of verb transfers action to a direct object?

3. What are the core parts of a Pattern 2 sentence?

4. What are the core parts of a Pattern 1 sentence?

5. What kind of pronoun would you use as a direct object?

6. What are the seven object pronouns?

7. What are the three simple verb tenses?

8. Do regular or irregular verbs form their past tense by adding an -ed ending to the main verb?

9. Do regular or irregular verbs form their past tense by making a spelling change to the main verb?

Outlines

Outlining is one of the most important skills you can learn because it helps you organize ideas and information in the correct order for writing or speaking. Making an outline gives you a visual map of what is read or heard. It is easy to study from outlines because ideas are grouped together in an organized pattern to show their relationship to one another. Outlines make excellent study tools because they keep you focused.

Reference 151

Topic Outline with Main Points and Subtopics

The **topic outline** is the easiest and most commonly used outline. In a topic outline, information is written in single words or phrases—not complete sentences.

An outline organizes information into categories, much like a computer organizes information into file folders. These categories are **main points** (*or topics*) and **subtopics**.

1. **Main Points** (two or more main points about the topic)

   → Use Roman numerals (I. II. III.) for main points. You must have two or more main points.

   → Capitalize the first word but do not use an end mark.

   → Line up the periods after the Roman numerals, one under the other.

   Pet Chores for Kids

I. Cat chores	MAIN POINT
II. Dog chores	MAIN POINT

2. Subtopics (information that supports a main point)

➜ Use capital letters (A. B. C.) for subtopics.
You must have two or more subtopics.

➜ Line up subtopics under the first word of the main point.

➜ Line up the periods after the capital letters.

➜ Capitalize the first word but do not use an end mark.

I. Cat chores — **MAIN POINT**

A. **Feed cat** — **SUBTOPIC**

B. **Change water** — **SUBTOPIC**

C. **Clean litter box** — **SUBTOPIC**

II. Dog chores — **MAIN POINT**

A. **Food** — **SUBTOPIC**

B. **Water** — **SUBTOPIC**

C. **Exercise** — **SUBTOPIC**

The Outline Example

The outline below contains information in one organized, easy-to-read place.

Pet Chores for Kids — **Title**

I. Cat chores — **I. Main Point**

A. Feed cat — **A. Subtopic**

B. Change water — **B. Subtopic**

C. Clean litter box — **C. Subtopic**

II. Dog chores — **II. Main Point**

A. Food — **A. Subtopic**

B. Water — **B. Subtopic**

C. Exercise — **C. Subtopic**

Name: _____ Date:_____

SKILLS:

Exercise 1: Put the information into outline form, following the rules for outlining.

Outline:

_____

_____

_____

_____

Kinds of Games
That Use Balls
Main points
outside games
inside games

_____

_____

Subtopics
soccer
golf
tennis
baseball

_____

_____

football
bowling
basketball
volleyball
jacks

_____

_____

_____

_____

_____

_____

Word Time

Rev Up Your Writing with Power Words

Recite these Power Words with your teacher to help you make good word choices.

Set 7:	Power Words		
NOUNS	VERBS	ADJECTIVES	ADVERBS
traveler	shouted	rich	happily
drifter	squealed	wealthy	gleefully
guest	talked	playful	awfully
visitor	whispered	bouncy	dreadfully

Melody jumped and **squealed** in horror during the **dreadfully** scary movie.

Writing Time

Lesson 1

WA8

Prose

You have learned that **prose** is any type of writing that is arranged in sentences, paragraphs, essays, or books. *Prose* is the most widely used type of writing, and some forms include stories, essays, articles, letters, diaries, journals, and books. A short story is a kind of *prose*.

In this lesson, you will write an independent short story with dialogue. Think about the writing assignment, prepare your story elements map, and write a rough draft.

Writing Assignment 8: Independent Short Story with Dialogue
Steps 1 & 2: Making a Story Elements Map and Writing a Rough Draft

Purpose: to entertain
Genre: narrative
Audience: classmates

Choose the writing prompt or one of the writing topics. Write your story in third person. Make sure your story has all five Story Elements. Use description to help you describe the action, establish the setting, and to introduce the main characters. Use the characters' actions, thoughts, and feelings to aid in the development of the plot.

Be as entertaining as possible!

PROMPT: Everyone knew that Rosa was a "dog person," because she loved every dog she met. Rosa desperately wanted a dog of her own, but her mom was allergic to dog fur! Write a short story about how Rosa and her mom find a solution that makes both of them happy.

WRITING TOPICS:

1. Alex's hot-air balloon adventure
2. Brandon and his secret backyard project
3. A whole weekend without electricity
4. Brainstorm for other ideas, individually or in groups

SPECIAL INSTRUCTIONS:

1. Follow the Prewriting Checklist in Reference 59 on pages Q18–Q19.
2. Follow the Rough Draft Checklist in Reference 61 on pages Q20–Q21.
3. Use Reference 133 on page 427 to help you write a short story with dialogue.
4. Utilize a dictionary and thesaurus (in print or digital) to look up word meanings, spellings, and synonyms to help you write your rough draft.
5. Put your story elements map and your rough draft in your Rough Draft folder.

During this lesson, your teacher will conference with you individually about your previous writing assignment. After your writing conference, continue working on your independent writing assignment.

Writing Strategy: Using Reflection (Book)

As you have learned, to *reflect* means to think carefully about something and write your thoughts and feelings about it. When you write a reflection of a book, it usually includes your opinion about one or more of these elements: setting, main character or characters, plot, main idea or theme of the book, and the author's tone or writing voice. Your reflection may help you recognize the writing styles of different authors.

JOURNAL WRITING 22

Student Note:
Capitalize the first word and all important words in titles of books. Use italics when you type titles of books; underline book titles when you write them by hand.

Write an entry in your notebook journal or digital journal. Your entry should include your reflections of your favorite book. Read the writing strategy again to help you decide which area you want to include in your reflection. Give reasons for your feelings and support your opinions with details from the book. Would you end the book the same way the author ended it? Why or why not? Do you see room for improvement? Can you recognize the writing style of your favorite author?

Rev Up Your Writing with Power Words

Review these Power Words with your teacher to help you make good word choices.

Set 7: NOUNS	VERBS	ADJECTIVES	ADVERBS
traveler ⚡ drifter	shouted ⚡ squealed	rich ⚡ wealthy	happily ⚡ gleefully
guest ⚡ visitor	talked ⚡ whispered	playful ⚡ bouncy	awfully ⚡ dreadfully

Using Precise Language

How would you compare the word *talked* with the Power Word *whispered* in these sentences?

Brad **talked** to his cousin about his plans.

Brad **whispered** to his cousin about his plans.

DISCUSSION:

What mental picture does each word create?

Thinking process

There's more precise meaning in the word *whispered*. The word *whispered* suggests that Brad was speaking in a quieter voice than just *talking* would imply.

 **Double Negatives**

A very common mistake in writing is using **double negatives**. This means using two negatives—or words that mean "*no*" or "*not*"—in the same sentence. Study the reference to learn more about this writing no-no.

 Reference 152

Double Negatives

Double means **TWO**. Negative means **NO** or **NOT**.

A double-negative mistake occurs when two negative words are used in the same sentence. Two negative words in a sentence make the sentence confusing.

Negative Words That Begin with the Letter N

neither	never
nobody	not (n't)
no one	nothing
no	none
nowhere	

Contractions That End in –n't Because –n't Stands for Not

didn't
haven't
wasn't
can't
isn't
couldn't

Negative Prefixes

dis
non
un

Words with Negative Meanings

barely
hardly
scarcely

Three Ways to Correct a Double Negative

RULE 1   Change the second negative to a positive.

> **INCORRECT**   Dad **couldn't** find **nothing** in his closet.

Dad couldn't find **anything** in his closet.

TOOL: The second negative word, *nothing*, was changed to a positive word, *anything*.

RULE 2   Remove the negative part of a contraction.

> **INCORRECT**   Dad **couldn't** find **nothing** in his closet.

> **CORRECT**   Dad **could** find **nothing** in his closet.

TOOL: The *–n't* was removed from *couldn't*, leaving *could* in its place.

RULE 3   Remove the first negative word. (Possible subject-verb agreement change)

> **INCORRECT**   Dad **couldn't** find **nothing** in his closet.

> **CORRECT**   Dad **finds** **nothing** in his closet.

TOOL: The first negative word, *couldn't*, was removed. The verb *find* was changed to *finds* to make the subject and verb agree.

Changing Negative Words to Positive Words:

no or none ⟹ **any**   no one ⟹ **anyone**   nobody ⟹ **anybody**

nothing ⟹ **anything**   nowhere ⟹ **anywhere**   never ⟹ **ever**

neither ⟹ **either**   remove the **n't** from a contraction

Changing Negative Words to Positive Words

Directions: Underline the negative words in each sentence. Rewrite each sentence and correct the double-negative mistake as indicated by the rule number.

1. They <u>haven't</u> done <u>nothing</u> about the leak.

   (USE RULE 1)   **They haven't done anything about the leak.**

2. I <u>can't</u> <u>hardly</u> wait for tomorrow.

   (USE RULE 2)   **I can hardly wait for tomorrow.**

3. He <u>doesn't</u> have <u>no</u> money to spend.

   (USE RULE 3)   **He has no money to spend.**

Guided Practice

Directions: Underline the negative words in each sentence. Rewrite each sentence and correct the double-negative mistake as indicated by the rule number.

1. I never ate nothing for lunch.

   (USE RULE 3) _____

2. We aren't going nowhere tonight.

   (USE RULE 2) _____

3. Tina hasn't gotten no sleep.

   (USE RULE 1) _____

Lesson 2

Name: _____ Date:_____

SKILLS:

Exercise 1: Underline the negative words in each sentence. Rewrite each sentence and correct the double-negative mistake as indicated by the rule number.

RULE 1 Change the second negative to a positive.
RULE 2 Take out the negative part of a contraction.
RULE 3 Remove the first negative word. (possible verb change)

1. We never go nowhere during the holidays.

(USE RULE 1) _____

2. Sandy couldn't carry nothing heavy.

(USE RULE 1) _____

3. Seth hasn't never been to the new park.

(USE RULE 2) _____

4. We don't have no tests today.

(USE RULE 3) _____

5. They don't have no syrup for the pancakes.

(USE RULE 3) _____

Classroom Practice 55B

SKILLS:

Exercise 2: Underline the negative words in each sentence. Rewrite each sentence and correct the double-negative mistake as indicated by the rule number.

> **RULE 1** Change the second negative to a positive.
> **RULE 2** Take out the negative part of a contraction.
> **RULE 3** Remove the first negative word. (possible verb change)

1. There isn't no more cake.

(USE RULE 2) _____

2. Cindy never wants nothing for breakfast.

(USE RULE 1) _____

3. We don't have no money.

(USE RULE 3) _____

4. Wesley hasn't never played this game.

(USE RULE 2) _____

5. He hasn't done nothing today.

(USE RULE 1) _____

EDITING:

Exercise 3: Capitalize and punctuate the quotations.
Editing Guide: Paragraph 1: 15 mistakes   Paragraph 2: 15 mistakes

mr martin do you need someone to mow your yard asked

george my prices are very reasonable and i will do a very good job

mr martin replied yes george i would like for you to mow

my yard can you start this saturday

Publishing Time

STEP 6

Publishing

It's time to share your writing with others by publishing it.
Follow the publishing step in the writing assignment box.

Writing Assignment 7: Personal Narrative or
Step 6: Publishing   Short Story with Dialogue

SPECIAL INSTRUCTIONS:
The publishing step is your chance to share your writing with others.
To publish WA 7, follow these steps:

1. Rewrite your graded paper in ink or type it on a computer.
   Be sure to correct any mistakes.

2. Give your teacher your stapled papers. Your papers should
   include the rubrics, your graded final paper, your revised and
   edited rough draft, and your prewriting map.

3. There are many ways to publish your work.
   Choose one of the ways listed below.

Publishing Ideas

▶ Make a book of your story to take home. You can also add
   pages of illustrations.

▶ Put your writing in the classroom library or school library for checkout.

▶ Type your story and email it to a friend or relative. You can even
   illustrate it using imaging software.

▶ Send your story to a school newspaper, local newspaper, or magazine
   to be printed.

▶ Dramatize your story in the form of a one-person play, puppet show,
   or radio broadcast. (See Guidelines for Video Presentations on page Q40.)

▶ Share your writing with others during an oral presentation in a small
   or large group. (See the Guidelines for an Oral Presentation in Reference 85
   on page Q29.)

▶ Choose another publishing form that is not listed.

Word Time

Rev Up Your Writing with Power Words

Review these Power Words with your teacher to help
you make good word choices.

Set 7: **Power Words**			
NOUNS	**VERBS**	**ADJECTIVES**	**ADVERBS**
traveler ⚡ drifter	shouted ⚡ squealed	rich ⚡ wealthy	happily ⚡ gleefully
guest ⚡ visitor	talked ⚡ whispered	playful ⚡ bouncy	awfully ⚡ dreadfully

Using a Word Ladder for Degrees of Meaning

Study the following words:
beautiful, stunning, pretty, attractive,
good-looking, dazzling, cute, nice-looking

Study the Word Ladder example to the
left. Discuss how the words on the
ladder have similar meanings but vary
in intensity. Make a word ladder of
your own, using the following words:
beautiful, stunning, pretty,
attractive, good-looking,
dazzling, cute, nice-looking

Writing Time

Today, you will choose a writing assignment (WA 2, 4, 6, or 8) from your Rough Draft folder to revise and edit. Then, you will write a final paper. Use the writing checklists on pages Q23–Q25 and Q27 in the back of your book. After you have finished your final paper, read it to others in small groups, display it in the classroom, or place it in a class booklet for others to read and enjoy.

Writing Time

Team Writing
Prewriting - Persuasive/Argumentative

Today, you will start a team writing project. It will last several days, but you will only do a few steps of the writing process at a time. After you have been assigned to a team, discuss each other's strengths in the writing process. For example, some students are good at editing, and others are good at prewriting and planning. As a group, you might decide to let the prewriting expert lead the group during the first step of the writing process and let the editing expert lead the group when it's time to edit.

Before you begin your Team Writing Project, study the guidelines for respect, teamwork, and rules for discussion.

Guidelines for Respect and Teamwork

Respect means showing people that they are important through your words, actions, and attitude. When you are interacting with people, it is important that you treat them with respect.

➡ **Respect your teacher.** Listen to your teacher's instructions. Ask questions if you are not sure about something, but don't grumble or complain.

➡ **Respect your teammates.** Listen to what they have to say and really think about their ideas. Don't interrupt, criticize, or put down your teammates.

➡ **Respect the other teams.** Speak softly within your team so that you don't disturb the other groups.

➡ **Respect yourself.** Don't put yourself down. Your ideas are important; share them with the group.

CONTINUED ON NEXT PAGE ▶

Teamwork means working closely with others to reach a goal. Teamwork and respect go hand-in-hand. When teammates respect each other, they make an effort to work together to reach their goals.

1. **Participate.** Focus on the goals of the project. Think about the best way you can help your team reach its goals.

2. **Communicate.** Share your ideas and opinions and listen respectfully to your teammates' ideas and opinions.

3. **Cooperate.** Work together with your teammates to sort through everyone's ideas. Some ideas will be used; some ideas will not be used. If your idea is not used, you should move on with a good attitude.

Review: Rules for Discussion

Rules for Discussion are guidelines that will help you know how to participate in a discussion. These rules can be used for class discussions, small group discussions, or one-on-one discussions.

RULE 1 **Be prepared.** Study the required assignment.

RULE 2 **Participate.** Contribute when it is your turn.

RULE 3 **Be attentive.** Look at the speaker and listen carefully.

RULE 4 **Respect others.** Wait for your turn; do not interrupt another speaker.

RULE 5 **Gain the floor.** Follow the class rules for gaining the floor.

RULE 6 **Stay on topic.** Make sure your comments contribute to the topic.

RULE 7 **Ask questions.** Ask the speaker to explain anything you do not understand.

RULE 8 **Link your comments.** Respond to specific questions or comments of others. Put what a speaker says in your own words to clarify it.

RULE 9 **Review key ideas.** Consider the main points and details presented in order to draw a conclusion.

RULE 10 **Adapt speech.** Use casual (informal) language in pairs or small groups, but use formal English in whole class discussions or presentations.

Student Tip...

The examples below show you how to link your ideas and comments to what others are saying.

When you agree:

"**I like the point** (name of speaker) **made because....**"

"(Name of speaker) **is correct in saying** _____, **because....**"

"**When** (name of speaker) **said** _____, **I agreed because....**"

When you disagree:

"(Name of speaker) **makes a good point, but I think....**"

"(Name of speaker) **may be right about** _____, **but what about....?**"

"**When** (name of speaker) **said** _____, **I disagreed because....**"

When you are confused:

"**Excuse me,** (name of speaker), **what did you mean when you said...?**"

"**When** (name of speaker) **said** _____, **I got confused because....**"

As you start your Team Writing Project, everyone in your group should work together. Read and follow the directions below for your Team Writing Project.

 **Part 1**
PERSUASIVE

Making a Prewriting Map

Each team selects

➡ a member to copy and complete the Team Writing Record.

➡ a member to write a prewriting map.

➡ a member to verify that all members have signed their names on the papers and to give all papers to the teacher.

Topics:

• Why everyone should have (or not have) a pet

• Why families should (or should not) play sports together

• Why obeying parents is important

As a team,

➡ select a topic or writing prompt to explain or defend.

➡ brainstorm together to develop ideas for the persuasive essay.

➡ make a prewriting map, with all members contributing ideas.

• Why our school needs more play equipment

• Why eating breakfast is important

• Why recesses are important

• Select a persuasive topic of your own.

WRITING PROMPTS

Your teacher has decided to bring a snack to class, but only if the whole class agrees on which snack they want. Right now, everyone wants a different snack—which means there will be no snack at all. Choose one of these prompts:

 Choose your favorite snack and try to get all your classmates to choose it, too. Write a persuasive essay to your class, giving three good reasons for your choice of snack and supporting each reason with facts.

 Instead of choosing your favorite, try to think of a snack that everyone is likely to agree on. Write a persuasive essay to your class, giving three good reasons for your choice of snack and supporting each reason with facts.

Part 1 of Team Writing Record

1. Kind of writing __**Persuasive**_____

2. Team writers 1. _____ 2. _____ 3. _____

3. Writing Prompt #_____

4. Title of writing piece _____

5. Team writing record written by _____

6. Prewriting map written by _____

7. All papers verified and turned in by _____

8. Was a team leader selected for Part 1?   **YES   NO**

   Name _____

Review: Elements of Persuasive Writing by Team Members

Persuasion is getting other people to see things your way. Persuasive/argumentative writing helps you to state an opinion and back it up with well-thought-out reasons, examples, facts, and details in order to persuade your audience to agree with you.

Elements of Persuasive Writing

- Opinion statement
- Convincing reasons to back up the opinion statement
- Supporting examples, facts, and details to support each reason
- A call-to-action

One of the best ways to present your persuasive argument is by organizing your writing into three main parts.

CONTINUED ON NEXT PAGE

Introduction

The **Introduction** is the first part and lets the reader know your opinion and lists the reasons you will use.

Paragraph 1: **Opinion statement** (topic sentence)
Information sentence (extra information)
List-of-reasons sentence (reasons)

Body

The **Body** is the middle and most important part because it contains the reasons and supporting evidence for your opinion.

Paragraph 2: **First-reason sentence** (1st reason)
Supporting sentences (example, fact, or detail)

Paragraph 3: **Second-reason sentence** (2nd reason)
Supporting sentences (example, fact, or detail)

Paragraph 4: **Third-reason sentence** (3rd reason)
Supporting sentences (example, fact, or detail)

Conclusion

The **Conclusion** is the last part.
It contains a summary and a *call-to-action* sentence.

Paragraph 5: **Summary sentence** (restate the opinion)
Restatement-of-reasons sentence(s) (three reasons)
Call-to-action sentence (ask the reader to act)

Student Tip...

1. It is VERY important to consider who your audience/readers are and to use arguments that will appeal to them.

2. Use words that signal an opinion: *think, believe, feel, hope, seem, best, better, worse, worst, probably, excellent, terrible, should, love,* and *hate.*

3. Transition words are especially important in persuasive writing and are used to link reasons, examples, facts, and details. Some useful transition words are listed below.
for example, for instance, in addition, as well, also, next, another, along with, besides, in other words, truly, again, for this reason, in fact, not only that...but also

Conference Questions:

1. How is choosing a topic and making a prewriting map in a team different from doing it individually?

2. What kind of difficulties or differences did your team encounter? How did you resolve them?

3. Did your team choose a person to lead this part of the project?

4. How did your team divide the work on this part of the project? Did each person have his or her own special task, or did everyone share all the work?

5. For the Prewriting Step, were team members assigned tasks according to their strengths, like leading discussions, brainstorming for ideas, or organizing thoughts on paper? Explain.

6. What suggestions do you have that would help you and your team work together more effectively?

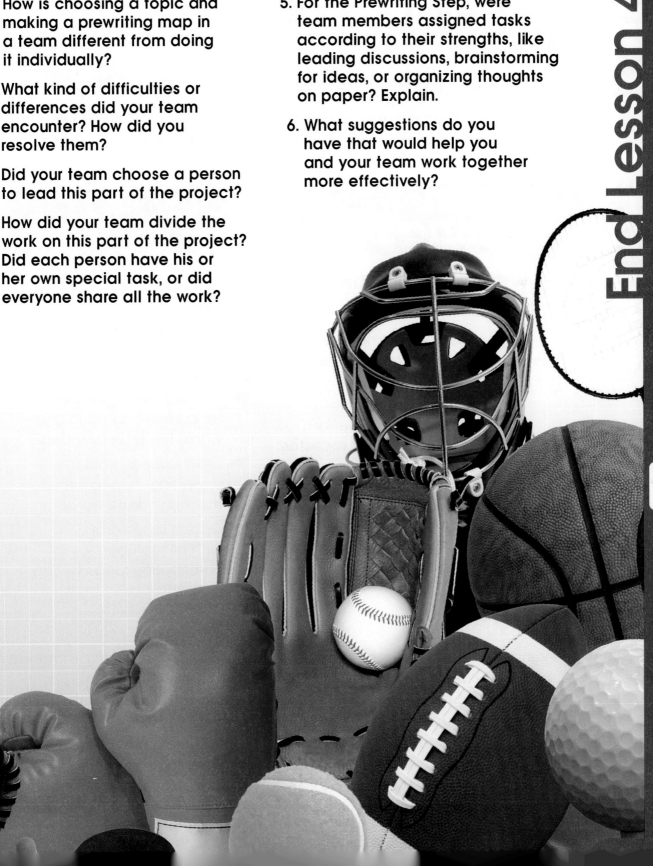

Writing Time

Team Writing: Write a Rough Draft

Even though your persuasive essay has three authors, it should only have one opinion statement. Your readers should not be able to tell that it was written by three people.

Team Writing **Tw** — Part 2

PERSUASIVE

Writing a Rough Draft

Each team selects

➡ a member to copy and complete Part 2 of the Team Writing Record.

➡ a member to write the rough draft on paper or type it on a word processor.

➡ a member to verify that all members have signed their names on the papers and to give all papers to the teacher.

As a team,

➡ make sure everyone's individual role is defined and understood.

➡ set your own deadlines for completing each goal within the time provided.

➡ use the ideas from the prewriting map to write the rough draft.

➡ write a rough draft, with all members contributing ideas.

Team Strategy

A visual aid can make a big difference in how well your reader comprehends your argument. As you write your persuasive essay, think of specific information that would be easier to understand if it were accompanied by a chart, graph, or other illustration. Sketch the appropriate visual aid in your rough draft and draw or print a more detailed version on a separate sheet of paper for your final paper. You may wish to use a digital camera to take an appropriate picture for an illustration, or you may use publishing software to create a digital chart or graph. Print the visual aid and keep it with your final paper.

Student Tip...

As you work in your groups, apply the guidelines you learned about respect, teamwork, and rules of discussion. Set deadlines for each task, and stick to your individual role.

Part 2 of Team Writing Record

1. Kind of writing ___**Persuasive**_____

2. Team writers 1. _____ 2. _____ 3. _____

3. Writing Prompt #_____

4. Title of writing piece _____

5. Team writing record written by _____

6. Rough draft written or typed by _____

7. All papers verified and turned in by _____

8. Was a team leader selected for Part 2? **YES   NO**

   Name _____

Conference Questions:

1. How is writing a rough draft in a team different from doing it individually?

2. What kind of difficulties or differences did your team encounter? How did you resolve them?

3. Did your team choose a person to lead this part of the project?

4. In what way did everyone participate in this part of the team writing project? Did everyone understand his or her individual role?

5. For the Rough Draft Step, were team members assigned tasks according to their strengths, like making decisions, recording information, or keeping things focused and running smoothly?

6. What suggestions do you have that would help you and your team work together more effectively?

Writing Time

Team Writing:
Revise, Edit, and Write a Final Paper

Today, work on your Team Writing Project again. Read and follow the directions below for this part of the Team Writing Project.

Part 3

PERSUASIVE

Revising, Editing, and Writing a Final Paper

Each team selects

➡ a member to copy and complete Part 3 of the Team Writing Record.

➡ a member to write the revising and editing corrections on the rough draft.

➡ a member to write the final paper or type it on a word processor.

➡ a member to verify that all members have signed their names on the papers and to give all papers to the teacher.

As a team,

➡ make sure everyone's individual role is defined and understood.

➡ set your own deadlines for completing each goal within the time provided.

➡ read through the rough draft your team wrote earlier.

➡ discuss ways to revise the rough draft, using the Revising Checklist on pages Q23–Q24.

➡ edit and make corrections to the rough draft, using the Editing Checklist on page Q25.

➡ make sure the group's revisions and corrections are added to the final paper.

Student Tip...

1. As you work in your groups, apply the guidelines you learned about respect, teamwork, and rules of discussion.

2. Utilize a dictionary (in print or digital) to look up word meanings, spellings, and synonyms to help you revise and edit.

Part 3 of Team Writing Record

1. Kind of writing __Persuasive_____

2. Team writers 1. _____ 2. _____ 3. _____

3. Writing Prompt #_____

4. Title of writing piece _____

5. Team writing record written or typed by _____

6. Revising and editing written on the rough draft by _____

7. All papers verified and turned in by _____

8. Was a team leader selected for Part 3? **YES NO**

   Name _____

9. Final paper written or typed by _____

Conference Questions:

1. How is revising, editing, and writing a final paper in a team different from doing it individually?

2. What kind of difficulties or differences did your team encounter? How did you resolve them?

3. Did your team choose a person to lead this part of the project?

4. How did your team divide the work on this part of the project? Were the individual roles well defined? How did you decide who would produce the final draft?

5. For the Revising and Editing Step, were team members assigned tasks according to their strengths, like finding misspelled words or grammar mistakes, thinking of more descriptive words, typing the final draft, or keeping things focused and running smoothly?

6. What suggestions do you have that would help you and your team work together more effectively?

Writing Time

Team Writing:
Plan for Your Group Presentation

Today, work on your Team Writing Project again. Read and follow the directions below for this part of the Team Writing Project.

Team Writing Tw **Part 4**
PERSUASIVE

Planning Your Group Presentation

Each team selects

➡ a member to copy and complete Part 4 of the Team Writing Record.

➡ a member to verify that all members have signed their names on the writing record and to give it to the teacher.

As a team,

➡ make sure everyone's individual role is defined and understood.

➡ set your own deadlines for completing each goal within the time provided.

➡ read through the final paper your team wrote earlier.

➡ brainstorm how your group will present the paper to the class.

➡ decide what each member's job will be during the presentation.

Team Strategy

In the next lesson, you will present your final paper to the class as a group presentation. Discuss how your group will present its project.

• Will one person read the essay, or will you take turns reading the paragraphs to the class?

• Will you show charts, graphs, or other illustrations that support the opinion statement and reasons presented?

• Will you use publishing software to create a digital chart or graph?

• Will you have a narrator to explain the flow of information if you use a digital format?

• Will you incorporate technology and convert your argument into a slide presentation?

• Will you use audio recordings to enhance your presentation?

• Discuss other presentation ideas that suit your topic.

Part 4 of Team Writing Record

1. Kind of writing __**Persuasive**_____

2. Team writers 1. _____ 2. _____ 3. _____

3. Writing Prompt #_____

4. Title of writing piece _____

5. Team writing record written by _____

6. Presentation plans listed below. Each team member's assignment included.

7. Was a team leader selected for Part 4? **YES   NO**

   Name _____

Conference Questions:

1. How is planning a presentation in a team different from doing it individually?

2. What kind of difficulties or differences did your team encounter? How did you resolve them?

3. Did your team choose a person to lead this part of the project?

4. What kind of plans have you made for presenting your team writing paper? What part of the presentation are you most excited about? Are you nervous about any part of the presentation?

5. What kind of technology has your team decided to use to present your paper? How did you come to this decision? What extra preparation will you need to use this technology?

6. For the Publishing Step, were team members assigned tasks according to their strengths, like helping with technology, making creative suggestions, pinning down details, or helping the group come to an agreement?

7. What suggestions do you have that would help you and your team work together more effectively?

Team Writing: Give a Group Presentation

It's presentation day! Today is the day that you finally get to share what you and your writing team have been working on for several days. Read and follow the directions below for this part of the Team Writing Project.

Part 5

PERSUASIVE

Publishing

Follow the Presentation Guidelines for speaker presentation and audience response.

PRESENTATION GUIDELINES: PERSUASIVE WRITING

Speaker

1. Have your presentation ready when it is your turn.

2. Make sure everyone on the team knows what to do.

3. Make sure your digital presentation works before your presentation.

4. Tell the title of your presentation.

5. Tell the purpose and type of writing used.

6. Use appropriate facts and details to support your main ideas.

7. Make sure you speak clearly and at an understandable pace. Maintain eye contact with your audience.

8. Speak in complete sentences and use formal English when presenting to an audience.

9. Take questions from the audience and answer them to the best of your ability.

Audience

1. Look at the speaker.

2. Turn your body toward the speaker.

3. Listen attentively. Do not let your thoughts wander.

4. Do not distract the speaker or other listeners.

5. Show interest in what the speaker is saying.

6. Silently summarize what the speaker is saying to help you understand the topic.

7. Show appreciation by clapping after the speaker has finished.

8. If there is time for questions, raise your hand and wait to be called on before asking your question.

9. Ask questions to check your understanding of the topic or to request further details. Link your own ideas about the topic to comments of others.

Conference Questions:

1. How is giving a presentation in a team different from doing it individually?

2. What kind of difficulties or differences did your team encounter? How did you resolve them?

3. Did your team choose a person to lead this part of the project?

4. What did you learn about working in a group to get a project done?

5. What suggestions do you have that would help you and your team work together more effectively?

Student Tip...

Whether you are the speaker or a member of the audience, remember to speak in complete sentences. Even a simple "yes or no" question can be answered thoroughly; elaborate on the answer, provide interesting details, and explain *why*!

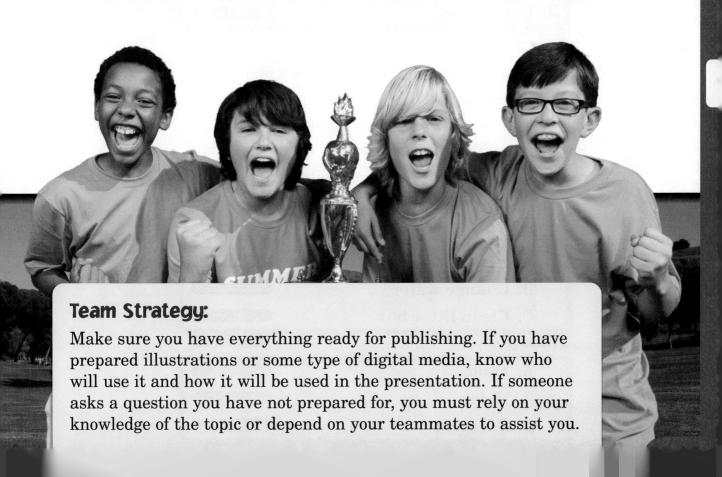

Team Strategy:

Make sure you have everything ready for publishing. If you have prepared illustrations or some type of digital media, know who will use it and how it will be used in the presentation. If someone asks a question you have not prepared for, you must rely on your knowledge of the topic or depend on your teammates to assist you.

Skill Time

Review: Topic Outline with Main Points and Subtopics

Outlining helps you group related ideas and information together in an organized pattern to show their relationship to one another.

1. **Main Points** (two or more main points about the topic)

   → Use Roman numerals (I. II. III.) for main points.
   You must have two or more main points.

   → Capitalize the first word but do not use an end mark.

   → Line up the periods after the Roman numerals, one under the other.

   Pet Chores

I. Cat chores	**MAIN POINT**
II. Dog chores	**MAIN POINT**

2. **Subtopics** (information that supports a main point)

   → Use capital letters (A. B. C.) for subtopics.
   You must have two or more subtopics.

   → Line up subtopics under the first word of the main point.

   → Line up the periods after the capital letters.

   → Capitalize the first word but do not use an end mark.

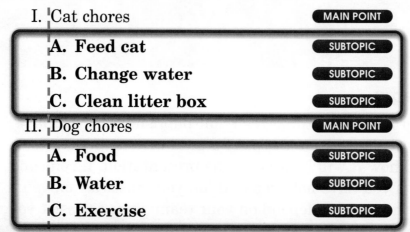

Name: _____ Date:_____

Exercise 1: Put the information into outline form, following the rules for outlining.

Outline:

_____

_____

_____

_____

_____

_____

_____

_____

_____

_____

_____

Different Kinds of Insects

-Main points
flying insects
crawling insects

-Subtopics
butterfly
moth

bee
mosquito
fly

ant
beetle
roach
cricket

End Lesson 9

Jingle Time
Listening and Speaking

Jingle 23   The Indirect Object Jingle

Indirect, oh, indirect, oh, indirect object.
Give me that indirect, oh, indirect, oh, indirect object.

An indirect object is a NOUN or a PRONOUN
That receives what the direct, the direct object names.
An indirect object is found between the verb, **verb-transitive**,
And the direct object.

> To find the indirect object,   *(sha-bop)*
> Ask **TO WHOM** or **FOR WHOM**   *(sha-bop)*
> After the direct object.   *(sha-bop)*

> An indirect, indirect, indirect, indirect, yeah!
> An indirect object!
> *Just give me that indirect,*
> *oh, indirect,*
> *oh, indirect object.*
> *Give me that indirect,*
> *oh, indirect,*
> *oh, indirect object.*
> *Give me that object,*
> *oh, indirect,*
> *oh, indirect object.*
> An **INDIRECT OBJECT!**

Time

Review: Sentence Patterns 1-2

➜ **Pattern 1 core: noun-verb** (SN V)

➜ **Pattern 2 core: noun-verb-noun** (SN V-t DO)

Today, you will learn another sentence pattern, **Pattern 3**, which has three nouns and a verb (**noun-verb-noun-noun**) for its core. To understand Pattern 3, you must first understand its core parts, the subject noun, transitive verb, indirect object, and direct object: **SN V-t IO DO**.

Reference 153

Indirect Object, Verb-transitive, and Pattern 3

Indirect Objects

1. An **indirect object** is a noun or pronoun that is located *after* the verb and *before* the direct object.

2. An indirect object receives the direct object.

3. To find the indirect object, ask ***to whom*** or ***for whom*** AFTER identifying the direct object. If the indirect object word is not a person, ask ***to what*** or ***for what***.

4. An **indirect object** is labeled with the abbreviation **IO**.

➥ Example 1: **SN   V-t   IO A DO**
   Mom made me a cake.

➥ **Mom made a cake for whom?** me - indirect object

➥ Example 2: **SN   V-t   A   IO   A DO**
   Marty gave the puppy a treat.

➥ **Marty gave a treat to what?** puppy - indirect object

Transitive Verbs

1. A sentence with an indirect object also has a direct object. If there is a direct object, the verb is a transitive verb. Therefore, a Pattern 3 sentence has a transitive verb.

2. A **transitive verb** is labeled with the abbreviation **V-t**.

Pattern 3

1. Sentence Patterns identify the order of the core parts of sentences. The third pattern, **Pattern 3**, has *four* core parts: a Subject Noun (**SN**), a Verb-transitive (**V-t**), an Indirect Object (**IO**), and a Direct Object (**DO**).

2. **Pattern 3** is identified by its core parts: **SN V-t IO DO P3** (*Subject Noun, Verb-transitive, Indirect Object, Direct Object, Pattern 3*).

Adding Indirect Objects to the Question and Answer Flow

Sample Sentence: **Holly read them a story.**

1. Who read them a story?
   Holly – Subject Noun . . . . (Write **SN** above *Holly.*)

2. What is being said about *Holly*?
   Holly read – Verb . . . . (Write **V** above *read.*)

3. Holly read what? **story – verify the noun**

4. Does *story* mean the same thing as *Holly*? **No**

5. **Story – Direct Object** . . . . (Write **DO** above *story.*)

6. **Read – Verb-transitive** . . . . (Write **-t** above *read.*)

7. Holly read story to whom?
   them – Indirect Object . . . . (Write **IO** above *them.*)

8. **A – Article Adjective** . . . . (Write **A** above *a.*)

9. **Subject Noun, Verb-transitive, Indirect Object, Direct Object, Pattern 3**
   (Write **SN V-t IO DO P3** in the blank.)

10. **Skill Check!**
    ➡ **Verb-transitive – check again**
    ➡ **No prepositional phrases**

CONTINUED ON NEXT PAGE >>>

➥ **Period, statement, declarative sentence**
(Write **D** at the end of the sentence.)

➥ Go back to the verb.
Divide the complete subject from the complete predicate.

➥ Is this sentence in a natural or inverted order? **Natural - no change**

SN V-t
IO DO P3

SN   V-t   IO   A   DO
Holly / read   them   a   story. **D**

Discussion Questions:

1. What is a noun or pronoun called that receives a direct object?

2. Where is an indirect object located?

3. What kind of verb is used with an indirect object?

4. What are the core parts of a Pattern 3 sentence?

5. What are the pattern labels in a Pattern 3 sentence?

Review: Sentence Patterns

→ **Pattern 1** is **SN V**.
It has a **noun-verb (N V)** core.

→ **Pattern 2** is **SN V-t DO**.
It has a **noun-verb-noun (N V N)** core.

→ **Pattern 3** is **SN V-t IO DO**.
It has a **noun-verb-noun-noun (N V N N)** core.

The location of a noun determines its job in a sentence. Only certain noun jobs form the pattern parts of a sentence. A noun that is an object of the preposition is not part of a sentence pattern.

Classifying Sentences

Classify the Introductory Sentences with your teacher, using the Question and Answer Flow. Classifying these sentences will help you learn indirect objects.

Introductory Sentences
ORAL PARTICIPATION

1. _____ Jennie gave me a cookie.

2. _____ At lunch, Jennie gave me an oatmeal cookie.

3. _____ Yesterday, Dad bought Scott and me a cute little puppy.

Word Study

Compare Sentence 1 to Sentence 2. The sentences mean basically the same thing, but Sentence 2 is more appealing because of the added details. Notice how adjectives, adverbs, and prepositional phrases are used to improve and expand the meaning of the original sentence. Name the words and phrases in Sentence 2 that are used to add more details. When you write, ask yourself this question: Have I used enough adjectives, adverbs, and prepositional phrases to make my sentences interesting? Brainstorm and make a list of interesting adjectives, adverbs, and prepositional phrases that can be used for elaboration.

Noun Check
Adding Indirect Objects

Now that you have classified the Introductory Sentences, it is time to do a Noun Check. During a Noun Check, you identify nouns in different noun jobs. Today, the indirect object is added to the Noun Check. You must decide whether the indirect object is a noun or a pronoun. If it is a noun, it will be circled. If it is a pronoun, it will not be circled. Now, recite the Noun Check with your teacher.

Noun Check Introductory Sentences

Sentence 1: (Jennie) gave me a (cookie.)

> Subject Noun **Jennie**, *yes, it is a noun;*
> Indirect Object **me**, *no, it is a pronoun;*
> Direct Object **cookie**, *yes, it is a noun.*

Sentence 2: At (lunch,) (Jennie) gave me an oatmeal (cookie.)

> Object of the Preposition **lunch**, *yes, it is a noun;*
> Subject Noun **Jennie**, *yes, it is a noun;*
> Indirect Object **me**, *no, it is a pronoun;*
> Direct Object **cookie**, *yes, it is a noun.*

Sentence 3: Yesterday, (Dad) bought (Scott) and me a cute little (puppy.)

> Subject Noun **Dad**, *yes, it is a noun;*
> Compound Indirect Object **Scott**, *yes, it is a noun;*
> Compound Indirect Object **me**, *no, it is a pronoun;*
> Direct Object **puppy**, *yes, it is a noun.*

Are there any Possessive Nouns in the sentences? **No**

Bringing It All Together
The Noun Chart Adding Indirect Objects

The Noun Chart below adds the indirect object and reviews the other information about nouns that you have learned. Discuss the Noun Chart below with your teacher.

Reference 154

noun Chart

              Adv   SN   V-t   CIO   C CIO A Adj

3. $\underset{\text{IO DO P3}}{\text{SN V-t}}$ Yesterday, Dad / bought Scott and me a cute

        Adj   DO
        little puppy.   D

Directions: Use the sentence above to complete the table below.

LIST THE NOUNS USED	NOUN JOB	SINGULAR or PLURAL	COMMON or PROPER	SIMPLE SUBJECT	SIMPLE PREDICATE
Dad	SN	S	P	Dad	bought
Scott	CIO	S	P		
puppy	DO	S	C		

Guided Practice

Directions: Classify these sentences on notebook paper.

	A	SN	V-t	PPA	IO	PPA	DO

<u>SN V-t</u>   The   students / showed   their   parents   their   art.
IO DO P3

_____   Mandy   knitted   me   a   hat.

_____   Mom   gave   us   a   taste   of   her   pie.

Directions: Use the sentences above to answer the following questions.

1. What are the subjects? **students, Mandy, Mom**

2. What are the indirect objects?

3. What are the direct objects?

4. What are the transitive verbs?

JOURNAL WRITING 23

Write an entry in your notebook journal or digital journal. Before you begin your journal entry, write one or two sentences with an indirect object. As a challenge, try to write one sentence for each of the three patterns. Can you identify different sentence patterns in your entry?

Jingle Time

Listening and Speaking

Practice Jingle 23 in the Jingle Section. **PAGE Q11**

Grammar Time

Classifying Sentences

Classify the Practice Sentences with your teacher, using the Question and Answer Flow.

Practice Sentences
ORAL PARTICIPATION

1. _____ Aunt Laura fed the hungry girls cookies and milk for a snack.

2. _____ Yesterday, our teacher read us an exciting story about wild horses.

3. _____ Yummy! Nana baked Erika and me blueberry muffins for breakfast!

Word Study

Informal family words like *Nana* in Sentence 3 are very common. The words and their meanings vary greatly from region to region and even from family to family. Have you ever heard of *Gran-Gran*, *Granny*, *Nana*, *Mimi*, *Pops*, *Gramps*, *Paw-Paw*, and *Granddaddy*? What special words do you use to talk about your parents, brothers, sisters, grandparents, aunts, uncles, and other favorite relatives?

Review: Transitive and Intransitive Verbs

A **transitive verb** is an action verb that shows a complete action with a direct object. Any sentence that has a direct object will have a transitive verb to transfer the action from the subject to the direct object. Verbs in Patterns 2 and 3 show action with direct objects; therefore, they are transitive verbs.

An **intransitive verb** is an action verb that shows a complete action without a direct object. Verbs in Pattern 1 sentences show action without direct objects; therefore, they are intransitive verbs.

In the sentences that you just classified, which verbs are transitive? Explain. Are there any intransitive verbs? Explain.

Today, you will review pronoun cases and add indirect objects to the objective case.

Lesson 2

Pronoun Cases, Adding Indirect Objects

Pronoun Cases

1. **Subjective Case Pronouns**
   Pronouns that are used as **subjects** are in the subjective case.

   ➡ SP: **He went to work.**

   > **Subjective Case:**
   > **I, we, he, she, it, they,** and **you**

2. **Objective Case Pronouns**
   Pronouns that are used as **objects of the prepositions**, **direct objects**, and **indirect objects** are in the objective case.

   ➡ OP: **The principal talked to me after class.**
   ➡ DO: **Mom took me to the zoo.**
   ➡ IO: **Leslie drew me a picture.**

   > **Objective Case:**
   > **me, us, him, her, it, them,** and **you**

3. **Possessive Case Pronouns**
   Pronouns that are used to **show ownership** are in the possessive case.

   ➡ PPA: **Luke walked to his office.**

   > **Possessive Case:**
   > **my, our, his, her, its, their,** and **your**

Compound Pronouns

Many people often confuse subject pronouns and object pronouns when they are compound. Reading the sentence with only the first pronoun is a quick way to determine if you are using the correct case.

Examples: ➤ Write **S** for subjective, **O** for objective, or **P** for possessive in the blank. Underline the correct pronoun in parentheses.

__S__ 1. (**She and I**, Her and me) drove home.

__O__ 2. Dora looked for (he and I, **him and me**).

__O__ 3. Lucy phoned (she and I, **her and me**) today.

__O__ 4. Dad bought (he and I, **him and me**) a present.

Case Check

After you have classified the Practice Sentences, you will do a **Case Check**. During a Case Check, you will say the pronoun, identify its job, and then tell its case. **Subject** pronouns are in the subjective case, **possessive** pronouns are in the possessive case, and **object** pronouns are in the objective case. Now, recite the Case Check, adding pronouns used as indirect objects.

 Practice Sentences

Sentence 1: Aunt Laura fed the hungry girls cookies and milk for a snack.

None

Sentence 2: Yesterday, our teacher read us an exciting story about wild horses.

our: possessive pronoun, *possessive case*

us: indirect object pronoun, *objective case*

Sentence 3: Yummy! Nana baked Erika and me blueberry muffins for breakfast.

me: indirect object pronoun, *objective case*

REMINDER: Any pronoun that uses the letter **O** as part of its classified label is in the objective case because the **O** stands for *object*: **IO** for indirect *object*, **DO** for direct *object*, and **OP** for *object* of the preposition.

Noun Check
Adding Pronouns as Indirect Objects

Now, it is time to do a Noun Check. During a Noun Check, you identify nouns in different noun jobs. You must decide whether the indirect object is a noun or a pronoun. If it is a noun, it will be circled. If it is a pronoun, it will not be circled. Now, recite the Noun Check with your teacher.

Noun Check Practice Sentences

Circle the nouns in the sentences.

Sentence 1: (Aunt Laura) fed the hungry (girls)(cookies) and (milk) for a (snack)

Subject Noun **Aunt Laura**, *yes, it is a noun;*

Indirect Object **girls**, *yes, it is a noun;*

Compound Direct Object **cookies**, *yes, it is a noun;*

Compound Direct Object **milk**, *yes, it is a noun;*

Object of the Preposition **snack**, *yes, it is a noun.*

Sentence 2: Yesterday, our (teacher) read us an exciting (story) about wild (horses.)

Subject Noun **teacher**, *yes, it is a noun;*

Indirect Object **us**, *no, it is a pronoun;*

Direct Object **story**, *yes, it is a noun;*

Object of the Preposition **horses**, *yes, it is a noun.*

Sentence 3: Yummy! (Nana) baked (Erika) and me blueberry (muffins) for (breakfast!)

Subject Noun **Nana**, *yes, it is a noun;*

Compound Indirect Object **Erika**, *yes, it is a noun;*

Compound Indirect Object **me**, *no, it is a pronoun;*

Direct Object **muffins**, *yes, it is a noun;*

Object of the Preposition **breakfast**, *yes, it is a noun.*

Are there any Possessive Nouns in the sentences? **No**

Skill Time

Review: Simple Verb Tenses

The word **tense** means *time*. The three simple verb tenses show that an action takes place in the present, past, or future.

1. A verb in the simple **present** tense shows that an action is happening now.

2. A verb in the simple **past** tense shows that an action has already happened.

3. A verb in the simple **future** tense shows that an action will happen later.

Review: Regular and Irregular Verbs

Verbs are divided into two groups: **regular** and **irregular**.

A verb is **regular** if it is made past tense by adding an *–ed* ending to the main verb.

A verb is **irregular** if it is made past tense by making a spelling change.

Recite the Verb Chant with your teacher.

Verb Chart for Regular Verbs

COLUMN 1 PRESENT TENSE	COLUMN 2 PAST TENSE	COLUMN 3 HV PLUS AN -ED MAIN VERB	COLUMN 4 HV PLUS AN -ING MAIN VERB
start	started	(has, have, had) started	(am, is, are, was, were) starting
try	tried	(has, have, had) tried	(am, is, are, was, were) trying

Verb Chart for Irregular Verbs

COLUMN 1 PRESENT TENSE	COLUMN 2 PAST TENSE	COLUMN 3 HV PLUS A 3RD COLUMN MAIN VERB	COLUMN 4 HV PLUS AN -ING MAIN VERB
ring	rang	(has, have, had) rung	(am, is, are, was, were) ringing
rise	rose	(has, have, had) risen	(am, is, are, was, were) rising
run	ran	(has, have, had) run	(am, is, are, was, were) running
say	said	(has, have, had) said	(am, is, are, was, were) saying
see	saw	(has, have, had) seen	(am, is, are, was, were) seeing
sell	sold	(has, have, had) sold	(am, is, are, was, were) selling
sing	sang	(has, have, had) sung	(am, is, are, was, were) singing
sink	sank	(has, have, had) sunk	(am, is, are, was, were) sinking
swim	swam	(has, have, had) swum	(am, is, are, was, were) swimming
write	wrote	(has, have, had) written	(am, is, are, was, were) writing

End Lesson 2

Name: _____ Date:_____

GRAMMAR:

Exercise 1: Classify each sentence.

1. _____ Jennie loaned me her umbrella.

2. _____ Mom and Dad bought us a new puppy!

Exercise 2: Use **Sentence 1** above to complete the table below.

LIST THE NOUNS USED	NOUN JOB	SINGULAR or PLURAL	COMMON or PROPER	SIMPLE SUBJECT	SIMPLE PREDICATE

Exercise 3: Write the labels for the eight parts of speech.

1. _____ 2. _____ 3. _____ 4. _____ 5. _____ 6. _____ 7. _____ 8. _____

SKILLS:

Exercise 4: Write the four parts of the verbs **join** and **know**.

FIRST PRESENT TENSE	SECOND PAST TENSE	THIRD HV PLUS A 3RD COLUMN MAIN VERB	FOURTH HV PLUS AN -ING MAIN VERB

Jingle Time

Listening and Speaking

Practice Jingle 23 in the Jingle Section. **PAGE Q11**

Grammar Time

Classifying Sentences

Classify the Practice Sentences with your teacher, using the Question and Answer Flow.

Practice Sentences   ORAL PARTICIPATION

1. _____ Hand me the hammer and screwdriver from the toolbox.

2. _____ Dad gave our tour guide a huge tip for all his help.

3. _____ Ouch! The nurse at the health clinic gave me my allergy shot.

Case Check

After you have classified the Practice Sentences, recite a Case Check and a Noun Check with your teacher. These checks help you analyze nouns and pronouns and understand how they are used in sentences.

Case Check Practice Sentences

Sentence 1: Hand me the hammer and screwdriver from the toolbox.

> **(You):** understood subject pronoun, *subjective case*
>
> **me:** indirect object pronoun, *objective case*

Sentence 2: Dad gave our tour guide a huge tip for all his help.

> **our:** possessive pronoun, *possessive case*
>
> **his:** possessive pronoun, *possessive case*

Sentence 3: Ouch! The nurse at the health clinic gave me my allergy shot.

> **me:** indirect object pronoun, *objective case*
>
> **my:** possessive pronoun, *possessive case*

REMINDER: Any pronoun that uses the letter **O** as part of its classified label is in the objective case because the **O** stands for *object*: **IO** for indirect *object*, **DO** for direct *object*, and **OP** for *object* of the preposition.

Noun Check

Now that you have classified the Practice Sentences, it is time to do a Noun Check. A Noun Check helps you identify information about each noun in a sentence. Recite the Noun Check with your teacher.

Noun Check

☐ 1. **Identify the nouns in a Noun Check.**
(Say the job and the noun. Circle each noun.)

☐ 2. **Identify the nouns as singular or plural.**
(Write **S** or **P** above the noun.)

☐ 3. **Identify the nouns as common or proper.**
(Write **C** or **P** above the noun.)

Review: Parts of Speech

REMINDER: How a word is used in a sentence determines its part of speech. What are the eight parts of speech?

What are the labels for the eight parts of speech?

 **Time**

Review: Simple Verb Tenses

The word **tense** means *time*. The three simple verb tenses show that an action takes place in the present, past, or future.

1. A verb in the simple **present** tense shows that an action is happening now.

2. A verb in the simple **past** tense shows that an action has already happened.

3. A verb in the simple **future** tense shows that an action will happen later.

Review of Regular and Irregular Verbs

Verbs are divided into two groups: **regular** and **irregular**.

A verb is **regular** if it is made past tense by adding an *–ed* ending to the main verb.

A verb is **irregular** if it is made past tense by making a spelling change.

Recite the Verb Chants with your teacher.

Verb Chart for Regular Verbs

COLUMN 1 PRESENT TENSE	COLUMN 2 PAST TENSE	COLUMN 3 HV PLUS AN -ED MAIN VERB	COLUMN 4 HV PLUS AN -ING MAIN VERB
look	looked	(has, have, had) looked	(am, is, are, was, were) looking
open	opened	(has, have, had) opened	(am, is, are, was, were) opening

Verb Chart for Irregular Verbs

COLUMN 1 PRESENT TENSE	COLUMN 2 PAST TENSE	COLUMN 3 HV PLUS A 3RD COLUMN MAIN VERB	COLUMN 4 HV PLUS AN -ING MAIN VERB
cut	cut	(has, have, had,) cut	(am, is, are, was, were,) cutting
do	did	(has, have, had) done	(am, is, are, was, were) doing
drink	drank	(has, have, had) drunk	(am, is, are, was, were) drinking
drive	drove	(has, have, had) driven	(am, is, are, was, were) driving
eat	ate	(has, have, had) eaten	(am, is, are, was, were) eating
fall	fell	(has, have, had) fallen	(am, is, are, was, were) falling
fly	flew	(has, have, had) flown	(am, is, are, was, were) flying
freeze	froze	(has, have, had) frozen	(am, is, are, was, were) freezing

FALLING

Changing the Tense of Verbs in Paragraphs

When you write, it is important to keep your verbs in the proper tense because they tell the reader the time period in which an event takes place. Use verbs in the same tense when you are describing events that occur at the same time. When you write about things that are happening now, use present-tense verbs. Use past-tense verbs when you write about things that have happened in the past.

To check the tense of your writing, you must check each verb to make sure it is written in the tense you have chosen. It helps to read a paragraph aloud so you can train your ear to hear the tense of the verbs. Also, make sure your adverbs and prepositional phrases match your verb tenses. For example, you would not say, **"Tomorrow, I hiked with my dad."** or **"Yesterday, I will hike with my dad."**

Student Tip...

Usually, you should use one verb tense for consistency. However, you may change tenses to show that one action or event happens before or after another.

Yesterday, I played at the park, but now I am playing at home.

Reference 156

Changing the Tense of Verbs in Paragraphs

Use consistent tenses to show actions that occur at the same time. Paragraph 1 shows actions that are happening now; therefore, the verbs are in present tense.

PARAGRAPH 1: PRESENT TENSE

Troy's dad **keeps** a steady pace as he **throws** sacks of feed in the back of the farm truck. Sweat **pours** down Troy's face as he **struggles** to keep up with his dad. Troy **strains** as he **lifts** the fifty-pound sacks, one after another. He **is gaining** new respect for his dad as they **work** without a break.

Tip for checking the verb tense

To make sure each verb in Paragraph 1 is written in the present tense, identify each verb and check for present tense. You must make sure there are no past-tense forms mixed with your present-tense verbs. It is best to separate the verbs from the paragraph so that you can check each verb individually. (*keeps, throws, pours, struggles, strains, lifts, is gaining, work*)

Paragraph 2 shows actions that have happened in the past; therefore, the verbs are in past tense. Notice how the present-tense verbs from Paragraph 1 have been changed to past-tense verbs in Paragraph 2.

PARAGRAPH 2: PAST TENSE

Troy's dad **kept** a steady pace as he **threw** sacks of feed in the back of the farm truck. Sweat **poured** down Troy's face as he **struggled** to keep up with his dad. Troy **strained** as he **lifted** the fifty-pound sacks, one after another. He **was gaining** new respect for his dad as they **worked** without a break.

Tip for changing the verb tense

If you want to change a present-tense paragraph to a past-tense paragraph, you must change each verb to past tense, one at a time. Again, it is best to separate the verbs from the paragraph so that you can check each verb individually. (*keeps-kept, throws-threw, pours-poured, struggles-struggled, strains-strained, lifts-lifted, is gaining-was gaining, work-worked*)

Classroom Practice 58

Name: _____ Date:_____

GRAMMAR:

Exercise 1: Classify each sentence.

1. _____ Today, Jalen and Rosa told me some funny jokes.

2. _____ At halftime, I will bring the team snacks and drinks.

Exercise 2: Write **S** for subjective, **O** for objective, or **P** for possessive in the blank.
Underline the correct answer in parentheses.

____ 1. (**Him, His**) family will meet us at the game.

____ 2. Robby and (**me, I**) went to the library today.

____ 3. Mr. Green gave (**Brian and I, Brian and me**) good directions.

____ 4. Lucy played checkers with (**Holly and I, Holly and me**).

SKILLS:

Exercise 3: Change the **present-tense** verbs in Paragraph 1 to **past-tense** verbs in Paragraph 2.

PARAGRAPH 1: **Present Tense**

After her nap, my cat [1. **stretches**] and [2. **yawns**].
She [3. **feels**] playful, so she [4. **gets**] up and [5. **walks**] to the den.
She [6. **checks**] several hiding places before she [7. **finds**] what
she [8. **is**] searching for—a toy mouse!

PARAGRAPH 2: **Past Tense**

After her nap. my cat [1. _____] and [2. _____].
She [3. _____] playful, so she [4. _____] up and [5. _____] to the den.
She [6. _____] several hiding places before she [7. _____] what
she [8. _____] searching for—a toy mouse!

End Lesson 3

Listening and Speaking

Practice Jingles 20–23 in the Jingle Section. PAGES Q9-Q11

Mixed Patterns

 Reference 157

Mixed Patterns 1–3

Study the three sentence patterns shown. As you classify the sentences, pay close attention to the core parts of each sentence. This will help you decide which pattern to choose.

→ **Pattern 1 is SN V.**
It has a **noun-verb (N V)** core.

> SN V
> ↑ ↑
> N V

➤ Example:

                A SN   V   P A Adj OP

<u>SN V</u>   The boys / played (on the baseball field). **D**
P1

→ **Pattern 2 is SN V-t DO.**
It has a **noun-verb-noun (N V N)** core.

> SN V-t DO
> ↑ ↑ ↑
> N V N

➤ Example:

              A SN   V-t   DO

<u>SN V-t</u>   The boys / played baseball. **D**
DO P2

→ **Pattern 3** is **SN V-t IO DO**.
It has a **noun-verb-noun-noun** (**N V N N**) core.

SN V-t IO DO
↕ ↕ ↕ ↕
N V N N

➥ Example:

PPA SN   V-t IO A   DO
SN V-t   My friend / threw me the baseball. **D**
IO DO P3

Classifying Mixed Patterns 1-3

Classify the Introductory Sentences with your teacher, using the Question and Answer Flow.

Introductory Sentences   ORAL PARTICIPATION

1. _____ Give Brittany your recipe, please.

2. _____ The boys won the footrace.

3. _____ Will you toss me a dry towel?

4. _____ We camped along the river.

Word Study

Look at the word *please* in Sentence 1. The word *please* is called a **function** word of politeness because it is used to help "soften" a command so that it sounds like a courteous request. If the word "please" is used in the last position of the sentence, it is set off by a comma and is considered a tag word for politeness. The word *please* is classified as an adverb.

Review: Transitive and Intransitive Verbs

Transitive verbs are action verbs with a direct object. They are used in Pattern 2 and 3 sentences. **Intransitive verbs** are action verbs without a direct object. They are used in Pattern 1 sentences.

In the sentences that you just classified, which verbs are transitive? Explain. Which verb is intransitive? Explain.

Case Check

After you have classified the Introductory Sentences, recite a Case Check and a Noun Check with your teacher. These checks help you analyze nouns and pronouns and understand how they are used in sentences.

Case Check Introductory Sentences

Sentence 1: Give Brittany your recipe, please.

(You): understood subject pronoun, *subjective case*

your: possessive pronoun, *possessive case*

Sentence 2: The boys won the footrace.

None

Sentence 3: Will you toss me a dry towel.

You: subject pronoun, *subjective case*

me: indirect object pronoun, *objective case*

Sentence 4: We camped along the river.

We: subject pronoun, *subjective case*

Noun Check

REMINDER: Any pronoun that uses the letter **O** as part of its classified label is in the objective case because the **O** stands for *object*: **IO** for indirect *object*, **DO** for direct *object*, and **OP** for *object* of the preposition.

Noun Check
Do a Noun Check with the sentences just classified.

1. **Identify the nouns in a Noun Check.**
   (Say the job and the noun. Circle each noun.)

2. **Identify the nouns as singular or plural.**
   (Write **S** or **P** above the noun.)

3. **Identify the nouns as common or proper.**
   (Write **C** or **P** above the noun.)

Skill Time

Review: Simple Verb Tenses

The word **tense** means *time*. The three simple verb tenses show that an action takes place in the present, past, or future.

1. A verb in the simple **present** tense shows that an action is happening now.

2. A verb in the simple **past** tense shows that an action has already happened.

3. A verb in the simple **future** tense shows that an action will happen later.

Review of Regular and Irregular Verbs

Verbs are divided into two groups: **regular** and **irregular**.

A verb is **regular** if it is made past tense by adding an *–ed* ending to the main verb.

A verb is **irregular** if it is made past tense by making a spelling change.

In writing, one of the most common mistakes made is mixing present-tense and past-tense verbs. This is called inappropriate shifts in verb tenses. Today, you will learn how to recognize and correct mixed tenses in a paragraph. Recite the Verb Chant with your teacher.

Verb Chart for Regular Verbs

COLUMN 1 PRESENT TENSE	COLUMN 2 PAST TENSE	COLUMN 3 HV PLUS AN -ED MAIN VERB		COLUMN 4 HV PLUS AN -ING MAIN VERB	
help	helped	(has, have, had)	helped	(am, is, are, was, were)	helping
jog	jogged	(has, have, had)	jogged	(am, is, are, was, were)	jogging

Verb Chart for Irregular Verbs

COLUMN 1 PRESENT TENSE	COLUMN 2 PAST TENSE	COLUMN 3 HV PLUS A 3RD COLUMN MAIN VERB		COLUMN 4 HV PLUS AN -ING MAIN VERB	
become	became	(has, have, had)	become	(am, is, are, was, were)	becoming
begin	began	(has, have, had)	begun	(am, is, are, was, were)	beginning
blow	blew	(has, have, had)	blown	(am, is, are, was, were)	blowing
break	broke	(has, have, had)	broken	(am, is, are, was, were)	breaking
bring	brought	(has, have, had)	brought	(am, is, are, was, were)	bringing
buy	bought	(has, have, had)	bought	(am, is, are, was, were)	buying
choose	chose	(has, have, had)	chosen	(am, is, are, was, were)	choosing
come	came	(has, have, had)	come	(am, is, are, was, were)	coming

Name: _____ Date:_____

GRAMMAR:

Exercise 1: Classify each sentence.

1. _____ Cole and I gave him a hat at the ballpark.

2. _____ Will we need new luggage for our trip to Europe?

3. _____ Ouch! I stepped on a rusty nail in that board!

SKILLS:

Exercise 2: Change the **past-tense** verbs in Paragraph 1 to **present-tense** verbs in Paragraph 2.

PARAGRAPH 1: Past Tense

Our hometown parade [1. **was**] a big event in our town. My family [2. **arrived**] early because we [3. **wanted**] good seats. We [4. **placed**] our chairs close to the curb and [5. **waited**] for the parade to begin. My little sister [6. **wiggled**] and [7. **squirmed**] until a clown [8. **stopped**] and [9. **gave**] her a pink balloon. Then, we [10. **heard**] the marching bands in the distance. The parade [11. **was**] beginning!

PARAGRAPH 2: Present Tense

Our hometown parade [1. ____] a big event in our town. My family [2. ____] early because we [3. ____] good seats. We [4. ____] our chairs close to the curb and [5. ____] for the parade to begin. My little sister [6. ____] and [7. ____] until a clown [8. ____] and [9. ____] her a pink balloon. Then, we [10. ____] the marching bands in the distance. The parade [11. ____] beginning!

Jingle Time

Listening and Speaking

Practice Jingles 21–23 in the Jingle Section. **PAGES Q10-Q11**

Grammar Time

Mixed Patterns 1-3

Classify the Practice Sentences with your teacher, using the Question and Answer Flow.

Practice Sentences   ORAL PARTICIPATION

1. _____ Yikes! That scary movie will give me nightmares tonight!

2. _____ Tonight, we went to my uncle's new restaurant for dinner.

3. _____ Will you mow our neighbor's yard during the summer?

4. _____ The mother bird fed her babies several bugs from the garden.

Review: Transitive and Intransitive Verbs

Transitive verbs are action verbs with a direct object. They are used in Pattern 2 and 3 sentences. **Intransitive verbs** are action verbs without a direct object. They are used in Pattern 1 sentences.

In the sentences that you just classified, which verbs are transitive? Explain. Which verb is intransitive? Explain.

Reference 158

Identifying Pattern Numbers Only for Patterns 1-3

When identifying mixed patterns, you must concentrate on the core of each sentence. Since the core is the pattern of the sentence, classify only the main parts (**SN V**), (**SN V-t DO**), and (**SN V-t IO DO**) without classifying all the other words in the sentence. Classify the core parts, determine the pattern, and write only the pattern number in the blank. With practice, you will be able to identify the pattern by sight.

Example: ▶ Write the correct pattern number in each blank.
(**P1 = SN V, P2 = SN V-t DO, P3 = SN V-t IO DO**)

P3 1. Dora gave me a party.

P1 2. The baby cried for her mother.

P3 3. Will you give us a ride to the gym?

P2 4. Mom wrote a note to my teacher.

Guided Practice

Exercise 1: Write the correct pattern number in each blank.
(**P1 = SN V, P2 = SN V-t DO, P3 = SN V-t IO DO**)

P2 1. I put my lunch in my backpack.

_____ 2. My friends and I played until dark.

_____ 3. Patty sang her mom a song.

_____ 4. I jumped into the cold water.

_____ 5. Hand me the keys to David's car.

_____ 6. Dad grilled hotdogs for us.

Exercise 2: Write the main verbs in Exercise 1 and identify them with a **T** for transitive or an **I** for intransitive. Then, think of other sentences that use transitive and intransitive verbs.

VERBS	T OR I	VERBS	T OR I	VERBS	T OR I
1. **put**	**T**	3.		5.	
2.		4.		6.	

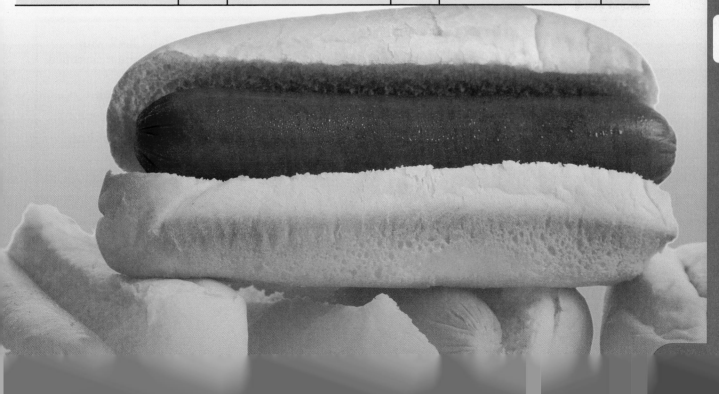

Case Check

After you have classified the Practice Sentences, recite a Case Check and a Noun Check with your teacher. These checks help you analyze nouns and pronouns and understand how they are used in sentences.

Case Check Practice Sentences

Sentence 1: Yikes! That scary movie will give me nightmares tonight!

me: indirect object pronoun, *objective case*

Sentence 2: Tonight, we went to my uncle's new restaurant for dinner.

We: subject pronoun, *subjective case*

my: possessive pronoun, *possessive case*

Sentence 3: Will you mow our neighbor's yard during the summer?

You: subject pronoun, *subjective case*

our: possessive pronoun, *possessive case*

Sentence 4: The mother bird fed her babies several bugs from the garden.

her: possessive pronoun, *possessive case*

Noun Check

REMINDER: Any pronoun that uses the letter **O** as part of its classified label is in the objective case because the **O** stands for *object*: **IO** for indirect *object*, **DO** for direct *object*, and **OP** for *object* of the preposition.

Noun Check

Do a Noun Check with the sentences just classified.

☐ 1. **Identify the nouns in a Noun Check.**
(Say the job and the noun. Circle each noun.)

☐ 2. **Identify the nouns as singular or plural.**
(Write **S** or **P** above the noun.)

☐ 3. **Identify the nouns as common or proper.**
(Write **C** or **P** above the noun.)

Skill Time

Shifts in Verb Tenses

One of the most common mistakes made in writing is mixing present-tense and past-tense verbs. This is called inappropriate shifts in verb tenses. Remember to use verbs in the same tense if you are describing events that occur at the same time. Today, you will learn how to recognize and correct mixed tenses in a paragraph.

Reference 159

Recognizing and Correcting Shifts in Verb Tenses

Change the underlined mixed-tense verbs in Paragraph 1 to **past-tense** verbs in **Paragraph 2** and to **present-tense** verbs in **Paragraph 3**.

PARAGRAPH 1: Mixed Tenses

My new puppy, Rufus, ^{1.}**sniffs** everything and ^{2.}**ran** all around his new home. We ^{3.}**had** a great time. But when night ^{4.}**comes** , Rufus ^{5.}**missed** his mother. He ^{6.}**cries** a lot. My mom ^{7.}**takes** an alarm clock and a hot water bottle to Rufus's bed. She ^{8.}**placed** them under his blanket. Rufus ^{9.}**went** right to sleep because these things ^{10.}**remind** him of his mother!

CONTINUED ON NEXT PAGE

PARAGRAPH 2: Past Tense

My new puppy, Rufus [1. **sniffed**] everything and [2. **ran**] all around his new home. We [3. **had**] a great time. But when night [4. **came**], Rufus [5. **missed**] his mother. He [6. **cried**] a lot. My mom [7. **took**] an alarm clock and a hot water bottle to Rufus's bed. She [8. **placed**] them under his blanket. Rufus [9. **went**] right to sleep because these things [10. **reminded**] him of his mother!

PARAGRAPH 3: Present Tense

My new puppy, Rufus, [1. **sniffs**] everything and [2. **runs**] all around his new home. We [3. **have**] a great time. But when night [4. **comes**], Rufus [5. **misses**] his mother. He [6. **cries**] a lot. My mom [7. **takes**] an alarm clock and a hot water bottle to Rufus's bed. She [8. **places**] them under his blanket. Rufus [9. **goes**] right to sleep because these things [10. **remind**] him of his mother!

Name: _____ Date: _____

GRAMMAR:

Exercise 1: Classify each sentence.

1. _____ Did Isabella go to the movie tonight?

2. _____ Robert asked the teacher a very good question.

3. _____ Cool! Billy told Nate and me about his secret cave!

Exercise 2: Write the correct pattern number in each blank.
(P1 = SN V, P2 = SN V-t DO, P3 = SN V-t IO DO)

_____ 1. May I borrow this movie tonight?

_____ 2. We are leaving in one hour.

_____ 3. Send us a card from Sweden.

_____ 4. Did Dad give you the message?

_____ 5. Isabella drew a picture of her cat.

_____ 6. My favorite baseball team won!

End Lesson 5

SKILLS:

> **Exercise 3:** ▶ Change the **mixed-tense** verbs in **Paragraph 1** to **past-tense** verbs in **Paragraph 2**.

PARAGRAPH 1: **Mixed Tenses**

My family [1. **owns**] a restaurant. My dad [2. **is**] the manager, and he [3. **keeps**] us busy. My uncle [4. **cooked**], and my brother and I [5. **help**] him in the kitchen. My aunt [6. **serves**] the food, and my three sisters [7. **helped**] her. My mom [8. **has**] the best job of all. She [9. **collects**] the money and [10. **hears**] the compliments from the customers for such a good meal.

PARAGRAPH 2: **Past Tense**

My family [1. _____] a restaurant. My dad [2. _____] the manager, and he [3. _____] us busy. My uncle [4. _____], and my brother and I [5. _____] him in the kitchen. My aunt [6. _____] the food, and my three sisters [7. _____] her. My mom [8. _____] the best job of all. She [9. _____] the money and [10. _____] the compliments from the customers for such a good meal.

Word Time

Vocabulary and Analogy

Word 19 → **identical** (ī děn′ tǐ kŭl)

Definition: alike in every way; similar; twin

Synonym: alike   **Antonym:** different

Sentence: The magician held up a card **identical** to the one I had picked!

Analogy → **correct : accurate :: similar : alike**

Relationship: Synonym

Thinking Process: Just as **correct** means about the same as **accurate**, **similar** means about the same as **alike**. Therefore, this is a **synonym** analogy.

ACTIVITY   Draw a picture or write a poem or story in your Vocabulary Notebook to help you remember the word identical.

(Picture Idea: Draw several sets of items that are identical.)

Spelling

Study this Spelling Rule to help you become a better speller.

Spelling Rule 7 — Making Irregular Nouns Plural

Some nouns are made plural by spelling the word differently instead of adding **-s** or **-es**.

➡ Example: **man** ⟶ **men**

Sometimes a word is spelled exactly the same, whether singular or plural.

➡ Example: **deer** ⟶ **deer**   **fish** ⟶ **fish**

Spelling Words For each pair of words: **Recite**, **Spell**, and **Repeat**.

Recite woman - women   **Spell** w-o-m-e-n   **Repeat** women

1. **woman - women**
2. **mouse - mice**
3. **ox - oxen**
4. **child - children**
5. **sheep - sheep**
6. **fish - fish**

fish   fish

Jingle Time

Listening and Speaking

Practice Jingles 21 and 23 in the Jingle Section. **PAGES Q10-Q11**

Grammar Time

Mixed Patterns 1-3

Classify the Practice Sentences with your teacher, using the Question and Answer Flow.

Practice Sentences

1. _____ I shopped yesterday at the new supermarket.

2. _____ Will you give Anna and me a ride to school in the morning?

3. _____ Look at the bottom of the page for the answer.

4. _____ The small donkey carried a huge load of supplies.

Review: Transitive and Intransitive Verbs

Transitive verbs are action verbs with a direct object. They are used in Pattern 2 and 3 sentences. **Intransitive verbs** are action verbs without a direct object. They are used in Pattern 1 sentences.

In the sentences that you just classified, which verbs are transitive? Explain. Which verbs are intransitive? Explain.

Checks and Chants

After you have classified the Practice Sentences, recite a Case Check and a Noun Check with your teacher. These checks help you analyze nouns and pronouns and understand how they are used in sentences.

Case Check Practice Sentences

Sentence 1: I shopped yesterday at the new supermarket.

I: subject pronoun, *subjective case*

Sentence 2: Will you give Anna and me a ride to school in the morning?

you: subject pronoun, *subjective case*

me: compound indirect object pronoun, *objective case*

Sentence 3: Look at the bottom of the page for the answer.

(You): understood subject pronoun, *subjective case*

Sentence 4: The small donkey carried a huge load of supplies.

None

REMINDER: Any pronoun that uses the letter **O** as part of its classified label is in the objective case because the **O** stands for *object*: **IO** for indirect *object*, **DO** for direct *object*, and **OP** for *object* of the preposition.

Noun Check
Do a Noun Check with the sentences just classified.

1. **Identify the nouns in a Noun Check.**
   (Say the job and the noun. Circle each noun.)

2. **Identify the nouns as singular or plural.**
   (Write **S** or **P** above the noun.)

3. **Identify the nouns as common or proper.**
   (Write **C** or **P** above the noun.)

Skill Time

Review: Simple Verb Tenses

The word **tense** means *time*. The three simple verb tenses show that an action takes place in the present, past, or future.

1. A verb in the simple **present** tense shows that an action is happening now.

2. A verb in the simple **past** tense shows that an action has already happened.

3. A verb in the simple **future** tense shows that an action will happen later.

Review of Regular and Irregular Verbs

Verbs are divided into two groups: **regular** and **irregular**.

A verb is **regular** if it is made past tense by adding an *–ed* ending to the main verb.

A verb is **irregular** if it is made past tense by making a spelling change.

Recite the Verb Chant with your teacher.

Verb Chart for Regular Verbs

COLUMN 1 PRESENT TENSE	COLUMN 2 PAST TENSE	COLUMN 3 HV PLUS AN *-ED* MAIN VERB	COLUMN 4 HV PLUS AN *-ING* MAIN VERB
play	played	(has, have, had) played	(am, is, are, was, were) playing
spell	spelled	(has, have, had) spelled	(am, is, are, was, were) spelling

Verb Chart for Irregular Verbs

COLUMN 1 PRESENT TENSE	COLUMN 2 PAST TENSE	COLUMN 3 HV PLUS A 3RD COLUMN MAIN VERB	COLUMN 4 HV PLUS AN *-ING* MAIN VERB
get	got	(has, have, had) gotten	(am, is, are, was, were) getting
give	gave	(has, have, had) given	(am, is, are, was, were) giving
go	went	(has, have, had) gone	(am, is, are, was, were) going
grow	grew	(has, have, had) grown	(am, is, are, was, were) growing
know	knew	(has, have, had) known	(am, is, are, was, were) knowing
lose	lost	(has, have, had) lost	(am, is, are, was, were) losing
make	made	(has, have, had) made	(am, is, are, was, were) making
ride	rode	(has, have, had) ridden	(am, is, are, was, were) riding

Name: _____ Date:_____

GRAMMAR:

Exercise 1: Classify each sentence.

1. _____ Brad and Paula rode their bikes to town.

2. _____ Curtis and I played in the park until dark.

3. _____ Today, Mom and Dad gave us several chores.

Exercise 2: Write the correct pattern number in each blank.
(**P1 = SN V, P2 = SN V-t DO, P3 = SN V-t IO DO**)

_____ 1. We waited for the bus.

_____ 2. The cows ran to the pond.

_____ 3. Make him a good lunch.

_____ 4. Cody tapped his foot impatiently.

_____ 5. My sister took a very short nap.

_____ 6. Did Sam give you the note?

SKILLS:

Exercise 3: Change the **mixed-tense** verbs in **Paragraph 1** to **present-tense** verbs in **Paragraph 2**.

PARAGRAPH 1: Mixed Tenses

Mom ^{1.} **taught** me how to be organized. It ^{2.} **was** easy if I ^{3.} **get** everything ready for school the night before. First, I ^{4.} **placed** all my finished homework in my book bag. My homework ^{5.} **is** ready. After that, I ^{6.} **select** the clothes I ^{7.} **wanted** to wear. Next, I ^{8.} **took** my bath and ^{9.} **brush** my teeth. Finally, I ^{10.} **crawled** sleepily into bed. I ^{11.} **love** being organized because I ^{12.} **felt** in control and that ^{13.} **made** me happy.

PARAGRAPH 2: Present Tense

Mom ^{1.} _____ me how to be organized. It ^{2.} _____ easy if I ^{3.} _____ everything ready for school the night before. First, I ^{4.} _____ all my finished homework in my book bag. My homework ^{5.} _____ ready. After that, I ^{6.} _____ the clothes I ^{7.} _____ to wear. Next, I ^{8.} _____ my bath and ^{9.} _____ my teeth. Finally, I ^{10.} _____ sleepily into bed. I ^{11.} _____ being organized because I ^{12.} _____ in control and that ^{13.} _____ me happy.

Chapter 14

Word Time

Vocabulary and Analogy

Word 20 **similar** (SIHM uh ler)

Definition: having some of the same traits; having a likeness or resemblance

Synonym: alike   **Antonym:** different

Sentence: A radish is **similar** to a beet because it grows underground.

Etymology **Word History of similar**

Latin Root: assimilares (uh SIHM uh LAR ays)

Definition: being similar or about the same

Other words from the root: similarity, facsimile

Analogy **similar : same :: different : varied**

Relationship: Synonym

Thinking Process: Just as **similar** means about the same as **same**, **different** means about the same as **varied**. Therefore, this is a **synonym** analogy.

ACTIVITY
Draw a picture or write a poem or story in your Vocabulary Notebook to help you remember the word similar.

(Picture Idea: Draw a picture of two objects that share similar traits, such as a butterfly/moth, a pen/pencil, or a car/truck. Draw symbols or use colors to show which parts are similar.)

Spelling

It's time to review what you've learned about spelling!

Spelling Rule 7 — Making Irregular Nouns Plural

Some nouns are made plural by spelling the word differently instead of adding **-s** or **-es**.

➡ Example: **man** ⟹ **men**

Sometimes a word is spelled exactly the same, whether singular or plural.

➡ Example: **deer** ⟹ **deer**   **fish** ⟹ **fish**

Spelling Words For each pair of words: **Recite**, **Spell**, and **Repeat**.

Recite woman - women   **Spell** w-o-m-e-n   **Repeat** women

1. woman - women
2. mouse - mice
3. ox - oxen
4. child - children
5. sheep - sheep
6. fish - fish

fish   fish

Classifying Mixed Patterns 1-3

Classify the Practice Sentences with your teacher,
using the Question and Answer Flow.

Practice Sentences   ORAL PARTICIPATION

1. _____ Play us a soothing song on the piano after dinner.

2. _____ The baby monkey hugged Amber tightly
around her neck.

3. _____ Mmm! The tender steaks sizzled invitingly
on the grill.

4. _____ The pet store down the street gave our
puppies special treats.

Review: Transitive and Intransitive Verbs

Transitive verbs are action verbs with a direct object. They are used in
Pattern 2 and 3 sentences. **Intransitive verbs** are action verbs without
a direct object. They are used in Pattern 1 sentences.

In the sentences that you just classified, which verbs are transitive? Explain.

Which verb is intransitive? Explain.

Review: Parts of Speech

REMINDER: How a word is used in a sentence determines its part of speech.
What are the eight parts of speech?

What are the labels for the eight parts of speech?

Writing Time

Blueprint for Building a Sentence

Today, you will learn how to add an Indirect Object and Verb-transitive to your blueprint labels to write an original sentence.

Reference 160

Designing a Sentence Blueprint,
Adding Indirect Objects

Design and build your sentence on Classroom Practice 62.

1. Use the core labels, **SN/SP**, **V-t**, **IO**, and **DO**, only once and **in that order**.

2. The other labels, **Adj**, **Adv**, **A**, **P**, **OP**, **PPA**, **C**, **HV**, **I**, and **PNA**, can be used as many times as you wish, in any order you wish, *as long as they make sense*. (REMEMBER: Complete sense is one of the five parts of a complete sentence.)

3. **Instructions for the new label, IO:** First, think of a transitive verb that makes sense with an indirect object, such as "*gave*," "*told*," "*handed*," "*sang*," and so on. Write your transitive verb under the **V-t** label. Then, think of a noun or object pronoun that tells to whom or for whom the action of the verb is done. Write your noun or object pronoun under the **IO** label.

4. Write the labels in the order you choose on the **Labels** line.

5. Write a word that makes sense for each label.

After writing your original sentence on Classroom Practice 62, use the revision strategies on page 620 to help you make revisions.

Use Revision Strategies to Revise Your Original Sentence

REMEMBER: **Revising** means looking for ways to improve your writing. As you revise your Original Sentence, write the abbreviation of the revision strategy you used under each word in your Revised Sentence.

1 Synonym (syn) **2** Antonym (ant) **3** Word Change (wc)

4 Added Word (add) **5** Deleted Word (delete) **6** No Change (nc)

When you have finished, your paper should resemble the example below.

Labels:	A	SN	V-t	PPA	IO	A	Adj	DO
Original Sentence:	The	leader	gave	his	men	a	loud	order.
Revised Sentence:	The	captain	gave	his	crew	a	bold	command.
Revision Strategy:	(nc)	(syn)	(nc)	(nc)	(syn)	(nc)	(wc)	(syn)

Student Tip...

1. Use your Vocabulary Words, Power Words, a thesaurus, and a dictionary to help you write your Original and Revised Sentences.

2. As you go through each word of your Original Sentence, think about the changes and improvements you want to make.

3. To help you improve your sentence, use your revision strategies.

4. As you revise your original sentence, keep this information in mind:

   • Antonyms and Word Changes will change your sentence's meaning.

   • Synonyms and No Changes will keep the meaning of the original sentence.

   • Added Words and Deleted Words can change the meaning of your sentence or keep it the same, depending on the words you choose to add or delete.

Name: _____ Date: _____

Exercise 1: Write your own blueprint labels. Use the labels to write an original sentence. Then, revise your sentence, writing the abbreviation of the revision strategy under each word.

Labels:

Original Sentence:

Revised Sentence:

Revision Strategy:

Labels:

Original Sentence:

Revised Sentence:

Revision Strategy:

Exercise 2: Rewrite your revised sentence on the lines below. Use the checklist to check your sentence.

_____

_____

Sentence Checklist: ☐ Capital letter ☐ Subject ☐ Verb ☐ Complete sense ☐ End mark

Lesson 7

Writing a *Mover* & **Shaker** Sentence in Your Journal:

Skip two lines below your last entry and write the date and chapter number. Then, skip one line and write a Mover & Shaker Sentence with a **repeated verb**. This is an amazing strategy that allows a writer to add more description with a distinctive flair. Repeat the verb at the end of a sentence; then, add more information about the repeated verb.

> **Simple Sentence:** The apes at the zoo just kept chattering.
>
> **Mover & Shaker Sentence:** The apes at the zoo just kept chattering, chattering and swinging from tree to tree.

Compare all of the Mover & Shaker Sentences you have written so far.

JOURNAL WRITING 24

Write an entry in your notebook journal or digital journal. Use the spelling pattern in Spelling Rule 7 to help you spell words correctly.

Grammar Time

Classifying Mixed Patterns 1-3

Classify the Practice Sentences with your teacher,
using the Question and Answer Flow.

Practice Sentences   ORAL PARTICIPATION

1. _____ Write your mom and dad a poem for
their anniversary.

2. _____ Did Randy talk to Wesley and Angela
during recess?

3. _____ Someday, Carlos will teach me a Spanish song.

4. _____ Bobby and I ate a salad with our pizza today.

Writing Time

Review: Writing the Four Kinds of Sentences

Choose one of the following options:

1. Write a *declarative, exclamatory, interrogative,* and *imperative* sentence,
   using a different spelling word in each sentence. (*See Chapter 2 for a
   review of the four kinds of sentences.*)

CONTINUED ON NEXT PAGE

2. Write a declarative sentence, using one of your spelling words. Then, change that sentence to the other three kinds of sentences (*exclamatory, interrogative, and imperative*).

3. Write a compound or complex declarative sentence, using at least one of your spelling words. (*See Chapter 7 for a review of compound and complex sentences.*)

For your sentences, use the spelling words from Rule 7: **women, mice, oxen, children, sheep, fish**.

The Reading Club is a time to get into small groups and share a favorite book with others. Use the suggestions below to help you share your book.

♦ Give the title and author of the book. Show the book if you still have it.

♦ Describe a particular setting that is important to the story and tell where it is found in the book.

♦ Describe the main characters and tell something about them and discuss the specific evidence from the book that helps you focus your impressions about them.

♦ Tell what happens to the characters as the plot progresses. Be brief. Don't tell too much.

♦ Tell why you liked the book.

Write down the title and author of any book that you would like to read. Follow the **Rules for Discussion** and listen respectfully to other members of your group as different books are shared.

⚡Challenge Tell how the characters responded to challenges. Would your response have been different? How would you have responded?

Name: _____ Date:_____

GRAMMAR:

Exercise 1: Classify each sentence.

1. _____ Take Papa some cookies and a glass of milk.

2. _____ Today, the two frisky mares galloped around the field.

3. _____ Did Mr. Hanks bring this delicious dessert for us?

Exercise 2: Write the correct pattern number in each blank.
(P1 = SN V, P2 = SN V-t DO, P3 = SN V-t IO DO)

_____ 1. Ed told me a funny story.

_____ 2. Allie rode to town with us.

_____ 3. His bike has a flat tire.

_____ 4. Talk to your brothers today.

_____ 5. Matt gave me a new CD.

_____ 6. They built a new brick house.

Exercise 3: Write the main verbs in Exercise 2 and identify them with a **T** for transitive or an **I** for intransitive.

VERBS	T OR I	VERBS	T OR I	VERBS	T OR I
1.		3.		5.	
2.		4.		6.	

Exercise 4: Write **S** for subjective, **O** for objective, or **P** for possessive in the blank. Underline the answer in parentheses.

____ 1. (**Him, His**) football was in the backyard.

____ 2. Ethan played football with (**Abe and I, Abe and me**).

____ 3. Nathan and (**me, I**) rode bikes in the park.

____ 4. Aunt Emma made (**she and I, her and me**) chocolate brownies.

SKILLS:

Exercise 5: Change the **mixed-tense** verbs in **Paragraph 1** to **past-tense** verbs in **Paragraph 2**.

PARAGRAPH 1: Mixed Tenses

My brother [1. **finds**] a snake by the garage. He [2. **yelled**] excitedly for everyone. Everyone [3. **comes**] very fast. We all [4. **stand**] back until Dad [5. **looked**] at the snake very carefully. The snake [6. **is**] only a little garden snake this time. But my brother [7. **is**] wise when he [8. **calls**] for an older person. My dad [9. **is**] proud of him and [10. **tells**] him so. My brother [11. **grins**] and [12. **walked**] off. He [13. **is**] looking for another snake!

PARAGRAPH 2: Past Tense

My brother [1. _____] a snake by the garage. He [2. _____] excitedly for everyone. Everyone [3. _____] very fast. We all [4. _____] back until Dad [5. _____] at the snake very carefully. The snake [6. _____] only a little garden snake this time. But my brother [7. _____] wise when he [8. _____] for an older person. My dad [9. _____] proud of him and [10. _____] him so. My brother [11. _____] and [12. _____] off. He [13. _____] looking for another snake!

Exercise 6: Fill in the circle beside each correct answer.

1. Antonym for: **similar** ◯ alike ◯ different
2. Definition: alike in every way ◯ identical ◯ different
3. similar : same :: different : ◯ alike ◯ varied

WRITING:

Exercise 7: Write one of the four types of sentences (*declarative, exclamatory, interrogative,* or *imperative*), using the vocabulary word **identical**.

_____

_____

Oral Review Time

With your teacher, read the questions below. Do you know all the answers? Listen carefully for answers you do not know. After the review, you will have a chapter test.

1. What word receives what the direct object names?

2. Where is an indirect object located in a sentence?

3. What type of verb is used with an indirect object?

4. What are the core parts of a Pattern 3 sentence?

5. What are the three simple verb tenses?

6. What kind of verb makes the past tense by adding an -ed ending?

7. What kind of verb makes the past tense by a spelling change?

8. What tense shows that an action is happening now?

9. What tense shows that an action has already happened?

10. What tense shows that an action will happen later?

Time to evaluate your goals!

Check your study-skills progress. Are you staying organized? Do you listen carefully and write things down? Are you using your time wisely? Write a paragraph evaluating your short-term and long-term goals. Be sure to include any changes you have made to your goals.

Skill Time

Making an outline gives you a visual map of what is read or heard. It is easy to study from outlines because ideas are grouped together in an organized pattern to show their relationship to one another.

Reference 161

Topic Outline, Adding Details

1. Main Points *(two or more main points about the topic)*

→ Use Roman numerals (I. II. III.) for main points.
   You must have two or more main points.

→ Capitalize the first word but do not use an end mark.

→ Line up the periods after the Roman numerals, one under the other.

Pet Chores

| I. Cat chores | MAIN POINT |
| II. Dog chores | MAIN POINT |

2. Subtopics *(information that supports a main point)*

→ Use capital letters (A. B. C.) for subtopics.
   You must have two or more subtopics.

→ Line up subtopics under the first word of the main point.

→ Line up the periods after the capital letters.

→ Capitalize the first word but do not use an end mark.

I. Cat chores   MAIN POINT

A. Feed cat	SUBTOPIC
B. Change water	SUBTOPIC
C. Clean litter box	SUBTOPIC

3. Details (*information that supports a subtopic*)

→ Use Arabic numerals for details. You must have two or more details.

→ Line up details under the first word of the subtopic.

→ Line up periods after the Arabic numerals.

→ Capitalize the first word but do not use an end mark.

II. Dog chores   `MAIN POINT`

   A. Food   `SUBTOPIC`

   B. Water   `SUBTOPIC`

   C. Exercise   `SUBTOPIC`

     1. Go for a walk   `DETAIL`

     2. Play games   `DETAIL`

The Outline Example

The outline below contains information in one organized, easy-to-read place.

Pet Chores   `Title`

  I. Cat chores   `I. Main Point`

    A. Feed cat   `A. Subtopic`

    B. Change water   `B. Subtopic`

    C. Clean litter box   `C. Subtopic`

  II. Dog chores   `II. Main Point`

    A. Food   `A. Subtopic`

    B. Water   `B. Subtopic`

    C. Exercise   `C. Subtopic`

      1. Go for a walk   `1. Detail`

      2. Play games   `2. Detail`

Name: _____ Date: _____

SKILLS:

Exercise 1: ▸ Put the information into outline form, following the rules for outlining.

Outline:

Chores at Home
Main points
inside chores
outside chores

Subtopics
keep bedroom neat
clean kitchen
take out trash

yard
garden
Details
make bed

hang clothes
empty dishwasher
load dishwasher
wipe counters

mow grass
rake leaves
pull garden weeds
pick vegetables

_____

_____

_____

_____

_____

_____

_____

_____

_____

_____

_____

_____

_____

_____

_____

_____

_____

Jingle Time

Listening and Speaking

Practice Jingle 4 in the Jingle Section. **PAGE Q3**

Jingle 24 — The Predicate Noun Jingle

A predicate, predicate noun
    Is a special, special noun
        In the predicate, predicate, predicate
            That means the **same as the subject**,
                The simple, simple subject.

        A predicate, predicate noun
            Follows after a linking verb.

To locate a predicate noun,
    Ask **WHAT** or **WHO** after the verb and verify the answer.
        Verify that the noun in the predicate means
        the same thing as the subject,
            The simple, simple subject.

Review: Sentence Patterns 1-3

→ **Pattern 1 core:** noun-verb (**SN V**)

→ **Pattern 2 core:** noun-verb-noun (**SN V-t DO**)

→ **Pattern 3 core:** noun-verb-noun-noun (**SN V-t IO DO**)

Today, you will learn another sentence pattern, **Pattern 4**, which has two nouns and a linking verb (noun-linking verb-noun) for its core. To understand Pattern 4, you must first understand its core parts, *the subject noun, linking verb,* and *predicate noun:* **SN LV PrN**.

Reference 162

Predicate Noun, Linking Verb, and Pattern 4

Predicate Noun

A **predicate noun** is a noun in the predicate that means the same thing as the subject noun.

To find a predicate noun, ask **what** or **who** AFTER the verb.

A **predicate noun** is labeled with the abbreviation **PrN**.

➡ Example 1:
                    SN   LV   PrN
Brandon's father is a pilot.

➡ Example 2:
       SN LV   PrN
Texas is a big state.

➡ Example 3:
           SN   LV   PrN
Strawberries are my favorite fruit.

In the examples, *father* and *pilot* mean the **same person**; *Texas* and *state* mean the **same place**; *strawberries* and *fruit* mean the **same thing**. In each sentence, the subject noun and the predicate noun are connected by a linking verb.

CONTINUED ON NEXT PAGE ▶

Linking Verbs

A **linking verb links** the subject to a predicate noun. A predicate noun is always located after a **linking verb**.

A linking verb is not an action verb because it shows a state of being. It tells what the subject **is** instead of *what* the subject does.

A **linking verb** is labeled with the abbreviation **LV**.

Examples of linking verbs: *am, is, are, was, were, being, been, appear, become, feel, grow, look, remain, seem, smell, sound,* and *taste.*

Pattern 4

Sentence Patterns identify the order of the core parts of sentences. The fourth pattern, **Pattern 4**, has *three* core parts: a Subject Noun (**SN**), a Linking Verb (**LV**), and a Predicate Noun (**PrN**).

Pattern 4 is identified by its core parts: **SN LV PrN P4** (*Subject Noun, Linking Verb, Predicate Noun, Pattern 4*).

Adding Predicate Nouns to the Question and Answer Flow

Sample Sentence: Madelyn is a talented dancer.

1. Who is a talented dancer?
   Madelyn - Subject Noun............................(Write **SN** above *Madelyn.*)

2. What is being said about Madelyn?
   Madelyn is - Verb................................(Write **V** above *is.*)

3. Madelyn is who? **dancer - verify the noun**

4. Does *dancer* mean the same thing as *Madelyn*? **Yes**

5. **Dancer - Predicate Noun**............................(Write **PrN** above *dancer.*)

6. **Is - Linking Verb**................................(Write **L** above *is.*)

7. What kind of dancer? **talented - Adjective**........(Write **Adj** above *talented.*)

8. **A - Article Adjective**..............................(Write **A** above *a.*)

9. **Subject Noun, Linking Verb, Predicate Noun, Pattern 4**
   (Write **SN LV PrN P4** in the blank.)

CONTINUED ON NEXT PAGE >>>

10. **Skill Check!**
> **Linking Verb – check again**
> (This check is to make sure the "**L**" is added to the verb.)

> **No prepositional phrases**

> **Period, statement, declarative sentence**
> (Write **D** at the end of the sentence.)

> Go back to the verb.
> Divide the complete subject from the complete predicate.

> Is this sentence in a natural or inverted order? **Natural – no change**

	SN		LV	A	Adj		PrN	

SN LV
PrN P4
Madelyn / is a talented dancer. **D**

Watch for Predicate Pronouns

Predicate Pronoun

A **predicate pronoun** is a pronoun in the predicate that means the same thing as the subject.

To find a predicate pronoun, ask *what* or *who* AFTER the verb.

Predicate pronouns come from the subject pronoun list, because they are the same thing as the subject. The subject pronouns are *I*, *we*, *you*, *he*, *she*, *it*, and *they*.

A **predicate pronoun** is labeled with the abbreviation **PrP**.

Discussion Questions:

1. What is a noun called that renames the subject in a sentence?

2. Where is a predicate noun located?

3. What kind of verb shows a state of being and connects the subject noun to the predicate noun?

4. What are the core parts of a Pattern 4 sentence?

5. What is the pattern in a Pattern 4 sentence?

Review: Sentence Patterns

→ **Pattern 1** is **SN V**.
It has a **noun-verb (N V)** core.

→ **Pattern 2** is **SN V-t DO**.
It has a **noun-verb-noun (N V N)** core.

→ **Pattern 3** is **SN V-t IO DO**.
It has a **noun-verb-noun-noun (N V N N)** core.

→ **Pattern 4** is **SN LV PrN**.
It has a **noun-linking verb-noun (N LV N)** core.

The location of a noun determines its job in a sentence. Only certain noun jobs form the pattern parts of a sentence. For each pattern, the order of the core nouns does not change. A noun that is an object of the preposition is not part of a sentence pattern.

Classifying Sentences

Classify the Introductory Sentences with your teacher, using the Question and Answer Flow. Classifying these sentences will help you learn predicate nouns and linking verbs.

Introductory Sentences

1. _____ My dad is a firefighter.

2. _____ My dad and uncle are firefighters in a large city.

3. _____ Popcorn is Jermaine's favorite snack.

Lesson 1

Word Study

Compare Sentence 1 to Sentence 2. The sentences mean basically the same thing, but Sentence 2 is more appealing because of the added details. Notice how adjectives, adverbs, and prepositional phrases are used to improve and expand the meaning of the original sentence. Name the words and phrases in Sentence 2 that are used to add more details. When you write, ask yourself this question: Have I used enough adjectives, adverbs, and prepositional phrases to make my sentences interesting? Brainstorm and make a list of interesting adjectives, adverbs, and prepositional phrases that can be used for elaboration.

Noun Check:
Adding Predicate Nouns

Now that you have classified the Introductory Sentences, it is time to do a Noun Check. During a Noun Check, you identify nouns in different noun jobs. Today, the predicate noun is added to the Noun Check. You must decide whether the predicate noun is a noun or a pronoun. If it is a noun, it will be circled. If it is a pronoun, it will not be circled. Now, recite the Noun Check with your teacher.

Noun Check Introductory Sentences

Circle the nouns in the sentences.

Sentence 1: My (dad) is a (firefighter.)

Subject Noun **dad**, *yes, it is a noun;*
Predicate Noun **firefighter**, *yes, it is a noun.*

Sentence 2: My (dad) and (uncle) are (firefighters) in a large (city.)

Compound Subject Noun **dad**, *yes, it is a noun;*
Compound Subject Noun **uncle**, *yes, it is a noun;*
Predicate Noun **firefighters**, *yes, it is a noun;*
Object of the Preposition **city** *yes, it is a noun.*

Sentence 3: (Popcorn) is Jermaine's favorite (snack.)

Subject Noun **popcorn**, *yes, it is a noun;*
Predicate Noun **snack**, *yes, it is a noun.*

Are there any Possessive Nouns in the sentences? **Yes**
Name it. **Jermaine's**

Bringing It All Together
The Noun Chart
Adding Predicate Nouns

The Noun Chart below adds the predicate noun and reviews
the other information about nouns that you have learned.
Discuss the Noun Chart below with your teacher.

 Reference 163

Noun Chart

       PPA CSN   C   CSN   LV   PrN
<u>SN LV</u> My dad and uncle / are firefighters
PrN P4

        P A Adj   OP
      (in a large city). D

Directions: Use the sentence above to complete the table below.

LIST THE NOUNS USED	NOUN JOB	SINGULAR or PLURAL	COMMON or PROPER	SIMPLE SUBJECT	SIMPLE PREDICATE
dad	CSN	S	C	dad, uncle	are
uncle	CSN	S	C		
firefighters	PrN	P	C		
city	OP	S	C		

End Lesson 1

Guided Practice

Directions: Classify these sentences on notebook paper.

	SN	LV	PPA	Adj	PrN

<u>SN LV</u>
PrN P4   Tony / is   my   best   friend. **D**

           SN   LV   A   PrN   P   OP

<u>SN LV</u>
PrN P4   Uncle Ray / is   a   detective (in   Dallas.)   **D**

           SN   LV   Adj   PrN

<u>SN LV</u>
PrN P4   Roses / are   beautiful   flowers.   **D**

Directions: Use the sentences above to answer the following questions.

1. What are the subjects? **Tony, Uncle Ray, roses**

2. What are the predicate nouns? friend, detective, flowers

3. What are the linking verbs? is, is, are

JOURNAL WRITING 25

Write an entry in your notebook journal or digital journal. Before you begin your journal entry, write one or two sentences with a predicate noun. As a challenge, try to write one sentence for each of the four patterns. Can you identify different sentence patterns in your entry?

Listening and Speaking

Practice Jingle 24 in the Jingle Section. **PAGE Q12**

Classifying Sentences

Classify the Practice Sentences with your teacher, using the Question and Answer Flow.

Practice Sentences

ORAL PREPARATION

1. _____ Wow! My friend is a really great soccer player!

2. _____ In our kindergarten class, Dillon was the tallest boy.

3. _____ On our trip, my favorite city was London.

4. _____ The judges for the best costume will be she and I.

Word Study

Loanwords are words that come directly from another language. In Sentence 2, *kindergarten* is a loanword from the German language. The literal meaning of *kindergarten* is *"children's garden."* Can you guess which part of *kindergarten* means *"children's"* and which part means *"garden"*? *kinder = children's, garten = garden*

Review: Linking Verbs

A **linking verb** is not an action verb because it shows a state of being. It tells what the subject **is** instead of what the subject **does**. If a sentence has a predicate noun, it will have a linking verb. The linking verb links the subject and the predicate noun. All verbs in Pattern 4 sentences are linking verbs.

In the sentences that you just classified, which verbs are linking? Explain. Are there any transitive or intransitive verbs? Explain.

Today, you will review pronoun cases and add predicate pronouns to the subjective case.

Reference 164

Pronoun Cases, Adding Predicate Pronouns

Pronoun Cases

1. **Subjective Case Pronouns**
   Pronouns that are used as **subjects** are in the subjective case.

   ➤ SP: **He went to work.**
   ➤ PrP: **The first person at work is he.**

   A **predicate pronoun** is a pronoun in the predicate that means the same thing as the subject.

> Subjective Case:
> **I, we, he, she, it, they,** and **you**

2. Objective Case Pronouns

Pronouns that are used as **objects of the prepositions**, **direct objects**, and **indirect objects** are in the objective case.

➡ OP: **The principal talked to** me **after class.**
➡ DO: **Mom took** me **to the zoo.**
➡ IO: **Leslie drew** me **a picture.**

Objective Case:

me, us, him, her, it, them, and you

3. Possessive Case Pronouns

Pronouns that are used to **show ownership** are in the possessive case.

➡ PPA: **Luke walked to** his **office.**

Possessive Case:

my, our, his, her, its, their, and your

Compound Pronouns

Many people often confuse subject pronouns and object pronouns when they are compound. Reading the sentence with only the first pronoun is a quick way to determine if you are using the correct case.

Directions: Write **S** for subjective, **O** for objective, or **P** for possessive in the blank. Underline the correct pronoun in parentheses.

S 1. (**She and I**, **Her and me**) drove home.

O 2. Dora looked for (**he and I**, **him and me**).

S 3. The fastest runners are (**he and I**, **him and me**) today.

O 4. Dad bought (**he and I**, **him and me**) a present.

Review: Case Check

Subject pronouns and **predicate** pronouns are in the subjective case, **possessive** pronouns are in the possessive case, and **object** pronouns are in the objective case.

After you have classified the Practice Sentences, you will do a Case Check. During a Case Check, you will say the pronoun, identify its job, and then tell its case. Now, recite the Case Check.

Case Check Practice Sentences

Sentence 1: Wow! My friend is a really great soccer player!

my: possessive pronoun, *possessive case*

Sentence 2: In our kindergarten class, Dillon was the tallest boy.

our: possessive pronoun, *possessive case*

Sentence 3: On our trip, my favorite city was London.

our: possessive pronoun, *possessive case*

my: possessive pronoun, *possessive case*

Sentence 4: The judges for the best costume will be she and I.

she: compound predicate pronoun, *subjective case*

I: compound predicate pronoun, *subjective case*

REMINDER: Since a predicate pronoun means the same thing as the subject, it is in the subjective case and must be one of these subject pronouns: *I, we, he, she, it, they,* and *you*.

Noun Check

Now, it is time to do a Noun Check. During a Noun Check, you identify nouns in different noun jobs. Predicate nouns are circled because they are nouns. Predicate pronouns are not circled because they are not nouns. Now, recite the Noun Check with your teacher.

Noun Check Practice Sentences

Circle the nouns in the sentences.

Sentence 1: Wow! My (friend) is a really great soccer (player!)

Subject Noun **friend**, *yes, it is a noun;*

Predicate Noun **player**, *yes, it is a noun.*

Sentence 2: In our kindergarten (class,) (Dillon) was the tallest (boy.)

Object of the Preposition **class**, *yes, it is a noun;*

Subject Noun **Dillon**, *yes, it is a noun;*

Predicate Noun **boy**, *yes, it is a noun.*

Sentence 3: On our (trip,) my favorite (city) was (London.)

Object of the Preposition **trip**, *yes, it is a noun;*

Subject Noun **city**, *yes, it is a noun;*

Predicate Noun **London**, *yes, it is a noun.*

Sentence 4: The (judges) for the best (costume) will be she and I.

Subject Noun **judges**, *yes, it is a noun;*

Object of the Preposition **costume**, *yes, it is a noun;*

Compound Predicate Pronoun **she**, *no, it is a pronoun;*

Compound Predicate Pronoun **I**, *no, it is a pronoun.*

Are there any Possessive Nouns in the sentences? **No**

 **Time**

Degrees of Adjectives and Adverbs

You know that adjectives and adverbs are words that describe things. Today, you will learn how to use adjectives and adverbs to compare two or more things that you describe. This description is called **degrees of comparison**.

 Reference 165

Degrees of Comparison of Adjectives and Adverbs

Adjectives and adverbs can describe in a special way called **degrees of comparison**. The term **degrees of comparison** means that two or more things are being compared as they are described.

Study the three degrees of comparison below.

Simple Form: This form is the one used most often because it describes ONE person or thing. Use the simple form when no comparison is being made.

Simple Adjectives	Simple Adverbs
Carl is a **fast** swimmer.	Carl swims **fast**.
The **loud** dog barked.	The dog barked **loudly**.

Comparative Form: This form is used to compare TWO things. To make the comparative form, add *–er* or ***more*** to the simple form. Use *–er* with short adjectives or adverbs (one or two syllables). Use ***more*** with longer adjectives or adverbs (two or more syllables).

Comparative Adjectives	Comparative Adverbs
Carl is a **faster** swimmer than Tim.	Carl swims **faster** than Tim does.
He is a **louder** dog than your dog.	He barked **more loudly** than my dog.

Superlative (sŭ per' lŭ tĭv) **Form:** This form is used to compare THREE or more things. To make the superlative form, add **–est** or **most** to the simple form. Use **–est** with short adjectives and adverbs (one or two syllables). Use **most** with longer adjectives and adverbs (two or more syllables).

Superlative Adjectives	Superlative Adverbs
Carl is the **fastest** swimmer on the team.	Carl swims the **fastest** of anyone on the team.
He is the **loudest** dog in the neighborhood.	He barked **most loudly** of all the dogs.

Irregular Adjectives and Adverbs that Must be Memorized

A few adjectives and adverbs have irregular comparative and superlative forms. You will need to memorize them.

Adjectives		
Simple	Comparative	Superlative
good, well	better	best
bad, ill	worse	worst
little	less	least
little	lesser	least
much, many	more	most

Adverbs		
Simple	Comparative	Superlative
well	better	best
badly	worse	worst
little	less	least
much	more	most

GRAMMAR AVE.
SKILL ST.

Guided Practice

Directions: Write the correct form of each adjective or adverb in parentheses.

1. Our new car is _____**better**_____ than our old car! (**good**)

2. This trail is the _____ trail on the mountain. (**difficult**)

3. Katherine is _____ than her sister. (**helpful**)

Student Tip... Avoid double comparisons.

Never use both -er and more to make the comparative form.

(INCORRECT) That bird is more prettier than this one.

Likewise, never use -est and most to make the superlative form.

(INCORRECT) My bird is the most prettiest of all.

End Lesson 2

Name: _____ Date: _____

GRAMMAR:

Exercise 1: Classify each sentence.

1. _____ Martina is the new dental assistant for Dr. Kline.

2. _____ Hurray! Lucas and I were the first two picks

by the team captain!

Exercise 2: Use **Sentence 2** above to complete the table below.

LIST THE NOUNS USED	NOUN JOB	SINGULAR or PLURAL	COMMON or PROPER	SIMPLE SUBJECT	SIMPLE PREDICATE

SKILLS:

Exercise 3: Write the different forms for the adjectives and adverbs below.

Simple Form Rule 1	Comparative Form Rule 2: -er, more	Superlative Form Rule 3: -est, most
1. silly		
2. serious		
3. shy		
4. good		
5. worried		

Exercise 4: Write the correct form of each adjective or adverb in parentheses.

1. Frank is the_____ of my three brothers. (**old**)

2. Art is _____ to me than sports. (**interesting**)

3. The spotted gray kitten is the _____ one in the whole litter. (**cute**)

Listening and Speaking

Jingle 25 The Noun Job Jingle

Nouns will give you a run for your money.
  They do so many jobs
    That it's not even funny.

A noun — person, place, thing, or idea —
  Is very appealing.
    But it's the noun job *(noun job)*
      That is so revealing.

To find the nouns in a sentence,
  Go to their jobs *(go to their jobs)*.

Nouns can do objective jobs *(objective jobs)*.
  They're the **IO** *(IO)*, **DO** *(DO)*, and **OP** jobs *(OP jobs)*.

And nouns can do subjective jobs *(subjective jobs)*.
  They're the **SN** *(SN)* and **PrN** jobs *(PrN jobs)*.
    Jobs. Jobs. Noun Jobs! Yeah!

Grammar Time

Classifying Sentences

Classify the Practice Sentences with your teacher,
using the Question and Answer Flow.

Practice Sentences
ORAL PARTICIPATION

1. _____ My doctor is a nice man with white hair.

2. _____ Trey is the top detective in the police
department.

3. _____ The books on this shelf are classic stories
by C.S. Lewis.

4. _____ Our new friends across the street are
he and she.

Case Check

After you have classified the Practice Sentences, recite a Case Check and a Noun Check with your teacher. These checks help you analyze nouns and pronouns and understand how they are used in sentences.

Case Check Practice Sentences

Sentence 1: My doctor is a nice man with white hair.

my: possessive pronoun, *possessive case*

Sentence 2: Trey is the top detective in the police department.

None

Sentence 3: The books on this shelf are classic stories by C.S. Lewis.

None

Sentence 4: Our new friends across the street are he and she.

our: possessive pronoun, *possessive case*

he: predicate pronoun, *subjective case;*

she: predicate pronoun, *subjective case*

Noun Check

1. **Identify the nouns in a Noun Check.**
   (Say the job and the noun. Circle each noun.)
2. **Identify the nouns as singular or plural.**
   (Write **S** or **P** above the noun.)
3. **Identify the nouns as common or proper.**
   (Write **C** or **P** above the noun.)

REMINDER: Since a predicate pronoun means the same thing as the subject, it is in the subjective case and must be one of these subject pronouns: *I, we, he, she, it, they,* and *you.*

Noun Jobs

You have been using the eight parts of speech for several weeks. As you know, a noun is one of the eight parts of speech. You have learned different jobs for the nouns. Most sentences include more than one noun job.

Reference 166

noun Jobs

Every word in a sentence has a job. A word's position and function in a sentence determine its job. If you can recognize noun jobs in a sentence, you will identify nouns more accurately.

> ### noun Jobs:
>
> **SN - subject noun • OP - object of the preposition**
> **DO - direct object • IO - indirect object • PrN - predicate noun**

In the sentences below, the word **Sally** is used in different noun job positions and in one adjective position.

Noun job positions include **SN**, **OP**, **DO**, **IO**, and **PrN**.

1. <u>Sally</u> jumped in the leaves.
   Sally – SN
   leaves – OP

   > **Sally – SN**
   > (subject noun = noun job)

2. Troy raked leaves with <u>Sally</u>.
   Troy – SN
   leaves – DO
   Sally – OP

   > **Sally – OP**
   > (object of the preposition = noun job)

3. Troy rolled <u>Sally</u> in the leaves.
   Troy – SN
   Sally – DO
   leaves – OP

   > **Sally – DO**
   > (direct object = noun job)

4. Troy bought **Sally** a warm jacket.

Troy – SN
Sally – IO
jacket – DO

Sally – IO
(indirect object = noun job)

5. Troy's sister is **Sally**.

sister – SN
Sally – PrN

Sally – PrN
(predicate noun = noun job)

6. Troy told Mom his **Sally** story.

Troy – SN
Mom – IO
Sally – Adj
Story – DO

Sally – Adj
(adjective = not a noun job)

Student Tip...

1. Finding a noun is easy if you know the noun job. The nouns below are just nouns until you label each noun with a special name that identifies its job.

NOUN	NOUN	NOUN	NOUN	NOUN
sister	sister	sister	sister	sister
SN	OP	DO	IO	PrN

SN
My sister works with me.

OP
I ride to work with my sister.

DO
I admire my sister.

IO
I bought my sister lunch today.

PrN
My best friend is my sister.

2. As you review each pattern, notice how the Shurley patterns relate to the traditional patterns.

	Pattern 1	Pattern 2	Pattern 3	Pattern 4
Traditional:	N V	N V N	N V N N	N LV N
Shurley:	SN V	SN V-t DO	SN V-t IO DO	SN LV PrN

GRAMMAR AVE.

SKILL ST.

Guided Practice

Directions: In each blank, write the noun job label for the underlined noun.

1. Cody's sister is a <u>teacher</u>. _____

2. Donovan draws <u>horses</u> in art class. _____

3. Our <u>band</u> practices in the garage. _____

4. Will you read <u>Lucy</u> a story tonight? _____

5. We went to the <u>zoo</u> with our class. _____

Review: Parts of Speech

REMINDER: How a word is used in a sentence determines its part of speech. What are the eight parts of speech?

What are the labels for the eight parts of speech?

Review: Degrees of Comparison

1. Get with a partner and write three sentences, one each to demonstrate the simple, comparative, and superlative forms of comparison for adjectives or adverbs.

2. Discuss your sentences with other groups, using the Rules for Discussion.

Name: _____ Date:_____

GRAMMAR:

Exercise 1: Classify each sentence.

1. _____ We are the best hockey team in the whole league!

2. _____ New York is my favorite state in the United States.

Exercise 2: In each blank, write the noun job label for the underlined noun.

1. Kevin is a very good **friend**.   _____

2. He plays **ball** with me every day.   _____

3. We have campouts in the **summer**.   _____

4. My **brother** plays with us.   _____

5. Kevin treats us like **brothers**.   _____

6. Friends are important **people**!   _____

SKILLS:

Exercise 3: Write the different forms for the adjectives and adverbs below.

Simple Form Rule 1	Comparative Form Rule 2: -er, more	Superlative Form Rule 3: -est, most
1. rowdy		
2. normal		
3. closely		
4. fine		

Exercise 4: Write the correct form of each adjective or adverb in parentheses.

1. America is one of the _____ countries in the world. (**rich**)

2. The hand is _____ than the eye. (**quick**)

3. Traveling by car is _____ than traveling by bicycle. (**fast**)

4. The hungry coyotes yipped _____ than ever! (**loud**)

Chapter 15

Listening and Speaking

Practice Jingles 24–25 in the Jingle Section. **PAGES Q12–Q13**

Mixed Patterns

Reference 167

Mixed Patterns 1–4

Study the four sentence patterns shown. As you classify the sentences, pay close attention to the core parts of each sentence. This will help you decide which pattern to choose.

→ **Pattern 1** is **SN V**.
It has a **noun-verb (N V)** core.

➡ Example:

A   SN   V   P A   Adj   OP
The boys / played **(on the baseball field).** **D**

$\frac{\text{SN V}}{\text{P1}}$

→ **Pattern 2** is **SN V-t DO**.
It has a **noun-verb-noun (N V N)** core.

➡ Example:

A   SN   V-t   DO
The boys / played baseball. **D**

$\frac{\text{SN V-t}}{\text{DO P2}}$

→ **Pattern 3** is **SN V-t IO DO**.
It has a **noun-verb-noun-noun (N V N N)** core.

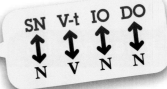

➡ Example:

　　　　　　　　PPA　SN　　V-t　IO　A　　DO
<u>SN V-t</u>　My friend / threw me the baseball.　**D**
IO DO P3

→ **Pattern 4** is **SN LV PrN**.
It has a **noun-linking verb-noun (N LV N)** core.

➡ Example:

　　　　　　　　PPA　SN　LV　A　Adj　PrN
<u>SN LV</u>　My　friend / is　the　new　pitcher.　**D**
PrN P4

Classifying Mixed Patterns 1–4

Classify the Introductory Sentences with your teacher, using the Question and Answer Flow.

Introductory Sentences
ORAL PARTICIPATION

1. _____ My puppy looked for the toy.

2. _____ My puppy chased the toy.

3. _____ My puppy brought me the toy.

4. _____ My puppy is my best friend.

Review: Transitive, Intransitive, and Linking Verbs

Pattern 1 sentences have intransitive verbs that show action but have no direct objects. Patterns 2 and 3 sentences have transitive verbs that show action and have direct objects. Pattern 4 sentences have linking verbs that show a state of being (no action) and have predicate nouns/pronouns.

In the sentences that you just classified, which verbs are transitive? Explain. Which verb is intransitive? Explain. Which verb is linking? Explain.

Reference 168

Identifying Pattern Numbers Only for Patterns 1-4

When identifying mixed patterns, you must concentrate on the core of each sentence. Since the core is the pattern of the sentence, classify only the main parts (**SN V**), (**SN V-t DO**), (**SN V-t IO DO**), and (**SN LV PrN**) without classifying all the other words in the sentence. Classify the core parts, determine the pattern, and write only the pattern number in the blank. With practice, you will be able to identify the pattern by sight.

Example: Write the correct pattern number in each blank.
(**P1 = SN V, P2 = SN V-t DO, P3 = SN V-t IO DO, P4 = SN LV PrN**)

__P2__ 1. I like our school carnival.

__P1__ 2. I go to the carnival with my friends.

__P3__ 3. Teachers give us candy and drinks.

__P4__ 4. Our carnivals are great fundraisers.

Guided Practice

Exercise 1: Write the correct pattern number in each blank.
(**P1 = SN V, P2 = SN V-t DO, P3 = SN V-t IO DO, P4 = SN LV PrN**)

_____ 1. John is a very talented artist.

_____ 2. Paul caught the ball.

_____ 3. Did you sleep through breakfast?

_____ 4. He made her a paper airplane.

_____ 5. Pizza is my favorite food.

_____ 6. Take Jim some water.

Exercise 2: Write the main verbs in Exercise 1 and identify them with a **T** for transitive, **I** for intransitive, or **L** for linking.

VERBS	T, I, OR L	VERBS	T, I, OR L	VERBS	T, I, OR L
1.		3.		5.	
2.		4.		6.	

Name: _____ Date:_____

GRAMMAR:

Exercise 1: Classify each sentence.

1. _____ Marsha and Sue gave Amy her birthday present today.

2. _____ That pile of snow and ice is melting very slowly.

3. _____ Will Bill be our guide for the tour through the caverns?

Exercise 2: Write the correct pattern number in each blank.
(P1 = SN V, P2 = SN V-t DO, P3 = SN V-t IO DO, P4 = SN LV PrN)

_____ 1. Terri is a talented singer.   _____ 4. I must shampoo my hair today.

_____ 2. Turn off the porch light.   _____ 5. My sister loaned me some money.

_____ 3. Will you bring your project?   _____ 6. Gymnastics is a challenging sport.

SKILLS:

Exercise 3: Write the different forms for the adjectives and adverbs below.

Simple Form Rule 1	Comparative Form Rule 2: -er, more	Superlative Form Rule 3: -est, most
1. cuddly		
2. sharp		
3. incredible		

Exercise 4: Write the correct form of each adjective or adverb in parentheses.

1. Friendship is _____ than gold! (**valuable**)

2. Spinach is my _____ of all leafy vegetables. (**favorite**)

3. A male bluebird has a _____ blue color than the female. (**bright**)

Word Time

Vocabulary and Analogy

Word 21 ➤ **erode** (ē rōd´)

Definition: the wearing away of something over time

Synonym: wear down   **Antonym:** build up

Sentence: Winds and water **erode** the soil and rocks over time.

Analogy ➤ **shoelace : shoe :: button : shirt**

Relationship: Part-to-Whole

Thinking Process: Just as a **shoelace** is part of a **shoe**, a **button** is part of a **shirt**. Therefore, this is a part-to-whole analogy.

🔧 **ACTIVITY**   Draw a picture or write a poem or story in your Vocabulary Notebook to help you remember the word **erode**.
(Picture Idea: Draw a canyon, a cave in a mountain, or a crack (crevice) in a boulder to demonstrate the word erode.)

Spelling

Study this Spelling Rule to help you become a better speller.

Spelling Rule 8 — Keeping Doubled Letters

When adding a prefix or suffix that causes a doubled letter, keep both of the letters.

➡ Example: **mis + spell** ⟹ **misspell**

➡ Example: **real + ly** ⟹ **really**

Spelling Words
For each word: **Recite**, **Spell**, and **Repeat**.

Recite co + operate = cooperate

Spell c-o-o-p-e-r-a-t-e   **Repeat** cooperate

1. co + operate = cooperate
2. graceful + ly = gracefully
3. re + elected = reelected
4. cool + ly = coolly
5. un + needed = unneeded
6. ski + ing = skiing

Listening and Speaking

Practice Jingles 24–25 in the Jingle Section. **PAGES Q12–Q13**

Classifying Mixed Patterns 1-4

Classify the Practice Sentences with your teacher,
using the Question and Answer Flow.

Practice Sentences   ORAL PARTICIPATION

1. _____ Maria's uncle is a very good dentist for children.

2. _____ Today, my friends and I are going to the fair.

3. _____ For lunch, Tina's mother has made us soup
and sandwiches.

4. _____ Thomas broke his arm during recess today!

Word Study

Homonym alert! Can you spot the homonym in Sentence 2? That's right—*I*
is a homonym of *eye*; *to* is a homonym of *two* and *too*; and *fair* is a homonym
of *fare*. Can you find two more homonyms in the sentences? (*for / four / fore,
made / maid*)

Review: Transitive, Intransitive, and Linking Verbs

Pattern 1 sentences have intransitive verbs that show action but have no direct objects. Patterns 2 and 3 sentences have transitive verbs that show action and have direct objects. Pattern 4 sentences have linking verbs that show a state of being (*no action*) and have predicate nouns/pronouns.

In the sentences that you just classified, which verbs are transitive? Explain. Which verb is intransitive? Explain. Which verb is linking? Explain.

Case Check

After you have classified the Practice Sentences, recite a Case Check and a Noun Check with your teacher. These checks help you analyze nouns and pronouns and understand how they are used in sentences.

Case Check Practice Sentences

Sentence 1: Maria's uncle is very good dentist for children.

None

Sentence 2: Today, my friends and I are going to the fair.

my: possessive pronoun, *possessive case*
I: subject pronoun, *subjective case*

Sentence 3: For lunch, Tina's mother has made us soup and sandwiches.

us: indirect object pronoun, *objective case*

Sentence 4: Thomas broke his arm during recess today!

his: possessive pronoun, *possessive case*

Noun Check

1. **Identify the nouns in a Noun Check.**
   (Say the job and the noun. Circle each noun.)
2. **Identify the nouns as singular or plural.**
   (Write **S** or **P** above the noun.)
3. **Identify the nouns as common or proper.**
   (Write **C** or **P** above the noun.)

Name: _____ Date: _____

GRAMMAR:

Exercise 1: Classify each sentence.

1. _____ Jefferson City is the capital of Missouri.

2. _____ Yikes! Mr. Green gave us a pop quiz in math class today!

3. _____ May we watch cartoons on Saturday morning?

Exercise 2: Write the correct pattern number in each blank.
(**P1 = SN V, P2 = SN V-t DO, P3 = SN V-t IO DO, P4 = SN LV PrN**)

_____ 1. The grandfather clock chimed.   _____ 4. Music is food for the soul!

_____ 2. A mouse ran up the clock!   _____ 5. Today is the longest day of summer.

_____ 3. The mouse gave us a fright.   _____ 6. We have peach pie for dessert.

SKILLS:

Exercise 3: Write the different forms for the adjectives and adverbs below.

Simple Form Rule 1	Comparative Form Rule 2: -er, more	Superlative Form Rule 3: -est, most
1. clear		
2. scary		
3. important		

Exercise 4: Write the correct form of each adjective or adverb in parentheses.

1. Missouri is one of the _____ states in the midwest. (**humid**)

2. Some whole grains are _____ than others. (**healthy**)

3. School starts _____ than usual this fall. (**late**)

Word Time

Vocabulary and Analogy

Word 22 **contrast** (kŏn' trăst and kŭn trăst')

Definition: to examine how two things are different

Synonym: differ   **Antonym:** compare

Sentence: The teacher **contrasted** the meanings of the two words.

Etymology **Word History of contrast**

Latin Root: contra (kŏn trŭ)

Definition: against

Other words from the root: contrary, contradict

Analogy **flock : dock :: blank : tank**

Relationship: Rhyming

Thinking Process: Just as **flock** rhymes with **dock**, **blank** rhymes with **tank**. Therefore, this is a **rhyming** analogy.

ACTIVITY   Draw a picture or write a poem or story in your Vocabulary Notebook to help you remember the word **contrast**.

*(Picture Idea: A Venn diagram is the graphic organizer used for comparison / contrast writing. Draw a Venn diagram. Color one circle red; color the other circle blue. The intersecting space between the two circles should end up being a purplish color. Above the two circles, write the word Contrast. Inside the intersecting shape (in light purple), write the word **Compare**.)*

Spelling

It's time to review what you've learned about spelling!

Spelling Rule 8 **Keeping Doubled Letters**

When adding a prefix or suffix that causes a doubled letter, keep both of the letters.

➡ Example: **mis + spell ⟹ misspell**

➡ Example: **real + ly ⟹ really**

Spelling Words For each word: **Recite**, **Spell**, and **Repeat**.

Recite co + operate = cooperate

Spell c-o-o-p-e-r-a-t-e **Repeat** cooperate

1. **co + operate = cooperate**
2. **graceful + ly = gracefully**
3. **re + elected = reelected**
4. **cool + ly = coolly**
5. **un + needed = unneeded**
6. **ski + ing = skiing**

Grammar Time

Classifying Mixed Patterns 1-4

Classify the Practice Sentences with your teacher, using the Question and Answer Flow.

Practice Sentences   ORAL PARTICIPATION

1. _____ May I listen to your new CD with you?

2. _____ Shawn's dad is the owner of the local newspaper.

3. _____ Over the weekend, Mom and Dad gave us several extra chores.

4. _____ Hey! Charles broke my expensive model airplane!

Review: Transitive, Intransitive, and Linking Verbs

Pattern 1 sentences have intransitive verbs that show action but have no direct objects. Patterns 2 and 3 sentences have transitive verbs that show action and have direct objects. Pattern 4 sentences have linking verbs that show a state of being (no action) and have predicate nouns/pronouns.

In the sentences that you just classified, which verbs are transitive? Explain. Which verb is intransitive? Explain. Which verb is linking? Explain.

Review: Parts of Speech

REMINDER: How a word is used in a sentence determines its part of speech. What are the eight parts of speech? What are the labels for the eight parts of speech?

Blueprint for Building a Sentence

Today, you will learn how to add a predicate noun and linking verb to your blueprint labels to write an original sentence.

 Reference 169

Designing a Sentence Blueprint,
Adding Predicate Nouns and Linking Verbs

Design and build your sentence on Classroom Practice 69.

1. Use the core labels, **SN/SP**, **LV**, and **PrN**, **only once** and **in that order**.

2. The other labels, **Adj**, **Adv**, **A**, **P**, **OP**, **PPA**, **C**, **HV**, **I**, and **PNA**, can be used as many times as you wish, in any order you wish, as long as they make sense. (**REMEMBER:** Complete sense is one of the five parts of a complete sentence.)

3. **Instructions for the new labels, LV and PrN:** First, think of a linking verb that makes sense with a predicate noun, such as "*am*," "*is*," "*are*," "*was*," and so on. Write your linking verb under the **LV** label. Then, think of a predicate noun that renames the subject. Write your predicate noun under the **PrN** label.

4. Write the labels in the order you choose on the **Labels** line.

5. Write a word that makes sense for each label.

After writing your original sentence on Classroom Practice 69, use the revision strategies to help you make revisions.

Use Revision Strategies to Revise Your Original Sentence

REMEMBER: **Revising** means looking for ways to improve your writing. As you revise your Original Sentence, write the abbreviation of the revision strategy you used under each word in your Revised Sentence.

1 Synonym (syn) **2** Antonym (ant) **3** Word Change (wc)

4 Added Word (add) **5** Deleted Word (delete) **6** No Change (nc)

When you have finished, your paper should resemble the example below.

Labels:	A	Adj	SN	LV	A	Adj	PrN	P	A	Adj	OP
Original Sentence:	A	bright	fire	was	a		guide	to	the	lost	hikers.
Revised Sentence:	The	roaring	blaze	was	a	clear	beacon	for	the	missing	backpackers.
Revision Strategy:	(wc)	(wc)	(syn)	(nc)	(nc)	(add)	(syn)	(wc)	(nc)	(syn)	(syn)

Student Tip...

1. Use your Vocabulary Words, Power Words, a thesaurus, and a dictionary to help you write your Original and Revised Sentences.

2. As you go through each word of your Original Sentence, think about the changes and improvements you want to make.

3. To help you improve your sentence, use your revision strategies.

4. As you revise your original sentence, keep this information in mind:

   • Antonyms and Word Changes will change your sentence's meaning.

   • Synonyms and No Changes will keep the meaning of the original sentence.

   • Added Words and Deleted Words can change the meaning of your sentence or keep it the same, depending on the words you choose to add or delete.

Name: _____

Date: _____

Exercise 1: Write your own blueprint labels. Use the labels to write an original sentence. Then, revise your sentence, writing the abbreviation of the revision strategy under each word.

Labels:

Original Sentence:

Revised Sentence:

Revision Strategy:

Labels:

Original Sentence:

Revised Sentence:

Revision Strategy:

Exercise 2: Rewrite your revised sentence on the lines below. Use the checklist to check your sentence.

_____

_____

Sentence Checklist: ☐ Capital letter ☐ Subject ☐ Verb ☐ Complete sense ☐ End mark

Writing a *Mover* & **Shaker** Sentence in Your Journal:

Skip two lines below your last entry and write the date and chapter number. Then, skip one line and write a Mover & Shaker Sentence **with an appositive phrase**. An appositive phrase adds more description to a noun in the sentence. It follows the noun it describes and is set off by commas. This strategy allows a writer to add more description anywhere in the sentence.

Simple
Sentence: **I ride the city bus to work every day.**

Mover & **Shaker**
Sentence: **I ride the city bus**, the one that goes by the river market, **to work every day.**

Compare all of the Mover & Shaker Sentences you have written so far.

JOURNAL WRITING 26

Write an entry in your notebook journal or digital journal. Use the spelling pattern in Spelling Rule 8 to help you spell words correctly. As you write your entry, use the simple, comparative, and superlative forms of adjectives and adverbs.

Classifying Mixed Patterns 1-4

Classify the Practice Sentences with your teacher,
using the Question and Answer Flow.

Practice Sentences   ORAL PARTICIPATION

1. _____ Did a large dog chase you home yesterday?

2. _____ My new poodle from the shelter is a
very smart dog.

3. _____ On Friday, Toby and I are going to the movies.

4. _____ At Wayne's school, the teachers give
the students tons of homework.

Review: The Four Kinds of Sentences

Choose one of the following options:

1. Write one each of the four kinds of sentences (*declarative, exclamatory, interrogative, or imperative*), using a different spelling word in each sentence. (*See Chapter 2 for a review of the four kinds of sentences.*)

2. Write a declarative sentence, using one of your spelling words. Then, change that sentence to the other three kinds of sentences (*exclamatory, interrogative, and imperative*).

3. Write a compound or complex declarative sentence, using at least one of your spelling words. (*See Chapter 7 for a review of compound and complex sentences.*)

For your sentences, use the spelling words from Rule 8:
cooperate, gracefully, reelected, coolly, unneeded, skiing.

The Reading Club is a time to get into small groups and share a favorite book with others. Use the suggestions below to help you share your book.

- ◆ Give the title and author of the book. Show the book if you still have it.
- ◆ Describe a particular setting that is important to the story and tell where it is found in the book.
- ◆ Describe the main characters and tell something about them and discuss the specific evidence from the book that helps you focus your impressions about them.
- ◆ Tell what happens to the characters as the plot progresses. Be brief. Don't tell too much.
- ◆ Tell why you liked the book.

Write down the title and author of any book that you would like to read. Follow the Rules for Discussion and listen respectfully to other members of your group as different books are shared.

Challenge

1. Tell whether you agree or disagree with the way the characters responded to different events in the story. Explain what you would do if you were in a similar situation.

2. Explain how the events of the story build on earlier events.

Name: _____ Date:_____

GRAMMAR:

Exercise 1: Classify each sentence.

1. _____ Winnie the Pooh is a character by A. A. Milne.

2. _____ Bring black coffee to work with you.

3. _____ Did your nephew bring you a souvenir from the state fair?

4. _____ Clover and wildflowers grew in the fields

around the little farm.

Exercise 2: In each blank, write the noun job label for the underlined noun.

_____ 1. Mattie planted <u>sunflowers</u>.   _____ 4. Mattie gave <u>me</u> some seeds.

_____ 2. They grew into tall <u>plants</u>.   _____ 5. We roasted the <u>seeds</u>.

_____ 3. The <u>flowers</u> faced the sun.   _____ 6. The seeds are a yummy <u>snack</u>.

Exercise 3: Write the correct pattern number in each blank.
(P1 = SN V, P2 = SN V-t DO, P3 = SN V-t IO DO, P4 = SN LV PrN)

_____ 1. Rover likes beef bones.   _____ 4. My two sisters are twins.

_____ 2. The honey bees buzzed loudly.   _____ 5. Do you collect coins?

_____ 3. Bill tossed me the ball.   _____ 6. Oh, no! The window shattered!

Exercise 4: Write the main verbs in Exercise 3 and identify them with a **T** for transitive,
I for intransitive, or **L** for linking.

VERBS	T, I, L	VERBS	T, I, L	VERBS	T, I, L
1.		3.		5.	
2.		4.		6.	

SKILLS:

Exercise 5: ▶ Select the sentence below that creates the best mental picture.

○ Three soft baby geese swam in the pond.

○ Three soft, fuzzy goslings waddled into the old farm pond.

Exercise 6: ▶ Write the different forms for the adjectives and adverbs below.

Simple Form Rule 1	Comparative Form Rule 2: -er, more	Superlative Form Rule 3: -est, most
1. soft		
2. good		
3. terrible		

Exercise 7: ▶ Write the correct form of each adjective or adverb in parentheses.

1. A microwave oven cooks food _____ than a conventional oven. (**fast**)

2. Panthers are among the _____ of wild cats. (**cunning**)

3. One side of the moon is _____ than the other side. (**dark**)

Exercise 8: ▶ Fill in the circle beside each correct answer.

1. **Definition:** wearing away over time   ○ contrast   ○ erode

2. Black and white are colors that _____.   ○ contrast   ○ erode

3. Shoelace : shoe :: _____ : shirt   ○ button   ○ pants

WRITING:

Exercise 9: ▶ Write one of the four types of sentences (*declarative, exclamatory, interrogative,* or *imperative*), using the vocabulary word **contrast**.

_____

_____

Oral Review Time

With your teacher, read the questions below. Do you know all the answers? Listen carefully for answers you do not know. After the review, you will have a chapter test.

1. What are the three kinds of verbs you have studied?

2. What kind of verb shows a state of action and tells what the subject does?

3. What kind of verb shows a state of being and tells what the subject is?

4. What is a special noun in the predicate that renames the subject noun?

5. What are the core parts of a Pattern 1 sentence?

6. What are the core parts of a Pattern 2 sentence?

7. What are the core parts of a Pattern 3 sentence?

8. What are the core parts of a Pattern 4 sentence?

9. What are the three degrees of comparison for adjectives?

10. Which degree of comparison is used to compare three or more nouns?

11. Which degree of comparison is used to compare two nouns?

12. Which degree of comparison is used to describe a single noun?

13. What are the three degrees of the adjective happy?

14. What are the three degrees of the word *good*?

Review: Topic Outline

Outlining is one of the most important skills you can learn because it helps you organize ideas and information in the correct order for writing or speaking.

1. Main Points *(two or more main points about the topic)*

→ Use Roman numerals (I. II. III.) for main points.
You must have two or more main points.

→ Capitalize the first word but do not use an end mark.

→ Line up the periods after the Roman numerals, one under the other.

Pet Chores

I. **Cat chores**	**MAIN POINT**
II. **Dog chores**	**MAIN POINT**

2. Subtopics *(information that supports a main point)*

→ Use capital letters (A. B. C.) for subtopics.
You must have two or more subtopics.

→ Line up subtopics under the first word of the main point.

→ Line up the periods after the capital letters.

→ Capitalize the first word but do not use an end mark.

I. Cat chores   **MAIN POINT**

A. **Feed cat**	**SUBTOPIC**
B. **Change water**	**SUBTOPIC**
C. **Clean litter box**	**SUBTOPIC**

CONTINUED ON NEXT PAGE

3. Details (*information that supports a subtopic*)

→ Use Arabic numerals for details. You must have two or more details.

→ Line up details under the first word of the subtopic.

→ Line up periods after the Arabic numerals.

→ Capitalize the first word but do not use an end mark.

II. Dog chores   **MAIN POINT**

    A. Food   **SUBTOPIC**

    B. Water   **SUBTOPIC**

    C. Exercise   **SUBTOPIC**

       1. Go for a walk   **DETAIL**

       2. Play games   **DETAIL**

Parallel Form

Using **parallel form** means to begin individual sections of the outline with the same part of speech.

In order for an outline to be well organized and easy to read, the items must be parallel in form. This means that each section in an outline should begin in the same way: all nouns, all verbs, all noun phrases, all verb phrases, all prepositional phrases, etc.

Reference 170

Parallel Form in Topic Outlines

When you first make an outline, it probably will not be parallel. After you organize the ideas, then you can go back and change or rearrange the words in your outline so they are parallel.

1. Main Points

To be parallel, all main points must begin with the same part of speech. It does not matter how the main points begin; it is just important that they begin the same way.

> **Example 1:**
> I. Cat chores
> II. Dog chores

> **Example 2:**
> I. Do my cat chores
> II. Do my dog chores

> **Example 3:**
> I. Do my cat chores
> II. Dog chores

Look at the examples under Main Points.

1. Do the main points in Example 1 begin with the same part of speech?
2. Which part of speech is used?
3. Are they parallel? Why?
4. Do the main points in Example 2 begin with the same part of speech?
5. Which part of speech is used?
6. Are they parallel? Why?
7. Do the main points in Example 3 begin with the same part of speech?
8. Which parts of speech are used?
9. Are they parallel? Why?

Lesson 9

2. Subtopics

To be parallel, all subtopics under a specific main point must begin with the same part of speech. It does not matter how the subtopics begin; it is just important that they begin the same way.

Example 5:

A. Food

B. Water

C. Litter

Example 4:

A. **Feed** cat

B. **Change** water

C. **Clean** litterbox

Example 6:

A. **Feed** cat

B. **Fresh** water

C. **Litter**

Look at the examples under Subtopics.

1. Do the subtopics in Example 4 begin with the same part of speech?
2. Which part of speech is used?
3. Are they parallel? Why?
4. Do the subtopics in Example 5 begin with the same part of speech?
5. Which part of speech is used?
6. Are they parallel? Why?
7. Do subtopics in Example 6 begin with the same part of speech?
8. Which parts of speech are used?
9. Are they parallel? Why?

3. Details

To be parallel, all details under a specific subtopic must begin with the same part of speech. It does not matter how the details begin; it is just important that they begin the same way.

Example 7:

1. Go for a walk
2. Play games

Example 8:

1. Daily walk
2. Fun games

Example 9:

1. Go for a walk
2. Fun games

Look at the examples under Details.

1. Do the details in Example 7 begin with the same part of speech?
2. Which part of speech is used?
3. Are they parallel? Why?
4. Do the details in Example 8 begin with the same part of speech?
5. Which part of speech is used?
6. Are they parallel? Why?
7. Do details in Example 9 begin with the same part of speech?
8. Which parts of speech are used?
9. Are they parallel? Why?

Student Tip...

All items under a specific section should be parallel. For example, under Roman numeral I, the subtopics could begin with adjectives or verbs to make them parallel. Under Roman numeral II, the subtopics could begin with prepositions or nouns and still remain parallel.

End Lesson 9

Name: _____ Date: _____

SKILLS:

Exercise 1: Put the information into outline form, following the rules for outlining.
Three items are not parallel. Make them parallel in the outline.

Movie Time
Main Points
things to buy in the theater lobby
things to do inside the theater

Subtopics
ticket
popcorn
buy drink
hot dog

get candy
find a good seat
turn off cell phone
snacks
enjoy movie

Details
with butter
without butter
chocolate mints
candy bar

in the center
on the top row

Outline:

_____

_____

_____

_____

_____

_____

_____

_____

_____

_____

_____

_____

_____

_____

_____

_____

Jingle Time

Listening and Speaking

Practice Jingle 4 in the Jingle Section. **PAGE Q3**

Jingle 26 The Predicate Adjective Jingle

A predicate, predicate, predicate adjective
Is a special, special adjective
In the predicate, predicate, predicate
That modifies, modifies, **modifies**
The simple, simple **subject**.

A predicate, predicate, predicate adjective
Follows after a linking verb.
To find a predicate adjective,
Ask **WHAT KIND** of subject
And verify the answer.

Verify that the adjective in the predicate
Modifies, modifies, modifies
The simple, simple subject.

Flamingos look pink.

Review: Sentence Patterns 1-4

→ **Pattern 1 core:** noun-verb (**SN V**)

→ **Pattern 2 core:** noun-verb-noun (**SN V-t DO**)

→ **Pattern 3 core:** three nouns and a transitive verb (**SN V-t IO DO**)

→ **Pattern 4 core:** two nouns and a linking verb (**SN LV PrN**)

Today, you will learn another sentence pattern, **Pattern 5**, which has one noun, a linking verb, and a predicate adjective (**noun-linking verb-adjective**) for its core. To understand Pattern 5, you must first understand its core parts, the *subject noun*, *linking verb*, and *predicate adjective*: **SN LV PA**.

Reference 171

Predicate Adjective, Linking Verb, and Pattern 5

Predicate Adjectives

A **predicate adjective** is an adjective in the predicate that modifies or describes the subject. It tells *what kind* of subject.

To find a predicate adjective, ask ***what kind*** **AFTER** the verb.

A **predicate adjective** is labeled with the abbreviation **PA**.

> ➡ Example 1:
>   SN   LV PA
> The circus clowns are funny.

> ➡ Example 2:
>   SN   LV PA
> Flamingos look pink.

> ➡ Example 3:
>   SN   LV PA
> Blueberries are blue.

In the examples, *funny describes clowns*; *pink describes flamingos*; and *blue describes blueberries*. In each sentence, the subject noun and the predicate adjective are connected by a **linking verb**.

Linking Verbs

A **linking verb links** the subject to a predicate adjective.
A predicate adjective is always located after a **linking verb**.

A linking verb is not an action verb because it shows a state of being. It tells what the subject **is** instead of *what* the subject does.

A **linking verb** is labeled with the abbreviation **LV**.

Examples of linking verbs: *am, is, are, was, were, being, been, appear, become, feel, grow, look, remain, seem, smell, sound,* and *taste.*

Pattern 5

Sentence Patterns identify the order of the core parts of sentences. The fifth pattern, **Pattern 5**, has *three* core parts: a Subject Noun (**SN**) a Linking Verb (**LV**), and a Predicate Adjective (**PA**).

Pattern 5 is identified by its core parts: **SN LV PA P5** (*Subject Noun, Linking Verb, Predicate Adjective, Pattern 5*).

Adding Predicate Adjectives to the Question and Answer Flow

Sample Sentence:	My brother is very smart.

1. Who is very smart? **brother - Subject Noun**..........(Write **SN** above *brother.*)
2. What is being said about brother? **brother is - Verb** .. (Write **V** above *is.*)
3. Brother is what? **smart - verify the adjective**
4. What kind of brother?
   smart - Predicate Adjective.........................(Write **PA** above *smart.*)
5. Is - Linking Verb ....(Write **L** above *is.*)
6. How smart?
   very - Adverb.....................................(Write **Adv** above *very.*)

CONTINUED ON NEXT PAGE >>>

Lesson 1

7. Whose brother?
   my – Possessive Pronoun Adjective................(Write **PPA** above *my*.)

8. **Subject Noun, Linking Verb, Predicate Adjective, Pattern 5**
   (Write **SN LV PA P5** in the blank.)

9. **Skill Check!**
   ➡ **Linking Verb – check again**
   (This check is to make sure the "**L**" is added to the verb.)

   ➡ **No Prepositional Phrases**

   ➡ **Period, statement, declarative sentence**
   (Write **D** at the end of the sentence.)

   ➡ Go back to the verb.
   Divide the complete subject from the complete predicate.

   ➡ Is this sentence in a natural or inverted order? **Natural - no change**

SN LV PA P5	PPA SN	LV Adv PA
	My brother /	is very smart. D

Discussion Questions:

1. What is an adjective called that is located in the predicate and modifies the subject?

2. Where is a predicate adjective always located?

3. What is the pattern in a Pattern 5 sentence?

4. What are the core parts of a Pattern 5 sentence?

Review: Sentence Patterns

→ **Pattern 1** is **SN V**.
It has a **noun-verb (N V)** core.

→ **Pattern 2** is **SN V-t DO**.
It has a **noun-verb-noun (N V N)** core.

→ **Pattern 3** is **SN V-t IO DO**.
It has a **noun-verb-noun-noun (N V N N)** core.

→ **Pattern 4** is **SN LV PrN**.
It has a **noun-linking verb-noun (N LV N)** core.

→ **Pattern 5** is **SN LV PA**.
It has a **noun-linking verb-adjective (N LV Adj)** core.

Classifying Sentences

Classify the Introductory Sentences with your teacher, using the Question and Answer Flow. Classifying these sentences will help you learn predicate adjectives and linking verbs.

Introductory Sentences ORAL PARTICIPATION

1. _____ A wild rose is very beautiful.

2. _____ The wild roses behind our house are very beautiful.

3. _____ My older brother is very smart.

Word Study

Compare Sentence 1 to Sentence 2. The sentences mean basically the same thing, but Sentence 2 is more appealing because of the added details. Notice how adjectives, adverbs, and prepositional phrases are used to improve and expand the meaning of the original sentence. Name the words and phrases in Sentence 2 that are used to add more details. When you write, ask yourself this question: Have I used enough adjectives, adverbs, and prepositional phrases to make my sentences interesting? Brainstorm and make a list of interesting adjectives, adverbs, and prepositional phrases that can be used for elaboration.

Noun Check

Now that you have classified the Introductory Sentences, it is time to do a Noun Check. During a Noun Check, you identify nouns in different noun jobs. Predicate adjectives are not circled in a Noun Check because they are not nouns. Now, recite the Noun Check with your teacher.

Noun Check Introductory Sentences

Circle the nouns in the sentences.

Sentence 1: A wild ⟨rose⟩ is very beautiful.

Subject Noun **rose**, *yes, it is a noun.*

Sentence 2: The wild ⟨roses⟩ behind our ⟨house⟩ are very beautiful.

Subject Noun **roses**, *yes, it is a noun;*
Object of the Preposition **house**, *yes, it is a noun.*

Sentence 3: My older ⟨brother⟩ is very smart.

Subject Noun **brother**, *yes, it is a noun.*

Are there any Possessive Nouns in the sentences? **No**

Bringing It All Together
The Noun Chart

The Noun Chart below reviews the other information about nouns that you have learned. Discuss the Noun Chart below with your teacher.

Reference 172

Noun Chart

	A	Adj	SN	P	PPA	OP
SN LV	The	wild	roses	**(behind**	our	house**)**
PA P5						

	LV	Adv	PA
/	are	very	beautiful. **D**

Directions: Use the sentence above to complete the table below.

LIST THE NOUNS USED	NOUN JOB	SINGULAR or PLURAL	COMMON or PROPER	SIMPLE SUBJECT	SIMPLE PREDICATE
roses	SN	P	C	roses	are
house	OP	S	C		

Guided Practice

Directions: Classify these sentences on notebook paper.

	PPA	SN	LV	PA
SN LV PA P5	My	dog / is	healthy.	**D**

_____ Lee is very cheerful.

_____ Butterflies are pretty.

Directions: Use the sentences above to answer the following questions.

1. What are the subjects? **dog, Lee, butterflies**

2. What are the predicate adjectives?

3. What are the linking verbs?

JOURNAL WRITING 27

Write an entry in your notebook journal or digital journal. Before you begin your journal entry, write a sentence with a predicate adjective. As a challenge, try to write one sentence for each of the five patterns. Can you identify different sentence patterns in your entry?

Listening and Speaking

Practice Jingle 26 in the Jingle Section. **PAGE Q14**

Classifying Sentences

Classify the Practice Sentences with your teacher, using the Question and Answer Flow.

Practice Sentences   ORAL PARTICIPATION

1. _____ My bed is really warm and cozy.

2. _____ Peter's dogs are very unhappy today.

3. _____ Oh, man! The front tire on my bike is flat again!

Word Study

The word *unhappy* in Sentence 2 is very broad and non-specific. It is always better to use more specific words in your writing. With a partner, make a list of synonyms of the word *unhappy*. Read Sentence 2 with each of your synonyms in place of *unhappy* and see how much more interesting the sentence becomes!

Review: Linking Verbs

A **linking verb** is not an action verb because it shows a state of being. It tells what the subject **is** instead of what the subject **does**. If a sentence has a predicate adjective, it will have a linking verb. The linking verb links the subject and the predicate adjective. All verbs in Pattern 5 sentences are linking verbs.

In the sentences that you just classified, which verbs are linking? Explain. Are there any transitive or intransitive verbs? Explain.

Review: Case Check

Subject pronouns and **predicate** pronouns are in the subjective case, **possessive** pronouns are in the possessive case, and **object** pronouns are in the objective case.

After you have classified the Practice Sentences, recite a Case Check and a Noun Check with your teacher. These checks help you analyze nouns and pronouns and understand how they are used in sentences.

Case Check Practice Sentences

Sentence 1: My bed is really warm and cozy.

  my: possessive pronoun, *possessive case*

Sentence 2: Peter's dogs are very unhappy today.

  None

Sentence 3: Oh, man! The front tire on my bike is flat again!

  my: possessive pronoun, *possessive case*

Noun Check

Noun Check Practice Sentences

Circle the nouns in the sentences.

Sentence 1: My (bed) is really warm and cozy.

Subject Noun **bed**, *yes, it is a noun.*

Sentence 2: Peter's (dogs) are very unhappy today.

Subject Noun **dogs**, *yes, it is a noun.*

Sentence 3: Oh, man! The front (tire) on my (bike) is flat again!

Subject Noun **tire**, *yes, it is a noun;*

Object of the Preposition **bike**, *yes, it is a noun.*

Are there any Possessive Nouns in the sentences? **Yes**
Name it. **Peter's**

Skill Time

Pronouns and Their Antecedents

The most common pronouns are known as personal pronouns. A personal pronoun refers to the one speaking (*first person*), the one spoken to (*second person*), or the one spoken about (*third person*).

Reference 173

Personal Pronouns and Their Antecedents

Any time a personal pronoun is used in a sentence, it refers to a noun. The noun to which a pronoun refers is called the **antecedent** (ănt′ ŭ sē′ dŭnt) of that pronoun. The antecedent usually comes before a pronoun and can even be in a preceding sentence.

➡ Examples: **The little boy loved his new puppy.**

antecedent   pronoun

The little boy laughed. He loved his new puppy.

Since antecedents determine the pronouns used, it is important for the pronoun to agree with the antecedent in number (singular/plural) and gender (male/female). See the two following rules for number and gender.

1. Number: Decide if the antecedent is singular or plural; choose the pronoun that agrees in number.

➡ If the antecedent is singular, the pronoun must be singular. (For the antecedent **man**, use **he**, **him**, **his**.)

➡ If the antecedent is plural, the pronoun must be plural. (For the antecedent **men**, use **they**, **them**, **their**.)

2. Gender: Decide if the antecedent is male or female; choose the pronoun that agrees in gender.

➥ If the antecedent is male, the pronoun must be male. (antecedent **boy**—pronoun **he**)

➥ If the antecedent is female, the pronoun must be female. (antecedent **girl**—pronoun **she**)

➥ If the antecedent is not a person, use the pronouns **it**, **they**, **them**, etc.
The chickens scratched around the yard.
They came running at feeding time!
(antecedent **chickens**—pronoun **they**)

GRAMMAR AVE.
SKILL ST.

Guided Practice

Directions: Complete the table. Then, underline the correct pronoun in the parentheses that agrees with its antecedent.

PRONOUN-ANTECEDENT AGREEMENT	ANTECEDENT	SINGULAR or PLURAL	PRONOUN S or P
1. Cindy ate every bite of (**their**, <u>**her**</u>) cake.	Cindy	S	S
2. Boots and Mugs played before (**his**, **their**) dinner.			
3. The hilltop was known for (**their**, **its**) view!			

 ACTIVITY

Get with a partner and write a sentence(s), using the new skills:

• Pronoun-Antecedent Agreement in gender and number.

Discuss your sentences with other groups, using the Rules for Discussion.

Extending the Lesson:
Reviewing Personal Pronouns

Study the table below to review the types of personal pronouns and their uses. Then, divide into small groups. With your group, write a sentence, using as many pronouns as you can from the chart.

Our chickens ran eagerly to **me** when I fed **them**!

For a challenge, write a sentence using as many pronouns as you can from one column. Share your group's sentences with the class.

	First Person		Second Person		Third Person	
	SINGULAR	PLURAL	SINGULAR	PLURAL	SINGULAR	PLURAL
Subject Pronouns	I	we	you	you	he, she, it	they
Possessive Pronouns	my, mine	our, ours	your, yours	your, yours	his, her, hers, its	their, theirs
Object Pronouns	me	us	you	you	him, her, it	them

Name: _____ Date:_____

GRAMMAR:

Exercise 1: Classify each sentence.

1. _____ My best friend is very special to me.

2. _____ The breeze feels so refreshing today!

Exercise 2: Use **Sentence 1** above to complete the table below.

LIST THE NOUNS USED	NOUN JOB	SINGULAR or PLURAL	COMMON or PROPER	SIMPLE SUBJECT	SIMPLE PREDICATE

SKILLS:

Exercise 3: Complete the table. Then, underline the correct pronoun in the parentheses that agrees with its antecedent.

PRONOUN-ANTECEDENT AGREEMENT	ANTECEDENT	SINGULAR or PLURAL	PRONOUN S or P
1. Rosa shared (**her, their**) recipe with me.			
2. The puppy chased (**its, their**) tail.			
3. My aunts announced (**their, her**) retirement.			
4. Toby and Jason waited for (**his, their**) uncle.			
5. Ann called David at (**his, their**) house.			

Exercise 4: Write the correct form of each adjective or adverb in parentheses.

1. A mouse is _____ than a rat. (**small**)

2. A tarantula is a _____ spider. (**large**)

3. This has been the _____ summer ever! (**hot**)

Chapter 16

Listening and Speaking

Practice Jingles 25–26 in the Jingle Section. **PAGES Q13–Q14**

Classifying Sentences

Classify the Practice Sentences with your teacher, using the Question and Answer Flow.

Practice Sentences   ORAL PARTICIPATION

1. _____ Today at the doctor's office, Tim was nervous.

2. _____ In the winter, the trees in the park are bare.

3. _____ My favorite snack is sweet and salty.

Word Study

There are many different ways that adjectives can modify a noun. The adjective *nervous* in Sentence 1 modifies *Tim* by describing his state of mind. Other examples of "state-of-mind" adjectives include *confident, lonely, drowsy, afraid, happy, sad, depressed,* and *giddy.* The adjectives *sweet* and *salty* in Sentence 3 modify *snack* by describing its taste. Can you think of other examples of "taste" adjectives?

Case Check

After you have classified the Practice Sentences, recite a Case Check and a Noun Check with your teacher. These checks help you analyze nouns and pronouns and understand how they are used in sentences.

Case Check Practice Sentences

Sentence 1: Today at the doctor's office, Tim was nervous.

None

Sentence 2: In the winter, the trees in the park are bare.

None

Sentence 3: My favorite snack is sweet and salty.

my: possessive pronoun, *possessive case*

Noun Check

Noun Check

1. **Identify the nouns in a Noun Check.**
   (Say the job and the noun. Circle each noun.)

2. **Identify the nouns as singular or plural.**
   (Write **S** or **P** above the noun.)

3. **Identify the nouns as common or proper.**
   (Write **C** or **P** above the noun.)

Review: Parts of Speech

REMINDER: How a word is used in a sentence determines its part of speech. What are the eight parts of speech?

What are the labels for the eight parts of speech?

Indefinite Pronouns, Singular and Plural

A pronoun that does not refer to a definite or specific person, place, or thing is called an **indefinite pronoun**. These words are indefinite pronouns: *everyone, nobody, something, each,* and *several.*

In order to prevent problems in subject-verb agreement and in pronoun-antecedent agreement, it is important to know which indefinite pronouns are always singular, which indefinite pronouns are always plural, and which indefinite pronouns can be either singular or plural.

The indefinite pronouns in the singular chart are always singular. If they are used as subjects, use a singular verb.

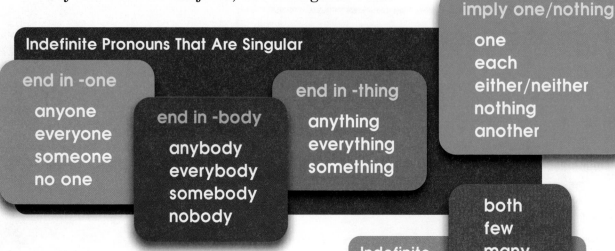

Indefinite Pronouns That Are Singular

end in -one
anyone
everyone
someone
no one

end in -body
anybody
everybody
somebody
nobody

end in -thing
anything
everything
something

imply one/nothing
one
each
either/neither
nothing
another

Indefinite Pronouns That Are Plural
both
few
many
others
several

The indefinite pronouns in the plural chart are always plural. If they are used as subjects, use a plural verb.

Subject-Verb Agreement of Singular and Plural Indefinite Pronouns

For singular indefinite pronouns, use singular verbs.
For plural indefinite pronouns, use plural verbs.

> **Singular: Everyone** in town **shops** at the local stores.
> **Plural: Many** in town **shop** at the local stores.

Pronoun-Antecedent Agreement of Singular and Plural Indefinite Pronouns

When singular indefinite pronouns are antecedents, use singular personal pronouns for agreement.

> **Singular: Everyone** has **his** assignment completed.

When plural indefinite pronouns are antecedents, use plural personal pronouns for agreement.

> **Plural: Several** have **their** assignments completed.

Ways Indefinite Pronouns Can Be Used

Singular indefinite pronouns are used in noun positions as subjects, objects, or predicate nouns.

As a subject: Everyone in the class was excited.

As an object: They heard somebody outside.

As a predicate noun: She is someone in my class.

Plural indefinite pronouns are also used in noun positions as subjects, objects, or predicate nouns.

As a subject: Few are going to the concert.

As an object: The volunteer helps several of the students.

As a predicate noun: The toys were many.

Pronoun or **Adjective?** Sometimes, words used as indefinite pronouns can also be used as adjectives. If an indefinite word is used as an adjective, it is an indefinite adjective, not an indefinite pronoun. Study the examples to help you know whether these words are used as adjectives or indefinite pronouns.

As an indefinite pronoun: Many are going to the play.

As an adjective: Many students are going to the play.

GRAMMAR AVE.
SKILL ST.

Guided Practice

Directions: Write the indefinite pronoun used as the subject. Identify it as **S** for singular or **P** for plural. Then, write the correct verb that agrees with the subject.

SUBJECT	S or P	VERB AGREEMENT
Everybody	S	likes

1. Everybody (**like, likes**) my brownie recipe.

2. Several of the students (**is, are**) early today.

3. Someone in the class (**have, has**) the flu.

ACTIVITY Write a sentence using a singular indefinite pronoun. Then, write another sentence using a plural indefinite pronoun.

Classroom Practice 73

Name: _____ Date:_____

GRAMMAR:

Exercise 1: Classify each sentence.

1. _____ Today, Paul and Sam were unbeatable in the

100-meter dash.

2. _____ Outdoor games are fun for the kids in my neighborhood.

SKILLS:

Exercise 2: Identify these indefinite as **S** for singular or **P** for plural.

_____ 1. few _____ 3. nothing _____ 5. someone

_____ 2. nobody _____ 4. everybody _____ 6. several

Exercise 3: Write the indefinite pronoun used as the subject. Identify it as **S** for singular or **P** for plural. Then, write the correct verb that agrees with the subject.

SUBJECT	S or P	VERB AGREEMENT

1. Everyone (**need, needs**) food.

2. Several (**know, knows**) the answer.

3. No one (**arrive, arrives**) on time.

4. Few (**laugh, laughs**) at his jokes.

5. Everybody (**is, are**) laughing at my joke!

Exercise 4: Complete the table. Then, underline the correct pronoun in the parentheses that agrees with its antecedent.

PRONOUN-ANTECEDENT AGREEMENT	ANTECEDENT	SINGULAR or PLURAL	PRONOUN S or P
1. Walt took off (**their, his**) shoes.			
2. Two robins built (**themselves, itself**) a nest.			
3. My friend played (**their, her**) piano solo.			
4. The girls said (**her, their**) favorite color is pink.			

Listening and Speaking

Practice Jingles 24–26 in the Jingle Section. **PAGES Q12–Q14**

Mixed Patterns

Reference 175

Mixed Patterns 1–5

Study the five sentence patterns shown. As you classify the sentences, pay close attention to the core parts of each sentence. This will help you decide which pattern to choose.

→ **Pattern 1** is **SN V**.
  It has a **noun-verb** (**N V**) core.

SN V
↑ ↑
N V

  ➡ Example:

                  A SN   V   P A Adj OP
$\dfrac{\text{SN V}}{\text{P1}}$ The boys / played (on the baseball field). **D**

→ **Pattern 2** is **SN V-t DO**.
  It has a **noun-verb-noun** (**N V N**) core.

SN V-t DO
↑ ↑ ↑
N V N

  ➡ Example:

                  A SN   V-t   DO
$\dfrac{\text{SN V-t}}{\text{DO P2}}$ The boys / played baseball. **D**

→ **Pattern 3** is **SN V-t IO DO**.
It has a **noun-verb-noun-noun (N V N N)** core.

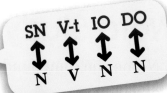

➥ Example:

PPA SN V-t IO A DO

<u>SN V-t</u> My friend / threw me the baseball. **D**
IO DO P3

→ **Pattern 4** is **SN LV PrN**.
It has a **noun-linking verb-noun (N LV N)** core.

➥ Example:

PPA SN LV A Adj PrN

<u>SN LV</u> My friend / is the new pitcher. **D**
PrN P4

→ **Pattern 5** is **SN LV PA**.
It has a **noun-linking verb-adjective (N LV Adj)** core.

➥ Example:

PPA Adj SN LV Adv PA

<u>SN LV</u> Our baseball coach / is very good. **D**
PA P5

Classifying Mixed Patterns 1-5

Classify the Introductory Sentences with your teacher, using the
Question and Answer Flow.

Introductory Sentences   ORAL PARTICIPATION

1. _____ Danny and I are quite good at card games.

2. _____ Paul caught the baseball in mid-air.

3. _____ Lisa slept through the boring movie.

4. _____ Did Julie make you a beaded bracelet today?

5. _____ Peaches and strawberries are my favorite desserts.

6. _____ Mmm! Mother's oatmeal cookies are absolutely delicious!

Word Study

1. Name the compound words in this set of sentences.

2. Name the word with a hyphen and tell whether it is a noun or an adjective.

3. What is the difference in the words *dessert* and *desert*?

4. Use a hard-copy or online dictionary to look up the words *mid-air*, *dessert*, and *desert*. Draw a picture in your journal to help you remember the meanings of these words.

Review: Transitive, Intransitive, and Linking Verbs

Pattern 1 sentences have intransitive verbs that show action but have no direct objects. Patterns 2 and 3 sentences have transitive verbs that show action and have direct objects. Patterns 4 and 5 sentences have linking verbs that show a state of being (no action) and have predicate nouns/pronouns or predicate adjectives.

In the sentences that you just classified, which verbs are transitive? Explain. Which verb is intransitive? Explain. Which verb is linking? Explain.

Identifying Pattern Numbers Only for Patterns 1-5

When identifying mixed patterns, you must concentrate on the core of each sentence. Since the core is the pattern of the sentence, classify only the main parts (**SN V**), (**SN V-t DO**), (**SN V-t IO DO**), (**SN LV PrN**), and (**SN LV PA**) without classifying all the other words in the sentence. Classify the core parts, determine the pattern, and write only the pattern number in the blank. With practice, you will be able to identify the pattern by sight.

Example: Write the correct pattern number in each blank. (**P1 = SN V, P2 = SN V-t DO, P3 = SN V-t IO DO, P4 = SN LV PrN, P5 = SN LV PA**)

__P4__ 1. My new kitten is Princess.

__P5__ 2. Princess is gray and white.

__P3__ 3. Mom bought her a pink collar.

__P3__ 4. We gave Princess a bed with a pillow.

__P1__ 5. She sleeps in bed with me anyway!

__P2__ 6. She purrs and wakes me up every day.

Guided Practice

Exercise 1: Write the correct pattern number in each blank. (**P1 = SN V, P2 = SN V-t DO, P3 = SN V-t IO DO, P4 = SN LV PrN, P5 = SN LV PA**)

__P2__ 1. Yea! Mom is making tacos!

_____ 2. Will you hand me a napkin?

_____ 3. Dana's dad is a racecar driver.

_____ 4. Later, we can walk to the waterfall.

_____ 5. Most babies are really cute!

_____ 6. My dad told us a tale about his dog.

Exercise 2: Write the main verbs in Exercise 1 and identify them with a **T** for transitive, **I** for intransitive, or **L** for linking.

VERBS	T, I, L	VERBS	T, I, L	VERBS	T, I, L
1. **making**	**T**	3.		5.	
2.		4.		6.	

Name: _____ Date:_____

GRAMMAR:

Exercise 1: Classify each sentence.

1. _____ Trisha and Steven worked on their art project together.

2. _____ Wait! I forgot my lunch on the kitchen counter!

3. _____ The hot, dry climate of the desert is perfect for cactus.

4. _____ My oldest brother is a first-year medical student.

Exercise 2: Write the correct pattern number in each blank. (**P1 = SN V, P2 = SN V-t DO, P3 = SN V-t IO DO, P4 = SN LV PrN, P5 = SN LV PA**)

_____ 1. Jamie enjoys craft shows.

_____ 2. The ball bounced over the fence.

_____ 3. This honey tastes very sweet.

_____ 4. Give me a hand with this project.

_____ 5. My sister is a talented singer.

_____ 6. Rosa hates turnips.

SKILLS:

Exercise 3: Identify these indefinite as **S** for singular or **P** for plural.

_____ 1. few

_____ 2. someone

_____ 3. nothing

_____ 4. anything

_____ 5. everyone

_____ 6. both

Exercise 4: Write the indefinite pronoun used as the subject. Identify it as **S** for singular or **P** for plural. Then, write the correct verb that agrees with the subject.

SUBJECT	S or P	VERB AGREEMENT

1. Everyone (**like, likes**) the new student.

2. Only a few (**dislike, dislikes**) chocolate.

3. Several (**is, are**) entered in the race.

Word Time

Vocabulary and Analogy

Word 23 **legend** (lej' ŭnd)

Definition: a fictional story built on a grain of historical truth

Synonym: fiction   **Antonym:** nonfiction

Sentence: Have you ever heard of the **legend** of King Arthur?

Analogy **sweet : sour :: rough :: smooth**

Relationship: Antonym

Thinking Process: Just as **sweet** is the opposite of **sour**, **rough** is the opposite of **smooth**. Therefore, this is an **antonym** analogy.

🔧 ACTIVITY

Draw a picture or write a poem or story in your Vocabulary Notebook to help you remember the word legend.

*(Picture Idea: Draw a picture of a famous legend like Robin Hood, Bigfoot, or the Loch Ness Monster. Label the picture with the label **legend**.)*

Spelling

Study this Spelling Rule to help you become a better speller.

Spelling Rule 9 — Spelling Words Ending in the K Sound

For words that end with the **k** sound:
Rule: Use **-ck** after a **single short vowel.**
➡ Examples: **lack, pick**

Rule: Use **-ke** after a **single long vowel.** (makes a **CVCe** pattern)
➡ Examples: **lake, pike**

Rule: Use **-k** after a **long vowel team.**
➡ Examples: **peak, soak**

Spelling Words For each word: Recite, Spell, and Repeat.

Rule: use **-ck** after a **single short vowel.**

Recite shack   **Spell** s-h-a-c-k   **Repeat** shack

Rule: use **-ke** after a **single long vowel** (makes a **CVCe** pattern)

Recite make   **Spell** m-a-k-e   **Repeat** make

Rule: use **-k** after a **long vowel team.**

Recite seek   **Spell** s-e-e-k   **Repeat** seek

1. shack	3. seek	5. rock
2. make	4. croak	6. broke

We took
a stack
of thick
books to
the lake
shack.

Listening and Speaking

Practice Jingles 24–26 in the Jingle Section. **PAGES Q12-Q14**

Classifying Mixed Patterns 1-5

Classify the Practice Sentences with your teacher, using the
Question and Answer Flow.

Practice Sentences   ORAL PARTICIPATION

1. _____ Monica's friends are very polite girls.

2. _____ Yikes! This scary movie could give me nightmares!

3. _____ The outside temperature is too cold for the children.

4. _____ During the fall, we hike and camp in Colorado.

5. _____ Yesterday, my brothers and I were late for school.

6. _____ During English class, Antonio and Phillip wrote a very funny poem.

Word Study

1. Homonym alert! Can you spot the six homonyms in these sentences?

2. A **concrete** noun names a person, place, or thing that can be identified by one of the senses (sight, hearing, taste, touch, and smell), such as desk, friend, or brownie. Use a concrete noun in a sentence.

3. An **abstract** noun names a thought, idea or feeling, such as freedom, a dream, or happiness.
   Can you find an abstract noun in the Practice Sentences?
   Use an abstract noun in a sentence.

Review: Transitive, Intransitive, and Linking Verbs

Pattern 1 sentences have intransitive verbs that show action but have no direct objects. Patterns 2 and 3 sentences have transitive verbs that show action and have direct objects. Patterns 4 and 5 sentences have linking verbs that show a state of being (no action) and have predicate nouns/pronouns or predicate adjectives.

In the sentences that you just classified, which verbs are transitive? Explain. Which verb is intransitive? Explain. Which verb is linking? Explain.

Case Check

After you have classified the Practice Sentences, recite a Case Check and a Noun Check with your teacher. These checks help you analyze nouns and pronouns and understand how they are used in sentences.

Case Check Practice Sentences

Sentence 1: Monica's friends are very polite girls.

None

Sentence 2: Yikes! This scary movie could give me nightmares!

me: indirect object pronoun, *objective case*

Sentence 3: The outside temperature is too cold for the children.

None

Sentence 4: During the fall, we hike and camp in Colorado.

we: subject pronoun, *subjective case*

Sentence 5: Yesterday, my brothers and I were late for school.

my: possessive pronoun, *possessive case*

I: subject pronoun, *subjective case*

Sentence 6: During English class, Antonio and Phillip wrote a very funny poem.

None

REMINDER: Since a predicate pronoun means the same thing as the subject, it is in the subjective case and must be one of these subject pronouns: *I, we, he, she, it, they,* and *you.*

Noun Check

☐ 1. **Identify the nouns in a Noun Check.**
(Say the job and the noun. Circle each noun.)

☐ 2. **Identify the nouns as singular or plural.**
(Write **S** or **P** above the noun.)

☐ 3. **Identify the nouns as common or proper.**
(Write **C** or **P** above the noun.)

Name: _____ Date:_____

GRAMMAR:

Exercise 1: Classify each sentence.

1. _____ Sweep the snow off the front porch.

2. _____ Mother's pet parakeet chattered and talked loudly to me.

3. _____ Squash, carrots, and potatoes are garden vegetables.

4. _____ Yum! Mom's blueberry pie tastes wonderful!

Exercise 2: Write the correct pattern number in each blank. (**P1 = SN V, P2 = SN V-t DO, P3 = SN V-t IO DO, P4 = SN LV PrN, P5 = SN LV PA**)

_____ 1. Phil loves jellybeans!   _____ 4. Our trees are bare in the winter.

_____ 2. Will Mary go to college in the fall?   _____ 5. Salsa is a tasty treat with chips.

_____ 3. Read us a bedtime story.   _____ 6. Did you let the cat out?

SKILLS:

Exercise 3: Identify these indefinite pronouns as **S** for singular or **P** for plural.

_____ 1. both   _____ 3. somebody   _____ 5. several

_____ 2. anyone   _____ 4. everyone   _____ 6. few

Exercise 4: Complete the table. Then, underline the correct pronoun in the parentheses that agrees with its antecedent.

PRONOUN-ANTECEDENT AGREEMENT	ANTECEDENT	SINGULAR or PLURAL	PRONOUN S or P
1. James loaned me (**his, their**) pen.			
2. Four men shaved (**his, their**) beards.			
3. The cat licked (**their, its**) paws slowly.			

Word Time

Vocabulary and Analogy

Word 24 → **exaggerate** (ĕks ăj' er āt)

Definition: to overstate the facts; enhance

Synonym: elaborate   **Antonym:** understate

Sentence: Susan exaggerated the details of her story.

Etymology → **Word History of exaggerate**

Latin Root: exaggerare
(ĕks ăj' ŭ rar' ā)

Definition: to heap up or enlarge

Other words from the root: exaggeration

Analogy → **taut : caught :: battery :: flattery**

Relationship: Rhyming

Thinking Process: Just as **taut** rhymes with **caught**, **battery** rhymes with **flattery**. Therefore, this is a **rhyming** analogy.

ACTIVITY   Draw a picture or write a poem or story in your Vocabulary Notebook to help you remember the word **exaggerate**.

*(Picture Idea: Draw a picture of a fisherman holding his arms out wide as if exaggerating how big the fish was that got away! Label the picture with the word **exaggerate**.)*

Spelling

It's time to review what you've learned about spelling!

Spelling Rule 9 — Spelling Words Ending in the K Sound

For words that end with the **k** sound:

Rule: Use **-ck** after a **single short vowel.**
➥ Examples: **lack, pick**

Rule: Use **-ke** after a **single long vowel.** (makes a **CVCe** pattern)
➥ Examples: **lake, pike**

Rule: Use **-k** after a **long vowel team.**
➥ Examples: **peak, soak**

Spelling Words

For each word: **Recite**, **Spell**, and **Repeat**.

Rule: use **-ck** after a **single short vowel.**

Recite shack   **Spell** s-h-a-c-k   **Repeat** shack

Rule: use **-ke** after a **single long vowel** (makes a **CVCe** pattern)

Recite make   **Spell** m-a-k-e   **Repeat** make

Rule: use **-k** after a **long vowel team.**

Recite seek   **Spell** s-e-e-k   **Repeat** seek

1. **shack**
2. **make**
3. **seek**
4. **croak**
5. **rock**
6. **broke**

Classifying Mixed Patterns 1-5

Classify the Practice Sentences with your teacher, using the Question and Answer Flow.

Practice Sentences   ORAL PARTICIPATION

1. _____ Will Billy and Kim open their anniversary present today?
2. _____ Our new puppy was very playful and curious.
3. _____ Sydney is a very large city in Australia.
4. _____ After the long trip, Mom and Dad were exhausted.
5. _____ Did the waiter bring you a fork and knife at lunch?
6. _____ Ask for a large popcorn and soda at the movies tonight.

Word Study

Use context clues or a dictionary to study multiple-meaning words like *present*. What is your definition of *present*? How many definitions do you think it has? How many definitions does the dictionary give? Use context clues to choose the meaning of *present* as it is used in Sentence 1.

Review: Transitive, Intransitive, and Linking Verbs

Pattern 1 sentences have intransitive verbs that show action but have no direct objects. Patterns 2 and 3 sentences have transitive verbs that show action and have direct objects. Patterns 4 and 5 sentences have linking verbs that show a state of being (no action) and have predicate nouns/pronouns or predicate adjectives.

In the sentences that you just classified, which verbs are transitive? Explain. Which verbs are intransitive? Explain. Which verbs are linking? Explain.

Review: Parts of Speech

REMINDER: How a word is used in a sentence determines its part of speech. What are the eight parts of speech?

What are the labels for the eight parts of speech?

Blueprint for Building a Sentence

Today, you will learn how to add a predicate adjective to your blueprint labels to write an original sentence.

 Reference 177

Designing a Sentence Blueprint,
Adding Predicate Adjectives

Design and build your sentence on Classroom Practice 76.

1. Use the core labels, **SN/SP**, **LV**, and **PA**, only once and in that order.

2. The other labels, **Adj**, **Adv**, **A**, **P**, **OP**, **PPA**, **C**, **HV**, **I**, and **PNA**, can be used as many times as you wish, in any order you wish, as long as they make sense. (REMEMBER: Complete sense is one of the five parts of a complete sentence.)

3. **Instructions for the new labels, LV and PA:** First, think of a linking verb that will make sense with a predicate adjective, such as "*am,*" "*is,*" "*are,*" "*was,*" and so on. Write your linking verb under the **LV** label. Then, think of a predicate adjective that describes the subject. Write your predicate adjective under the **PA** label.

4. Write the labels in the order you choose on the Labels line.

5. Write a word that makes sense for each label.

After writing your original sentence on Classroom Practice 76, use the revision strategies to help you make revisions.

Use Revision Strategies to Revise Your Original Sentence

REMEMBER: Revising means looking for ways to improve your writing. As you revise your Original Sentence, write the abbreviation of the revision strategy you used under each word in your Revised Sentence.

1 **Synonym** (syn)   **2** **Antonym** (ant)   **3** **Word Change** (wc)

4 **Added Word** (add)   **5** **Deleted Word** (delete)   **6** **No Change** (nc)

When you have finished, your paper should resemble the example below.

Labels:	A	Adj	SN	LV	PA	P	A	Adj	OP
Original Sentence:	The	small	pond	was	peaceful	in	the	late	afternoons.
Revised Sentence:	The	large	lake	was	tranquil	in	the	early	mornings.
Revision Strategy:	(nc)	(ant)	(syn)	(nc)	(syn)	(nc)	(nc)	(ant)	(ant)

Student Tip...

1. Use your Vocabulary Words, Power Words, a thesaurus, and a dictionary to help you write your Original and Revised Sentences.

2. As you go through each word of your Original Sentence, think about the changes and improvements you want to make.

3. Knowing the revision strategies gives you more flexibility as you work to improve your sentences.

4. As you revise your original sentence, keep this information in mind:

   • Antonyms and Word Changes will change your sentence's meaning.

   • Synonyms and No Changes will keep the meaning of the original sentence.

   • Added Words and Deleted Words can change the meaning of your sentence or keep it the same, depending on the words you choose to add or delete.

Lesson 6

Name: _____

Date: _____

Exercise 1: Write your own blueprint labels. Use the labels to write an original sentence. Then, revise your sentence, writing the abbreviation of the revision strategy under each word.

Labels:

Original Sentence:

Revised Sentence:

Revision Strategy:

Labels:

Original Sentence:

Revised Sentence:

Revision Strategy:

Exercise 2: Rewrite your revised sentence on the lines below. Use the checklist to check your sentence.

_____

_____

Sentence Checklist: ☐ Capital letter ☐ Subject ☐ Verb ☐ Complete sense ☐ End mark

Writing a *Mover & Shaker* Sentence in Your Journal:

Skip two lines below your last entry and write the date and chapter number. Then, skip one line and write a Mover & Shaker Sentence **with a repeated predicate adjective**. This strategy allows a writer to emphasize specific adjectives in a dramatic way. Repeat the predicate adjective at the end of a sentence; then, add another adjective.

Simple Sentence: Nancy's little car is cute.

Mover & Shaker Sentence: Nancy's little car is cute, cute and sporty.

Compare all of the Mover & Shaker Sentences you have written so far.

JOURNAL WRITING 28

Write an entry in your notebook journal or digital journal. Use the spelling pattern in Spelling Rule 9 to help you spell words correctly.

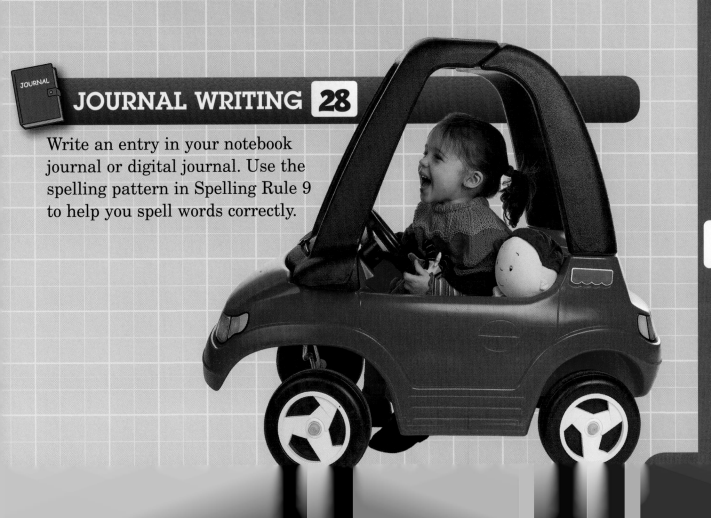

Classifying Mixed Patterns 1-5

Classify the Practice Sentences with your teacher,
using the Question and Answer Flow.

Practice Sentences

1. _____ Today, the mailman brought a large package to our house.

2. _____ Christy's vacation at Gulf Shores in Alabama was very relaxing.

3. _____ Wow! That huge stone in Aunt Laura's ring is a real diamond!

4. _____ A bank robber led the police on a high-speed chase!

5. _____ Tell Jack and Marion your exciting story during lunch.

6. _____ Bonnie and I are walking to school with Larry and Terry tomorrow.

Word Study

Use context clues or a dictionary to study multiple-meaning words like *ring*. What is your definition of *ring*? How many definitions do you think it has? How many definitions does the dictionary give? Use context clues to choose the meaning of *ring* as it is used in Sentence 3.

Review: Writing the Four Kinds of Sentences

Choose one of the following options:

1. Write one each of the four kinds of sentences *(declarative, exclamatory, interrogative, or imperative)*, using a different spelling word in each sentence. *(See Chapter 2 for a review of the four kinds of sentences.)*

2. Write a declarative sentence, using one of your spelling words. Then, change that sentence to the other three kinds of sentences *(exclamatory, interrogative, and imperative)*.

3. Write a compound or complex declarative sentence, using at least one of your spelling words. *(See Chapter 7 for a review of compound and complex sentences.)*

For your sentences, use the spelling words from Rule 9:
shack, make, seek, croak, rock, broke

Lesson 7

The Reading Club is a time to get into small groups and share a favorite book with others. Use the suggestions below to help you share your book.

◆ Give the title and author of the book. Show the book if you still have it.

◆ Describe a particular setting that is important to the story and tell where it is found in the book.

◆ Describe the main characters and tell something about them and discuss the specific evidence from the book that helps you form your impressions about them.

◆ Tell what happens to the characters as the plot progresses. Be brief. Don't tell too much.

◆ Discuss any major themes from your book.

◆ Tell why you liked the book.

Write down the title and author of any book that you would like to read. Follow the Rules for Discussion and listen respectfully to other members of your group as different books are shared.

 Challenge

1. Describe your favorite setting from a book and explain how it helped you understand the story or how it caused certain characters to play the role they played in the story. If your book contains illustrations, explain how they played an important part in the story.

2. As you read your story a second or third time, locate specific instances when the author used examples of figurative language that you liked, such as similes and personification. Give the chapter and page location, as well as the particular paragraph or sentence in which you found the figurative language.

Name: _____ Date:_____

GRAMMAR:

Exercise 1: Classify each sentence.

1. _____ Grandpa handed me a crisp new twenty-dollar bill

for my birthday.

2. _____ Grandma and her friends met for a movie and dinner.

3. _____ The movie showed incredible underwater creatures!

4. _____ Crabs and lobsters are my favorite seafood.

5. _____ In the fall, the locusts in our backyard are quite noisy!

Exercise 2: Write the correct pattern number in each blank. (**P1 = SN V, P2 = SN V-t DO, P3 = SN V-t IO DO, P4 = SN LV PrN, P5 = SN LV PA**)

_____ 1. Tarantulas look scary. _____ 4. Daryl's music is too loud!

_____ 2. The dog growled fiercely. _____ 5. Lucy is my cousin.

_____ 3. We took a ride on our bikes. _____ 6. Jump off the diving board.

Exercise 3: Write the main verbs from Exercise 2 and identify them with a **T** for transitive, **I** for intransitive, or **L** for linking.

VERBS	T, I, L	VERBS	T, I, L	VERBS	T, I, L
1.		3.		5.	
2.		4.		6.	

OVER

SKILLS:

Exercise 4: Write the indefinite pronoun used as the subject. Identify it as **S** for singular or **P** for plural. Then, write the correct verb that agrees with the subject.

SUBJECT	S or P	VERB AGREEMENT

1. No one in the class (**like, likes**) broccoli.

2. Can anyone (**hear, hears**) me?

3. Both of us (**eat, eats**) carrots.

4. Everyone in the concert (**sing, sings**) well.

Exercise 5: Complete the table. Then, underline the correct pronoun in the parentheses that agrees with its antecedent.

PRONOUN-ANTECEDENT AGREEMENT	ANTECEDENT	SINGULAR or PLURAL	PRONOUN S or P
1. Janie had (**their, her**) cast removed.			
2. The dog ran to (**their, its**) bed.			
3. Jackie gave the cats (**its, their**) toys.			

Exercise 6: Fill in the circle beside each correct answer.

1. **Antonym:** *legend*   ○ nonfiction   ○ fiction

2. **Synonym:** *exaggerate*   ○ elaborate   ○ understate

3. Grandpa told us the ____ of Sleepy Hollow.   ○ exaggerate   ○ legend

WRITING:

Exercise 7: Write a sentence for this vocabulary word: **legend**.

_____

_____

_____

With your teacher, read the questions below. Do you know all the answers? Listen carefully for answers you do not know. After the review, you will have a chapter test.

1. What are the three kinds of verbs you have studied?

2. What kind of verb shows a state of action and tells what the subject does?

3. What kind of verb shows a state of being and tells what the subject is?

4. What is a special adjective in the predicate that describes the subject noun?

5. What are the core parts of a Pattern 1 sentence?

6. What are the core parts of a Pattern 2 sentence?

7. What are the core parts of a Pattern 3 sentence?

8. What are the core parts of a Pattern 4 sentence?

9. What are the core parts of a Pattern 5 sentence?

10. What are the indefinite pronouns that are always singular?

11. What are the indefinite pronouns that are always plural?

Posttest

It is time to take the Posttest. Work very carefully and think about what you are doing. After everyone has finished, you will compare your Pretest and Posttest. If this is your first year in Shurley English, you should see a huge difference. If you have had several years of Shurley, even your Pretest should show how well you are remembering the skills you have learned.

JOURNAL WRITING 29

Write an entry in your notebook journal or digital journal. After you complete your Posttest, tell how your Pretest compared with your Posttest. Is there a big difference? What improvements have you made? Do you feel more confident in grammar and writing? Why?

Skill Time

Review: Topic Outline

Outlining helps you group related ideas and information together in an organized pattern to show their relationship to one another.

1. **Main Points** *(two or more main points about the topic)*

   → Use Roman numerals (I. II. III.) for main points.
   You must have two or more main points.

   → Capitalize the first word but do not use an end mark.

   → Line up the periods after the Roman numerals, one under the other.

   Pet Chores

I. **Cat chores**	MAIN POINT
II. **Dog chores**	MAIN POINT

2. **Subtopics** *(information that supports a main point)*

   → Use capital letters (A. B. C.) for subtopics.
   You must have two or more subtopics.

   → Line up subtopics under the first word of the main point.

   → Line up the periods after the capital letters.

   → Capitalize the first word but do not use an end mark.

   I. Cat chores   MAIN POINT

A. **Feed cat**	SUBTOPIC
B. **Change water**	SUBTOPIC
C. **Clean litter box**	SUBTOPIC

CONTINUED ON NEXT PAGE

3. Details (*information that supports a subtopic*)
- → Use Arabic numerals for details. You must have two or more details.
- → Line up details under the first word of the subtopic.
- → Line up periods after the Arabic numerals.
- → Capitalize the first word but do not use an end mark.

II. Dog chores   MAIN POINT
    A. Food   SUBTOPIC
    B. Water   SUBTOPIC
    C. Exercise   SUBTOPIC
      1. Go for a walk   DETAIL
      2. Play games   DETAIL

Review: Parallel Form

Using **parallel form** means that each section in an outline should begin in the same way: all nouns, all verbs, all noun phrases, all verb phrases, all prepositional phrases, etc. When you first make an outline, it probably will not be parallel. After you organize the ideas, then you can go back and change or rearrange the words in your outline so they are parallel.

Parallel Form for Main Points

To be parallel, all main points must begin with the same part of speech. It does not matter how the main points begin; it is just important that they begin the same way.

I. Do cat chores
II. Dog chores

Discussion Questions:

1. Are these main points in parallel form?

2. How can we make them parallel, using adjectives?

3. How can we make them parallel, using verbs?

4. How can we make them parallel, using pronouns?

Parallel Form for Subtopics

To be parallel, all subtopics under a specific main point must begin with the same part of speech. It does not matter how the subtopics begin; it is just important that they begin the same way.

A. **Feed** cat

B. **Fresh** water

C. **Litter**

Discussion Questions:

1. Are these subtopics in parallel form?

2. How can we make them parallel, using adjectives?

3. How can we make them parallel, using verbs?

4. How can we make them parallel, using prepositions?

Parallel Form for Details

To be parallel, all details under a specific subtopic must begin with the same part of speech. It does not matter how the details begin; it is just important that they begin the same way.

1. **Go** for a walk

2. **Fun** games

Discussion Questions:

1. Are these details in parallel form?

2. How can we make them parallel, using verbs?

3. How can we make them parallel, using adjectives?

4. How can we make them parallel, using nouns?

End Lesson 10

Name: _____ Date:_____

SKILLS:

Exercise 1: Put the information into outline form, following the rules for outlining. Four items are not parallel. Make them parallel in the outline.

Uses of Horses
Main Points
in the past
in the present

Subtopics
for travelingfor hunting
battles
to round up livestock
to pull loads
for police work

farm work
for fun
Details
on roads
over land

forests
wagons
carriages
plows
to work livestock

to check fences
horse races
horseback riding
rodeo
local parades

Outline:

_____
_____
_____
_____
_____
_____
_____
_____
_____
_____
_____
_____
_____
_____
_____
_____
_____
_____
_____
_____
_____
_____

Reading Time

Did you know that there are different speeds for reading? Learn how reading speeds should be adjusted according to your reason for reading.

Reference 178

Reasons for Reading

Reasons for Reading:	Reading Speeds:
For enjoyment ⇨	Read at a comfortable pace, enjoying the author's style.
For understanding ⇨	Read slowly and thoroughly, learning new information, remembering main ideas and details.
For a general idea ⇨	Read quickly over titles, subtitles, headings, key words, and captions, getting a general idea of the text.
For locating answers ⇨	Read quickly over titles, subtitles, headings, underlined and bold type to find the key words in specific questions. Then, read slowly to find the answer.

As your reading skills grow, learning new reading strategies will help you become an even more effective reader. A reading strategy is a plan that helps you read different kinds of texts. Reading strategies and reading speeds work together.

Sometimes, the best reading strategy is a combination of fast and slow reading. When reading school textbooks, magazine articles, and other materials that are packed with information, try using a combination of the reading strategies listed in Reference 179.

Lesson 1

Four Reading Strategies: Skim, Question, Read, Scan

When you read complicated subject matter, such as topics in the areas of science and social studies, **you should know how to use a combination of reading strategies**. Study the four reading strategies below.

1 → SKIM –
Read quickly to get a general idea of the text.
Skimming is a quick way for you to know what is in each section before you read it. To skim, quickly look over the titles, headings, subheadings, and key words in bold print to get a general idea of the text.

2 → QUESTION –
Turn headings into questions to give you a reason for reading.
As you skim, turn headings and bold words into **questions** to make it easier to remember the main ideas and key words.

3 → READ –
Read subject matter slowly to understand the information under each heading and to get definitions for key words.
Reading helps you understand the main ideas and key words in the article.

4 → SCAN –
Look for key headings and words that will signal sections where you will find answers to questions.
Scanning helps you find sections in the text to look for answers to questions. Scan headings, key words in bold print, underlined words, and topic sentences to help you find the answers you need.

Discussion Questions:

Skim

1. Why do you skim?

2. What is the reading speed for the skimming strategy?

3. What do you look at when skimming?

Question

4. Why do you form questions?

5. What do you turn into questions in the questioning strategy?

Read

6. Why do you read subject matter slowly?

Scan

7. Why do you scan?

8. What is the reading speed for the scanning strategy?

9. What do you look at when scanning?

Use Reference 180 to answer the questions below.

Reference 180

Article for Reading Strategies

First, skim headings and key words in bold print. Second, form questions from the headings and key words. Third, read the text, reading closely to understand information about headings and key words. Fourth, scan headings and key words again to find answers to questions.

Butterflies and Moths

SECTION 1 **How Butterflies and Moths Are Alike**

Butterflies and moths are alike in many ways. One way they are alike is that they are both **insects**. Insects are small animals that have six legs, wings, and antennae. **Antennae** are thin feelers on their head that are used for smelling. Another way they are alike is they both drink nectar from plants. **Nectar** is the sweet liquid inside flowers. In addition, butterflies and moths both have a caterpillar stage. While

CONTINUED ON NEXT PAGE

they are caterpillars, also called the **larval stage**, they look like fat, colorful worms. They eat and grow during this stage. Last of all, both butterflies and moths are found everywhere in the world.

SECTION 2 **How Butterflies and Moths Are Different**

Even though butterflies and moths are very similar, there are a few ways that they are different. One difference in butterflies and moths is their **body shape**. Butterflies have long, slender bodies, and moths have short, chubby bodies. Another way that butterflies and moths are different is their antennae. Butterflies have smooth antennae with knobs on the end. Moths have feathery antennae without knobs. The way butterflies and moths hold their wings when they rest shows another difference. Butterflies rest with their wings folded up while moths rest with their wings spread out. Finally, butterflies and moths are active at different times. The butterfly is active during the daytime, but a moth is active at night.

Strategy 1 **Using the Skimming Strategy**

The purpose of *skimming* is to get a general idea of the article before you actually read it. Use titles, headings, subheadings, and key words to help you.

1. What is the title of the article?

2. Name the headings.

3. What are the bold-type words in each section?

4. What is the main idea of the article?

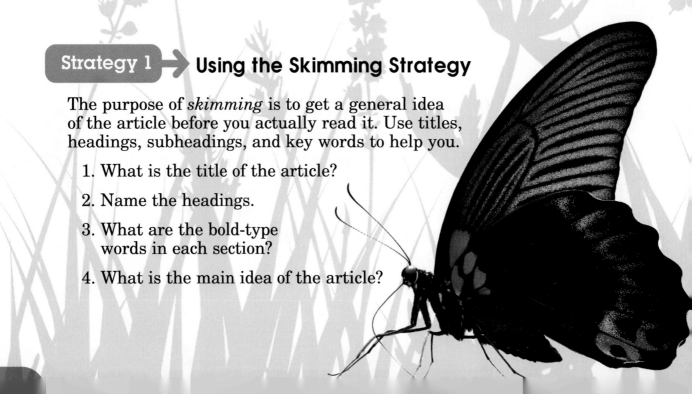

Strategy 2 → Using the Questioning Strategy

The purpose of *questioning* is to get your mind ready for information. It gives you a reason for reading and makes it easier to remember main ideas and understand key words. Turn headings and key words in the article into questions.

1. How are butterflies and moths alike?

2. What is an insect?

3. What are antennae?

4. What is nectar?

5. What is the larval stage?

6. How are butterflies and moths different?

7. What is body shape?

Strategy 3 → Using the Reading Strategy

The purpose of *reading* is to understand the information under headings and to get definitions for key words. Now, read the article.

Strategy 4 → Using the Scanning Strategy

The purpose of *scanning* is to help you use headings and key words to find answers to questions. Scan headings, key words in bold print, underlined words, and topic sentences to help you find the answers to the questions below.

1. How are butterflies and moths alike?

2. Which section contains these bold-type words: *insect, antennae, nectar, and larval stage?*

3. What is an insect?

4. What are antennae?

5. What is nectar?

6. What is the larval stage?

7. How are butterflies and moths different?

8. Which section contains the words *body shape* in bold-type?

9. What is body shape?

Extending the Lesson:

Learning Roman Numerals 1-5

Roman and Arabic numerals **one** through **five**:

Roman:	I	II	III	IV	V
Arabic:	1	2	3	4	5

→ The Arabic number system uses numerals for counting. Each numeral has a certain value.

➡ Example: 1=one, 2=two, 3=three, 4=four, and 5=five

→ The Roman number system uses capital letters to stand for numerals. Each capital letter has a certain value.

➡ Example: **I**=1, **II**=2, **III**=3, **IV**=4, and **V**=5

How to Write Roman Numerals for 1-5

→ In the Roman numeral system, you can never use more than three of the same letters in a row.

The capital **I** is used for the numbers 1–3.

➡ Examples: **I**=1

　　　　　　II=2

　　　　　　III=3

→ Anytime a lesser value is used in front of a greater value, it means to subtract. Since you cannot use **IIII** to represent the number 4, you use an **I** in front of the **V**. Therefore, subtract **I** (1) from **V** (5) to get 4.

➡ Example: **IV**=4

The capital **V** is used for the number 5.

➡ Example: **V**=5

 ACTIVITY　　Roman Numerals

Make a set of Roman numerals in bold type on large cardstock. Arrange them out of order either on the floor, table, or on a shelf. If possible, use Velcro tape on the wall and affix the cards to it with Velcro dots. By turn, invite individual students or small groups of students to re-arrange them in the proper order.

Name: _____ Date:_____

SKILLS:

Exercise 1: Underline the key word(s) in each question. The words *butterflies* and *moths* cannot be used as key words. Scan for the answers in the article in Reference 180. Write only the section number where you will find the answer.

Section:_____ 1. What is one way that butterflies and moths are alike?

Section:_____ 2. What is one way that butterflies and moths are different?

Section:_____ 3. How are the antennae of butterflies and moths different?

Section:_____ 4. What is nectar?

Exercise 2: Using Reference 180, write the answers in the blanks below and put the numbers of the sections where the answers were found.

Answer List:

wings	antennae	long	spread	nectar
chubby	short	legs	folded up	slender

Section:_____ 1. Insects have six _____ and usually have _____.

Section:_____ 2. A butterfly's body is _____ and _____.

Section:_____ 3. Both butterflies and moths have _____ for smelling.

Section:_____ 4. A moth's body is _____ and _____.

Section:_____ 5. Both butterflies and moths drink _____, the sweet liquid in flowers.

Section:_____ 6. Butterflies rest with their wings _____, but moths rest with their wings _____.

Exercise 3: Using the article in Reference 180, write the answers in the blanks below and put the number of the section where it is found.

Section:_____ 1. Give two ways that butterflies and moths are alike.

_____

_____

Section:_____ 2. Give two ways that butterflies and moths are different.

_____

_____

_____

_____

Review: Roman Numerals 1–5

Roman and Arabic numerals **one** through **five**:

Roman:	I	II	III	IV	V
	↕	↕	↕	↕	↕
Arabic:	1	2	3	4	5

REMEMBER: Outlining helps you organize ideas and information in the correct order for writing or speaking. Making an outline gives you a visual map because ideas are grouped together in an organized pattern to show their relationship to one another. Outlines make excellent study tools because they keep you focused, whether you are reading, writing, speaking, listening, or studying.

Review: Topic Outline

In a topic outline, information is written in single words or phrases—not complete sentences. An outline organizes information into categories, much like a computer organizes information into file folders. These categories are *main points (or topics), subtopics,* and *details.*

1. **Main Points** *(two or more main points about the topic)*

   → Use Roman numerals (I. II. III.) for main points.
   You must have two or more main points.

   → Capitalize the first word but do not use an end mark.

   → Line up the periods after the Roman numerals, one under the other.

   Pet Chores

I. Cat chores	MAIN POINT
II. Dog chores	MAIN POINT

2. Subtopics *(information that supports a main point)*

→ Use capital letters (A. B. C.) for subtopics.
  You must have two or more subtopics.

→ Line up subtopics under the first word of the main point.

→ Line up the periods after the capital letters.

→ Capitalize the first word but do not use an end mark.

I. Cat chores — **MAIN POINT**

  A. **Feed cat** — **SUBTOPIC**

  B. **Change water** — **SUBTOPIC**

  C. **Clean litter box** — **SUBTOPIC**

3. Details *(information that supports a subtopic)*

→ Use Arabic numerals for details. You must have two or more details.

→ Line up details under the first word of the subtopic.

→ Line up periods after the Arabic numerals.

→ Capitalize the first word but do not use an end mark.

II. Dog chores — **MAIN POINT**

  A. Food — **SUBTOPIC**

  B. Water — **SUBTOPIC**

  C. Exercise — **SUBTOPIC**

  1. **Go for a walk** — **DETAIL**

  2. **Play games** — **DETAIL**

Review: Parallel Form

Using **parallel form** means that each section in an outline should begin in the same way: all nouns, all verbs, all noun phrases, all verb phrases, all prepositional phrases, etc. What part of speech does each section begin with in the example to make it parallel?

The Outline Example

The outline below contains information in one organized, easy-to-read place.

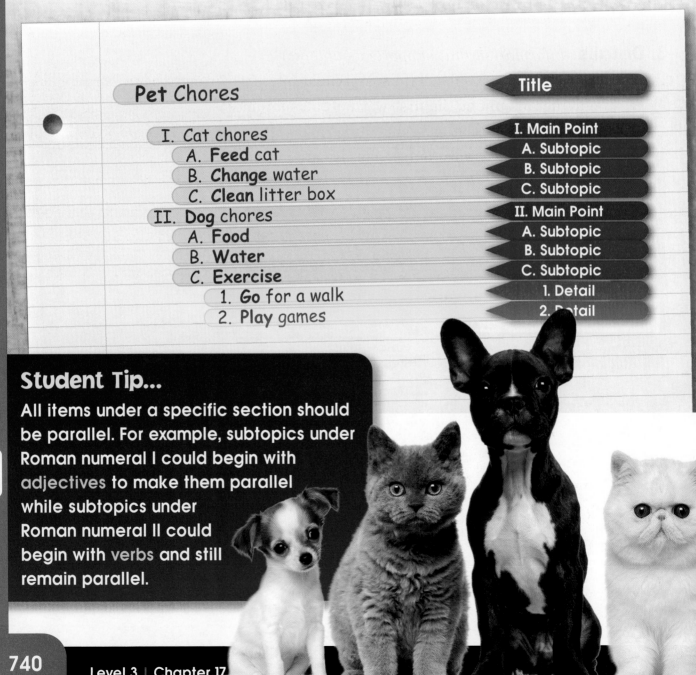

Pet Chores ◄ Title

I. **Cat** chores — I. Main Point
  A. **Feed** cat — A. Subtopic
  B. **Change** water — B. Subtopic
  C. **Clean** litter box — C. Subtopic
II. **Dog** chores — II. Main Point
  A. **Food** — A. Subtopic
  B. **Water** — B. Subtopic
  C. **Exercise** — C. Subtopic
    1. **Go** for a walk — 1. Detail
    2. **Play** games — 2. Detail

Student Tip...

All items under a specific section should be parallel. For example, subtopics under Roman numeral I could begin with adjectives to make them parallel while subtopics under Roman numeral II could begin with verbs and still remain parallel.

Name: _____ Date:_____

SKILLS:

Exercise 1: ▶ Put the information into outline form, following the rules for outlining.
Four items are not parallel. Make them parallel in the outline.

Sea Animals
Main Points
large sea animals
small sea animals

Subtopics
whales
sharks
big walrus
clownfish
seahorses
pretty butterflyfish

Details
blue whale
orca whale
gray whale
humpback whale
great white shark
hammerhead shark
goblin shark
blue shark

live in warm
ocean waters
have bright colors
have head like
a horse
long, curly tails
have body shaped
like angelfish
patterns of
bright colors

Outline:

_____
_____
_____
_____
_____
_____
_____
_____
_____
_____
_____
_____
_____
_____
_____
_____
_____
_____
_____
_____
_____
_____
_____
_____
_____
_____

End Lesson 2

Review: Roman Numerals 1–5

Roman and Arabic numerals **one** through **five**:

Roman:	I	II	III	IV	V
	↕	↕	↕	↕	↕
Arabic:	1	2	3	4	5

Review: Outlines

→ Write a title for your outline.

→ Use only words or phrases in a **topic outline**—not complete sentences.

→ Know that you cannot have an I without an II, an A without a B, or a 1 without a 2.

→ Although you must have at least two items in each category, you can have as many items as necessary to fit the information you want to outline.

→ Use Roman numerals for main points, capital letters for subtopics, and Arabic numerals for details.

→ Put periods after Roman numerals, capital letters, and Arabic numerals.

→ Capitalize the first word of each entry and any word that would be capitalized in a sentence.

→ Keep the items in each section parallel.

MCMXXVI

Classroom Practice 81

Name: _____ Date:_____

SKILLS:

Exercise 1: Put the information into outline form, following the rules for outlining. Four items are not parallel. Make them parallel in the outline.

Thanksgiving Traditions
Main Points
food
Get-togethers

Subtopics
turkey
dressing
several vegetables
breads
desserts
family
close friends

Details
green beans
potatoes
sweet-potato casserole
cranberry sauce

rolls
biscuits
loaf
pumpkin pie
pecan pie
chocolate cake

carrot cake
cookies
parents
children
grandparents
relatives

Outline:

_____
_____
_____
_____
_____
_____
_____
_____
_____
_____
_____
_____
_____
_____
_____
_____
_____
_____
_____
_____
_____
_____
_____
_____
_____
_____
_____

Skill Time

Review: Roman Numerals 1-5

Roman and Arabic numerals **one** through **five**:

Roman:	I	II	III	IV	V
	↕	↕	↕	↕	↕
Arabic:	1	2	3	4	5

Review: Outlines

→ Write a title for your outline.

→ Use only words or phrases in a **topic outline**—not complete sentences.

→ Know that you cannot have an *I* without an *II*, an *A* without a *B*, or a *1* without a *2*.

→ Although you must have *at least* two items in each category, you can have as many items as necessary to fit the information you want to outline.

→ Use Roman numerals for main points, capital letters for subtopics, and Arabic numerals for details.

→ Put periods after Roman numerals, capital letters, and Arabic numerals.

→ Capitalize the first word of each entry and any word that would be capitalized in a sentence.

→ Keep the items in each section parallel.

You already know how to use outlines as a graphic organizer to help you begin writing. Today, you will learn how to use outlining as a study aid to help you understand a written article.

Reference 181

Steps to Outline the Body of an Article

First, read the introduction and conclusion to get the main idea of the article. Then, read the body to get the main points and details of the article. Use the steps below to outline the body of an article.

For the Body

→ Scan each paragraph in the body of the article for the main points. Write each main point beside a Roman numeral on separate sheets of paper. Make the main points parallel.

→ Read the first paragraph in the body of the article and find the subtopics for the first main point. List the subtopics under the first main point. Use capital letters and make the subtopics parallel. Leave a few empty lines between the subtopics for any details.

→ Read the first paragraph again, looking for details. List any details under the appropriate subtopic. Use Arabic numerals and make the details parallel.

→ Repeat these steps for each paragraph in the body of the article.

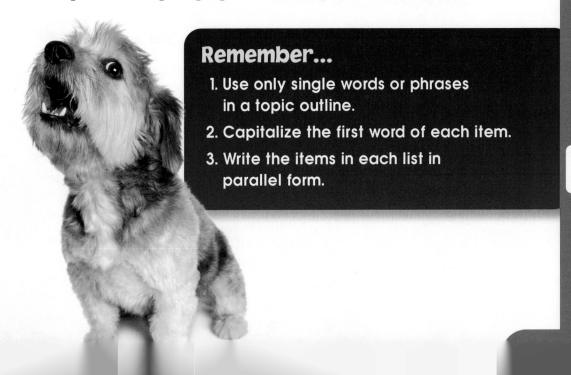

Remember...

1. Use only single words or phrases in a topic outline.

2. Capitalize the first word of each item.

3. Write the items in each list in parallel form.

Read the following article and compare it to the outline. Compare the main points, subtopics, and details in the article to those in the outline to see how the article was outlined. Pay special attention to the colors of each section.

 Reference 182

How to Outline a Sample Four-Paragraph Article
Differences Between Rabbits and Squirrels

Rabbits and squirrels are cute, furry little animals. Even though they are easily recognized, there are two main differences between them. Rabbits and squirrels look different and live in different places.

First, they look different. Rabbits have large back feet, large ears, and a tiny tuft of a tail. Squirrels, on the other hand, have small feet and small ears, and a huge, fluffy tail.

Second, they live in different places. Rabbits live on the ground and sleep in burrows. Squirrels, on the other hand, live in the trees. They sleep in nests of twigs and leaves.

Both rabbits and squirrels are cute little woodland creatures. Even though they look different and live in different places, rabbits and squirrels are fun to watch.

Sample Outline

Differences Between Rabbits and Squirrels	Title
I. Look different	I. Main Point
A. Rabbits	A. Subtopic
1. Large back feet	1. Detail
2. Large ears	2. Detail
3. Tiny tuft of a tail	3. Detail
B. Squirrels	B. Subtopic
1. Small feet	1. Detail
2. Small ears	2. Detail
3. Huge, fluffy tail	3. Detail
II. Live in different places	II. Main Point
A. Rabbits	A. Subtopic
1. Live on the ground	1. Detail
2. Sleep in burrows	2. Detail
B. Squirrels	B. Subtopic
1. Live in the trees	1. Detail
2. Sleep in nests of twigs and leaves	2. Detail

Lesson 4

Student Tip...
Remember: Outlines may not be parallel the first time. After you organize the ideas, then you can go back and change or rearrange the words in your outline to make them parallel.

You already know how to use outlines as a graphic organizer to help you begin writing. Today, you will learn how to use outlining as a study aid to help you understand a written article.

 Reference 183

The Introduction and Conclusion of an Article

As you read the introduction and conclusion of articles, notice how they are written. The suggestion below is one way to help you write your own introduction and conclusion.

Features of the Introduction

→ The first sentences of an introduction should spark interest and give extra information about the topic. These sentences can include a question, a fact, a definition, a quote, a general comment, or a personal observation.

→ The last sentence of an introduction should include the main points about the topic to get the reader ready for the body.

Use the introduction from Reference 182 to answer the questions below.

1. Which sentence(s) in the introduction sparks interest and gives extra information about the topic?

2. Which sentence includes the main points about the topic?

Features of the Conclusion

→ The sentences in the conclusion should review what the article is about and should restate the main points in a different way.

Use the conclusion from Reference 182 to answer the questions below.

1. Which sentence(s) in the conclusion reviews what the article is about?

2. Which sentence restates the main points about the topic?

Name: _____ Date: _____

SKILLS:

Exercise: Read the article below. Outline the article.
If needed, change the wording in the outline to make sure it is in parallel form.

A Four-Paragraph Article to Outline:

Whales and Fish in the Ocean

The ocean is home to many living creatures of all kinds. Many of these sea animals are fish, but a whale is one of the animals that lives in the sea that is not a fish. It is interesting to learn how whales and fish are alike and how they are different.

Do you know how whales and fish are alike? First, they both live in the ocean. Second, they eat similar food, such as smaller fish, shrimp, squid, and plankton. Finally, whales and fish move by swimming. They use their fins and tails to swim.

Do you know how whales and fish are different? One way they are different is their body coverings. A whale has skin, and most fish have scales. Another way they are different is their tails. A whale's tail moves up and down, and a fish's tail moves side to side. The third way they are different is their breathing. Whales have a blowhole on the top of their head to breathe air into their lungs, but fish have gills that allow them to breathe under water.

Whales and fish are truly amazing animals that live in the ocean! The next time you see a picture of a whale or visit an ocean aquarium, remember that whales and fish are alike in some ways and different in other ways.

Sample Outline:

_____

_____

_____

_____

_____

_____

_____

_____

_____

_____

_____

_____

_____

_____

_____

_____

_____

_____

_____

_____

_____

_____

_____

_____

_____

_____

_____

_____

_____

Time

Review: Roman Numerals 1-5

Roman and Arabic numerals **one** through **five**:

Roman:	I	II	III	IV	V
	↕	↕	↕	↕	↕
Arabic:	1	2	3	4	5

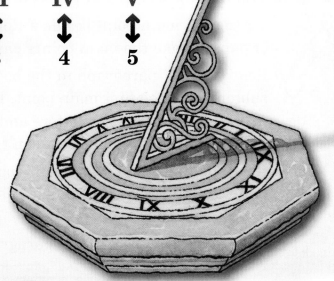

Review: Outlines

→ Write a title for your outline.

→ Use only words or phrases in a **topic outline**—not complete sentences.

→ Know that you cannot have an *I* without an *II*, an *A* without a *B*, or a *1* without a *2*.

→ Although you must have at least two items in each category, you can have as many items as necessary to fit the information you want to outline.

→ Use Roman numerals for main points, capital letters for subtopics, and Arabic numerals for details.

→ Put periods after Roman numerals, capital letters, and Arabic numerals.

→ Capitalize the first word of each entry and any word that would be capitalized in a sentence.

→ Keep the items in each section parallel.

Review: Steps to Outline the Body of an Article

First, read the introduction and conclusion to get the main idea of the article. Then, read the body to get the main points and details of the article. Use the steps below to outline the body of an article.

For the Body

→ Scan each paragraph in the body of the article for the main points. Write each main point beside a Roman numeral on separate sheets of paper. Make the main points parallel.

→ Read the first paragraph in the body of the article and find the subtopics for the first main point. List the subtopics under the first main point. Use capital letters and make the subtopics parallel. Leave a few empty lines between the subtopics for any details.

→ Read the first paragraph again, looking for details. List any details under the appropriate subtopic. Use Arabic numerals and make the details parallel.

→ Repeat these steps for each paragraph in the body of the article.

Remember...

1. Use only single words or phrases in a topic outline.
2. Capitalize the first word of each item.
3. Write the items in each list in parallel form.
4. After you organize the ideas, go back and change the words in your outline to make them parallel.

Name: _____ Date:_____

SKILLS:

Exercise: Study the article below. Then, outline the article.
If needed, change the wording in the outline to make sure it is in parallel form.

A Four-Paragraph Article to Outline:

The Right Tools for School

A carpenter or mechanic needs the right tools to build a house or to fix a car. In the same way, a student needs the right tools to do well in school. A student needs tools for writing and tools for organizing things.

First, students need tools for writing. Pencils are necessary for written work. Pens and computers could also be used. Highlighters are very handy for color-coding notes. A good mix of highlighter colors includes yellow, blue, and pink.

Next, students need tools for organizing. Good organizational tools include a pencil pouch, pocket folders, and a large binder. A pencil pouch holds pencils, pens, highlighters, glue, rulers, and scissors. Pocket folders can organize a student's spare paper, study notes, homework assignments, and graded assignments. The large binder organizes class subjects, the pencil pouch, and the pocket folders. Backpacks provide a way to organize items you carry from one place to another, such as books, supplies, and homework.

Having the right tools makes doing a job easier. Students need the proper tools, too. Schoolwork will be easier to do if students have the tools they need for writing and organizing things.

Sample Outline:

_____
_____
_____
_____
_____
_____
_____
_____
_____
_____
_____
_____
_____
_____
_____
_____
_____
_____
_____
_____
_____
_____
_____
_____
_____
_____
_____
_____
_____
_____
_____

Lesson 5

Extending the Lesson:
Review the Introduction and Conclusion of the Article in the Assessment

Features of the Introduction

→ The first sentences of an introduction should spark interest and give extra information about the topic. These sentences can include a question, a fact, a definition, a quote, a general comment, or a personal observation.

→ The last sentence of an introduction should include the main points about the topic to get the reader ready for the body.

Use the introduction from Classroom Practice 83 to answer the questions below.

1. Which sentence(s) in the introduction sparks interest and gives extra information about the topic?

2. Which sentence includes the main points about the topic?

Features of the Conclusion

→ The sentences in the conclusion should review what the article is about and should restate the main points in a different way.

Use the conclusion from Classroom Practice 83 to answer the questions below.

1. Which sentence(s) in the conclusion reviews what the article is about?

2. Which sentence restates the main points about the topic?

Writing an Article from an Outline

You have been learning how to read an article and outline it. This is called taking notes in outline form. Now, you will do the opposite: you will use an outline to write an article.

Steps for Your Writing Assignment

1. Study the outline provided for your topic.

2. Pay attention to the main points and the supporting points in each section of the outline. Your outline will tell you the information that will be in your article and a logical order for it to be presented.

3. Do extra research on the topic. During this time, you may change the outline to better fit your research. If you find more information you want to include, add it to the outline. If you need to delete or rearrange information in the outline, just make sure it makes sense.

4. During your research time, you should also take notes on information you want to use in your introduction and conclusion.

5. The place you go to find information during your research is called a source. Sources could be a site on the Internet, an encyclopedia, a book, or a magazine. You should write down information about the source in case you want to refer back to it and also to give the author credit for the material you use. Write down the title of the article or book, the author (if given), the publisher or website, and the date it was published (if given).

6. Use the information in Reference 184 to help you write an article from your outline.

Reference 184

Writing an Article from an Outline

You will write the body of the article first. Then, you will write the introduction and conclusion. You will write each of these sections on a separate sheet of paper: Body, Introduction, and Conclusion.

The Body

→ Study the main points beside the two Roman numerals. These points will tell you what each paragraph will be about.

→ Then, study the subtopics (A., B., C., etc.) and details (1., 2., 3, etc.) under each main point (Roman numeral). This information will support each main point.

→ As you study the information listed in the outline, think how you will turn the words and phrases into sentences.

For Paragraph 1

• First, turn the first main point into a sentence, using the information beside Roman Numeral I.

• Next, write supporting sentences, using the information from the subtopics and details under Roman Numeral I.

• Make sure you indent and put your sentences in paragraph form.

For Paragraph 2

• First, turn the second main point into a sentence, using the information beside Roman Numeral II.

• Next, write supporting sentences, using the information from the subtopics and details under Roman Numeral II.

• Make sure you indent and put your sentences in paragraph form.

Introduction

→ Take notes for information you want to use for your introduction.

→ Write your introduction on a separate sheet of paper. Be sure to indent.

→ Think about the topic and main points of your article. Write one or two sentences that will capture the interest of your readers and give them extra information about the topic. These sentences can include a question, a fact, a definition, a quote, a general comment, or a personal observation.

→ Then, write a sentence that tells the main points about the topic to prepare the reader for the information contained in the body.

Conclusion

→ Take notes for information you want to use for your conclusion.

→ Write your conclusion on a third sheet of paper. Be sure to indent.

→ Write sentences that review what the paragraph is about and that restate the main points in a different way.

Revision and Editing

→ Revise and edit the introduction, body, and conclusion. Use the Revision and Editing Checklists on pages Q23–Q25 to help you.

Final Paper

→ After you have made corrections, rewrite your article on one sheet of paper, putting the introduction, body, and conclusion in order.

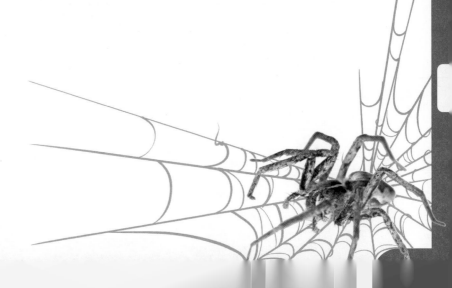

Name: _____ Date:_____

SKILLS: Writing an article from an outline

Directions: Study the outline below. Then, write an article on notebook paper, using the outline. Use Reference 184 to guide you.

Outline:

Two Types of Spiders

    I. Poisonous spiders

      A. Black widow

        1. Black body

        2. Red spot shaped like hourglass on belly

      B. Brown recluse

        1. Brown body

        2. Fiddle-shaped mark on back

    II. Non-poisonous spiders

      A. House spider

        1. Is harmless

        2. Can grow very large

        3. Is scary-looking

        4. Prefers to stay away from people

      B. Garden spider

        1. Builds large circular webs to catch flying insects

        2. Eats flies, moths, grasshoppers, bees, wasps

Explanatory Writing

You have learned about descriptive, persuasive, and narrative writing. Now, it's time to learn another genre: *explanatory writing*. Most nonfiction writing falls into this genre. When you tell about things that are true, you are using explanatory writing. **Explanatory writing** is any kind of writing *that explains something or shares facts and information about a topic.*

This type of writing covers a broad area. For example, you can use explanatory writing to write personal essays, to explain how to do something, or to give facts about different topics. Since this type of writing is so varied, it can be called explanatory, expository, informative, how-to, process, comparison, or report writing.

Reference 185

Three Main Parts of Explanatory Writing

Explanatory writing focuses on explaining or sharing information. Because it is very important for your reader to understand the information you are sharing, good explanatory writing should be clear, concise, and organized. All explanatory writing contains three main parts.

1 The **Introduction** is the first part and lets the reader know what to expect and lists the points that will be presented.

2 The **Body** is the middle and most important part because it contains the main points and supporting details.

3 The **Conclusion** is the last part. It summarizes the piece and restates the three main points.

CONTINUED ON NEXT PAGE

Paragraphs in an Explanatory Essay

An explanatory essay usually has one *introductory* paragraph and one *concluding* paragraph plus the paragraphs in the *body* of the essay. The number of paragraphs in the *body* depends on the number of main points you present. The body can have two, three, four, or more paragraphs. If the body has three paragraphs, you have a five-paragraph essay. If the body has four paragraphs, you have a six-paragraph essay.

Reference 186

Organizing Explanatory Writing

There are many ways to organize information in explanatory writing. The easiest and most direct way is a main-point system. A **main-point system** *lists the number of main points you will use in your essay*. It can be two or more points, depending on the amount of information that you wish to present. First, determine the number of main points you will need. Then, use that number as you organize the introduction, body, and conclusion.

Three main points are used in the body of the example on the next page. Each main point forms a paragraph of the body. With the three main points, plus the introduction and conclusion, the essay will have five paragraphs.

The introduction has

→ a *topic sentence* that tells what the essay is about.
→ an *information* sentence that gives a fact, a definition, a quote, or a personal observation.
→ a *main-point* sentence that names the main points in the order that they are presented.

Paragraph 1
Topic sentence
Information sentence
Main-point sentence

Paragraph 2
First main-point sentence
Supporting sentences
Paragraph 3
Second main-point sentence
Supporting sentences
Paragraph 4
Third main-point sentence
Supporting sentences

The body has:

→ *three main points* that tell about the topic.
→ *supporting sentences* that support each of the three main points. The number of supporting sentences may vary, according to the amount of information you have.

Paragraph 5
Summary
    sentence
"For this reason"
    sentence
Concluding
    main-point
    sentence

The conclusion has:

→ a *summary* sentence that restates what the essay is about.
→ a *"for this reason"* sentence that explains the importance of the topic.
→ a *concluding* main-point sentence that restates the three main points in a different way.

Student Tip...

An essay with three main points is called a five-paragraph essay:

• The *introduction* forms the first paragraph.

• The *body* forms the next three paragraphs.

• The *conclusion* forms the fifth paragraph.

Using Transition Words for Explanatory Writing

Use transition words that will help you connect ideas as you write the introduction, main points, supporting sentences, and the conclusion.

Introduction

to inform: *for example, for instance, in addition, as well, also, next, another, along with,* and *besides*

Main Points

to show time: *first, second, third, before, during, after, next, then,* and *finally*

to add: *in addition, as well, also, too, next, another, along with,* and *furthermore*

Supporting Sentences

to inform: *for example, for instance, in addition, as well, also, next, another, along with,* and *besides*

to clarify: *for example, for instance,* and *in other words*

to emphasize: *truly, again, for this reason,* and *in fact*

Conclusion

to summarize: *therefore, in conclusion, in summary,* and *finally, to sum it up, all in all, as a result,* and *last*

Personal Explanatory Essay

A *personal essay* is a type of explanatory writing. A **personal essay** is a well-organized piece of writing that reveals personal thoughts and observations on a particular subject. A prewriting map is used to organize the ideas for the body of a personal essay.

Reference 188

Prewriting Map for a Personal Explanatory Essay

Quigley's Prewriting Map:

Prewriting Map

Name: **Quigley Shurley**

Date: **Oct. 1**

TOPIC
favorite summer activities

Main Point 1
fishing

Main Point 2
camping

Main Point 3
rock climbing

Supporting Details:
- is a big bass in Grandpa's pond
- want to catch big bass in pond

Supporting Details:
- camp along Little Bear Creek
- have fun and learn outdoor things

Supporting Details:
- rock climbing hard work
- parents supervise and climb with me

Reference 189

Ways to Write the Main Points of a Personal Explanatory Essay

My Favorite Summer Activities

As you choose a way to introduce the points in your essay, you must be consistent. You cannot mix the different forms within the same essay.

Example 1 → begins with a possessive pronoun before the time order-words.

Example 2 → begins with time-order words.

Example 3 → begins with an article before the time-order words.

Example 4 → uses transition words.

Example 5 → begins with the main points.

Example 6 → has a pronoun, main point, and the word *because*.

Example 1 → Possessive Pronoun & time order

My first favorite summer activity is fishing.

My second favorite summer activity is camping.

My third favorite summer activity is rock climbing.

Example 2 → Time-order words only

First, I like to go fishing during the summer.

Next, I like camping with my family.

Finally, I like the exhilaration of rock climbing.

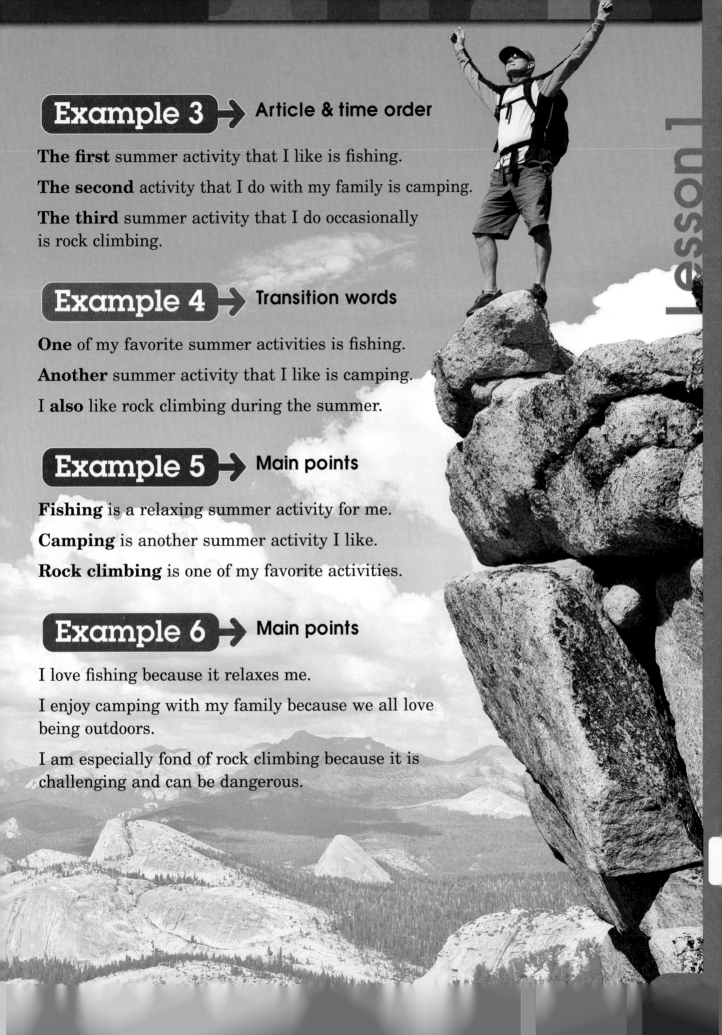

Example 3 → Article & time order

The first summer activity that I like is fishing.

The second activity that I do with my family is camping.

The third summer activity that I do occasionally is rock climbing.

Example 4 → Transition words

One of my favorite summer activities is fishing.

Another summer activity that I like is camping.

I **also** like rock climbing during the summer.

Example 5 → Main points

Fishing is a relaxing summer activity for me.

Camping is another summer activity I like.

Rock climbing is one of my favorite activities.

Example 6 → Main points

I love fishing because it relaxes me.

I enjoy camping with my family because we all love being outdoors.

I am especially fond of rock climbing because it is challenging and can be dangerous.

When writing an essay, it is important that you follow the format very closely so that the reader knows what to expect and can follow the information easily.

 Reference 190

Sentences in a Personal Explanatory Essay

Sentences in a Personal Explanatory Essay

Name: **Quigley Shurley**

Date: **Oct. 3**

Topic: _favorite summer activities_

Three Points: _fishing, camping, and rock climbing_

Title: _My Favorite Summer Activities_

1. Introduction:

Topic Sentence: _I have many fun things to do in the summertime._

Information Sentence: _In fact, there are three activities that I always love to do every summer._

Main-Point Sentence: _I can't wait until I can go fishing, camping, and rock climbing!_

2. Body

First Main-Point Sentence: _The first summer activity that I like is fishing._

• Supporting Sentence: _My grandpa has a pond on his farm, and he says there is a big bass in it that he wants on his dinner plate._

• Supporting Sentence: _I am going to catch that big bass this summer, so I go fishing every day!_

Second Main-Point Sentence: _The second activity that I do with my family is camping._

• Supporting Sentence: _My parents, my brother, and I camp along Little Bear Creek._

• Supporting Sentence: _We have a lot of fun, and I always learn how to do a lot of outdoor things._

Third Main-Point Sentence: _The third summer activity that I do occasionally is rock climbing._

• Supporting Sentence: _Rock climbing is hard work, but I feel so good when I make it to the top of the rocks._

• Supporting Sentence: _My parents supervise my climbing, and sometimes, they climb with me._

3. Conclusion

Summary Sentence: _When I think about my favorite summertime activities, I get so excited that I can't wait for summer each year._

"For this reason" Sentence: _For this reason, summer always has a special meaning for me._

Concluding Main-Point Sentence: _Believe me, I will be fishing, camping, and rock climbing as much as I can each and every summer for the rest of my life!_

When writing a personal explanatory essay, indent the first line of each paragraph, use the rules of convention, and organize your ideas for this type of essay.

Reference 191

Personal Explanatory Essay

My Favorite Summer Activities
by Quigley Shurley

I have many fun things to do in the summertime. In fact, there are three activities that I always love to do every summer. I can't wait until I can go fishing, camping, and rock climbing!

The first summer activity that I like is fishing. My grandpa has a pond on his farm, and he says there is a big bass in it that he wants on his dinner plate. I am going to catch that big bass this summer, so I go fishing every day!

The second activity that I do with my family is camping. My parents, my brother, and I camp along Little Bear Creek. We have a lot of fun, and I always learn how to do a lot of outdoor things.

The third summer activity that I do occasionally is rock climbing. Rock climbing is hard work, but I feel so good when I make it to the top of the rocks. My parents supervise my climbing, and sometimes, they climb with me.

When I think about my favorite summertime activities, I get so excited that I can't wait for summer each year. For this reason, summer always has a special meaning for me. Believe me, I will be fishing, camping, and rock climbing as much as I can each and every summer for the rest of my life!

Discussion Questions:

1. What is the topic of the sample explanatory essay?
2. What are the three main points in the sample essay?
3. Where is the introduction located?
4. What does the introduction tell?
5. Where is the body located?
6. What does the body tell?
7. Where is the conclusion located?
8. What does the conclusion tell?
9. What point of view is the essay written in?

Writing Time

Writing Assignment 10

Writing Assignment 10: **Personal Explanatory Essay**
Steps 1 & 2: Making a Prewriting Map and Writing a Rough Draft

Purpose: to inform
Genre: personal explanatory
Audience: classmates

Choose a writing prompt or one of the writing topics below. Make a prewriting map and write a personal explanatory essay with at least three main points. Then, support each main point with supporting details.

Be as informative as possible!

WRITING PROMPT 1:

We spend a lot of time with our family, but some things we do with our families are more exciting than others. Write an explanatory essay about three unique and fun ways you spend time with your family.

WRITING PROMPT 2:

The world is full of wonderful things, but some things could be improved to make it a better place for people to live. Write an explanatory essay, explaining three important things you think should be improved in our world to make it a better place for people to live.

WRITING TOPICS:

1. Reasons I like to go to the zoo, library, or park
2. People I would like to meet and why
3. Things I like about the city or country
4. Choose a topic of your own.

SPECIAL INSTRUCTIONS:

1. Make a prewriting map *(Reference 188)*.
2. Follow the Rough Draft Checklist in Reference 61 on pages Q20–Q21.
3. Use References 185–191 to help you write your personal explanatory essay.
4. Use a dictionary and thesaurus *(in print or digital)* to look up word meanings, spellings, and synonyms to help you write your rough draft.
5. Put your prewriting map and your rough draft in your Rough Draft folder.

Writing Time

Review: Explanatory Writing

Explanatory writing is any kind of writing that *explains something or shares facts and information about a topic*. When explanatory writing shares facts and information about a subject, it is sometimes called an informational or informative essay.

Three Main Parts of Explanatory Writing

1 The **Introduction** is the first part and lets the reader know what to expect and lists the points that will be presented. The introduction forms the first paragraph.

2 The **Body** is the middle and most important part because it contains the main points and supporting details. The body forms the middle paragraphs.

3 The **Conclusion** is the last part. It summarizes the piece and restates the three main points. The conclusion forms the last paragraph.

Using Transition Words for Informational Writing

Use transition words that will help you connect ideas as you write the introduction, main points, supporting sentences, and the conclusion.

Introduction

to inform: *for example, for instance, in addition, as well, also, next, another, along with,* and *besides*

Main Points

to show time: *first, second, third, before, during, after, next, then,* and *finally*

to add: *in addition, as well, also, too, next, another, along with,* and *furthermore*

Supporting Sentences

to inform: *for example, for instance, in addition, as well, also, next, another, along with,* and *besides*

to clarify: *for example, for instance,* and *in other words*

to emphasize: *truly, again, for this reason,* and *in fact*

Conclusion

to summarize: *therefore, in conclusion, in summary,* and *finally, to sum it up, all in all, as a result,* and *last*

Researching a Topic and Writing an Informational Essay

1 Choose a topic you want to learn more about.

2 Use at least two different sources to research your topic. Make sure you write down the following information about your sources.

→ the title of the article or book

→ the author (if given)

→ the publisher or website

→ the date it was published (if given)

3 Take notes by writing down information that you want to include about your topic.

→ Write **body** beside notes that you want to include in the *body*.

→ Write **introduction** beside notes that you want to include in the *introduction*.

→ Write **conclusion** beside notes that you want to include in the *conclusion*.

4 After you finish taking notes, use them to make an outline.

→ Write your main points beside **Roman numerals**.

→ Write supporting information about the main points beside the **subtopics** (capital letters).

→ Write supporting information about the subtopics beside the **details** *(numbers)*.

5 After you finish your outline, use it to write the rough draft for your informational essay.

Student Tip...

When writing an informational essay, indent the first line of each paragraph, use the rules of convention, and organize your ideas for this type of essay.

Writing Assignment 11: Informational Essay
Research a Topic

Purpose: to inform
Genre: informational
Audience: classmates

Write an informational essay. Choose one of the topics below or select your own. Make sure you follow the guidelines in Reference 192: research from two sources, take notes, make an outline, and write a rough draft.

WRITING TOPICS:

1. A topic from your science book
2. A topic from your social studies book
3. Kinds of Birds
4. African Animals
5. Porcupines
6. Sneezing
7. Invention of Cotton Candy
8. Notable People: Helen Keller, Henry Ford, or Alexander Graham Bell
9. Choose a topic of your own.

SPECIAL INSTRUCTIONS:

1. Use the instructions from Reference 192 for your informational essay.
2. Put your outline and rough draft in your Rough Draft folder.

Explanatory Writing: How-To

How-to essays are a form of explanatory writing because their purpose is **to inform**. A how-to essay provides instructions to help the reader complete a process. Because the directions are written *to the reader*, how-to essays are usually written in the **second person point of view**. How-to essays use imperative sentences and the personal pronouns *you* and *yours*.

 Reference 193

Guidelines for a How-To Essay

The following instructions will help you write a how-to essay.

1 Make sure your topic is something you know how to do.

2 Write a topic sentence that tells your reader two things:
  → what your topic is
  → why they should be interested in it.

3 Make a list of all the necessary materials your reader will need for the project, like tools, ingredients, and so on.

4 Make a list of the steps in the process, thinking through each step carefully in your mind. You don't want to get the steps out of order or leave anything out that would confuse your reader.

Chapter 18

Format for a How-To Essay

A notice or warning:
If needed, include a note of warning for specific allergic reactions, any safety issues, or other special concerns.

Introduction → The **introduction** of your essay should include your topic sentence and the list of materials needed.

Body → The **body** of your essay should include the steps in the process. Be sure to use transition words, clear examples, and detailed descriptions. If you are writing about a process with many steps in it, you should find logical dividing points and make several paragraphs in the body.

Conclusion → The **conclusion** should include a description of the final results, including a sentence about how the results will benefit the reader.

 Reference 194

Using Transition Words for How-To Essays

Transition words can show time, inform, contrast, compare, clarify, emphasize, and summarize. The steps in a how-to essay must be completed in a certain order, so **transition words that show time** will be most useful. They connect the steps in the order in which they occur, from first to last.

To Show Time and Order → like **first, second, third, before, during, after, next, then,** and **finally.**

also use transition phrases → such as **to begin, after that, the next step is,** etc.

➡ Examples: **First, brush your teeth. Then, comb your hair.**
To begin, open the package. After that, remove the toy.

A prewriting map is used to organize the ideas for the body of the how-to essay.

Prewriting Map for a How-to Essay

Prewriting Map

Name: **Quigley Shurley**

Date: **Oct. 10**

TOPIC
how to wash your dog

Materials

dog shampoo

an old towel

a large bathtub
or outside pen
and water hose

Notice/Warning

could get wet

Steps
- have all supplies needed
- place dog in bathtub or pen
  and wet hair
- apply shampoo and rub it in
- don't get soap in dog's eyes
  or ears
- rinse soap off dog
- watch for spray when dog
  shakes himself
- dry dog off with towel
- keep dog away from grass and
  dirt until dry

Lesson 4

How-To Essay

How to Wash Your Dog
by Quigley Shurley

Everyone enjoys a clean dog. They smell and look better, and they are more fun to pet. To wash your dog, you should have dog shampoo, an old towel, and a large bathtub or an outside pen and a water hose.

First, make sure you have all the supplies that are needed. Then, put your dog in the bathtub or pen and completely wet his hair. Next, apply the shampoo and rub it in. Be careful when washing your dog's head so that you do not get soap in his eyes or ears. After that, rinse all the soap off your dog but watch out for a spray of water when your dog shakes himself. You can help your dog dry off by rubbing him all over with an old towel. Last of all, keep your dog away from grass and dirt while his hair is still damp.

When you are finished, your dog's coat will be shiny and clean. He will smell much better, and everyone will want to play with him. This will make your dog and your family very happy!

Notice/Warning: You could get wet.

Discussion Questions:

1. **What point of view is used for the sample essay?**

2. **What is the topic of the essay?**

3. **What necessary materials are listed in the introduction of the essay?**

4. **How many paragraphs are in the introduction?**

5. **What transition words are used in the body of the essay?**

6. **What kind of transition words are they?**

7. **What warning is included at the end of the essay?**

Now, it's time to begin writing a how-to essay of your own. Use what you have learned about how-to writing in References 193–196 as a guide.

Writing Assignment 12

STEP 1
STEP 2

Writing Assignment 12: How-To Essay
Steps 1 & 2: Making a Prewriting Map and Writing a Rough Draft

Purpose: To give information about a process
Genre: how-to
Audience: a friend

TOPICS
Write a how-to essay explaining how to play a game or take care of a pet. You can write about how to wash the car, make a snowman, rake leaves, do the latest dance, ride a bike, make something, or practically anything else. Your directions must be complete and clear. Write your essay in second person point of view, directly to your reader.

SPECIAL INSTRUCTIONS:

1. Make a prewriting map (*Reference 195*).

2. Follow the Rough Draft Checklist in Reference 61 on pages Q20–Q21.

3. Use the information for a how-to essay in References 193–196.

4. Put your prewriting map and your rough draft in your Rough Draft folder.

Writing Strategy: Using Visual Aids

A visual aid can make a big difference in how well your reader comprehends your instructions. As you write your how-to essay, think of specific steps that could be illustrated to make it easier for the reader to understand. Sketch the illustration in your rough draft. Then, draw a more detailed version on a separate sheet of paper for your final paper. If you are not sure how to draw the illustration, try using a digital camera to take suitable pictures. Print the pictures and keep them with your final paper.

Explanatory Writing: Comparison-Contrast

Today, you will learn another type of explanatory writing: comparison. You will learn how to *compare* and *contrast* two subjects. To **compare** two things is *to tell how they are alike*. To **contrast** two things is *to tell how they are different*.

Reference 197

Venn Diagram for Comparison Writing

A **Venn diagram** is *a graphic organizer that can help you compare and contrast two subjects*. Ideas in the center section tell how both subjects are the same (comparison). Ideas in the outer sections tell how each subject is different from the other (contrast).

APPLES	fruit	ORANGES
red or green	produce juice	orange
thin skin	grow on trees	thick peel

You should always try to balance your Venn diagram by using almost the same number of ideas for each subject. Often, you can use the same kind of ideas, even if the facts are different—such as color (*red* or *orange*) and covering (*skin* or *peel*) in the example.

Other possible ideas for comparing and contrasting subjects are size, shape, texture, taste, behavior, purpose, location, degree of importance, ease of use, unusual facts, accomplishments, etc.

Organizing a Comparison Essay

A **comparison essay** *describes how two subjects are alike and how they are different.* Good comparison-contrast writing uses vivid details and/or concrete facts to keep the reader's attention while telling how the subjects are alike and different. Comparison essays will usually contain *four* paragraphs:

Four Main Paragraphs of a Comparison Essay

1 The **Introduction** should name the subjects to be compared and contrasted. A good introduction will also grab the reader's attention, perhaps with a question or an interesting fact.

2 The **Paragraph of Comparison** should tell how the two subjects are similar. Avoid simply listing facts. Try to connect your ideas logically and use plenty of transition words.

3 The **Paragraph of Contrast** should tell how the two subjects are different. Again, use a logical order of ideas and lots of transition words.

4 The **Conclusion** should summarize the essay, tie the ideas together, and draw the essay to a close.

Reference 199

Transition Words for Comparison Writing

Transition words are very important in a comparison essay. Use them to link similar ideas together (*comparing*), to link opposing ideas together (*contrasting*), and to present a final analysis (*concluding*). Learn the transition words below that can be used in a comparison essay.

To Compare: also, and, another, as, besides, furthermore, in addition, like, likewise, same, similarly, too, which, etc.

To Contrast: although, but, different, even though, however, in contrast, in other ways, on the other hand, otherwise, still, while, yet, etc.

To Conclude: all in all, as a result, finally, in conclusion, in summary, last, therefore, to sum it up, etc.

Comparison Essay

Comparing Apples and Oranges
by Quigley Shurley

Have you ever heard someone say, "It's like comparing apples and oranges"? Comparing apples and oranges is easy because they have many similar traits; however, they also have many traits that make them very different.

It is true that apples and oranges are similar in many ways. For instance, apples and oranges are both fruit. Also, they are both used to make juice for people to drink: apple juice and orange juice. Another similarity is that both apples and oranges grow on trees.

However, apples and oranges are also very different. First, apples are usually either red or green; sometimes they can be pink or yellow. Of course, oranges are always orange. In addition, apples have very thin, waxy skins covering them while oranges have a thick, porous peel for a covering.

In summary, apples and oranges are very different, despite their many similarities. So, next time someone says, "It's like comparing apples and oranges," tell them they should contrast apples and oranges, too.

Discussion Questions:

1. What is the title of the comparison essay?

2. What are the two subjects in the essay?

3. What are the similar traits?

4. What is in the introduction?

5. What is in the body?

6. What is in the conclusion?

Writing Assignment 13: **Comparison Essay**
Steps 1 & 2: **Making a Venn Diagram and Writing a Rough Draft**

Purpose: To compare and contrast
Genre: comparison
Audience: classmates

Write a comparison essay. Choose one of the topics below to compare and contrast or select your own. Choose topics that you are familiar with and use facts, details, or examples from your own experiences. Make a Venn diagram to organize your ideas before you write. Ideas in the center section tell how both subjects are the same (*compare*). Ideas in the outer sections tell how each subject is different from the other (*contrast*).

TOPICS

hotdogs and hamburgers

two types of
math problems

two flavors of ice cream

swimming and diving

cats and dogs

weeds and flowers

pens and pencils

two types of
playground equipment

light bulb and candle

sandals and boots

Grandma's home
and my home

two topics of your choice

SPECIAL INSTRUCTIONS:

1. Make a Venn diagram (*Reference 197*).
2. Follow the Rough Draft Checklist in Reference 61 on pages Q20–Q21.
3. Use the information for comparison writing in References 197–200.
4. Try adding illustrations, charts, graphs, and/or multimedia to your presentation.
5. Put your Venn diagram and your rough draft in your Rough Draft folder.

Student Tip...
Use a dictionary (in print or digital) to look up word meanings, spellings, and synonyms to help you write your rough draft.

Writing Time

Revising & Editing

Today, you will choose Writing Assignment 10, 11, 12, or 13 from your Rough Draft folder to revise, edit, and write a final paper. Choose the appropriate student rubric on the next several pages to evaluate your final paper.

Choose Writing Assignment 10, 11, 12, or 13 to Complete the Writing Process for your Explanatory Essay

Writing a Final Paper

1. Follow the Final Paper Checklist in Reference 77 on page WP11.
2. Use the Student Rubric to evaluate your Final Paper.
3. Put your stapled papers in your Final Paper folder.

Revising & Editing

1. **Individual Revision:** Read your rough draft silently. Then, use the revision questions in Reference 64 on pages Q23–Q24 to revise your rough draft.
2. **Individual Editing:** Now, go to the editing questions in Reference 66 on page Q25. Read your rough draft silently again, using the editing questions to edit your rough draft. Check thoroughly for errors.
3. **Partner Revision:** Get with your writing partner. Read each rough draft aloud. For each paper, ask the revision questions in Reference 64. Each partner should write revisions on his or her own paper.
4. **Partner Editing:** Using the editing questions in Reference 66, check each rough draft thoroughly for errors. Each partner should write corrections on his or her own paper.

After you write your final paper, choose the Student Rubric that matches your writing choice. Compare your writing to each section of the rubric. As you review each section, make any additional corrections that are needed. After you are finished, staple your papers together in this order: Prewriting map or Venn diagram on the bottom, rough draft in the middle, and final paper on top. Put them in your Final Paper folder.

STUDENT RUBRIC for Explanatory Writing

Name: _____ Date:_____

Directions: ▸ Put a checkmark beside each question that you answer with "yes."

Explanatory   SCORE [ ] (Count the checkmarks in this section.)

- [ ] 1. Have I presented clear main points to support the topic?
- [ ] 2. Have I used interesting details to support the main points?
- [ ] 3. Have I used appropriate transition words?
- [ ] 4. Have I developed the topic in a logical order that makes sense?

Ideas   SCORE [ ] (Count the checkmarks in this section.)

- [ ] 1. Is the topic and purpose of my paper clearly described in the topic sentence?
- [ ] 2. Have I narrowed or expanded my topic appropriately?
- [ ] 3. Have I used at least three main points to develop the topic of my paper?
- [ ] 4. Have I used at least one supporting detail to develop each of my main points?
- [ ] 5. Have I chosen a topic that is appropriate to my purpose, genre, and audience?

Organization   SCORE [ ] (Count the checkmarks in this section.)

- [ ] 1. Is my paper well organized and easy to follow?
- [ ] 2. Does my paper have a clear introduction, body, and conclusion?
- [ ] 3. Are my main points properly divided into paragraphs?
- [ ] 4. Does each paragraph have a main point that is supported by every sentence in that paragraph?
- [ ] 5. Is the organization of my essay appropriate for my purpose and audience?

Word Choice   SCORE [ ] (Count the checkmarks in this section.)

- [ ] 1. Have I used precise nouns and verbs to explain and describe my topic?
- [ ] 2. Have I used vivid adjectives and adverbs to create strong mental pictures?
- [ ] 3. Have I replaced unclear words with stronger words?
- [ ] 4. Have I deleted incorrect, repeated, or unnecessary words?
- [ ] 5. Have I used words appropriate to my purpose and audience?

Voice

SCORE ☐ (Count the checkmarks in this section.)

☐ 1. Have I developed a unique voice to show my style of writing?

☐ 2. Does my voice reflect my personality and feelings about the topic?

☐ 3. Do my individual word choices reflect my unique writing voice?

☐ 4. Have I used figures of speech (similes, metaphors, personification) to help develop my voice?

☐ 5. Have I used vocabulary appropriate for my purpose and audience?

Sentence Fluency

SCORE ☐ (Count the checkmarks in this section.)

☐ 1. Can a reader easily follow my ideas?

☐ 2. Have I combined short, choppy sentences to make my writing sound smooth?

☐ 3. Have I used different types of sentences (simple, compound, complex, Mover & Shaker)?

☐ 4. Have I used a variety of long and short sentences to add interest to my paper?

☐ 5. Have I used transition words to connect related sentences?

Convention

SCORE ☐ (Count the checkmarks in this section.)

☐ 1. Have I followed the conventions of capitalization?

☐ 2. Have I followed the conventions of punctuation?

☐ 3. Have I spelled every word correctly and corrected any mistakes in homonyms, contractions, possessives, or plural forms?

☐ 4. Have I corrected all usage mistakes, such as a/an mistakes and subject-verb agreement mistakes?

☐ 5. Have I corrected all sentence mistakes, such as run-ons, fragments, and comma splices?

Formatting

SCORE ☐ (Count the checkmarks in this section.)

☐ 1. Have I written neatly in pencil and used single-spaced lines and wide margins?

☐ 2. Have I written the title at the center of the top line, with my name under it?

☐ 3. Have I skipped a line under my name before writing my paper?

☐ 4. Have I indented the first line of each paragraph?

☐ 5. Does my whole paper look clean and neat?

Final Analysis

SCORE ☐ (Count the checkmarks in this section.)

☐ 1. Do I think my essay will be interesting and appealing to my audience?

☐ 2. Is my essay detailed enough to be effective?

☐ 3. Do my details give me a mental image of what I am explaining?

☐ 4. Does my essay flow smoothly when read aloud?

☐ 5. Does my essay fit into the proper genre?

STUDENT RUBRIC for How-To Writing

Name: _____ Date:_____

Directions: ▶ Put a checkmark beside each question that you answer with "yes."

How-To   SCORE [   ] (Count the checkmarks in this section.)

☐ 1. Have I given a list of materials needed for the process?

☐ 2. Have I explained the process in a clear, logical order?

☐ 3. Have I given detailed steps to explain the process?

☐ 4. Have I given clear examples and detailed descriptions?

☐ 5. Have I used appropriate transition words?

Ideas   SCORE [   ] (Count the checkmarks in this section.)

☐ 1. Is the purpose of my paper clearly described in the topic sentence?

☐ 2. Have I given a complete list of materials needed for the process?

☐ 3. Are there enough steps to explain the process?

☐ 4. Have I included a warning for special safety issues?

☐ 5. Have I chosen a process that is appropriate to my purpose, genre, and audience?

Organization   SCORE [   ] (Count the checkmarks in this section.)

☐ 1. Does my paper have a clear introduction, body, and conclusion?

☐ 2. Do all of my sentences support my topic? Have I deleted all non-supporting sentences?

☐ 3. Are my steps in a clear, logical order that is easy to follow?

☐ 4. If there are a lot of steps, have I divided them into paragraphs to make them easier to follow?

☐ 5. Are my directions appropriate for my purpose and audience?

Word Choice   SCORE [   ] (Count the checkmarks in this section.)

☐ 1. Have I used precise nouns and verbs to explain the process?

☐ 2. Have I used appropriate transitional words to help the reader follow the process?

☐ 3. Have I replaced unclear words with stronger words?

☐ 4. Have I deleted incorrect, repeated, or unnecessary words?

☐ 5. Have I used words appropriate to my purpose and audience?

Voice

SCORE ☐ (Count the checkmarks in this section.)

☐ 1. Have I developed a unique voice to show my style of writing?
☐ 2. Does my voice reflect my dedication to the process?
☐ 3. Do my individual word choices reflect my unique writing voice?
☐ 4. Have I used correct directional and transitional words to help develop my voice?
☐ 5. Have I used vocabulary appropriate for my purpose and audience?

Sentence Fluency

SCORE ☐ (Count the checkmarks in this section.)

☐ 1. Can a reader easily follow my directions?
☐ 2. Have I combined short, choppy sentences to improve my writing?
☐ 3. Have I used different types of sentences (simple, compound, complex, Mover & Shaker)?
☐ 4. Have I used a variety of long and short sentences to add interest to my paper?
☐ 5. Have I used transition words to connect related directions?

Conventions

SCORE ☐ (Count the checkmarks in this section.)

☐ 1. Have I followed the conventions of capitalization?
☐ 2. Have I followed the conventions of punctuation?
☐ 3. Have I spelled every word correctly and corrected any mistakes in homonyms, contractions, possessives, or plural forms?
☐ 4. Have I corrected all usage mistakes, such as a/an mistakes and subject-verb agreement mistakes?
☐ 5. Have I corrected all sentence mistakes, such as run-ons, fragments, and comma splices?

Formatting

SCORE ☐ (Count the checkmarks in this section.)

☐ 1. Have I written neatly in pencil and used single-spaced lines and wide margins?
☐ 2. Have I written the title at the center of the top line, with my name under it?
☐ 3. Have I skipped a line under my name before writing my paper?
☐ 4. Have I indented the first line of each paragraph?
☐ 5. Does my whole paper look clean and neat?

Final Analysis

SCORE ☐ (Count the checkmarks in this section.)

☐ 1. Is my paper interesting and easy to follow?
☐ 2. Does my knowledge about the topic come through clearly?
☐ 3. Are my directions detailed enough to be effective?
☐ 4. Do my directions give a mental image of what I am describing?
☐ 5. Does my description fit into the proper genre?

STUDENT RUBRIC for Comparison Writing

Name: _____ Date:_____

Directions: Put a checkmark beside each question that you answer with "yes."

Comparison   SCORE [   ] (Count the checkmarks in this section.)

- [ ] 1. Have I used a Venn diagram to create a well-planned essay?
- [ ] 2. Have I used appropriate transition words for each paragraph?
- [ ] 3. Have I used descriptive words to develop a strong comparison of my subjects?
- [ ] 4. Have I presented the information in a logical order that makes sense?
- [ ] 5. Have I compared and contrasted the two subjects in an interesting way?

Ideas   SCORE [   ] (Count the checkmarks in this section.)

- [ ] 1. Is the topic and purpose of my paper clearly described in the topic sentence?
- [ ] 2. Have I narrowed or expanded my subjects appropriately?
- [ ] 3. Have I compared and contrasted the two subjects in my paper?
- [ ] 4. Do I have several supporting details to develop each of my subjects?
- [ ] 5. Have I chosen two subjects that are appropriate to my purpose, genre, and audience?

Organization   SCORE [   ] (Count the checkmarks in this section.)

- [ ] 1. Is my paper well organized and easy to follow?
- [ ] 2. Does my paper have a clear introduction, body, and conclusion?
- [ ] 3. Are my ideas properly divided into paragraphs?
- [ ] 4. Have I discussed similarities in one paragraph and differences in another paragraph?
- [ ] 5. Is the organization of my sentences and paragraphs appropriate for my purpose and audience?

Word Choice   SCORE [   ] (Count the checkmarks in this section.)

- [ ] 1. Have I used precise nouns/verbs and vivid adjectives/adverbs to create strong mental pictures?
- [ ] 2. Have I used appropriate transitional words to help the reader follow my ideas?
- [ ] 3. Have I replaced unclear words with stronger words?
- [ ] 4. Have I deleted any incorrect, repeated, or unnecessary words?
- [ ] 5. Have I used words appropriate to my purpose and audience?

Voice   SCORE [ ] (Count the checkmarks in this section.)

- [ ] 1. Have I developed a unique voice to show my style of writing?
- [ ] 2. Does my voice reflect my personality and feelings about the topic?
- [ ] 3. Do my individual word choices reflect my unique writing voice?
- [ ] 4. Have I used figures of speech (similes, metaphors, personification) to help develop my voice?
- [ ] 5. Have I used vocabulary appropriate for my purpose and audience?

Sentence Fluency   SCORE [ ] (Count the checkmarks in this section.)

- [ ] 1. Can a reader easily follow my ideas?
- [ ] 2. Have I combined short, choppy sentences to make my writing sound smooth?
- [ ] 3. Have I used different types of sentences (simple, compound, complex, Mover & Shaker)?
- [ ] 4. Have I used a variety of long and short sentences to add interest to my paper?
- [ ] 5. Have I used transition words to connect related sentences?

Conventions   SCORE [ ] (Count the checkmarks in this section.)

- [ ] 1. Have I followed the conventions of capitalization?
- [ ] 2. Have I followed the conventions of punctuation?
- [ ] 3. Have I spelled every word correctly and corrected any mistakes in homonyms, contractions, possessives, or plural forms?
- [ ] 4. Have I corrected all usage mistakes, such as a/an mistakes and subject-verb agreement mistakes?
- [ ] 5. Have I corrected all sentence mistakes, such as run-ons, fragments, and comma splices?

Formatting   SCORE [ ] (Count the checkmarks in this section.)

- [ ] 1. Have I written neatly in pencil and used single-spaced lines and wide margins?
- [ ] 2. Have I written the title at the center of the top line, with my name under it?
- [ ] 3. Have I skipped a line under my name before writing my paper?
- [ ] 4. Have I indented the first line of each paragraph?
- [ ] 5. Does my whole paper look clean and neat?

Final Analysis   SCORE [ ] (Count the checkmarks in this section.)

- [ ] 1. Is my paper interesting and easy to follow?
- [ ] 2. Does my knowledge about the two topics come through clearly?
- [ ] 3. Are my comparisons detailed enough to be effective?
- [ ] 4. Do my descriptions give me a mental image of what I am comparing?
- [ ] 5. Does my comparison fit into the proper genre?

Writing a Research Report

When you are assigned a research report, you will gather information about your topic. This search for information is called research. A **research report** is *a very special kind of writing where you select a topic, gather information from various sources, analyze the information, and use it to write about the topic.* Research helps you learn facts and details about a topic that you did not know before. Then, when you write the report, you will help your readers learn about the topic, too.

Writing a research report is much like writing a five-paragraph explanatory essay, but there are some steps you will take before you begin writing your report. These steps are divided into stages, and you must complete each stage before going to the next stage.

Reference 201

Stages and Steps for Writing a Research Report

There are three stages to writing a research report. Each stage is described below.

Stage 1 Ideas

Select a topic, narrow the topic, and choose the main points you will research.

Stage 2 Research

Gather and record important information from several sources, citing your sources.

Stage 3 Writing

Organize the information and write a report, using the steps in the writing process to create a finished piece.

Each of the three stages has a number of steps necessary to complete the stage. Learning the stages and steps involved in writing a research report is important. The highlighted section will show you what will be studied in each lesson.

Stage 1: Ideas

STEP 1 Select a topic
STEP 2 Narrow the topic
STEP 3 Choose the main points

Stage 2: Research

STEP 1 Select sources
STEP 2 Record source information
STEP 3 Make note cards
STEP 4 Organize note cards

Stage 3: Writing

STEP 1 Write an outline
STEP 2 Write a rough draft
STEP 3 Revise & edit outline & draft
STEP 4 Write a final outline and report
STEP 5 Make a title page
STEP 6 Put research materials in order

Reference 202

Ideas Stage

STEP 1 Select a Topic

You can write a research report on just about anything. When it's time to select a topic for a research report, find a topic that interests you.

A topic usually fits into one of these categories: *people, places, things* or *industries, events, animals,* or *plants*. The Topic Guide gives you a general idea about what types of information can be found about these categories during your research. After you choose a category, use the Topic Guide and References 201–204 to help you narrow the topic and choose main points.

Topic Guide

People

Body: Choose one or more main points
1. Childhood: home, family, events
2. Adult: home, family, events
3. Interests, hobbies, or beliefs
4. Interesting traits or abilities
5. People who influenced his/her life
6. Occupations or career choices
7. Accomplishments
8. Contributions to mankind
9. Interesting facts
10. Think of your own main point to fit the topic.

Animals

Body: Choose one or more main points
1. Physical characteristics (what it looks like)
2. Habitat (where it lives)
3. What it eats and how it gets its food
4. Social habits (family groups/loners)
5. Predators or enemies
6. Ways of defending itself
7. Interesting traits, behaviors, or abilities
8. History or background
9. Relationship to humans
10. Interesting facts
11. Think of your own main point to fit the topic.

Plants

Body: Choose one or more main points
1. Physical appearance or identification (size, shape, looks, texture, color, etc.)
2. Parts of the plant
3. How the plant reproduces
4. Medical uses of the plant
5. Food uses of the plant
6. Other uses of the plant
7. Different types or varieties
8. History or background
9. Importance to humans
10. Interesting facts
11. Think of your own main point to fit the topic.

Places

Body: Choose one or more main points
1. Famous landmarks or tourist attractions
2. Major regions, mountain ranges, deserts, and other landforms
3. Bodies of water
4. Climate
5. National parks or natural resources
6. History/past events of the place
7. People or culture of the area
8. Common animals that live there
9. Major industries or products
10. Interesting facts
11. Think of your own main point to fit the topic.

Events

Body: Choose one or more main points
1. Causes of the event
2. People involved in the event
3. Things that happened during the event
4. Why the event was important
5. Results of the event
6. Historical consequences of the event
7. Things that can be learned from the event
8. Think of your own main point to fit the topic.

Things or Industries

Body: Choose one or more main points
1. Physical appearance, materials, or identification (size, shape, looks, texture, weight, color, etc.)
2. Parts or divisions
3. Important characteristics
4. Different types or varieties
5. History or background
6. Manufacturing information
7. Current Impact
8. Interesting facts
9. Think of your own main point to fit the to

Introduction: First paragraph
1. Write a topic sentence that tells what the essay is about.
2. Give extra information that can include a question, fact, definition, quote, general comment, or personal observation.

3. State the main points that will be presented in the essay.

Conclusion: Last paragraph
1. Summarize and review what the essay is abo
2. Restate main points presented in the essay

Ideas Stage

STEP 2 ▸ Narrow the Topic

Once you have selected the category for your topic, you need to narrow it. Most topics are too broad—this means they contain too much information to write about in one research report. For example, it would be very difficult to write a research report on animals because the topic is too broad. This broad topic needs to be narrowed several more times so that the information will fit in one report. Study the journey of a student writer as he goes through the narrowing process below.

The Narrowing Process

1. First, he went to the Topic Guide and chose the category **animals**.

2. The student was interested in *reptiles*, so he narrowed the topic *animals* to **reptiles**.

3. He then narrowed the topic *reptiles* to a specific *reptile*, **lizard**.

4. The student realized that the topic *lizard* was still pretty broad because there are many different kinds of *lizards*. He decided that he was most interested in the **glass lizard**. So, his narrowed topic became the **glass lizard**.

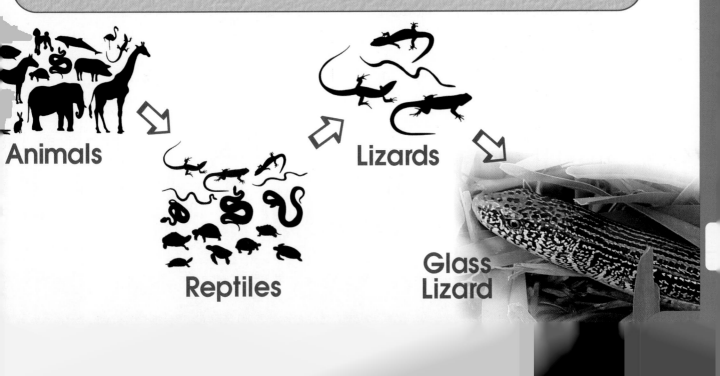

Animals

Reptiles

Lizards

Glass
Lizard

Lesson 1

Reference 204

Ideas Stage

STEP 3 ▶ Choose the Main Points

You have studied how a student chose and narrowed a topic. Now, you are ready for the main points. The student used the Topic Guide again to help him select the main points he wanted to research.

Most research reports present three main points about their topic. You can choose main points from the Topic Guide in two ways:

1. Choose three different main points from the Topic Guide.

2. Choose one point and expand it into three main points. For example, you could expand one main point, like Interesting traits, into three different *traits* and use them as your three main points.

Since the student was writing about the **glass lizard**, he looked at the Topic Guide to see if he could use any of the main points listed.

He decided that three main points could be **where it lives**, **what it looks like**, and **what it does**. These main points fit the topic, and they were interesting to him. The student jotted his narrowed topic and three main points on notebook paper.

Narrowed Topic
   the glass lizard

3 Main Points
   1. where it lives
   2. what it looks like
   3. what it does

Lesson 1

Student Tip...

1. The main points given in the Topic Guide are only suggestions. If you think of a main point for your topic that is not listed, feel free to use it.

2. As you progress through the Research Stage, you may need to change your main points. If you cannot find enough information on a main point, or if the information you find is not very interesting, you may change one or more of your main points. If you keep making changes to your main points, there is usually a problem with your topic. Therefore, you should consider selecting a different topic.

Exercise 1: Number 1–6 on your notebook paper. Study the topics below.
Write **N** if the topic is narrow enough for a research topic.
Write **B** if the topic is too broad for a research topic.

_____ 1. animals

_____ 2. large sea animals

_____ 3. food

_____ 4. breakfast food

_____ 5. types of clouds

_____ 6. two types of spiders

Exercise 2: On your notebook paper, outline the three stages for writing a research paper.
Use the information below. Check Reference 201 for the order of the subtopics
under each main point.

Main Points
Ideas stage
Research stage
Writing stage
Subtopics
Select a topic

Narrow your topic
Choose the
main points
Select sources
Record source
information

Make note cards
Organize note cards
Write an outline
Write a rough draft
Revise and edit

Write a final
outline and report
Make a title page
Put research
materials in order

_____

_____

_____

_____

_____

_____

_____

_____

_____

_____

_____

_____

_____

_____

_____

_____

_____

_____

_____

_____

_____

Writing Time

The Research Stage

Now, it is time to start the second stage of writing a research report, the Research Stage. This is the most important stage in the process because you cannot write a research report without doing the research. This is also the most exciting stage because it is your chance to discover new things about your topic.

Before you begin, review the stages and steps involved in writing a research report. The highlighted section will show you what will be studied in this lesson.

Stage 1: Ideas
- STEP 1 Select a topic
- STEP 2 Narrow the topic
- STEP 3 Choose the main points

Stage 2: Research
- STEP 1 **Select sources**
- STEP 2 **Record source information**
- STEP 3 Make note cards
- STEP 4 Organize note cards

Stage 3: Writing
- STEP 1 Write an outline
- STEP 2 Write a rough draft
- STEP 3 Revise & edit outline & draft
- STEP 4 Write a final outline and report
- STEP 5 Make a title page
- STEP 6 Put research materials in order

Reference 205

Main Sources Used to Research a Topic

You can use several types of **sources** to find information for your report: *nonfiction books, encyclopedias, websites, interviews,* and *magazines.* Each of these sources is useful in different ways. Using at least two sources when writing a research report is important. Using only one source limits the information available for your report.

CONTINUED ON NEXT PAGE

Lesson 2

An Encyclopedia Source

Encyclopedias make an excellent starting point for your research because you get a general introduction to your topic, along with specific details. Most current encyclopedias are also available online in public libraries. Encyclopedia articles on your topic are usually easy to find because they are listed alphabetically.

An Internet Source

Check Internet sources carefully to make sure they are reliable. Reliable sources often have domain names ending in **.edu** *(college and university sites)* or **.gov** *(United States government sites)*. Write down the Internet source for information that you use. If possible, print the information. Write the date you found the information because information on the Internet can change daily.

A Book Source

Use the card catalog in the library to find nonfiction books related to your topic. It is usually not necessary to read the whole book in order to locate specific information about your topic. Use the book's table of contents and index to find the information you need. If you see any chapter titles or words related to your topic in the index, skim the pages given to see if any information can be used.

A Magazine Source

Magazine articles can also give you information about your topic. Magazines can be found in the library or on the Internet.

An Interview Source

If you know a person who is an expert on your topic, you can interview him/her in person, by phone, or by e-mail.

Student Tip...

1. If you cannot find your narrowed topic in an encyclopedia, you may need to look under a broader topic.

   Example: Narrowed topic: Glass lizards
   Broader topic: Lizards

2. Do not rely too heavily on information from just one book, or you risk turning your research report into a book report on that book.

Reference 206

Research Stage

STEP 1 ▶ **Select Sources**

How to Find Information

1. **Skimming** is *reading only the key parts of a source to determine quickly if that source has information that will fit your topic and main points.* Skim key parts, such as titles, topic headings in boldface type, first sentences of paragraphs, underlined words, captions under pictures, text outlined by boxes, questions, and summaries.
One way to skim several paragraphs in a long article is to read the entire first paragraph because it usually contains a brief summary of the article. Then, read only the first sentence of each paragraph in the body of the article. This will give you a brief summary of each paragraph. Finally, read the entire last paragraph because it restates the most important points.

2. For a book, look at the pages given in the table of contents and index to find information about your topic. Skim those pages. If the information you are skimming is not about one of your main points, skip it.

3. For other sources that have information about your topic, start at the beginning of the article and read to the end, taking notes as needed.

4. Take advantage of **cross-referencing**. Watch for the words "See" or "See also." The information you find can make a source more useful or provide another useful source.

5. Look for a list of sources the author used to write the article or book. This list is usually found at the end of the article or book.

6. If you cannot find enough information about your topic and main points, go back to the Topic Guide and choose new main points. If you still cannot find enough information, you should choose a different topic and select main points for the new topic.

Student Tip...
Check out books and ask your librarian about printing copies of Internet or encyclopedia articles. Having a physical copy of a source can make research much easier.

Lesson 2

Lesson 2

Plagiarism

If you *use an author's words or ideas without giving the author proper credit*, you are guilty of **plagiarism**. Plagiarism is a form of dishonesty, like cheating on a test. That is why it is important to cite the sources you use in your report.

Citing Your Sources

Once you have decided to use a source, you need to *record the author and publishing details*. This is called **citing your sources**. Citing your sources lets a reader know where you found the information you used. A **citation** gives credit to another author for using his/her ideas. Write down the required information from each source you use to help you cite sources in your report.

Student Note:

When you begin your report, put all your work in your Research Report Folder.

Reference 207

Research Stage

STEP 2 ▶ Record Source Information

Encyclopedia Source

Author's Full Name: _not given_
(if given)

Title of Article: _"Glass Snake"_

Title of the Encyclopedia: _Encyclopaedia Britannica_

Publication Date: _2004 ed. CD ROM._

Internet Source

Author's Full Name: _Jeff LeClere_
(if given)

Title of Article: _"Slender Glass Lizard"_
(also called Page Title)

Title of the Website: _Herpnet.net_

Publication Date: _May 6, 2005_

Publisher (if given): _not given_

Date You Looked _May 15, 2007. Web._
Up the Article (day, month, and year)

Web Address (URL): _http://www.herpnet.net/Iowa-Herpetology_

Book Source

Author's Full Name: _D.M. Souza_

Title of Book: _Catch Me If You Can, A Book About Lizards_

Place Book was
was Published (City): _Minneapolis_

Publisher: _Carolrhoda Books, Inc_

Copyright: _1992. Print._
(year book was published)

Magazine Source

Author's Full Name: _R. D. Bartlett_

Title of Article: _"Thoughts on a Few Ophisaurus"_

Title of the Magazine: _Reptiles Magazine_

Publication Date: _March 2001_

Pages of Article: _92-105. Web._

Interview Source

Person's Full Name: _Teresa Reid_

Type of Interview: _Personal interview_
(personal, phone, etc.)

Date of Interview: _24 April 2012_

NOTE: Use the examples above to help you record the source information that you need.

Exercise 1: **Word Scramble:** Unscramble the five sources for a research report.

1. koob   _____

2. inetertn   _____

3. inezmaag   _____

4. iaclopedency   _____

5. inwterevi   _____

Exercise 2: **Outlining:** On your notebook paper, outline the three stages for writing a research paper. Put the information into outline form, following the rules for outlining. Two items are not parallel. Make them parallel in the outline.

Main Points
Ideas stage
Research stage
Writing stage
Subtopics
Select a topic

Narrow your topic
Choose the
main points
Select sources
Record source
information

Note cards
Organize note cards
Write an outline
Write a rough draft
Revise and edit

A final outline
and report
Make a title page
Put research
materials in order

Writing Time

Before you begin, it is important to review the stages and steps involved in writing a research report. The highlighted section will show you what will be studied in this lesson.

Stage 1: Ideas

STEP 1 Select a topic
STEP 2 Narrow the topic
STEP 3 Choose the main points

Stage 2: Research

STEP 1 Select sources
STEP 2 Record source information
STEP 3 **Make note cards**
STEP 4 **Organize note cards**

Stage 3: Writing

STEP 1 Write an outline
STEP 2 Write a rough draft
STEP 3 Revise & edit outline & draft
STEP 4 Write a final outline and report
STEP 5 Make a title page
STEP 6 Put research materials in order

Start Lesson 3

Reference 208

Research Stage

STEP 3 Make Note Cards

> **Introduction** 1
>
> is unusual animal
>
> is sometimes called a glass snake
>
> ("Glass Snake")

How to Label Note Cards

Since you will write your notes on note cards, you need to label them to keep them organized.

1. **Introduction**
   - → Write the word **Introduction** at the top of several blank note cards. Now, the cards are ready for information that will be used in the introduction.
   - → Write the topic sentence and the main-point sentence on the last two cards of the introduction. The main-point sentence does not require a citation source since it is a statement of your main points.

2. **Body**
   - → On several note cards, write **I.** and the first main point on the top line. Now, the cards are ready for supporting information.
   - → On several note cards, write **II.** and the second main point on the top line. Now, the cards are ready for supporting information.
   - → On several note cards, write **III.** and the third main point on the top line. Now, the cards are ready for supporting information.

3. **Conclusion**
   - → Write the word **Conclusion** at the top of blank note cards. Now, the cards are ready for information that will be used in the conclusion.

How to Write Notes on Note Cards

1. Each fact or piece of information that you might use should be recorded on a note card. When you write notes, you do not have to write in complete sentences—incomplete sentences, phrases, or even just a word or two can be enough. Just make sure you will understand it when you read it later.

2. Read the information and think about what it means. Then, write a sentence or phrase explaining the information in your own words.

3. If you use the exact words from a source, put them in quotation marks on your note card.

4. Put only one note from a source on a note card unless the notes are very closely related.

CONTINUED ON NEXT PAGE

Lesson 3

How to Write Sources on Note Cards

1. It is very important to list your sources, even if you put the information in your own words. The only information you do not have to cite is your own opinions, original ideas, or well-known facts.

2. At the bottom of every note card, write the author's last name and the page number where the information is found. Put parentheses around the author's last name and the page number.

3. If no author is given, write the title of the source and the page number. You may shorten a long title.

4. You will use the source information on your note cards to cite the sources in your report.

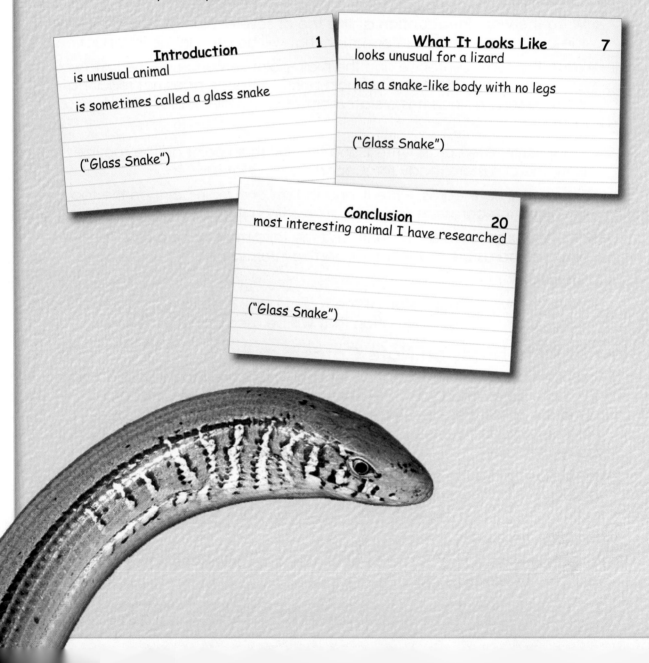

Introduction   1
is unusual animal

is sometimes called a glass snake

("Glass Snake")

What It Looks Like   7
looks unusual for a lizard

has a snake-like body with no legs

("Glass Snake")

Conclusion   20
most interesting animal I have researched

("Glass Snake")

Research Stage

STEP 4 ▸ Organize Note Cards

Student Tip...
The best way to make note cards is to take your notes from one source at a time.

Lesson 3

When you have read all your sources and made note cards for all the information you want to use in your report, you will have a lot of note cards. Most of them should already be labeled as *Introduction*, *the main points*, or *Conclusion*.

Now, it's time to organize the notes you have completed.

Student Tip...
Any information you use in your report needs to be recorded on a note card first.

1. Since you have written **Introduction**, **the main points**, and **Conclusion** at the top of your note cards, most of your information is already organized.

2. First, sort your note cards into piles according to the titles at the top of the note cards. You should have five piles: **introduction**, **first main point**, **second main point**, **third main point**, and **conclusion**.

3. Arrange the *introduction* note cards in the order you want for your introduction. Write **Paragraph 1** on the back of each introduction card.

4. Arrange the note cards for the first main point in the order you want for your report. Write **Paragraph 2** on the back of each first-point card.

5. Arrange the note cards for the second and third main points in the order you want for your report. Write **Paragraph 3** on the back of each second-point card. Write **Paragraph 4** on the back of each third-point card.

6. Arrange the conclusion note cards in the order you want for the conclusion. Then, write **Paragraph 5** on the back of each card.

7. Finally, number all your note cards (1, 2, 3, 4, etc.) in the upper right hand corner to prevent them from getting out of order.

8. Store all note cards in a plastic zip bag. If they get mixed up, use the numbers in the top-right corner to put them back in order. You will hand in your note cards with your final report.

Student Tip...
If you want to record information, but you are not sure where it would best fit in your report, just leave the top area blank. You can make the decision about which main point it fits as you organize your note cards.

Sample Note Cards

Lesson 3

Introduction   1

is unusual animal

is sometimes called a glass snake

("Glass Snake")

Introduction   2

how it gets its name:
its long tail is easily broken off
when chased or threatened

(LeClere 2)

Introduction   3

tail can break "into several wriggling
pieces" while rest of lizard escapes

(LeClere 3)

Introduction   4

commonly mistaken for a snake

(LeClere 1)

Introduction   5

Topic sentence:
The glass snake is a very unusual animal.

Introduction   6

Main-point sentence:
It's interesting to learn what a
glass lizard looks like, what it does,
and where it lives.

I. What It Looks Like   7

looks unusual for a lizard
has a snake-like body with no legs

("Glass Snake")

I. What It Looks Like   8

can grow up to 41 inches long

12 inches is body, rest is tail

("Glass

I. What It Looks Like   9

moves like a snake

(LeClere 2)

I. What It Looks Like   10

unlike a snake:
has ear opening on head
has moveable eyelids
has a groove on side of its body

(LeClere 2)

II. What It Does   11

is active during daytime from
April to October

(LeClere 2)

More Sample Note Cards

II. What It Does   12

hibernates during winter months

(LeClere 2)

III. Where It Lives   17

lives in burrows borrowed from
small mammals

(LeCle

II. What It Does   13

eats mostly insects:
grasshoppers, crickets, beetles

(LeClere 2)

III. Where It Lives   18

lives in loose soil found under rocks,
logs, and leaves

("Glass Lizard")

II. What It Does   14

eats small animals:
small snakes, lizards, mice, eggs

(LeClere 2)

III. Where It Lives   19

different kinds found in North America,
Europe, Asia, Africa

("Glass

Conclusion   20

most interesting animal I have researched

II. What It Does   15

lays 5 to 17 eggs that hatch in August

(LeClere 3)

Conclusion   21

want to see its tail break into
several pieces

II. What It Does   16

females guard eggs

(LeClere 3)

Conclusion   22

snake could be a glass lizard
saying: looks can be deceiving

Start Lesson 4

Before you begin, it is important to review the stages and steps involved in writing a research report. The highlighted section will show you what will be studied in this lesson.

Stage 1: Ideas

STEP 1 Select a topic
STEP 2 Narrow the topic
STEP 3 Choose the main points

Stage 2: Research

STEP 1 Select sources
STEP 2 Record source information
STEP 3 Make note cards
STEP 4 Organize note cards

Stage 3: Writing

STEP 1 Write an outline
STEP 2 Write a rough draft
STEP 3 Revise & edit outline & draft

STEP 4 Write a final outline and report
STEP 5 Make a title page
STEP 6 Put research materials in order

Your research is finished, and your note cards are organized. Now, you are ready to begin the final stage of a research report: the Writing Stage. You will begin your prewriting by writing an outline.

As you know, an **outline** is a graphic organizer that helps you see the order of your report before it is written. When you write a research report, your outline is the road map that helps you navigate through all the information you collected on your note cards. The outline helps you put all your information in one easy-to-read place.

Reference 210

Writing Stage

STEP 1 Write an Outline

To make an outline for your report, use the note cards that you have already organized. Keep in mind that you may not use all of your notes as you make your outline. Try to write items in parallel form. Follow the steps below to write an outline from your note cards.

Title

    Write your outline title on the top line of your paper. It should be the same as or similar to your narrowed topic.

First Main Point

    1. Write Roman numeral one (I.) for your first main point.

    2. Use the note cards titled **1st Main Point**.

    3. List supporting information as subtopics (A. B. C.) and details (1. 2. 3.).

    4. Capitalize the first word of the main point, subtopics, and details.

Second Main Point

    1. Write Roman numeral two (II.) for your second main point.

    2. Use the note cards titled **2nd Main Point**.

    3. List supporting information as subtopics (A. B. C.) and details (1. 2. 3.).

    4. Capitalize the first word of the main point, subtopics, and details.

Third Main Point

    1. Write Roman numeral three (III.) for your third main point.

    2. Use the note cards titled **3rd Main Point**.

    3. List supporting information as subtopics (A. B. C.) and details (1. 2. 3.).

    4. Capitalize the first word of the main point, subtopics, and details.

Note: You will write your introduction and conclusion during the rough-draft stage.

Using Note Cards to Write the 1st Main Point of Your Outline

1. Note Cards 7–10 for the *first main point* are used to write the first section of the outline.

2. **Roman numeral one (I.):** The first main point from the note cards is written beside Roman numeral one.

3. **Subtopics (A. B. C.):** Information about the main topic is transferred from the note cards to the outline as **subtopics**. Some notes may be changed slightly to keep the outline in parallel form.

4. **Details (1. 2. 3.):** Information about the subtopics is transferred from the note cards to the outline as **details**. Some notes may be changed slightly to keep the outline in parallel form.

5. Compare the note cards with the first section of the outline. Draw a line through any information that you decide not to use in your outline. Any information that is not in the outline will not be in the report.

Stage 2: Research

1st Main Point Note Cards:

I. What It Looks Like   7

looks unusual for a lizard
has a snake-like body with no legs

("Glass Snake")

I. What It Looks Like   8

can grow up to 41 inches long
~~12 inches is body, rest is tail~~

("Glass

I. What It Looks Like   9

moves like a snake

I. What It Looks Like   10

unlike a snake:
has ear opening on head
has moveable eyelids
has a groove on side of its body

(LeClere 2)

Stage 3: Writing

Outlining the 1st Main-Point From Your Note Cards

I. What the glass lizard looks like
  A. Like a snake
    1. Has a snake-like body with no legs
    2. Can grow up to 41 inches long
    3. Moves like a snake
  B. Unlike a snake
    1. Has an ear opening on its head
    2. Has movable eyelids
    3. Has a groove on the side

Using Note Cards to Write the 2nd Main Point of Your Outline

1. Note Cards 11–16 for the *second main point* are used to write the second section of the outline.

2. **Roman numeral two (II.):** The second main point from the note cards is written beside Roman numeral two.

3. **Subtopics (A. B. C.):** Information about the main topic is transferred from the note cards to the outline as **subtopics**. Some notes may be changed slightly to keep the outline in parallel form.

4. **Details (1. 2. 3.):** Information about the subtopics is transferred from the note cards to the outline as **details**. Some notes may be changed slightly to keep the outline in parallel form.

5. Compare the note cards with the second section of the outline. Draw a line through any information that you decide not to use in your outline. Any information that is not in the outline will not be in the report.

Stage 2: Research

2nd Main Point Note Cards:

II. What It Does   11

is active during daytime from April to October

II. What It Does   12

(LeCl

hibernates during winter months

II. What It Does   13

eats mostly insects: grasshoppers, crickets, beetles

(LeClere 2)

II. What It Does   14

eats small animals: small snakes, lizards, mice, eggs

II. What It Does   15

lays 5 to 17 eggs that hatch in August

(LeClere 3)

II. What It Does   16

females guard eggs

(LeClere 3)

CONTINUED ON NEXT PAGE

Lesson 4

II. What the glass lizard does
  A. Activity
    1. Is active during the daytime from April to October
    2. Hibernates in winter
  B. Food
    1. Insects, like grasshoppers, crickets, and beetles
    2. Animals, like small snakes, lizards, and mice
  C. Eggs
    1. Lays 5 to 17 eggs
    2. Hatch in August

Stage 3: Writing

Outlining the 2nd Main-Point From Your Note Cards

Using Note Cards to Write the 3rd Main Point of Your Outline

1. Note Cards 17–19 for the *third* main point are used to write the third section of the outline.

2. **Roman numeral three (III.):** The third main point from the note cards is written beside Roman numeral three.

3. **Subtopics (A. B. C.):** Information about the main topic is transferred from the note cards to the outline as **subtopics**. Some notes may be changed slightly to keep the outline in parallel form.

4. **Details (1. 2. 3.):** Information about the subtopics is transferred from the note cards to the outline as **details**. Some notes may be changed slightly to keep the outline in parallel form.

5. Compare the note cards with the third section of the outline. Draw a line through any information that you decide not to use in your outline. Any information that is not in the outline will not be in the report.

Stage 2: Research

3rd Main Point Note Cards:

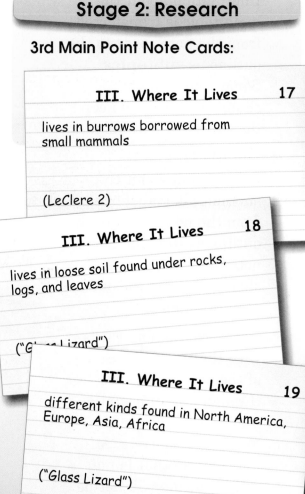

III. Where It Lives   17

lives in burrows borrowed from small mammals

(LeClere 2)

III. Where It Lives   18

lives in loose soil found under rocks, logs, and leaves

("Glass Lizard")

III. Where It Lives   19

different kinds found in North America, Europe, Asia, Africa

("Glass Lizard")

Stage 3: Writing

Outlining the 3rd Main-Point From Your Note Cards

III. Where the glass lizard lives
  A. In the loose soil found under rocks, logs, and leaves
  B. In North America, Europe, Asia, and Africa

Student Tip...

- Your outline is a "visual map" of your report.
  It will keep you going in the right direction. Keep it up-to-date.

- If you decide to change any main points, subtopics, or details, make the changes on your note cards AND your outline.

Example of an Outline

The Unusual Glass Lizard
I. What the glass lizard looks like
  A. Like a snake
    1. Has a snake-like body with no legs
    2. Can grow up to 41 inches long
    3. Moves like a snake
  B. Unlike a snake
    1. Has an ear opening on its head
    2. Has movable eyelids
    3. Has a groove on the side of its body
II. What the glass lizard does
  A. Activity
    1. Is active during the daytime from April to October
    2. Hibernates in winter
  B. Food
    1. Insects, like grasshoppers, crickets, and beetles
    2. Animals, like small snakes, lizards, and mice
  C. Eggs
    1. Lays 5 to 17 eggs
    2. Hatch in August
III. Where the glass lizard lives
  A. In the loose soil found under rocks, logs, and leaves
  B. In North America, Europe, Asia, and Africa

Student Tip...

1. As you complete your outline, you will see that some information does not belong and some important information may be missing. You may have made note cards for information that seemed important at the time, only to find that it does not flow well with the rest of your outline. Likewise, you may find gaps in your outline that require you to go back to your sources for more information. Adjust your note cards and outline as you add or delete information.

2. Your outline will be your guide as you begin writing your rough draft, but you will still need your note cards—so don't lose them!

Writing Time

Before you begin, it is important to review the stages involved in writing a research report. The highlighted section will show you what will be studied in this lesson.

Stage 1: Ideas

STEP 1 Select a topic
STEP 2 Narrow the topic
STEP 3 Choose the main points

Stage 2: Research

STEP 1 Select sources
STEP 2 Record source information
STEP 3 Make note cards
STEP 4 Organize note cards

Stage 3: Writing

STEP 1 Write an outline
STEP 2 **Write a rough draft**
STEP 3 Revise & edit outline & draft
STEP 4 Write a final outline and report
STEP 5 Make a title page
STEP 6 Put research materials in order

Reference 211

Writing Stage

How to Cite a Source in Your Rough Draft

It is very important to cite a source if you used information from it, even if you summarized or put the information in your own words. The only information you do not have to cite is your own opinions, original ideas, or well-known facts. Follow the directions below to cite your sources.

1. A citation is written inside parentheses at the end of the sentence. The end mark is placed after the parentheses.

2. The citation in parentheses has the author's last name and the page number where the information is found.

3. Your note cards have the citation information you will use *(author's name and page number).*

4. If the author is not given, write the title of the source and the page number. You may shorten a long title.

➥ Examples:

Citations

Book: The glass lizard is a very unusual animal (LeClere 2).

Encyclopedia: The glass lizard's looks are very unusual for a lizard ("Glass Snake").

Lesson 5

Lesson 5

Use your note cards and your outline to write your rough draft.

Reference 212

Writing Stage

STEP 2 ▶ **Write a Rough Draft**

Your research paper will be a five-paragraph report. You will have an introductory paragraph, three paragraphs in the body (a paragraph for each of the three main points), and a concluding paragraph. Skip every other line if handwritten or double space if typewritten. This will give you room to revise and edit your rough draft. You will write the body first. Then, you will write the introduction and conclusion on separate sheets of paper.

1. **1st Main Point**
   - → Use the first section of your outline and note cards to write the first paragraph of the body.
   - → The first sentence should state the first point, and the other sentences should support it.
   - → At the end of each sentence, cite your source and put it in parentheses.
   - → Make sure the sentences are arranged in the same order as your outline.

2. **2nd Main Point**
   - → Use the second section of your outline and note cards to write the second paragraph of the body.
   - → The first sentence should state the second point, and the other sentences should support it.
   - → At the end of each sentence, cite your source and put it in parentheses.
   - → Make sure the sentences are arranged in the same order as your outline.

3. **3rd Main Point**
   - → Use the third section of your outline and note cards to write the third paragraph of the body.
   - → The first sentence should state the third point, and the other sentences should support it.
   - → At the end of each sentence, cite your source and put it in parentheses.
   - → Make sure the sentences are arranged in the same order as your outline.

4. Introduction

→ Use the introduction section of your note cards to write the introductory paragraph.

→ The first sentence is a topic sentence that tells what your report is about.

→ The next sentences should capture the interest of your readers and give them extra information about the topic. These sentences can include a question, a fact, a definition, a quote, a general comment, or a personal observation.

→ If you used information from a source, cite the source and put it in parentheses.

→ The last sentence tells the main points of the topic to get the reader ready for the information contained in the body. This main-point sentence does not require a citation since it is a statement of the main points.

5. Conclusion

→ Use the conclusion section of your note cards to write the final paragraph.

→ The first sentence is used to summarize or restate the information in the introduction.

→ For the last sentences, use facts, personal opinions, or quotations that help you finalize the essay and restate the three main points.

→ If you used information from a source, cite your source and put it in parentheses. Otherwise, a conclusion usually comes from information previously cited or your own comments about the topic.

Student Tip...

1. You should write your report in your own words as you present facts and give examples. This will make your paper special because no one writes quite like you. Only quotes are written exactly as they are worded.

2. If you are citing a direct quotation, put the source after the quotation marks but before the end mark.

3. Remember that this is only a rough draft. Don't worry too much about mistakes. You will have time to find and correct them when you revise and edit.

Lesson 5

Using Your Outline and Note Cards to Write a Rough Draft

1st Main Point

Use your outline and note cards to write a paragraph for the first main point. Compare the note cards and your paragraph.

Stage 2: Research

1st Main Point Note Cards:

> **I. What It Looks Like**   7
>
> looks unusual for a lizard
> has a snake-like body with no legs
>
> ("Glass Snake")

> **I. What It Looks Like**   9
>
> moves like a snake
>
> (LeClere 2)

> **I. What It Looks Like**   8
>
> can grow up to 41 inches long
> ~~12 inches is body, rest is tail~~
>
> ("Glass Snake")

> **I. What It Looks Like**   10
>
> unlike a snake:
> has ear opening on head
> has moveable eyelids
> has a groove on side of its body
>
> (LeClere 2)

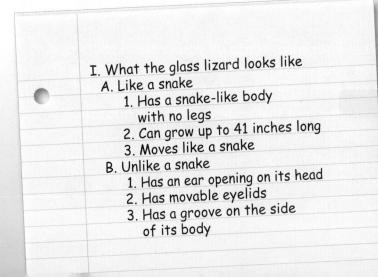

I. What the glass lizard looks like
  A. Like a snake
    1. Has a snake-like body
      with no legs
    2. Can grow up to 41 inches long
    3. Moves like a snake
  B. Unlike a snake
    1. Has an ear opening on its head
    2. Has movable eyelids
    3. Has a groove on the side
      of its body

Stage 3: Writing

Outline: First Section

Stage 3: Writing

Stage 3: Writing

1st Main Point of Rough Draft

The glass lizard's looks are very unusual for a lizard ("Glass Snake"). For one thing, it has a long snake-like body with no legs ("Glass Snake"). Its body and tail can grow as long as 41 inches ("Glass Snake"). Besides that, a glass lizard moves along the ground in an s-shape pattern, just like a snake. (LeClere 2). However, unlike snakes, glass lizards have ear openings, movable eyelids, and a groove down each side of their body (LeClere 2).

Using Your Outline and Note Cards to Write a Rough Draft

2nd Main Point

Use your outline and note cards to write a paragraph for the second main point. Compare the note cards and your paragraph.

Stage 2: Research

2nd Main Point Note Cards:

II. What It Does   11
is active during daytime from April to October
(LeClere 2)

II. What It Does   14
eats small animals: small snakes, lizards, mice, eggs
(LeClere 2)

II. What It Does   12
hibernates during winter months

II. What It Does   15
lays 5 to 17 eggs that hatch in August

II. What It Does   13
eats mostly insects: grasshoppers, crickets, beetles
(LeClere 2)

II. What It Does   16
~~females guard eggs~~
(LeClere 3)

II. What the glass lizard does
   A. Activity
      1. Is active during the daytime from April to October
      2. Hibernates in winter
   B. Food
      1. Insects, like grasshoppers, crickets, and beetles
      2. Animals, like small snakes, lizards, and mice
   C. Eggs
      1. Lays 5 to 17 eggs
      2. Hatch in August

The glass lizard does some very interesting things. Glass lizards are active during the daytime from April to October, and they hibernate in winter (LeClere 2). They eat mostly insects, like grasshoppers, crickets, and beetles (LeClere 2). However, glass lizards can also eat small animals, like snakes, lizards, and mice (LeClere 2). They lay 5 to 17 eggs that hatch in August (LeClere 3).

Using Your Outline and Note Cards to Write a Rough Draft

3rd Main Point

Use your outline and note cards to write a paragraph for the third main point. Compare the note cards and your paragraph.

Stage 2: Research

3rd Main Point Note Cards:

III. Where It Lives   17

~~lives in burroughs borrowed from small mammals~~

III. Where It Lives   18

lives in loose soil found under rocks, logs, and leaves

III. Where It Lives   19

different kinds found in North America, Europe, Asia, Africa

("Glass Lizard")

Stage 3: Writing

Outline: Third Section

III. Where the glass lizard lives
   A. In the loose soil found under rocks, logs, and leaves
   B. In North America, Europe, Asia, and Africa

Stage 3: Writing

3rd Main Point of Rough Draft

   The glass lizard lives in the loose soil underneath rocks, logs, and leaves ("Glass Lizard"). Different kinds of glass lizards have been found in parts of North America, Europe, Asia, and Africa ("Glass Lizard").

Using Note Cards to Write the Introduction

On another sheet of paper, use your note cards to write the introduction. Compare the note cards and the introduction. Draw a line through any information on your note cards that you do not use in your introduction.

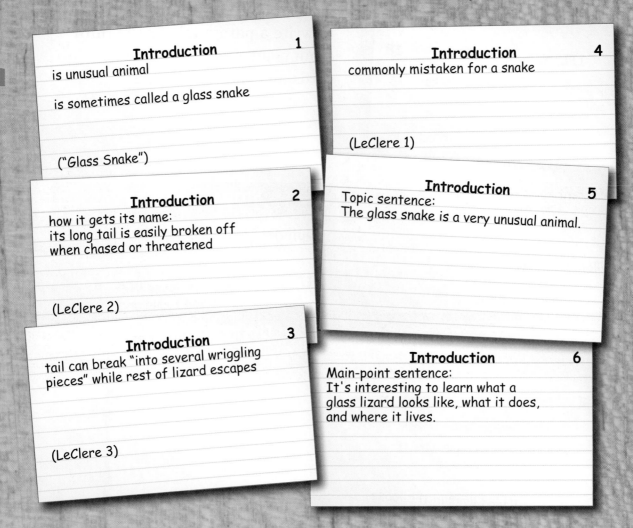

Introduction   1
is unusual animal

is sometimes called a glass snake

("Glass Snake")

Introduction   2
how it gets its name:
its long tail is easily broken off
when chased or threatened

(LeClere 2)

Introduction   3
tail can break "into several wriggling
pieces" while rest of lizard escapes

(LeClere 3)

Introduction   4
commonly mistaken for a snake

(LeClere 1)

Introduction   5
Topic sentence:
The glass snake is a very unusual animal.

Introduction   6
Main-point sentence:
It's interesting to learn what a
glass lizard looks like, what it does,
and where it lives.

Introduction

Introduction

The glass lizard is a very unusual animal ("Glass Snake").
It is not really made of glass, but the glass lizard gets its name
because its long tail is easily broken off when it is chased or
threatened (LeClere 2). Sometimes its tail breaks into "several
wriggling pieces" while the rest of the lizard scoots away to
safety (LeClere 3). In fact, the glass lizard is often mistaken
for a snake (LeClere 1). It's interesting to learn what a glass
lizard looks like, what it does, and where it lives.

Using Note Cards to Write the Conclusion

On another sheet of paper, use your note cards to write the conclusion. Compare the note cards and the conclusion. Draw a line through any information on your note cards that you do not use in your conclusion.

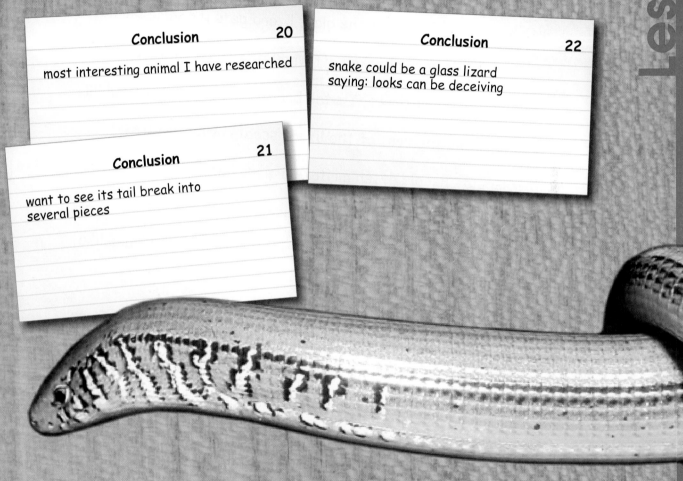

Conclusion   20

most interesting animal I have researched

Conclusion   22

snake could be a glass lizard
saying: looks can be deceiving

Conclusion   21

want to see its tail break into
several pieces

Conclusion

Conclusion
    I think that the glass lizard is one of the most interesting animals that I have researched. I would love to see a glass lizard's tail break into several pieces. Whenever I see a snake, I know that it could really be a glass lizard. As the saying goes, "Looks can be deceiving."

Example of a Rough Draft

The Unusual Glass Lizard

The glass lizard is a very unusual animal (LeClere 2). It is not really made of glass but the glass lizard gets its name because its long tail is easily broken off when it is chase or threatened (LeClere 2). Sometimes, it's tail breaks into "several wriggling pieces" while the rest of the lizard scoots away to safety (LeClere 3). People often mistake a glass lizard for a snake (LeClere 1). In fact, it is sometimes called a glass snake ("Glass Snake"). It's interesting to learn what a glass lizard looks like, what it does, and where it lives.

The glass lizard's looks are very unusal for a lizard ("Glass Snake"). For one thing, it has a long snake-like body with no legs ("Glass Snake"). Its body and and tail can grow as long as 41 inches ("Glass Snake"). Besides that, a glass lizard moves along the ground in an s-shape pattern, just like a snake. (LeClere 2). However, unlike snakes, glass lizards have ear openings, movable eyelids, and a groove down each side of their body (LeClere 3).

The glass lizard does some very interesting things. Glass lizards are active during the daytime from April to october, and they hibernate in winter (LeClere 2). They eat mostly insects,

like grasshoppers, crickets, and beetles (LeClere 2). Glass lizards
can also eat small animals, like snakes, lizards, and mice (LeClere 2).
They lay 5 to 17 eggs that hatch in August (LeClere 3).

The glass lizard lives in the loose soil underneath rocks, logs,
and leaves ("Glass Lizard"). Different kinds of glass lizards have
been found in parts of North America, Europe, Asia, and africa
("Glass Lizard").

I think that the glass lizard is one of the most interesting
animals that i have researched. I would love to see a glass
lizard's tail break into several pieces. Whenever I see a snake,
I know that it could really be a glass lizard. As the saying goes,
"Looks can be decieving."

Writing Time

Before you begin, it is important to review the stages and steps involved in writing a research report. The highlighted section will show you what will be studied in this lesson.

Stage 1: Ideas

STEP 1 Select a topic
STEP 2 Narrow the topic
STEP 3 Choose the main points

Stage 2: Research

STEP 1 Select sources
STEP 2 Record source information
STEP 3 Make note cards
STEP 4 Organize note cards

Stage 3: Writing

STEP 1 Write an outline
STEP 2 Write a rough draft
STEP 3 **Revise & edit outline & draft**
STEP 4 Write a final outline and report
STEP 5 Make a title page
STEP 6 Put research materials in order

The next step should be very familiar by now—you will revise and edit the rough draft of your research paper, just as you would revise and edit any writing assignment. Use Reference 213 below to help you revise and edit your rough draft.

Reference 213

Writing Stage

STEP 3 Revise and Edit
the Outline and Rough Draft

Outline

Use the checklist below to see if there are any changes you want to make to your outline.

☑ 1. **Is the information in your outline the same as the information in your rough draft?**

☑ 2. **Is the information in your outline in the same order as your rough draft?**

☑ 3. **Do you need to add, delete, or change any information in your outline?**

☑ 4. **Do you need to change the wording in your outline to make it parallel?**

☑ 5. **Have you used the correct outline form?**

You will write a final outline when you write your final report.

Rough Draft

Revise and edit your research report, using References 64 and 66 on pages Q23–Q25. In addition, use the following checklist below to help you revise and edit your rough draft.

☑ 1. **Have I checked for capitalization, punctuation, spelling, and usage mistakes?**

☑ 2. **Have I checked for the best wording of my sentences?**

☑ 3. **Have I presented clear main points to support the topic?**

☑ 4. **Have I used interesting details to support the main points?**

☑ 5. **Have I used appropriate transition words?**

☑ 6. **Have I developed the topic in a logical order that makes sense?**

☑ 7. **Have I followed my outline?**

☑ 8. **Have I put a citation for every sentence that needs one?**

☑ 9. **Have I put my citations in parentheses at the end of the sentence before the end mark?**

Example of a Revised and Edited Rough Draft

The Unusual Glass Lizard

The glass lizard is a very unusual animal (LeClere 2). It is not really made of glass, but the glass lizard gets its name because its long tail is easily broken off when it is chase or threatened (LeClere 2). Sometimes, it's tail breaks into "several wriggling pieces" while the rest of the lizard scoots away to safety (LeClere 3). People often mistake a glass lizard for a snake (LeClere 1). In fact, it is sometimes called a glass snake ("Glass Snake"). It's interesting to learn what a glass lizard looks like, what it does, and where it lives.

The glass lizard's looks are very unusal for a lizard ("Glass Snake"). For one thing, it has a long snake-like body with no legs ("Glass Snake"). Its body and and tail can grow as long as 41 inches ("Glass Snake"). Besides that, a glass lizard moves along the ground in an s-shape pattern, just like a snake. (LeClere 2). However, unlike snakes, glass lizards have ear openings, movable eyelids, and a groove down each side of their body (LeClere 3).

The glass lizard does some very interesting things. Glass lizards are active during the daytime from April to october, and they hibernate in winter (LeClere 2). They eat mostly insects, like grasshoppers, crickets, and beetles (LeClere 2). Glass lizards can also eat small animals, like snakes, lizards, and mice (LeClere 2). They lay 5 to 17 eggs that hatch in August (LeClere 3).

The glass lizard lives in the loose soil underneath rocks, logs, and leaves ("Glass Lizard"). Different kinds of glass lizards have been found in parts of North America, Europe, Asia, and africa ("Glass Lizard").

I think that the glass lizard is one of the most interesting animals that i have researched. I would love to see a glass lizard's tail break into several pieces. Whenever I see a snake, I know that it could really be a glass lizard. As the saying goes, "Looks can be decieving."

Writing Time

Before you begin, it is important to review the stages and steps involved in writing a research report. The highlighted section will show you what will be studied in this lesson.

Stage 1: Ideas

STEP 1 Select a topic
STEP 2 Narrow the topic
STEP 3 Choose the main points

Stage 2: Research

STEP 1 Select sources
STEP 2 Record source information
STEP 3 Make note cards
STEP 4 Organize note cards

Stage 3: Writing

STEP 1 Write an outline
STEP 2 Write a rough draft
STEP 3 Revise & edit outline & draft
STEP 4 Write a final outline and report
STEP 5 Make a title page
STEP 6 Put research materials in order

Reference 214

Writing Stage

STEP 4A Write a Final Outline

Use your edited rough-draft outline to write a final outline. You may write it in ink or type it on a computer. Both outlines will be handed in with your final report.

Example of a Final Outline

The Unusual Glass Lizard

I. What the glass lizard looks like
  A. Like a snake
    1. Has a snake-like body with no legs
    2. Can grow up to 41 inches long
    3. Moves like a snake
  B. Unlike a snake
    1. Has an ear opening on its head
    2. Has movable eyelids
    3. Has a groove on the side of its body
II. What the glass lizard does
  A. Activity
    1. Is active during the daytime from April to October
    2. Hibernates in winter
  B. Food
    1. Insects, like grasshoppers, crickets, and beetles
    2. Animals, like small snakes, lizards, and mice
  C. Eggs
    1. Lays 5 to 17 eggs
    2. Hatch in August
III. Where the glass lizard lives
  A. In the loose soil found under rocks, logs, and leaves
  B. In North America, Europe, Asia, and Africa

It is time to finish the final steps of your research paper.
Use Reference 215 below to make sure you write your final report correctly.

Reference 215

Writing Stage

STEP 4B Write a Final Report

Read over your rough draft one last time and make any necessary last-minute changes. Then, begin writing your final report neatly in ink or type it on a computer. If your teacher does not have specific requirements, use the general guidelines for handwritten or typed reports.

Handwritten

1. Write your report in blue or black ink.
2. Double-space your paper, leaving one-inch margins on each side and on the top and bottom.
3. Indent each paragraph.
4. Write your last name and the page number in the upper right corner on every page of your report.

Typewritten

1. Type your report in a 12 point common font, like Times New Roman.
2. Double-space your paper, leaving one-inch margins on each side and on the top and bottom.
3. Indent each paragraph five spaces.
4. Leave one space after every end mark.
5. Type your last name in the upper right corner of every page of your report. Add a page number if you have more than one page.

Word Processor

Follow the same directions for a typewritten report. Most of the formatting icons can be found on the task bar at the top of your computer screen. Ask your teacher for help with the task bar functions.

 NOTE: If you wish to include illustrations or visual aids, don't forget to add them to your final report. You will make a title page after you finish writing your final report. Before turning in your final report, proofread it one last time. Use the student rubric on pages 782–783 to evaluate your paper.

Example of a Final Report

The glass lizard is a very unusual animal. It is not really made of glass, but the glass lizard gets its name because its long tail is easily broken off when it is chased or threatened (LeClere 2). Sometimes its tail breaks into "several wriggling pieces" while the rest of the lizard scoots away to safety (LeClere 3). The glass lizard is also unusual because people often mistake it for a snake (LeClere 1). In fact, the glass lizard is sometimes called a "glass snake," but it is really a lizard ("Glass Snake").

The glass lizard's looks are very unusual for a lizard ("Glass Snake"). For one thing, it has a long snake-like body with no legs ("Glass Snake"). Its body and tail can grow as long as 41 inches ("Glass Snake"). Besides that, a glass lizard moves along the ground in an s-shape pattern, just like a snake. (LeClere 2). However, unlike snakes, glass lizards have ear openings, movable eyelids, and a groove down each side of their body (LeClere 3).

The glass lizard does some very interesting things. Glass lizards are active during the daytime from April to October, and they hibernate in winter (LeClere 2). They eat mostly insects, like grasshoppers, crickets, and beetles (LeClere 2). However, glass lizards can also eat small animals, like snakes, lizards, and mice (LeClere 2). They lay 5 to 17 eggs that hatch in August (LeClere 3).

The glass lizard lives in the loose soil underneath rocks, logs, and leaves ("Glass Lizard"). Different kinds of glass lizards have been found in parts of North America, Europe, Asia, and Africa ("Glass Lizard").

I think that the glass lizard is one of the most interesting animals that I have researched. I would love to see a glass lizard's tail break into several pieces. Whenever I see a snake, I know that it could really be a glass lizard. As the saying goes, "Looks can be deceiving."

Lesson 7

Research reports have special parts that normal explanatory essays do not have: *a title page* and *citations* within your report. You have already learned how to cite your sources in your report. Now, you will learn how to make a title page.

Reference 216

Writing Stage

STEP 5 Make a Title Page

The **title page** will be the first page of your report. If your teacher does not have specific requirements, follow the general guidelines below for a title page.

Title Page

1. Write your title page in ink or type it.

2. Skip five lines from the top line. On the sixth line, center the **title** of your report.

3. Skip ten more lines. Then, on the next line, center "**By** (and write your name)."

4. Skip one line, and on the next line, center "**For** (and write your teacher's name)."

5. Skip one line, and on the next line, center "**English**" as your subject.

6. Skip one line, and on the next line, center the **date**.

The Unusual Glass Lizard

By (First and Last Name)

For (Teacher's Name)

English

Date

Congratulations! You have just learned about the three stages for a research report. **There is only one more step** that must be completed before your report can be given to your teacher: put all research materials in the proper order.

Reference 217

Writing Stage

STEP 6 ▶ **Put Research Materials in Order**

Put your research materials in the order listed below, from top to bottom with Number 1 being the first page. After your papers are in the correct order, put everything in your Research Report Folder. Put the note cards and source information in the folder's left pocket and everything else in the folder's right pocket. Make sure your name is on the front of your folder.

Research Materials:

1. Title page
2. Final report
3. Illustrations and visual aids (optional)
4. Outlines (outline draft and final outline)
5. Rough draft
6. Source information
7. Note cards in plastic zip-bag

Schedule for Writing an Independent Research Report

Today, you will begin working on an independent research report. Use one of the topics listed or choose your own. Make sure your teacher approves your choice before you begin your research. Follow the writing schedule below as you research and write your report. Use the references listed in Chapter 19 to help you.

Reference 218

Independent Research Report

Select one of the report topics below or choose your own.

1. A city, state, or country
2. A famous scientist or inventor
3. A famous author
4. An interesting or unusual animal

5. A famous American in history
6. A team sport or individual sport
7. A famous singer or musician
8. A President
9. Flying machines

Writing Schedule:

Lesson 1 References 201-204
Pages 788-792

Stage 1: Ideas

- **STEP 1** Select a topic
- **STEP 2** Narrow the topic
- **STEP 3** Choose the main points

Lesson 2 References 205-207
Pages 795-798

Stage 2: Research

- **STEP 1** Select sources
- **STEP 2** Record source information

Lesson 3 References 208-209
Pages 801-805

Stage 2: Research

- **STEP 3** Make note cards
- **STEP 4** Organize note cards

Lesson 4 Reference 210
Pages 807-811

Stage 3: Writing

- **STEP 1** Write an outline

Lesson 5 References 211-212
Pages 813-823

Stage 3: Writing

- **STEP 2** Write a rough draft

Lesson 6 Reference 213
Pages 824-827

Stage 3: Writing

- **STEP 3** Revise and edit the outline and rough draft

Lesson 7 References 214-217
Pages 829-833

Stage 3: Writing

- **STEP 4** Write a final outline and report
- **STEP 5** Make a title page
- **STEP 6** Put research materials in order

Lesson 8

Share and Evaluate.

Lesson 9

Share and Evaluate.

Use the Presentation Guidelines when you present your research reports.

Presentation Guidelines for Research Reports

Speaker Presentation

1. Have your paper ready to read when it is your turn.

2. Give the title of your research report.

3. Tell the purpose of your report.

4. Stand with your feet flat on the floor and your shoulders straight. Do not shift your weight as you stand.

5. Hold your paper about chin high to help project your voice to your audience.

6. Read in a clear voice that can be heard so your audience does not have to strain to hear.

7. Make sure you do not read too fast.

8. Since you are presenting to an audience, use formal language.

Audience Response

1. Look at the speaker.

2. Turn your body toward the speaker.

3. Listen attentively. Do not let your thoughts wander.

4. Do not distract the speaker or other listeners.

5. Show interest in what the speaker is saying.

6. Silently summarize what the speaker is saying. Take notes if necessary.

7. Ask questions about anything that is not clear.

8. Show appreciation by clapping after the speaker has finished.

clap, clap, clap
clap, clap, clap

Extending the Lesson:
Evaluation and Commentary of a Classmate's Report

Choose a classmate's report for a commentary that you will write in your journal. A commentary is an essay that tells what you think about a person's work or presentation. At the top of a new journal page, write the date and title of your favorite presentation from today. Write a commentary that includes an introduction, a paragraph that tells why you liked the report, a paragraph that tells what you learned from it, and a conclusion.

Evaluation and Commentary of Your Report

Do this part only on the day you give your report. For your own report, write a commentary in your journal that includes the reasons why you liked your topic, some of the most interesting things you learned during your research, and an evaluation of your presentation.

Unit Studies

Table of Contents

Study Skills

The Study Skills with Quigley

Meet Quigley. When Quigley entered third grade, he was very worried. You see, Quigley had always had a huge problem with organization. And in the third grade, organization was very important.

Quigley was a bright student, but sometimes he could not keep up with his work at home or at school. At other times, he would get sidetracked, and he never seemed to have time to finish his schoolwork or do his chores. All this was because he could not get organized. When Quigley was unorganized and unprepared, he was stressed and felt terrible. This resulted in Quigley having **Un-Quigley** days because he was "**Un**-organized."

Sometimes, Quigley would buckle down and get organized and prepared. When he did, he felt in control and had confidence in himself. This resulted in Quigley having **O-Quigley** days because he was "**So**-organized."

Over time, Quigley began to realize that good study habits and good work habits were the keys to making his life easier and happier. The things Quigley learned can make your life easier and happier, too!

As you read about the Un-Quigley day, you will clearly see the trouble that Quigley has with organization. Poor Quigley! Then, Quigley has an O-Quigley day. Yea Quigley! As you study each one of Quigley's days, you will realize that being organized makes a huge difference in Quigley's attitude and the type of day he has.

Now, let's find out what happens to Quigley in the third grade.

Getting Organized

An Un-Quigley Day:

When Quigley Was Not Organized

Quigley walked nervously into the classroom. It was only the second week of school in third grade, and Quigley was already stressed out. Even though he liked his teacher, Ms. Garcia, she expected a lot from her students. Quigley knew that meant he should also learn a lot. Knowing that he would be expected to pull his own load scared Quigley because he was so unorganized and so unsure of himself.

As Ms. Garcia started math class, Quigley tried desperately to pull his math book from the pile of stuff in his desk. He frowned. His desk wasn't big enough! He couldn't find anything, and it was only the second week of school! Finally, he found his math book and some paper, but his paper was so wrinkled that he couldn't even read his math problems after he wrote them. Then, his pencil lead broke, and he didn't have an extra pencil. As he rushed to sharpen his pencil, Ms. Garcia was frowning. He was supposed to have three sharpened pencils in his desk at all times.

Oh, dear! What an awful day he was having! He couldn't wait to get home because one of his favorite movies would be on TV tonight. As he waited for the final bell, Quigley couldn't wait for the school day to end. When the bell finally rang, he rushed outside. He dreaded school, and didn't want to come back! Later, he would realize that he had forgotten to pack the books that he needed for his homework, and he didn't write down any of his homework assignments. What a day!

Discussion Questions:

1. Why was Quigley having such a bad day?

2. How would organizational skills help Quigley?

3. Have you ever gotten yourself into trouble by not being organized? How did it make you feel?

Now, you can learn some ways to improve your organizational skills.

How to Get Organized

Follow these steps to get organized!

1. **Write it down!**
   Keep an assignment notebook to record assignments, page numbers, and due dates.

2. **Put it away!**
   When you put things away, always put them in the same place. If you know where something goes before you put it away, you will already know where it is when you need it again.

3. **Organize your space!**
   Each time you put something in your desk, backpack, or locker, put it exactly where it goes. Avoid "stuffing" things in at random. Start today by having a complete cleanout and fix-up.

4. **Divide and conquer!**
   Keep each subject in a separate folder so that you can find papers easily. Put all folders and notebooks on one side of your desk, and put all textbooks on the other side. Small items should be kept in the front in a zippered bag.

5. **Keep it up!**
   Staying organized is easy if you take just a few minutes *every day* to reorganize. If you don't do it every day, you will get unorganized again in no time.

An O-Quigley Day:
When Quigley Was Organized

Quigley walked happily into the classroom. This was the second week of school in third grade, and Quigley loved every minute of it. He really liked his teacher, Ms. Garcia. She was a good teacher who expected a lot from her students. Quigley liked challenges and was learning a lot.

Quigley kept himself prepared each day. First, he organized his desk and materials so he would not waste time and energy looking for things. Then, he made a study chart so he could get the most done in the scheduled time. Quigley relaxed as Ms. Garcia started math class. He got his math book and math folder from his desk. The folder protected his paper, and he always knew where his math papers were. As he started his math problems, his pencil lead broke. He quickly reached inside his desk and pulled out one that was already sharpened. He was glad Ms. Garcia required three sharpened pencils in their desks at all times.

Wow! What a fantastic day he was having! He loved science class today. He couldn't wait to get home and try the experiment for extra points. As he waited for the final bell, Quigley made sure he had his homework assignments written down and the books and supplies he would need in his book bag. He also included a list of chores his mom wanted him to do. If he did his chores and homework as soon as he got home, he would have time to watch one of his favorite movies on TV tonight. When the bell finally rang, he made sure he had his book bag before he rushed outside. He loved school and couldn't wait to come back! What a day!

Discussion Questions:

1. Why do you think Quigley felt good about his day at school?

2. How does the organized Quigley differ from the unorganized Quigley?

3. How do you think good organizational skills could help you become a better student?

4. What other ideas do you have that would help you become better organized?

Listening

An Un-Quigley Day:
When Quigley Did Not Listen

Quigley had caught a praying mantis and had brought it to school in a large jar this morning. He knew he should be listening as Ms. Garcia explained the new schedule for today, but all he could think about was that praying mantis. It was HUGE! During a study period, Quigley went back to the science table to watch the praying mantis climb a stick. He was deep in thought and did not hear Ms. Garcia make her announcement.

"Line up, boys and girls. We're going for a nature walk."

Quigley didn't even notice everyone leaving the room. "I wonder what he eats?" thought Quigley to himself. He could hardly wait to read about the praying mantis in his insect book. When Quigley finally turned around to ask Ms. Garcia a question, his eyes opened wide in total surprise. His classmates and his teacher were gone! He looked frantically around. "Where is everyone?" he groaned out loud with a sick feeling in his stomach. He was in trouble again for sure. He couldn't understand why he had all the bad luck.

Discussion Questions:

1. Why was Quigley having another bad day?

2. How would listening skills help Quigley?

3. Have you ever wished that you had listened more carefully in a situation?

4. Have you ever felt left behind because you weren't focused? Explain.

Listening and being observant are necessary because you learn most of life's important information by doing both. **Observant** listeners know what is going on around them, and it makes learning easier.

Word Study

The word **observant** comes from the base word **observe** which means **to pay attention carefully with all of your senses.**

Now, you can learn some ways to improve your listening skills.

How to Become a Better Listener

Use these listening skills every day!

Student Tip...

Being a better listener is most important when someone is giving you directions or instructions. Listening and being observant are important skills that you will use all your life.

1. **Listen carefully!** Look directly at the speaker. Listen to every word, and focus your mind on what the speaker is saying. Don't fidget. Hearing happens in your ears, but listening happens in your brain.

2. **Think about it!** Think about what the speaker is saying. Does it make sense? Do you agree or disagree with the speaker's opinion? Can you repeat what the speaker said, but in your own words?

3. **Ask questions!** Try to understand what the speaker is saying. When the speaker says something you don't understand, raise your hand and ask the speaker to explain.

4. **Write it down!** Write down anything that you think you might forget. Write down important information like dates, times, addresses, and so on. Also, write down questions to ask the speaker later.

An O-Quigley Day:
When Quigley Listened Carefully

Quigley couldn't wait for class to begin. He just knew Ms. Garcia would comment on the huge praying mantis that he brought to school this morning. As always, he listened very carefully to everything Ms. Garcia said because she gave a lot of extra information and shared inside jokes if her students were listening. He loved her jokes! Finally, the moment Quigley had been waiting for came at last. Ms. Garcia complimented Quigley on the fine specimen that he had brought to class today. Then, she made a surprise announcement.

"Line up, boys and girls. We're going for a nature walk."

As he waited for the final bell, Quigley smiled happily. What could he say? It had been a fantastic day! Ms. Garcia had even let him show his praying mantis to his classmates and answer their questions. He loved school and couldn't wait to come back!

Discussion Questions:

1. Why was Quigley's day so fun?

2. How do you think listening helped Quigley become a better student?

3. How do you think listening could help you become a better student?

Using Time Wisely

An Un-Quigley Day:
When Quigley Did Not Use His Time Wisely

Since Quigley had so much to do this afternoon, he decided that homework could wait until later. After all, he needed to mow the yard while it was still daylight. After the lawnmower would not start, he suddenly remembered that he forgot to tell Mom that he needed gas for the lawnmower. Oh well! That job would have to wait until Saturday.

Now, he had time for that butterfly chase. Quigley's new net was terrific! He caught a Zebra Swallowtail. By the time he got it mounted and labeled, Mom was calling him to dinner. Then, Quigley decided he would do his homework as he watched a great special on TV about spiders and ants. After the program, Quigley's heart sank as he realized that he had only answered one question and still had a big stack of homework assignments to do. Before Quigley could finish his first assignment, his mother made him go to bed.

The next morning, Quigley looked at his unfinished homework papers scattered all over his desk. Oh, man! He could already see Ms. Garcia frowning and saying, "Quigley, why haven't you finished your homework?" Quigley moaned. He didn't want to go to school today. Why did everything have to happen to him?

Discussion Questions:

1. In what ways did Quigley show that he did not plan his time wisely?

2. How have Quigley's choices affected his day?

3. How would using his time wisely have helped Quigley?

4. Have you ever gotten yourself into trouble by not using your time wisely?

Time is very valuable, so you should never waste it. Proper planning and prioritizing can help you use your time more wisely. Now, you can learn some things to help you plan your time.

How to Use Your Time Wisely

Try these suggestions to make the most of each day!

1. **Plan ahead!**

   If you know you won't have time to do something later, do it now! If you don't have time now, plan to do it at a definite time, not just "later."

2. **Prioritize!**

   "Prioritize" is just a fancy word that means "do the most important thing first." When that is finished, do the next most important thing.

3. **Make a schedule!**

   Write down all of the things you have to do. Write down the time and the day you will do them. Check things off as you finish them.

4. **Think about homework before you leave school!**

   Check your assignment folder and decide what you need to take home. Put books and folders you will need in your book bag. At home, put your finished homework in your book bag, and you will always have it ready to take to school.

5. **Schedule a time and place to study!**

   Think about your family's routine and decide on a good study time away from distractions like TV and conversations. Have all the supplies you will need at your study area. Concentrate on what you are doing. Keep your eyes on your work and your pencil moving until you've finished the task at hand.

An O-Quigley Day:

When Quigley Used His Time Wisely

Quigley was very excited today. It was Friday, and his cousins were coming to visit. They had a full weekend planned, so Quigley knew that he needed to finish as much of his homework as possible. All during the day, Quigley used every free minute to work on his homework. By the end of the day, he only had two short assignments left to do.

As Quigley got ready to go home, he made sure he had his homework assignments written down and the books and supplies he would need in his book bag. He also included a list of chores to finish before his cousins arrived. This was going to be a great weekend, and he didn't want any unfinished jobs to distract him and mess things up.

As he waited for the final bell, Quigley couldn't wipe the grin off his face. He knew he had done a good job at school today, and he was ready for a wonderful weekend. He looked happily around at his friends and his teacher and knew that he would be ready to come back on Monday!

Discussion Questions:

1. What evidence in this story tells you that Quigley used his time wisely?

2. Which of Quigley's choices had a good effect on him?

3. How do you think good study skills have helped Quigley become a better student?

4. In what ways can you relate to Quigley?

5. What other ideas would help you use your time wisely?

Being a Successful Student

Now, you have seen how Quigley had O-Quigley days by using good study skills. As Quigley continues to use good study skills, those skills will become study habits, and he will use them every day without thinking about it. Every day will be an O-Quigley day, and Quigley will become a happier student.

Being a successful student involves more than just how fast you learn.

Most successful students know how to organize their materials, how to listen effectively, and how to make good use of their time. Because they practice good study skills, successful students usually enjoy school.

They pay attention in class and write things down. They take the time to keep their things organized, which makes their lives a lot easier. Good students don't work all the time. Instead, they work very hard so they can have plenty of free time to do fun things.

You are about to evaluate your current study habits. This evaluation is only a tool to help you find out which study skills you need to work on most. As you read each section, decide whether you think your study skills are excellent, average, or poor. Work hard on improving your poor and average study skills, and you should become a better student!

→ **Do you enjoy learning new things at school?**

→ **In your free time, do you feel proud of your finished work, or do you feel anxious because you have unfinished work to do?**

→ **Do you consider yourself a successful student?**

Student Tip...

Remember, study skills are easier when they become study habits. Habits are things you do every day without thinking about them. It usually takes about three or four weeks to turn a practice into a habit.

Study Skills Chart

Name: _____ Date:_____

Directions: Rate your skills in each category by marking the appropriate column with an **X**.

Getting Organized: Reference 2

	Excellent	Average	Poor
1. I write things down	☐	☐	☐
2. I put everything in its place	☐	☐	☐
3. I organize my space	☐	☐	☐
4. I keep subjects in separate folders	☐	☐	☐
5. I spend the time to stay organized	☐	☐	☐

Listening: Reference 3

	Excellent	Average	Poor
1. I listen carefully	☐	☐	☐
2. I think about what I hear	☐	☐	☐
3. I ask questions when I don't understand	☐	☐	☐
4. I write down important details	☐	☐	☐

Using Your Time Wisely: Reference 4

	Excellent	Average	Poor
1. I plan ahead	☐	☐	☐
2. I do important things first—prioritize	☐	☐	☐
3. I write down everything I have to do	☐	☐	☐
4. I take home what I need for homework	☐	☐	☐
5. I schedule a time and place to study	☐	☐	☐

If you marked any areas as "Average" or "Poor," look back at the references in those areas to help you find ways to improve. Find a study-skills partner to check your progress, to encourage you, and to give you advice and help.

ACTIVITY With the results of your Study-Skills Chart in mind, write a paragraph about your study skills. Include your study-skills strengths and weaknesses, as well as ideas for improving your weak areas and making full use of your strong areas.

To learn good
study habits:
**MAKE
A PLAN.**

STUDY PLANS

When you set a goal, think of that goal as the destination of your journey. You need a map to show you how to get there.

Your PLAN is that map.

To make a plan, just write down all of the steps you will need to achieve your goal. To follow a plan, simply do each step in the plan. You may want to check the steps off as you complete them.

A Plan for Organizing Schoolwork

If organization is your goal, use this plan to help you achieve it!

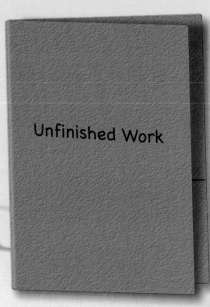

Unfinished Work

1. Decide where all of your school supplies will go and keep them in some kind of container. Keep it handy, and label it with your name and a list of what is inside.

2. Make a folder labeled **Unfinished Work**. Put all of your unfinished work for every subject in this folder so you can find it easily when you have time to work.

unday	Monday	Tuesday	Wednesday	Thursda
	1	2	3	4

3. Make several folders labeled **Finished Work**, using different colors for each subject. Put your finished work for each subject in the correct folder so that you will know where it is when your teacher asks for it. In one side of each of these subject folders, put your class notes, study guides, and other papers your teacher gives you, so you can find them later to study for tests.

4. Make a folder labeled **Progress**. Put graded work in this folder for your parents to view. The papers sent home in the Progress folder will help you and your parents keep track of your grades.

5. Make a folder labeled **Paper** to store your used and unused paper. Place clean sheets of unused paper in one pocket and keep it full at all times. Put scrap papers that need to be recycled in the other pocket. Empty this pocket at the end of every day. Do not stuff scrap paper in your subject folders or your desk!

6. Have a notebook labeled **Assignments**. Write down every assignment that your teacher gives you in this notebook. Include the day's date and the date the assignment is due. Check your assignment notebook whenever you have free time throughout the day and before you leave school in the afternoon.

Remember that a plan is the map to your goals. One of the best plans you can make is a daily routine. Doing the same thing every day will help you break bad habits and form good habits more quickly.

A Plan for a Daily Routine at School

Start your day the right way with this plan.

1. Always be on time; try to be early when you can.

2. Turn everything in on time. If you are absent, ask about make-up work and turn it in on time.

3. Develop a positive attitude. Every day, you are learning new things and improving your mind.

4. Keep your area organized.

5. Make the effort to listen.

6. Concentrate on what you're doing and use your time wisely.

7. Write it down! Write it down! Write it down! Make a habit of taking notes in class. Put the notes in the correct subject folder.

8. Be "in-the-know." Know what's on your "to-do" list, on your calendar, and in your assignment notebook.

9. Think before you leave school! Check your assignment notebook and decide what you need to take home. Put the books and folders you will need in your backpack so you won't forget them.

Your daily routine is just as important at home as it is at school. You are still a student, even when you get home.

A Plan for a Daily Routine at Home

Stick to this plan every evening!

1. Check your assignment notebook as soon as you get home. Use it to plan your evening.

2. Study a little bit every night. Don't wait until the last minute to study for a test. Studying is homework, too.

3. Schedule a time to study and do homework. Choose a study time based on your family's routine.

4. Use your study time for reviewing the day's lessons, completing assignments, or studying for a test.

5. Find a quiet place. Your studying area should be a DFZ (Distraction-Free Zone). Keep your homework and supplies in your study area.

6. Concentrate one hundred percent on your work. Don't let your mind wander. You'll be amazed how much you can accomplish in a short amount of time.

7. Set a time limit. Use a timer to see how long you can work without getting distracted; then, challenge yourself to concentrate even longer next time.

8. Discuss your progress and problems with your parents. Evaluate your own progress, and ask for your parents' input. Work hard to improve each of your study skills. You will get better!

Letter Writing

Friendly Letters

The Information Age has changed how we communicate with family and friends, so sending a handwritten letter, or a reply to one, is both rare and special. Although social networking sites and e-mail are immediate forms of keeping in touch with others, handwritten letters remain a great way to communicate with people you care about.

Tips for Writing Friendly Letters

A friendly letter is *a letter between friends or relatives.*
When you write a friendly letter…

➜ Write as if you were talking to the person face to face. For instance, you might tell stories or jokes, or you might share photographs, articles, or drawings.

➜ Don't write unkind things about the person you are writing to or about anyone else.

➜ If you are writing a return letter, be sure your letter is a good reply to the original letter. Repeat any question that was asked, and answer it appropriately.

➜ End your letter in a positive way so that your reader will want to write a return letter. One good way to ensure that you will get a letter in return is to ask a question or two at the end of your letter.

➜ The language used in a friendly letter is conversational and informal, but conventions of spelling, capitalization, and sentence structure are still important. Nobody wants a letter they can't understand.

The Five Parts of a Friendly Letter

The five parts of a friendly letter are the **heading**, **greeting (salutation)**, **body**, **closing**, and **signature**.

1. Heading

The heading is the full address of the writer of the letter, followed by the full date of the day the letter is written.

➡ Examples: 145 North Front Street
Midland, TX 79712
March 2, 2013

2. Greeting

The greeting is the salutation of a friendly letter. The greeting allows you to begin a letter without being abrupt. It's the written version of saying "hello" before starting a conversation. It always begins with the word *Dear* (capitalized), names the person receiving the letter, and ends with a comma.

➡ Examples: Dear Aunt Maria,

3. Body

The body is the main part of the letter. It is the conversation area of the letter. This is where you write what you want to say to the person receiving the letter. The body is made of one or more paragraphs.

4. Closing

The closing is a personal phrase at the end of the letter that lets the reader know the letter is over. It allows you to end the letter without being abrupt. It's the written version of saying "goodbye" before walking away. It always begins with a capital letter and ends with a comma.

➡ Examples: Your niece,

5. Signature

The signature provides a personal touch to the letter while also showing who wrote it. Your signature is your unique way of writing your name, usually in cursive. In a friendly letter, the signature is usually just your first name.

➡ Examples: *Lucy*

Example of a Friendly Letter

Friendly Letter Style
Start the heading, closing, and signature near the middle of the page. Indent each paragraph in the body and do not skip a line between paragraphs.

1. Heading:
- P.O. Box or Street Address of the writer
- City, State, and Zip Code of the writer
- Full date the letter was writte

2. Greeting (Salutation):
- Begins with **Dear**
- Names the person receiving the letter
- Ends in a comma

145 North Front Street
Midland, TX 79712
March 2, 2013

Dear Aunt Maria,

    I'm learning to write friendly letters in school. I think it would be fun to write each other, and it will help me practice my letter-writing skills.
    I hope we can write each other at least once a week. I have lots of family news that I will share in my next letter. I can hardly wait to get my first letter from you!

Your niece,
Lucy

3. Body:
- Indent paragraphs

4. Closing:
- Your choice of personal phrase
- Capitalize first word
- Ends in a comma

5. Signature:
- Names the writer of the letter
- Usually written in cursive

Addressing an Envelope

In order for the person to receive his or her letter, you have to send it in the mail. There are certain rules you must follow when addressing an envelope to be mailed.

Addressing an Envelope

Return Address

The return address goes in the upper-left corner on the front of the envelope and includes the following:

1. Name of the writer of the letter
2. P.O. box or street address of the writer
3. City, state, and zip code of the writer

Mailing Address

The mailing address goes in the center of the envelope and includes the following:

1. Full name of the person receiving the letter
2. P.O. box or street address of the person
3. City, state, and zip code of the person

Postage Stamp

The postage stamp goes in the upper-right corner of the envelope.

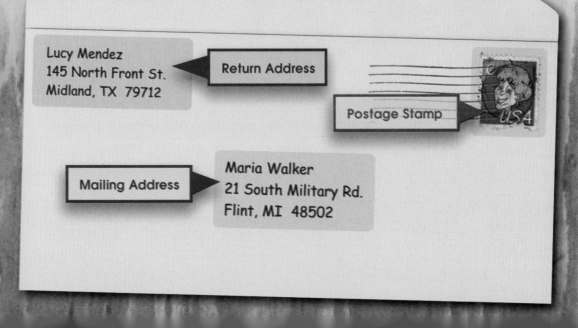

Lucy Mendez
145 North Front St.
Midland, TX 79712

Return Address

Postage Stamp

Mailing Address

Maria Walker
21 South Military Rd.
Flint, MI 48502

Knowing commonly used abbreviations is useful in letter writing.

Commonly Used Abbreviations

Postal Abbreviations for States

Alabama	AL	New Hampshire	NH
Alaska	AK	New Jersey	NJ
Arizona	AZ	New Mexico	NM
Arkansas	AR	New York	NY
California	CA	North Carolina	NC
Colorado	CO	North Dakota	ND
Connecticut	CT	Ohio	OH
Delaware	DE	Oklahoma	OK
Florida	FL	Oregon	OR
Georgia	GA	Pennsylvania	PA
Hawaii	HI	Rhode Island	RI
Idaho	ID	South Carolina	SC
Illinois	IL	South Dakota	SD
Indiana	IN	Tennessee	TN
Iowa	IA	Texas	TX
Kansas	KS	Utah	UT
Kentucky	KY	Vermont	VT
Louisiana	LA	Virginia	VA
Maine	ME	Washington	WA
Maryland	MD	West Virginia	WV
Massachusetts	MA	Wisconsin	WI
Michigan	MI	Wyoming	WY
Minnesota	MN		
Mississippi	MS		
Missouri	MO		
Montana	MT		
Nebraska	NE		
Nevada	NV		

Addresses

Apartment	Apt.
Avenue	Ave.
Building	Bldg.
Boulevard	Blvd.
Circle	Cir.
County	Co.
Court	Ct.
Drive	Dr.
Fort	Ft.
Headquarters	Hq.
Highway	Hwy.
Lane	Ln.
Mount	Mt.
Mountain	Mt./Mtn.
Parkway	Pkwy.
Place	Pl.
Point	Pt.
Post Office	P.O./PO
Road	Rd.
Route	Rt.
School	Sch.
Street	St.
Terrace	Terr./Ter.
University	Univ.

Directions

Direction	Abbr.	Direction	Abbr.
North	N	Northeast	NE
South	S	Northwest	NW
East	E	Southeast	SE
West	W	Southwest	SW

Days

Monday	Mon.
Tuesday	Tues.
Wednesday	Wed.
Thursday	Thurs.
Friday	Fri.
Saturday	Sat.
Sunday	Sun.

Titles

Attorney	Atty.
Doctor	Dr.
Governor	Gov.
Honorable	Hon.
Junior	Jr.
Manager	Mgr.
Miss/Mistress	Ms.
Missus/Mistress	Mrs.
Mister	Mr.
President	Pres.
Professor	Prof.
Representative	Rep.
Reverend	Rev.
Senator	Sen.
Senior	Sr.
Superintendent	Supt.

Business Titles

Company	Co.
Corporation	Corp.
Department	Dept.
Incorporated	Inc.

Military Titles

Admiral	Adm.
Captain	Capt.
Colonel	Col.
Commander	Cmdr.
Corporal	Cpl.
Ensign	Ens.
General	Gen.
Lieutenant	Lt.
Major	Maj.
Private	Pvt.
Sergeant	Sgt.
Specialist	Spec.

Months

January	Jan.
February	Feb.
March	Mar.
April	Apr.
May	—
June	—
July	—
August	Aug.
September	Sept.
October	Oct.
November	Nov.
December	Dec.

Math Abbreviations

foot	ft.
hour	hr.
inch	in.
mile	mi.
minute	min.
month	mo.
ounce	oz.
pint	pt.
pound	lb.
quart	qt.
second	sec.
week	wk.
yard	yd.
year	yr.

Others

District of Columbia	D.C./DC
afternoon	p.m.
before noon	a.m.

Thank-You Notes

A special kind of friendly letter is the thank-you note. A well-written and properly timed thank-you note is the proper response whenever anyone goes out of his or her way to do something nice for you. Writing a good thank-you note is simple. Keep the note short and tell the person three things:

1. Tell what specific gift or action you are thanking the person for.

2. Tell how the gift or action benefited you (brightened your day, changed your life).

3. Tell the person you appreciated the gift or action.

REMEMBER: Keep the note short and positive and use specific language. To format your note, use the same five parts that you use in any friendly letter: **heading**, **greeting**, **body**, **closing**, and **signature**.

Thank-You Notes

Gift Thank-You Note Example

112 Luke Road
Glenwood, TN 3724[
August 30, 2013

Dear Aunt Pam,

Thank you for the bottle-shaped bank. It's j[
what I needed to help me save my allowance! I rea[
appreciate your thoughtful birthday gift.

Your nephew,
Jackson

Action Thank-You Note Example

456 Concord Street
East Plains, MD 20115
March 6, 2013

Dear Mr. Travis,

Thank you for speaking to our class about fire safety. We learned so much during your talk, and we enjoyed touring and riding the fire truck. I want to be a firefighter when I grow up.

Your friend,
Carl

Writing Assignment

Writing Assignment:
Writing a Friendly Letter or Thank-You Note to Your Parents

SPECIAL INSTRUCTIONS:

1. Write a friendly letter or thank-you note to your parents. Follow the conventions of capitalization and punctuation and format your letter correctly. For the heading, use your school address as the return address.

2. When your letter is finished, read it carefully for convention errors. Once you have revised and edited the letter, fold it up and place it in your envelope.

3. Address the envelope, using your home address as the mailing address and your school address as the return address.

4. Draw a stamp on your envelope.

5. Have your teacher check your letter. Then, deliver the letter to your parents.

Student Tip...

Rules to remember when you write friendly letters or thank-you notes:

→ Capitalize the first word in the greeting (salutation) of a letter.

→ Use a comma after the greeting (salutation).

→ Indent each paragraph in the body of a letter.

→ Capitalize the first word in the closing of a letter.

→ Use a comma after the closing.

Review Questions

1. What kind of letter is written to or received from friends or relatives?

2. What are the five parts of a friendly letter?

3. What two kinds of addresses are used for an envelope?

4. What information is contained in the heading?

5. What punctuation mark is used after the greeting in a friendly letter?

6. Whose name appears in the greeting?

7. Why do you write a thank-you note?

Guided Practice

Even though the person receiving your letter is a friend or relative, you want to keep their respect when they read it. Do your best not to make mistakes in capitalization, punctuation, and spelling. The friendly letter for the Guided Practice contains many errors. Can you find and correct them?

Directions: Write the capitalization and punctuation corrections only.
**Editing Guide: End Marks: 4   Capitals: 18   Commas: 7
Apostrophes: 1**

228 flower drive

chicago il 00003

march 22 2_____

dear grandmother

    our plane leaves for tokyo japan on monday april 2 this will be an exciting trip i wish you could go with us ill write again soon

love

andy

Directions: Find Andy's address in the friendly letter and use it to address the envelope. Use your own address for Betty's address.

Andy Taylor

_____

_____

Betty Taylor

_____

_____

Classroom Activity for the Friendly Letter

First, glue the friendly letter below onto cardstock or construction paper. Next, cut the sections apart at the dotted lines. Then, glue or write the number and the title for each friendly-letter part on the back of the corresponding strip.

Divide into teams. Time each team as members put the pieces of the friendly-letter puzzle together and identify each part. Check the correct answers with the number and title on the back of each piece. The team that completes the puzzle correctly in the shortest time is the winner.

Friendly Letter

Titles: 1. Heading   2. Greeting or Salutation   3. Body   4. Closing   5. Signature

772 Queens Avenue
Goldberg, OH 00004
June 20, 20—

Dear Uncle Frank,

    Our new colts are wonderful. I can't wait for you to see them. In fact, we've named one of them Frankie, after you. I'm looking forward to seeing you in July.

Your nephew,

Roger

Invitations

With all the commercial cards available today, the art of writing personal, unique, and individual invitations is almost obsolete. However, learning to write invitations is an important skill. An invitation should follow the same form as a friendly letter: *heading, greeting, body, closing,* and *signature.*

Before you begin writing an invitation, it helps to make an outline that includes specific information (what, who, where, when) in any logical order. Study the example of the outline and the invitation below.

An invitation will sometimes contain an RSVP. This is an acronym for a French expression that means "please respond," and a reply is needed. If a phone number is included, reply by phone. Otherwise, a written reply is expected.

Invitation Outline

1. **What** . . . . Tell what the event or special occasion is. . . . . A pizza party
2. **Who** . . . . Tell whom the event is for. . . . . For Maria Lopez
3. **Where** . . . . Tell where the event will take place. . . . . At 13 Linda Lane
4. **When** . . . . Tell the date and time of the event. . . . . On Friday, July 22, at 6:00
5. **Whipped Cream** . . . . A polite statement written to make the person feel welcome. . . . We hope to see you there!

Sample Invitation

> 13 Linda Lane
> Brinkley, Arkansas 00003
> July 17, 20—
>
> Dear Tina,
>
> You are invited to a pizza party in honor of Maria Lopez. She has recently won a state art award. The party is at 6:00 on July 22, at our house on 13 Linda Lane. Lots of games are planned. We hope to see you there!
>
> Your friend,
> Jan and Dan Miller

✓ Check Your Understanding
Why do you send an invitation?

HANDS-ON ACTIVITIES

1. **Writing Connection:** Pretend you are giving a party or other event. First, make an invitation outline. Then, write, revise, edit, and illustrate an invitation for your event. (Ideas: costume or theme party, food-tasting party, sports party, book-club meeting, science/history/math/Spanish-club meeting, movie party, etc.)

2. **Literature Connection:** Create an invitation to ask your friends or family to join a book club.

3. **Social Studies/Science Connection:** Pretend you are having a show to display some of your science or social studies projects. Create an invitation to encourage your family and friends to attend.

Types of Business Letters

Not every letter you write should be as casual and informal as a friendly letter. When you write a letter about things that are serious or not personal, or when you must write a letter to someone you do not know, the voice and tone of your writing will be different. You will use your "business" voice by writing a business letter.

Four Types of Business Letters

1. Letter of Inquiry

Written when you want to ask for information
→ Be very clear about the information or answers you need.

2. Letter of Request or Order

Written when you want to purchase a product by mail
→ Be very clear about the product you wish to purchase.
→ Include information about how and where the product should be shipped and how you will pay for it.

3. Letter of Complaint

Written when you want to complain to a company about a product you have purchased
→ Be very clear about the product you want to complain about.
→ Describe the problem and what may have caused it.
→ Explain any actions you have already taken to solve the problem.
→ End your letter with a short explanation of what you would like the company to do to solve the problem.

4. Letter to an Editor or Official

Written when you want to express your opinion to the public or to the government
→ Be very clear about the situation you want to express an opinion about.
→ Offer your opinion, along with facts and examples to back it up.
→ Suggest possible causes for the situation, as well as your ideas for solving or improving it.

In any business letter, no matter its purpose, your reader will not have much time to read your letter, so always keep business letters short and to the point. Also, no matter what opinion you are expressing, always be polite and courteous.

Parts of a Business Letter

Business letters have six parts, and each part has a purpose and a specific placement on the page.

The Six Parts of a Business Letter

The six parts of a business letter are the **heading**, **inside address**, **salutation**, **body**, **closing**, and **signature**.

1. Heading

The heading is the full address of the writer of the letter, followed by the date the letter is written. Begin the heading about an inch from the top in the middle of the page.

2. Inside Address

The inside address includes the full name and address of the person and/or company receiving the letter. If the person has a title at the company, it should be placed after his/her name, separated by a comma. If the title is two or more words, place the title on the next line. Leave three blank lines between the heading and inside address.

➡ Examples: Mr. Clint Matthews, Sales
The Movie Warehouse
4200 Broadway
Buffalo, NY 14203

3. Greeting (Salutation)

The greeting of a business letter is formal. It should begin with Dear (capitalized) and end with a colon after the person's name or title. Leave one blank line between the inside address and the greeting.

➡ Examples: Mr. Matthews:

4. Body

The body is the main part of the letter. The information in the body should be clearly and briefly written. Leave one blank line between the greeting and the body.

5. Closing

The closing is a formal phrase that closes a business letter (*Very truly, Respectfully, Sincerely*). Place a comma at the end of the closing. Leave one blank line between the body and the closing. Begin the closing in the middle of the page. It should line up with the heading.

➡ Examples: Sincerely,   Best regards,

6. Signature

The signature shows who wrote the letter. The signature is your unique way of writing your name, usually in cursive. Leave three blank lines below the closing. Then, print your full name. Next, sign your name in ink above your printed name. If you are typing your letter, type your full name three blank lines beneath your closing and sign your name between the closing and your typed name.

> **Student Tip...**
> To find the middle of the page for your heading, closing, and signature, just fold your paper in half, lengthwise. When you unfold it, the crease will be in the middle.

Example Business Letter

1. Heading:
- P.O. Box or Street Address of the writer
- City, State, and Zip Code of the writer
- Full date the letter was written

106 Oak Street
Buffalo, NY 14203
November 29, 2013

Mr. Clint Matthews, Sales
The Movie Warehouse
4200 Broadway
Buffalo, NY 14203

2. Inside Address
- Full name and title of person receiving the letter
- Name of the company
- Address of the company

3. Formal Greeting (Salutation):
- Begins with **Dear**
- Names the person receiving the letter
- Ends in a colon

Dear Mr. Matthews:

The copy of *Robot Samurai Rabbits* that I rented from you on November 28th was damaged and would not play. I tried cleaning the disc, but it still did not work. I would like a refund for this movie rental. Thank you.

Sincerely,

Harry Hughes
Harry Hughes

4. Body:
- Indent paragraphs

5. Formal Closing:
- Capitalize first word
- Put a comma after closing

6. Signature:
- Name of the writer
- Written in cursive
- Printed or typed below signed name

Addressing a Business Envelope

There are certain rules you must follow when addressing a business letter to be mailed.

Parts of a Business Envelope

Return Address

The return address goes in the upper-left corner on the front of the envelope and includes the following:
1. Name of the writer of the letter
2. P.O. box or street address of the writer
3. City, state, and zip code of the writer

Student Note:

The Return Address should be the same as the address in the Heading of the letter. The Mailing Address should be the same as the Inside Address of the letter.

Mailing Address

The mailing address goes in the center of the envelope and includes the following:
1. Name and title of the person or department* receiving the letter, if known
2. Name of the company receiving the letter
3. Street address of the company receiving the letter
4. City, state, and zip code of the company receiving the letter

(*department: Sales, Shipping, Accounting, etc.)

Postage Stamp

The postage stamp goes in the upper-right corner of the envelope.

Harry Hughes
106 Oak Street
Buffalo, NY 14203

Return Address

Postage Stamp

Mailing Address

Mr. Clint Matthews, Sales
The Movie Warehouse
4200 Broadway
Buffalo, NY 14203

Review Questions

1. What kind of letter is written about something that is not personal in nature?

2. What are the four types of business letters?

3. What are the six parts of a business letter?

4. What information that is not contained in a friendly letter is added to the business letter?

5. What information is included in the inside address?

6. What two kinds of addresses are used for a business envelope?

7. What extra information is added to the mailing addresses of the business envelope?

8. What punctuation mark is used after the greeting in a business letter?

9. How should a business letter be signed?

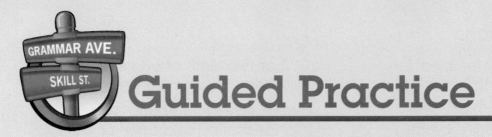

Guided Practice

You want the person receiving your business letter to take you and your letter seriously. Mistakes in capitalization, punctuation, and spelling could ruin your message. Many business people will simply throw away a letter at the first sign of an error. This is why you must edit business letters very carefully. The business letter in the Guided Practice contains many errors. Can you find and correct them?

Directions: Write the capitalization and punctuation corrections only.
Editing Guide: End Marks: 3   Capitals: 28   Commas: 4
Colons: 1   Periods: 6

po box 58

tampa fl 00011

march 21 2013

mr tony smith

37 north ave

austin tx 00099

dear mr smith

i am interested in the two week tour of mars and venus would you send me the pamphlets on these planets i would also like to make flight plans for july 15

sincerely yours

john t thomas

Envelope for Business Letter

Directions: Use the addresses in the business letter to address the envelope correctly.

John T. Thomas

_____

_____

USA

Mr. Tony Smith

_____

_____

Writing Assignment

Writing Assignment:
Writing a Business Letter to Your Principal

SPECIAL INSTRUCTIONS:

1. Write a business letter to your principal. Follow the conventions of capitalization and punctuation and format your letter correctly. For the heading, use your school address as the return address.

2. When your letter is finished, read it carefully for convention errors. Once you have revised and edited the letter, fold it and place it in your envelope.

3. Address the envelope, using your school address as your principal's mailing address and as the return address.

4. Draw a stamp on your envelope.

5. Have your teacher check your letter. Then, deliver the letter to your principal.

Student Tip...

Rules to remember when you write business letters:

→ Have a heading and inside address

→ Use a formal greeting

→ Use a colon after the greeting (salutation).

→ Indent each paragraph of a business letter.

→ Use a formal closing.

→ Print or typed name below signed name.

Classroom Activity for the Business Letter

First, glue the business letter below onto cardstock or construction paper. Next, cut the sections apart at the dotted lines. Then, glue or write the number and the title for each business-letter part on the back of the corresponding strip.

Divide into teams. Time each team as members put the pieces of the business-letter puzzle together and identify each part. Check the correct answers with the number and title on the back of each piece. The team that completes the puzzle correctly in the shortest time is the winner.

Business Letter

Titles: | 1. Heading | 2. Inside Address | 3. Salutation | 4. Body | 5. Closing | 6. Signature

756 Beech Road
Lawton, OK 00016
August 9, 20——

Senator Bill Holt
15 Fifth Avenue
Stillwell, OK 00097

Dear Senator Holt:

I am glad you are supporting the parks and wildlife in our area. Keep up the good work.

Sincerely yours,

Chris Brown
Chris Brown

Friendly-Letter Placement

Use the letter parts below to fill in the blanks of the friendly letter.

TITLE PARTS of a Friendly Letter:

Closing   **Signature**   **Heading**

Greeting   **Body**

SAMPLE PARTS of a Friendly Letter:

William   Dear Joey,   Pine Grove, TX 00067

Your friend,   May 3, 20___   208 Valley Drive

We want you to visit us soon. We will go fishing, have picnics, and ride our motorcycles. It will be a great summer break! Write back when you can.

Friendly Letter

1. Title: _____

3. Title: _____

4. Title: _____

5. Title: _____

6. Title: _____

Editing Practice

Directions: Write the capitalization and punctuation corrections only.

Editing Guide: End Marks: 6   Capitals: 28   Commas: 4

25 kingston road

new york city ny 00004

june 13 20____

dear mom and dad

    i am having a great time aunt sara and i are doing something new every day we went to the statue of liberty yesterday it was wonderful we are going to the rainbow chocolate company this afternoon we will spend the day at the atlantic ocean tomorrow

love you

holly

Editing Practice

Directions: Write the capitalization and punctuation corrections only.
Editing Guide: **End Marks: 6 Capitals: 17 Commas: 5 Apostrophes: 1**

408 linda lane

springhill ar 00287

october 14 20____

dear joseph

it was great to hear from you i will send you a picture of james and me riding our new fourwheeler we ve never had as much fun except for the times you were with us we put a new roof on the barn last week now the horses will have a dry place write soon

your cousin

waylon

Test

1616 tower lane

springfield mo 00054

may 3 2013

dear grandpa

i can t wait until our vacation this summer i know i will like staying at your house in dallas it will be fun to go to six flags over texas and to visit the stockyards in fort worth with you i ll bring my camera and lots of film we ll see you next month

with love

nick

Business-Letter Placement

Directions: Use the letter parts below to fill in the blanks of the business letter.

TITLE PARTS of a Business Letter:

Closing	Signature	Heading
Salutation	Body	Inside Address

SAMPLE PARTS of a Business Letter:

Sincerely yours,   Megan Wells   Wiggins Center
                                                141 Lincoln Street

Dear Sir or Madam: 66 Twin Oaks Avenue Chicago, IL 00060
May 13, 20—   Lewis Springs, IA 00012

I am interested in your new math games for computers. I am looking for something to help me with math facts. I am in the third grade. Please send me a catalog and a price list.

Business Letter

1. Title: _____

2. Title: _____

3. Title: _____

4. Title: _____

5. Title: _____

6. Title: _____

Editing Practice

Directions: Write the capitalization and punctuation corrections only.
Editing Guide: End Marks: 4   Capitals: 30   Commas: 6
Periods: 7   Colons: 1

po box 89

oklahoma city ok 00106

june 3 20____

mr jw rockwell

725 north ave

knoxville tn 00021

dear mr rockwell

    i want to enter my dog in your contest his name is jefferson jefferson saved matthew my little brother from drowning in our neighbors pool i love jefferson very much

sincerely yours

mary alexander

Editing Practice

Directions: Write the capitalization and punctuation corrections only.
Editing Guide: End Marks: 4   Capitals: 25   Commas: 4   Colons: 1

1213 pine street

harrison mo 00066

august 10 20_____

harper music company

4312 slate drive

penney nc 00192

dear sir or madam

    my sister bought a music box made by your company i would like to buy one also but the store where she bought hers no longer sells them can you tell me where i might find one thank you for your help

        sincerely

        sara barnes

Test

119 river ridge road

york pa 00200

april 5 20_____

joplin visitors center

602 s main street

joplin mo 00682

dear sir or madam

    i am excited about visiting your city the last two weeks in june for the airshow i have looked at your website and i am very interested in visiting three other attractions could you send information on the frisco greenway trail the reptile world zoo and the mineral museum thank you for your help

sincerely

elaine nelson

Elaine Nelson

Poetry

Poetry Elements

Poetry is a special form of literature that allows you to express emotions or experiences directly through words. A poet does not write *about* emotions or experiences, but pours them directly onto the page in such a way that the listener *feels* the emotions, too. Poetry is a direct and very powerful connection from the poet's heart to the listener's.

A poet is like a musician who uses words instead of musical notes. A musician can turn basic sounds into beautiful and moving pieces of art. A poet can do the same with words and sentences. And, just like music, a poem can be written on paper, but you need to listen to it to experience it fully.

Poetry is one of the oldest forms of literature. It is very compact and focused: each word in a poem is packed with meaning. In fact, many poets carefully choose each word for the effect its meaning and sound will have on their listeners. Poets choose words that will bring about sensory images in the imagination and emotional responses in the heart.

The words in a poem are grouped into **lines** of poetry, and the lines are grouped into one or more **stanzas**. When reading a poem out loud, you should pause briefly between stanzas and whenever you see a punctuation mark, such as a comma or a period.

Poetry Strategy: Sound Devices

Some poems contain **sound devices**, special tools the poet can use to create certain effects in the poem. There are four main sound devices: repetition, rhyme, alliteration, and assonance.

1. **Repetition** is the repeating of any words, phrases, sentences, or lines within a poem.

2. **Rhyme** is the matching vowel sounds at the end of words or lines.
   Example: **me, see** (**long e sounds**)

3. **Alliteration** is the repetition of the consonant sounds at the beginning of words.
   Example: **Five feathered pheasants** (**f sounds**)

4. **Assonance** is the repetition of vowel sounds within words.
   Example: **Long, low moan** (**o sounds**)

Figurative Language

Poetry often says things in a special way by using figurative language. **Figurative language** uses words to draw mental pictures of things being compared. There are three figures of speech that create images that compare one thing to another. They are *simile*, *metaphor*, and *personification*.

Simile compares two or more things by using the words **like** or **as**.

Examples:

➡ That candy is **as** hard **as** a rock.   ➡ My sister is **as** fast **as** the wind.   ➡ Kelly is sleeping **like** a baby.

Metaphor compares things by stating that one thing is something else. It uses linking verbs such as **am**, **is**, **are**, **was**, and **were**.

Examples:

➡ Dan's **strength is a rock** for his family.   ➡ The **snowfall was a blanket** over the earth.

Personification compares things by giving human qualities to something nonhuman.

Examples:

➡ The large oak **tree waved its arms** in the air.

Afternoon on a Hill

I will be the gladdest thing
Under the sun!
I will touch a hundred flowers
And not pick one.

I will look at cliffs and clouds
With quiet eyes,
Watch the wind bow down
the grass,
And the grass rise.

And when lights begin to show
Up from the town,
I will mark which must be mine
And then start down!

—Edna St. Vincent Millay

Discussion Questions for Afternoon on a Hill:

1. Who is the author of the poem, "Afternoon on a Hill"?

2. How many stanzas are in the poem?

3. In this poem, what does the wind do to the grass?

   a. parts it in unfamiliar patterns

   b. eats it on its way to the valleys

   c. bends it down, then allows it to rise again

4. How do you think the person in this poem feels about nature? Which line(s) and words from the poem helped you understand how the person feels about nature?

5. How many flowers does the narrator take home with her at evening time?
   a. six　　　　b. a dozen
   c. a handful　d. none

6. Why do you think the person in the poem does not pick the flowers?

7. Does the poem, "Afternoon on a Hill," use sound devices?

8. What are some examples of *rhyme*?

9. What are some examples of *alliteration*?

10. What are some examples of *assonance*?

11. What are some examples of *repetition*?

12. What does the word *contrasting* mean?

13. Discuss the contrasting elements in each stanza of this poem.

14. Describe what you think the hill looks like in the afternoon after reading this poem.

Comprehension Strategy: Mood in Stories, Poems, and Illustrations

Authors, poets, and illustrators use words and pictures to make you, the reader, feel a certain way about what you are reading. How you feel when you read a story or poem or see an illustration is called mood. You can even detect mood in the type of music that movie producers use in their motion pictures. How does the poem "Afternoon on a Hill" make you feel? Which words in the poem make you feel this way? Now, look at the illustration. How does the picture help create a mood for the poem?

Guidelines for Reading Poetry Aloud

Whenever you are asked to read aloud, you should always read with expression. This means making your speech sound interesting and using the tone of your voice to help your audience to comprehend the material better. This is true no matter what you're reading, be it a poem, a story, an essay, or even the definition of a word.

Writing Assignment

Choose one of the writing assignments below.

PROMPT 1

1. You have been studying a poem by Edna St. Vincent Millay. Look up more information about her, using the Internet, a poetry reference, and/or an encyclopedia. Write an informational paragraph that includes the following information:

Introduction: Tell who Edna St. Vincent Millay was and what she did.

Body: Tell one or more important or unusual facts about Edna St. Vincent Millay's early life.

Tell one or more important or unusual facts about Edna St. Vincent Millay's later life.

Mention one or more important works written by Edna St. Vincent Millay.

Conclusion: Give a summary, or wrap-up, of what you said about Edna St. Vincent Millay 's life.

PROMPT 2 In "Afternoon on a Hill," Edna St. Vincent Millay described her afternoon on a hill. Can you see what the hill looks like in the afternoon after reading this poem? Think of your favorite place. What makes it special? Think about how you would describe it. Write a poem in which you describe that place so others can see why it is special to you.

Extending the Lesson:
Enjoying Poetry

Use the resources in the library or on the Internet to look up poems by poets Dorothy Aldis and Maya Angelou. Pick out the poem you like the best and answer the following questions.

- Why do you like this poem?

- What do you think this poem is about (interpretation)?

- How is this poem similar to another poem or story you have read? Is there anything about this poem that reminds you of a personal experience?

- Give examples of some sound devices that were used in the poem.

- Read the poem aloud and discuss it with a partner. What does your partner think about the poem?

- With your partner, discuss what you like or dislike about the writing style of this poet.

- Compare the style of your favorite poet to the style of your friend's favorite poet.

Meter

Poetry is more like music than you may realize. Music and poetry are both artistic ways of organizing sounds. The sounds of the words in a line of poetry make a rhythm that is similar to the rhythm in music—the steady heartbeat underneath the other sounds. In poetry, this rhythm is established by stressed and unstressed syllables. The *pattern of stressed and unstressed syllables in a poem* is called its **meter**.

To understand meter, you have to *see* and *hear* it.

Look at the line of poetry below.

I will **be** the **glad**dest **thing**
Under the **sun**!

You can see the stressed and unstressed syllables. Read the line, stressing only the bold syllables. Can you hear the meter? Now, read the line below, stressing the bold syllables. Notice that the first two syllables are unstressed.

I will **touch** a **hun**dred **flowers**
And **not** pick **one**.

This line follows a similar—but slightly different—pattern from the line before it. Little variations like this keep the rhythm fun and exciting. As a class, read the first stanza of "Afternoon on a Hill," paying careful attention to the meter of the poem.

Afternoon on a Hill

I will **look** at **cliffs** and **clouds**

With quiet **eyes**,

Watch the **wind** bow
down the **grass**,

And the **grass rise**.

And when **lights** begin to **show**

Up from the **town**,

I will **mark** which **must** be **mine**

And then **start down**!

Reading Poetry Aloud

Reading poetry aloud can be fun,
especially if you **take the time to do it right**.

Practice ahead of time.

Read through the poem several times, pronouncing each word very
carefully and slowly at first.

Understand the poem.

If you know the meaning of the poem, you can use the inflections
of your voice effectively.

Read the following poems aloud, using the guidelines above.

A **couplet** has two lines that rhyme. Some poems are written
entirely in couplets. Other poems have only one couplet.
Couplets are often silly and are usually about one subject.

➡ Example:

I went to the store to buy a book.

I had no money; I could only look.

I went to the store to buy a book.

I had no money, so I could only look.

I found the book I wanted to buy.

But I must wait 'til my pockets aren't dry.

A **triplet** has three lines that rhyme.

➡ Example:

To the ice cream shop, we all went.

To buy our favorite, chocolate mint.

Now, our money is all spent!

A **quatrain** is a four-line poem with at least two lines that rhyme. There are several rhyming schemes possible. For example, the first and second lines rhyme, and the third and fourth lines rhyme (**aabb**). Some other rhyming combinations include **abab**, **abba**, **aaba**, **abcb**, etc.

➡ Example 1: (**aabb**)

    a) **Sometimes, when I'm on the bus,**

    a) **Tiny, tired babies begin to fuss.**

    b) **I think their moms ride through town**

    b) **Just trying to calm their babies down.**

➡ Example 2: (**abab**)

    a) **Ten red apples in a crate;**

    b) **I bet they taste delicious.**

    c) **If I had one now, it would be great**

    b) **Because they're so nutritious!**

The Difference in Prose and Poems

You have learned that **prose** is the type of writing that is used in stories, essays, articles, letters, diaries, journals, and books. A **poem** is arranged in verses and stanzas instead of sentences and paragraphs. You can tell a poem by how it is arranged. Poems also use many of the poetic elements that you have learned, such as sound devices, figures of speech, and meter.

Writing Assignment

Write a couplet, triplet, or quatrain of your own.
Read your poem aloud in a small group or to a partner.

Extending the Lesson:
Enjoying Poetry

1. Bring a poem in another language and share it with the class. After the poem is read aloud in the new language, translate it into English.

2. Select a poem to share from the book *The 20th Century Children's Poetry Treasury* by Jack Prelutsky.

3. Use the resources in the library or on the Internet to look up poems by poets James Tippet and Charlotte Pomerantz. Pick out the poem you like the best and answer the following questions.

   • Why do you like this poem?

   • What do you think this poem is about (interpretation)?

   • How is this poem similar to another poem or story you have read? Is there anything about this poem that reminds you of a personal experience?

   • Give examples of some sound devices that were used in the poem.

   • Read the poem aloud and discuss it with a partner.
     What does your partner think about the poem?

   • With your partner, discuss what you like or dislike about the writing style of this poet?

   • Compare the style of your favorite poet to the style of your friend's favorite poet.

Literature Time

Review: Reading Poetry Aloud

Reading poetry aloud can be really fun, especially if you **take the time to do it right.**

Practice ahead of time.
Read through the poem several times, pronouncing each word very carefully and slowly at first.

Understand the poem.
If you know the meaning of the poem, you can use the inflections of your voice effectively.

Read the following poems aloud, using the guidelines above.

Using Similes and Metaphors in Poetry

Color poems are a great way to demonstrate the use of similes and metaphors. To review, a **simile** is a figure of speech that uses *like* or *as* to compare two things that are different.

My horse runs **like** the wind.

A **metaphor** is a figure of speech that compares two different things by saying that one thing *is* something else. Metaphors are just like similes except that they don't use *like* or *as*.

My dad **is** a bear in the mornings.

Find the similes and metaphors in the color poems on the next page.

Color Poems

Directions: Pick a color as your title. Tell about your color in complete sentences. Your sentences do not have to rhyme.

Orange and the Senses

Orange looks like the glow of a setting sun.

Orange smells like freshly-polished furniture.

Orange tastes as good as a tall glass of orange juice.

Orange sounds like autumn leaves crunching underfoot.

Orange feels like a toasty campfire in the evening.

White is...

White is the color of my cat.

White is a soft blanket of snow.

It is clouds and cotton balls and dress shirts.

It is pillows, feathers, and sheep's wool.

White is a beautiful wedding gown.

White is my grandmother's hair.

White can be mixed with any other color.

Writing Assignment

Write a color poem of your own.
Read your poem aloud in a small group or to a partner.

Extending the Lesson:
Enjoying Poetry

1. Pick out a poem you like and record it. Listen to the poem several times to hear its rhythm. Do you like the way you recorded the poem? If not, record it again until the poem sounds right to you. Have your teacher, friends, and parents listen to your recording. Ask for their advice to improve your recording.

2. Use the resources in the library or on the Internet to look up poems by poets Lilian Moore and Dr. Seuss. Pick out the poem you like the best and answer the following questions.

   • Why do you like this poem?

   • What do you think this poem is about (interpretation)?

   • How is this poem similar to another poem or story you have read? Is there anything about this poem that reminds you of a personal experience?

   • Give examples of some sound devices that were used in the poem.

   • Read the poem aloud and discuss it with a partner. What does your partner think about the poem?

   • With your partner, discuss what you like or dislike about the writing style of this poet?

   • Compare the style of your favorite poet to the style of your friend's favorite poet.

Literature Time

The Land of Nod

From breakfast on through all the day
At home among my friends I stay.
But every night I go abroad
Afar into the land of Nod.

All by myself I have to go,
With none to tell me what to do—
All alone beside the streams
And up the mountain-sides of dreams.

The strangest things are there for me,
Both things to eat and things to see,
And many frightening sights abroad
Till morning in the land of Nod.

Try as I like to find the way,
I never can get back by day,
Nor can remember plain and clear
The curious music that I hear.

—*Robert Louis Stevenson*

Discussion Questions for Analyzing "The Land of Nod":

1. Who is the author of the poem, "The Land of Nod"?

2. How many stanzas are in the poem?

3. Look up the word *abroad*. What does it mean? Is *abroad* a word you would use in everyday language? What other word in the first stanza is a synonym of *abroad*? What is the dictionary definition of *afar*?

4. Where does the author go at night?
   a. home   b. traveling to other towns   c. The land of Nod

5. Which words best describe the way the poet feels about going?
   a. alone and afraid   b. excited and eager   c. tired and hungry

6. Look up the word "*nod*" in the dictionary.
   What does the Land of Nod stand for?
   a. another country   b. the land of dreams   c. his bedroom

7. In the last stanza, what describes what the author thinks about his dreams?
   a. he understands them
   b. he can't go back to Nod during the day
   c. he remembers his dreams

8. Does the poem, "The Land of Nod," use sound devices?

9. What are some examples of *rhyme*?

10. What are some examples of *repetition*?

11. What are some examples of *assonance*?

12. What are some examples of *alliteration*?

13. How would you describe this poem to a friend?

14. Which lines in the poem do you like the best? Explain.

15. Why do you think the author cannot go to the Land of Nod during the day?

16. How does this poem make you feel?
    Which words in the poem make you feel this way?

Review: Mood in Poetry

As you have learned, authors, poets, and illustrators use words and pictures to make you, the reader, feel a certain way about what you are reading. How you feel when you read a story or poem or see an illustration is called *mood*.

Writing Assignment

Choose one of the writing assignments below.

PROMPT 1 You have been studying a poem by Robert Louis Stevenson. Look up more information about him, using the Internet, a poetry reference, and/or an encyclopedia. Write an informational paragraph that includes the following information:

Introduction: Tell who Robert Louis Stevenson was and what he did.

Body: Tell one or more important or unusual facts about Robert Louis Stevenson's early life.

Tell one or more important or unusual facts about Robert Louis Stevenson's later life.

Mention one or more important works written by Robert Louis Stevenson.

Conclusion: Give a summary, or wrap-up, of what you said about Robert Louis Stevenson.

PROMPT 2 Write a poem of your own. Read your poem aloud in a small group or to a partner. Discuss the story told in your poem.

Extending the Lesson:
Enjoying Poetry

1. Select a song and record the lyrics as a poem. Do you like the way you recorded the lyrics? If not, record it again until the lyrics sound right to you. Have your teacher, friends, and parents listen to your recording. Ask for their advice to improve it.

2. Use the resources in the library or on the Internet to look up poems by poets Richard Armour and Kristine O'Connell George. Pick out the poem you like the best and answer the following questions.

   • Why do you like this poem?

   • What do you think this poem is about (interpretation)?

   • How is this poem similar to another poem or story you have read? Is there anything about this poem that reminds you of a personal experience?

   • Give examples of some sound devices that were used in the poem.

   • Read the poem aloud and discuss it with a partner. What does your partner think about the poem?

   • With your partner, discuss what you like or dislike about the writing style of this poet?

   • Compare the style of your favorite poet to the style of your friend's favorite poet.

Literature Time

Review: Reading Poetry Aloud

Reading poetry aloud can be really fun, especially if you **take the time to do it right.**

Practice ahead of time.
Read through the poem several times, pronouncing each word very carefully and slowly at first.

Understand the poem.
If you know the meaning of the poem, you can use the inflections of your voice effectively.

Acrostic Poem

In an **acrostic** poem, the letters that begin each line often spell the subject of the poem. To write an acrostic, think of an event, person, animal, or thing to describe. Write the letters of your topic vertically. Beside each letter, write an adjective or short phrase that starts with that letter to describe the person or thing.

Read the acrostic poems aloud, using the guidelines above.

➡ Acrostic Poem Example 1:

D Daring, determined, and decent
A Always cheerful
R Red hair like the blazing sun
E Eyes as blue as the ocean
N Never rude

➡ Acrostic Poem Example 2:

R Ribbons of color
A Arch in the sky
I Impressive
N Natural beauty
B Breathtaking
O Over the top
W Wonderful

Free Verse Made from Parts of Speech

Free Verse is a form of poetry that is usually unrhymed and without a fixed and traditional metrical pattern. Use the directions below to write a free-verse poem made from the parts of speech.

➡ Free Verse for a Person:

Line 1: Write your name.

Line 2: Write two adjectives that describe your personality.

Line 3: Write four words that describe your appearance: adjective, noun, adjective, noun.

Line 4: Write five nouns naming things you enjoy.

Line 5: Write any descriptive word you choose.

> Lance
>
> Loyal, trustworthy
>
> Kind eyes, freckled face
>
> Friends, swimming, soccer, reading, family
>
> Friendly

➡ Free Verse for a Topic:

Line 1: Write the name of the topic.

Line 2: Write two adjectives that describe the topic.

Line 3: Write a verb and prepositional phrase about the topic.

Line 4: Write two adverbs describing the verb.

Line 5: Write a sentence to describe the topic.

> Snow
>
> Soft and cold
>
> Falls on the ground
>
> Quietly and slowly
>
> Snow is a silent mystery.

Free Verse Made from Sentences

Free Verse is a form of poetry that is usually unrhymed and without a fixed and traditional metrical pattern. Write a free-verse poem made from sentences about a topic.

The Color Gray

Gray is an unusual color to like;
I think of fog and dreary days.
I think of storm clouds,
And strength and silver and steel.

But I also think of dolphins, which I love to watch;
Gray is the color of the owl outside my window at night.
My oldest pair of shoes is a soft and cozy gray.
They are comfortable, and I like them.

But best of all, gray describes my grandmother's hair;
She listens to me when no one else will.
She makes good-smelling things for me in her kitchen;
I love her, just as I love the color gray.

Writing Assignment

Choose a type of poem in this lesson and write one of your own.
Read your poem aloud in a small group or to a partner.

Extending the Lesson:
Enjoying Poetry

1. Write a poem and record it. Do you like the way you recorded the poem? If not, record it again until the poem sounds right to you. Have your teacher, friends, and parents listen to your recording. Ask for their advice to improve your poem or recording.

2. Use the resources in the library or on the Internet to look up poems by poets Richard Armour and Kristine O'Connell George. Pick out the poem you like the best and answer the following questions.

   • Why do you like this poem?

   • What do you think this poem is about (interpretation)?

   • How is this poem similar to another poem or story you have read? Is there anything about this poem that reminds you of a personal experience?

   • Give examples of some sound devices that were used in the poem.

   • Read the poem aloud and discuss it with a partner. What does your partner think about the poem?

   • With your partner, discuss what you like or dislike about the writing style of this poet?

   • Compare the style of your favorite poet to the style of your friend's favorite poet.

Analyzing Literature

The Little Red Hen

Long ago, back when birds and foxes and other animals could talk like people, there was a little Red Hen, who lived in a lovely little cottage on a deserted old farm, all by herself. All around, crickets chirruped and bees buzzed happily in the warm summer sun. It was all so calm and quiet. The Little Red Hen's cottage was just perfect for her with a big oak tree in front for shade, a neat little white picket fence all around it, and flowers blooming here, there, and yonder.

The Little Red Hen was a Rhode Island Red with fiery red feathers, and she was quite dainty and small. What Little Red lacked in size and strength, she made up for in cleverness. You see, she was a very smart bird.

An old Fox, crafty and sly, had a den in the rocks on a hill far away, but he knew where the Little Red Hen lived. Many nights the Fox lay awake and thought how good that Little Red Hen would taste.

But the sly old fox just wasn't crafty enough to catch the Little Red Hen. She was too wise for him. Whenever she went out, she usually locked the door behind her. When she came in again, she locked the door behind her and put the key in the apron pocket where she kept her scissors. The old fox had tried many times to catch the Little Red Hen, but she just flew into a tree until he left.

At last, the old Fox thought up a way to catch the little Red Hen. Early in the morning, he said to his old wife, "I'll be bringing the little Red Hen for supper." Then, he took a big bag and walked to the Little Red Hen's house. Hiding behind the woodpile next to the house, he waited for the Little Red Hen to come out of her house. He didn't have long to wait. Soon, Little Red came outside to pick up a few sticks for kindling. For the first time, she did not shut and lock her door since the sticks were just a few steps away.

As soon as she bent down to get the sticks, the old Fox slipped into her house and hid behind her chair. In a minute, the little Red Hen came quickly in and shut the door and locked it.

"I'm glad I'm safely in," she said. Just as she said it, she turned around, and there stood the ugly old Fox with his big bag over his shoulder. Little Red was so surprised and frightened that she dropped her sticks and flew up to the big beam across the ceiling. There she perched and called to the old Fox below, "You may as well go home for you can't get me!"

"Well, we will see about that!" replied the Fox.

So, what do you think the old fellow did? He began twirling round in a circle after his tail. As he spun faster and faster and faster, the poor Little Red Hen got so dizzy watching him that she couldn't hold on to her perch. She dropped off, and the old Fox picked her up and put her in his bag and started for home.

He had a very long way to go, and most of it was uphill. The Little Red Hen was still so dizzy that she could not think about what to do. When she finally came to her right mind, she whisked her little scissors out of her apron pocket and snipped a little hole in the bag. She poked her head out and looked around. As soon as they came to a good spot, she cut the hole bigger, jumped out, picked up a stone, and put it in the bag as quick as a wink. She hid until the fox was out of sight. Then, she ran as fast as she could till she

came to her own little farmhouse. She went in and locked the door. She felt so lucky. Then, she started laughing and couldn't quit.

The old Fox carried his bag with the stone inside to his home. "I've got the Little Red Hen. Let's cook her right now!" he exclaimed to his wife. "I will shake the bag so that the hen will fall in the boiling hot kettle of water when you lift the lid." The old Fox lifted the bag up until it was over the open pot and gave it a shake. Splash! Thump! Splash! In went the stone and out came hot water. The hot water soaked the fox. He was so surprised and in so much pain that he ran out of the house and disappeared down the road, his old wife hobbling after him. No one ever heard from them again! The Little Red Hen lived happily ever after in her own little farmhouse, feeling rather sly like a fox.

Analyzing a Setting

To *analyze* means to examine the elements that make up a larger whole. When you analyze literature, you examine one particular element of a story, such as a particular setting, character, theme, or plot.

The **setting** is the time and place of the story. It tells you where and when the action of the story takes place. The action of some stories moves from one place to another, giving the story more than one setting. Authors often establish the setting early in a story, building a mental image with sensory details, as in this example:

Story: The Little Red Hen

The Little Red Hen

Long ago, back when birds and foxes and other animals could talk like people, there was a little Red Hen, who lived in a lovely little cottage on a deserted old farm, all by herself. All around, crickets chirruped and bees buzzed happily in the warm summer sun. It was all so calm and quiet. The Little Red Hen's cottage was just perfect for her with a big oak tree in front for shade, a neat little white picket fence all around it, and flowers blooming here, there, and yonder.

A simple description of the setting of a little cottage might be like the one below.

> **where:** *in a cottage on a farm*
>
> **when:** *long ago*

However, a good story includes detailed descriptions to help the reader better imagine the setting. A better description of the same setting could be like the one below.

> **where:** *in a lovely little cottage on a deserted old farm*
>
> **when:** *long ago, back when birds and foxes and other animals could talk like people*

Now, that's a much better setting to picture in your mind!

As you begin analyzing a setting, begin by picking out specific words from the text that describe the time, place, and setting-related sensory details. Then, think about those words and generalize how the setting makes you feel before turning that "feeling" into a specific adjective. This adjective describes the *tone* or *mood* of the setting. Finally, your observations are put into complete sentences, forming an opinion that you support with details from the text.

Instructions for Analyzing a Setting

1. Look for words that describe the time and place that a story takes place. Pay special attention to sensory details.

TIME	PLACE	SIGHT DETAILS	SOUND DETAILS	FEEL DETAILS	OTHER DETAILS
• long ago	• cottage • on a deserted old farm	• lovely • neat little white picket fence • flowers blooming	• crickets chirruped • quiet • bees buzzing	• calm • warm summer sun	• perfect • oak tree for shade

2. Think about the time, place, and sensory details of a story's setting and tell how they make you feel.

   ➥ **How does the setting make you feel?**

3. After writing down all the words that tell how the setting makes you feel, pick out one or two words that BEST describe it.

   ➥ **What one or two adjectives best describe how the setting makes you feel?**

4. Write a paragraph about the setting. First, write a sentence that tells how the setting makes you feel, using some of the adjectives from your list. Then, write a sentence that summarizes the when and where of the setting. Finally, write a sentence that tells which sensory details support your evaluation of the setting.

   ➥ **How would you summarize the setting, using details from the text?**

Discussion Questions
to Help You Analyze Setting

1. When does the story take place?

2. Where does the story take place?

3. How does the author use details that can be seen?

4. How does the author use details that can be heard?

5. How does the author use details that can be felt?

6. How does the author use other details?

7. Could you picture in your mind what was described as if you were there?

8. Based on your study of the setting, choose one or two adjectives that best describe the feeling, or mood, that the setting creates.

Note: After each major detail of a setting, cite the sentence, chapter and page number for a book. Cite the stanza or scene for poems and plays.

**Recommended Reading List
for an Analysis of a Setting**

- *My Father's Dragon*
  by Ruth Stiles Gannett
- *The Fire Cat* by Esther Averill
- *Amos & Boris* by William Steig

Characters

Characters are the people who speak, think, and act in a story. In most stories, the characters are human beings. Fantasy stories or fairy tales may include characters that are animals or even objects. Science fiction stories can include characters that are robots, aliens, or even stranger things! A good rule of thumb is *"If it can talk or do things on its own, then it's probably a character."*

Character Traits

Everything you learn about characters can help you understand their traits. Characters have **physical traits** *(tall, thin, strong)* and **personality traits** *(brave, hardworking, smart)*. You can tell the traits of a person by the way they act, speak, and look. Sometimes, the author will mix personality and physical traits when describing a character. A character's traits can also change during a story. Authors use physical and personality traits to develop their characters and make them interesting, with believable thoughts, actions, and dialogue.

Developing a Character

An author usually begins with a simple idea for a character.

Character: litte red hen

Physical: small, not very strong, red feathers

Personality: clever, witty

Then, the author quickly moves the simple ideas to detailed descriptions to help the reader better imagine the physical and personality traits of the character.

Character: little red hen

Physical: The Little Red Hen was a Rhode Island Red with fiery red feathers, and she was quite dainty and small.

Personality: What Little Red lacked in size and strength, she made up for in cleverness. You see, she was a very smart bird.

Analyzing a Character

Remember: To **analyze** means *to examine the elements that make up a larger whole*. When you analyze literature, you examine one particular element of a story, such as a particular setting, character, theme, or plot.

Authors want the reader to get to know the characters in a story, so the reader will care about what happens to them and continue reading the story to find out.

Instructions for Analyzing a Character

1. Look for descriptive words that provide a mental image. Then, examine the character's spoken words, actions, feelings, and opinions for indirect characterization clues.

2. Think about how these clues come together to create a character. Write down a few words you might use to tell someone about the character.

   • How would you describe the character's personality?

3. Write a paragraph analyzing the character. Use the following guide to help you write your analysis.

   • Write one or two sentences that describe the physical traits of the character.

   • Write a statement that describes one or two personality traits of the character.

   • Write a sentence that introduces the details to support your analysis.

   • Then, use details from the story to support your analysis of the character's personality traits.

   The Little Red Hen is a small, dainty Rhode Island Red with fiery red feathers. She is also clever and smart. There are several details from the text that support my analysis that the red hen is clever and smart. Right from the beginning, we are told that "the sly old fox just wasn't crafty enough to catch the Little Red Hen. She was too wise for him." Other details that show that the Little Red Hen is clever and smart include keeping her door locked, flying up in a tree to get away from the fox, and putting a stone in the fox's bag to help her escape unnoticed.

Discussion Questions to Help You Analyze a Character

Character Being Analyzed: Little Red Hen

1. Is the character a person (boy, girl, man, woman), animal, or object?

2. Search the text and find a description of the character's physical traits.

3. What kind of picture does the physical description give you of the character?

4. Search the text and find how the author described the character's personality traits.

5. Based on your study of the character, choose one or two adjectives that best describe the character's personality.

Note: After each major detail of a character, cite the sentence, chapter, and page number for a book. Cite the stanza or scene for poems and plays.

Recommended Reading List for an Analysis of a Character

- *Henry and Mudge: The First Book of Their Adventures* by Cynthia Rylant
- *Tops and Bottoms* by Janet Stevens
- *The Raft* by Jim LaMarche

Plot

The **plot** is *what happens to the characters and what the characters do*—it is the action of a story. It shows the order of events and includes some kind of conflict or problem. In literature, you usually have to read the entire story in order to recognize which events are important and which events are not.

Suspense

One very important reason that we read stories is to learn what is going to happen next. The excited expectation you feel when you don't know what will happen next is called suspense (*dramatic tension*). Suspense is the whole reason we read stories or even watch movies or TV shows. To keep your reader's interest, you want your plot to be moving forward, and you want to keep the *suspense* building.

Structure of a Plot

Remember that **plot** is the order of events and experiences of the characters in a story. These events and experiences lead to a certain outcome. As events happen, they usually include some kind of **conflict or problem**. The structure of a plot includes a beginning, middle, and ending.

- The **beginning** introduces the characters, settings, and conflict, or problem.

- The **middle** continues developing the characters, and a series of events (*rising action*) now lead to the climax, which may also contain elements of surprise. The climax is the most important event in the story before the conflict is resolved.

- The **ending** resolves minor conflicts and answers most of the reader's questions (*falling action*). The ending also shows how the conflict is resolved (*resolution*) and tells the outcome of the story.

Instructions for Analyzing Plot

Beginning: Identify the Conflict

Every plot begins with some sort of conflict, or problem. The conflict creates dramatic tension so the reader wants to know how the problem will be solved.

- An old Fox, crafty and sly, had a den in the rocks on a hill far away, but he knew where the Little Red Hen lived. Many nights the Fox lay awake and thought how good that Little Red Hen would taste. **(initial conflict: Little Red Hen vs. the sly old fox)**

Middle: Identify the Rising Action

Every time something happens to the characters, or whenever the characters take action, *the conflict escalates and the dramatic tension and suspense increase.* This part of the plot is called the **rising action**. Depending on the length of the story, rising action may go on for paragraphs, pages, or chapters. Most stories present rising action through a series of events, each one more tense than the last.

- Many nights the Fox lay awake and thought how good that Little Red Hen would taste. The old fox had tried many times to catch the Little Red Hen, but she just flew into a tree until he left. **(rising action)**

- At last, the old Fox thought up a way to catch the little Red Hen. Early in the morning, he said to his old wife, "I'll be bringing the little Red Hen for supper." **(rising action)**

- For the first time, she did not shut and lock her door since the sticks were just a few steps away. As soon as she bent down to get the sticks, the old Fox slipped into her house and hid behind her chair. In a minute, the little Red Hen came quickly in and shut the door and locked it. **(rising action)**

- Just as she said it, she turned around, and there stood the ugly old Fox with his big bag over his shoulder. Little Red was so surprised and frightened that she dropped her sticks and flew up to the big beam across the ceiling. **(rising action)**

- So, what do you think the old fellow did? He began twirling round in a circle after his tail. As he spun faster and faster and faster, the poor Little Red Hen got so dizzy watching him that she couldn't hold on to her perch. **(rising action)**

CONTINUED ON NEXT PAGE

Middle: Identify the Climax

Readers can only stand so much dramatic tension, and eventually the story must end. The **climax** *is the most exciting part of the story*, and the dramatic tension is at its highest point: when the knight finally faces the evil dragon, or when the baseball team is trailing their rivals by one point in the final inning of the championship game. Most of the time, it can't get any more exciting than the climax. When the climax is over, readers know the final outcome of the conflict: the knight defeats the dragon, the pinch-hitter hits a home run to win the championship.

- She dropped off, and the old Fox picked her up and put her in his bag and started for home. (**climax**)

- When she finally came to her right mind, she whisked her little scissors out of her apron pocket and snipped a little hole in the bag. She poked her head out and looked around. As soon as they came to a good spot, she cut the hole bigger, jumped out, picked up a stone, and put it in the bag as quick as a wink. (**surprise action**)

Ending: Identify the Resolution

Some stories may end with a final resolution, which explains what happens to the characters after the problem is solved. This is often a very short part of the story, and it is almost always the last part. For example, the knight uses the magic key to unlock the dungeon and rescue the princess, and they get married and live happily ever after, or the baseball fans storm the field and carry the hero of the game on their shoulders, and people talk about the championship game for years. A good resolution leaves the reader feeling satisfied.

- The old Fox lifted the bag up until it was over the open pot and gave it a shake. Splash! Thump! Splash! In went the stone and out came hot water. The hot water soaked the fox. He was so surprised and in so much pain that he ran out of the house and disappeared down the road, his old wife hobbling after him. No one ever heard from them again! (**resolution**)

Recommended Reading List for an Analysis of Plot
- *The Lighthouse Family: The Storm* by Cynthia Rylant
- *The One-Eyed Giant (Book One of Tales from the Odyssey)* by Mary Pope Osborne
- *Cowgirl Kate and Cocoa* by Erica Silverman

Theme

Every piece of literature has a theme. The theme of a story or poem is a message or a lesson about life in general. The best stories are the ones that teach you something about yourself, your life, and other people. Reading stories allows you to make a connection to the characters that authors bring to life in their books.

Analyzing a Story for Its Theme

The **theme** of a book is *the message that the author wants you to learn about life or human nature*. When stories seem similar, it is because they share a common theme. When you understand the theme of a story, it helps you understand the entire story and its characters and their actions better.

Sometimes an author will tell you the theme of a story at the end, like Aesop does in his fables. However, the themes of most stories are not stated directly. You have to infer, or figure them out. For example, in the story *"The Lion and the Mouse"* by Aesop, you are not told the theme directly, but you can infer that the theme is "showing kindness works both ways."

How can you tell? When the lion showed mercy to the little mouse, the mouse was able to return the favor by saving the lion's life.

When you analyze a story for its theme, think about the settings, the characters, and the plot of the story. Decide what the characters learned about life. This will help you determine the theme. Most of the time, a theme can be stated in just one or two words that carry an overall message (*friendship, trust, loyalty, truth, keeping a promise*).

Draw a Theme Chart

A Theme Chart helps you chart the stories that you read. A theme chart will give you a quick summary of the overall message of a story. As you read poems, stories, and books, keep a theme chart to record the title, author, and theme. This will help you share your thoughts about certain books with others. Most people will not express themes the same way, but the general idea will be similar.

Theme Chart

Title	Theme
"The Little Red Hen" Public Domain, adapted by Center for Urban Education	Cleverness: You can usually figure something out if you remain calm
Mufaro's Beautiful Daughters by John Steptoe	Pride: Too much pride often causes big mistakes
Charlotte's Web by E. B. White	Friendship: Do what you can to help your friends.

More Examples of Story Themes

The Ugly Duckling	Do not judge by outward appearances. (acceptance)
Abel's Island	Too much leisure can make you lazy. (survival)
Woodsong	Life teaches you important lessons. (wisdom)

The Difference Between Main Idea and Theme

Sometimes, it is easy to confuse the theme of a story with its main idea (topic). But, if you remember that the theme is a message or a lesson about life in general, it will be easier to tell the difference. The main idea or topic of a story is directly related to the story so that you get the idea of that story specifically.

The **main idea** of *The Ugly Duckling* is do not judge by outward appearances.

The **theme** of *The Ugly Duckling* is acceptance.

Recommended Reading List for an Analysis of Theme

- *Meet Christopher Columbus (Landmark Books)* **by James T. de Kay**
- *Sequoyah: The Cherokee Man Who Gave His People Writing* **by James Rumford**
- *How We Crossed The West: The Adventures Of Lewis And Clark* **by Rosalyn Schanzer**

Compare and Contrast Two Books in a Series

Read two books in a series. The books should be about the same or similar characters. Use the books to complete the comparisons below. Make sure you refer to the details in the books to support your comparison.

Setting

- Compare the settings for each book. How are the settings from both books similar? How are they different?

- How are the settings of these two selections like real life? Are there any parts of the settings that are not like real life?

Character Traits

- Describe the main characters from both books. Use the character traits to help you. How are the main characters from each book similar? How are they different?

- How are you like the main characters in the selections you have read? Have you had any similar experiences? How are you different from the main characters in these selections?

- What situations, events, thoughts, or attitudes motivate (cause) the main characters to do what they do in the stories and say what they say? Discuss some of the author's specific words or some paragraphs that support your ideas about a character's motives.

- Is there anything you would want the author to change about the characters from these two selections?

- Do the main characters in these selections remind you of any characters from other books you have read?

Plot

- How are the plots of these two selections similar? How are they different? Which events in both of the stories are your favorites?

- Is there anything you would change about the plot of either book? Which book had the strongest or most exciting plot? Explain.

Theme

- What do you think is the main message or theme of these books? Which words, phrases, or sections helped you understand the theme?

- Are the themes of the two books similar or different? In what ways are they similar? In what ways are they different?

- Can you think of other books or stories with similar themes?

Taking a Closer Look

Some suggested books are listed below.
- *Fudge* by Judy Blume
- *Fudge-a-Mania* by Judy Blume
- *The Mysterious Benedict Society* by Trenton Lee Stewart
- *The Mysterious Benedict Society and the Perilous Journey* by Trenton Lee Stewart

- Are your reading selections arranged as a whole story or in chapters? How do the later chapters build on to the earlier chapters? Which events in the earlier chapters did the author include to help the later chapters make sense?

- Are there any sections in the stories that confused you? If so, what specific words, phrases, or paragraphs did you find hard to understand? Can you tell which words and phrases have a literal (real) meaning or non-literal (*figurative language*)? Explain.

- Do any of the illustrations (if there are illustrations) help you understand the stories better? If so, locate the illustrations and describe how they help the story make sense and how they make you feel.

- The word motivation means "the reasons why." Characters in stories are *motivated* by many things. Pay close attention to the reasons why characters act and talk the way they do in stories.

- Longer books are usually arranged in chapters. Poems and songs are arranged in stanzas. Plays are usually arranged by scenes. Pay special attention to the kind of text you are reading and to the way it is organized. Knowing these key details will help you become an even better reader.

- When you refer to longer books with chapters, always think about how the chapters work together to build a complete story.

Analyzing Informational Text

Organizational Strategies for Nonfiction Books

Fiction books contain stories that are not true. Nonfiction books contain true stories and factual information. Nonfiction books are written to share information about a topic. You can find nonfiction books about practically any subject: animals, oceans, planets, space, countries, history, and all kinds of other topics. Authors of nonfiction books organize ideas and information in a variety of ways.

How Information Is Organized in a Nonfiction Book

When you read information in nonfiction books, you expect it to be in an order that is easy to understand. Some ways to organize ideas and information are explained below.

Time Order

This organizational strategy is used when information is arranged according to time, using words like first, second, next, then, and finally. Time order is also used in step-by-step processes to describe how to do something. Time order is often used in biographies, autobiographies, instructions, events, and news accounts.

Comparison/Contrast

This organizational strategy is used when two or more things are compared to show how they are alike and how they are different. If they are alike, it is called comparing. If they are different, it is called contrasting. Comparison/contrast is used in informative and opinion articles.

Problem/Solution

This organizational strategy is used when a problem or a need is identified and a solution is needed or presented. Problem/solution is used most often in persuasive writing and in scientific writing.

Cause/Effect

This organizational strategy is used to explain why things happen. An event that makes something happen is called the *cause*. An event that is the *result* of another event is called the *effect*. Cause/effect is used most often in reporting, historical writing, and scientific writing.

Visual Information

Many books contain visual elements, such as pictures, charts, tables, graphs, diagrams, or timelines to display certain facts in an easy-to-understand format. Information that is displayed visually includes a short explanation, title, or key to explain it.

Comprehension Strategy: **Using Headings and Subheadings**

Sometimes, an author does not want to give his readers one paragraph after another without any breaks. Longer pieces of text are easier to write and to read when they are broken into smaller pieces. Most novels are divided into chapters for exactly this reason.

Nonfiction works may also have chapters, but even chapters can be long sometimes—so authors use headings and subheadings to break things down even further. You will know headings by the size and type of print used. Headings will usually have a larger or bolder font than subheadings. Subheadings are divisions of information smaller than headings, and the information they contain is often very specific. The use of headings and subheadings in writing is similar to the use of topics and subtopics in an outline—with smaller groups of information within larger groups of information.

- What is the main heading of this section?
- What is the subheading of this section?

Logical Reasoning

Reasoning is the way your brain "fills in the gaps" when you don't have all the information. Your reasoning is **logical** when it makes sense or has an order. Two different types of reasoning are **inductive** reasoning and **deductive** reasoning.

- Think of **Inductive** reasoning as adding up the small clues (bits of evidence) to reveal the BIG IDEA called a **generalization** (jĕn' er ŭ lŭ zā' shŭn).

- Think of **Deductive** reasoning as already seeing the BIG IDEA (the generalization) and using it to make specific predictions or to find new clues.

CAUTION: A generalization can be very tricky. Don't generalize too quickly; you might be putting the clues together in the wrong way.

Example of Inductive Reasoning

Last month, Stan had pizza from The Pizza Place, and he got sick. Last week, Stan had another pizza from The Pizza Place, and got sick again. Today, Stan had a third pizza from The Pizza Place, and he is sick yet again. Now, Stan has *reasoned* that the pizza at The Pizza Place makes him sick because all the clues point in that direction. Using the clues, Stan made a generalization: The Pizza Place's pizza makes him sick. He based his generalization on his observations and experience.

Example of Deductive Reasoning

Monica knows she gets sick every time she drinks milk. A few moments ago, she unthinkingly drank a glass of milk with her cookies. Now, she reasons that she will feel sick very soon. Monica has made a *prediction*: she will get sick soon. She based her prediction on a generalization.

Logic helps you make generalizations or predictions, but it can also help you with your reading and writing. Nonfiction books can be harder to read, but they are usually set up logically. As you read, ask yourself, "Is the information moving from a BIG IDEA to smaller clues, or from smaller clues to a BIG IDEA?"

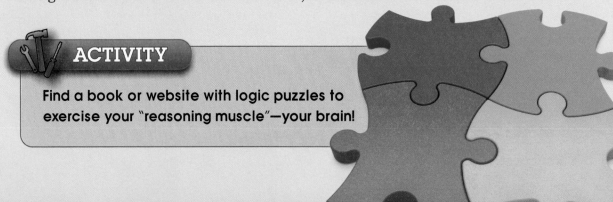

ACTIVITY

Find a book or website with logic puzzles to exercise your "reasoning muscle"—your brain!

Drawing on Experience

You live your life in the real world, and everything you experience—everything you see, hear, read, taste, smell, touch, and feel—affects who you are in some way, great or small. In the same way, your past experiences influence your future experiences. For example, you may not have thought much about the first wasp you ever saw—but if it stung you, you would see the next wasp a lot differently!

Authors try to use common experiences to relate to their readers before introducing new experiences. For example, C. S. Lewis's *The Lion, the Witch, and the Wardrobe* begins with children playing hide-and-seek inside on a rainy day—something you have probably experienced—before introducing his characters to the magical land of Narnia.

As you read the author's words, think about how they remind you of personal experiences in your life. A story set in a frozen wasteland will affect you much more if you have ever been camping in the wintertime, but any experience of feeling cold will work just as well. If you recall that experience as you read, you may even find yourself shivering.

Your experiences can help you relate to different types of writing. For example, as you were reading about fairy tales, you probably recalled fairy tales you have read or seen in a movie. Making connections between what you are reading and what you have already experienced can help you understand and remember the information.

Organizing and Reading
of Informational Text

As you read books throughout the year, use the guidelines below to help you achieve the goals of comprehending, summarizing, and analyzing the information you read. Some of the guidelines are used when working with single texts, and others are used when working with multiple texts.

Note: Use the recommended reading lists from your school district or the ones in the core standards.

Single Text: Determine the Main Idea and Tell How Details Support the Main Idea

1. What is the main idea of this text?

2. Which details in the text support the main idea?

3. After you determine the main idea and details, explain the text in your own words.

Single Text: To Understand a Text, Ask and Answer Questions, Referring to the Text for Answers

1. Change headings and bolded information into questions. Then, read the information to find the answers.

2. What specific details in the text helped you answer questions?

Single Text: Describe Relationships Between Events or Ideas Using Time, Sequence, and Cause and Effect

1. What major ideas, events, or procedures are explained in the text?

2. How would you describe the timing or sequence of events in a text?

3. Why do certain events happen and how do they cause other events to take place?

4. What is the final outcome, or result, of the events that take place?

5. How do the ideas or events in the text affect the outcome?

Single Text: Determine the Meaning of Academic and Domain-specific Words in a Text

1. Use vocabulary words to help you understand the topic. Make a list of these words.

2. Determine whether the domain-specific words help explain the information in the text.

3. Look for emphasized words: boldfaced, italicized, underlined, all caps, font size, captions, or headings.

4. Ways to determine the meanings of words in a text:
   • Look for definitions within the text.
   • Use context clues to determine meanings.
   • Use the dictionary or glossary to look up unknown words.

5. How do headings guide your reading and help you understand the topic?

Single Text: Use Text Features to Locate Information About a Topic Efficiently

1. What key words would you use to search for more information about the topic?

2. How would you use sidebars and hyperlinks to search for additional information about the topic?

3. What other resources could you use to find information about the topic?

Single Text: Distinguish Your Own Point of View from That of the Author

1. What is the author's point of view of the information in the text?

2. What is your point of view of the information in the text?

3. In what ways do you agree or disagree with the author's opinion or point of view?

Single Text: Use Information From Different Media or Formats to Understand a Topic

1. How do illustrations, such as maps, photographs, and other visual information, help you understand a topic?

2. How do words work with visual information in a text to help you understand it?

Single Text: Describe the Logical Connection Between Sentences and Paragraphs

1. What transition words and phrases are found in the text?

2. Use the transition words to help you decide if sentences and paragraphs are arranged in comparison, cause/effect, or time-order sequence.

Analyzing Multiple Texts

Multiple Texts: Compare and Contrast the Most Important Points in Two Texts About the Same Topic

1. What main points and details in both texts are similar?

2. What main points and details in both texts are different?

3. How does the overall information in the two texts compare?

Multiple Texts: Read and Comprehend Information Independently In Your Reading Range

1. Have you read a variety of science, social studies, history, and technical texts?

2. Which kind of text is easier for you to read and understand?

3. What strategies do you use to help you understand difficult text?

4. In what ways are you using domain-specific words in your reading, speaking, and writing?

Folktales, Proverbs, Idioms, and Theme

Literature Time

Idioms and Proverbs

The English language is full of interesting sayings that have become widely known and accepted by most people who speak English. **Proverbs** are *sayings that are easy-to remember and share a bit of wisdom or give you a good rule to live by*. They are often in sentence form.

An **idiom** is *a common saying that means something other than the literal meaning of its words*. When someone says, "I can't carry a tune in a bucket," that doesn't mean he can't carry a literal (*actual; real*) tune around in a literal (*actual; real*) bucket—it means that he can't sing very well. You have to look beyond the meaning of the actual words to understand what they really mean.

No doubt you have read many books by now, and you have probably noticed many of the special ways authors express their thoughts. Idioms and proverbs are some of the ways authors get their ideas across. These are sayings that, if used every once in a while, can add extra meaning to your writing.

IDIOM	MEANING
bite off more than you can chew	try to do more than you are able to do
get the ball rolling	to start an activity or action
jump the gun	to start before you should
put two and two together	to figure something out

PROVERB	MEANING
Don't count your chickens before they're hatched.	Don't depend on getting something before you actually have it.
Birds of a feather flock together.	People who are alike often become friends.

Birds of a feather flock together.

Folktales:
Legends, Myths, Tall Tales, and Fables

Human beings are natural-born story-tellers. We were telling stories long before we learned to write, passing stories down from generation to generation by **oral tradition**. This form of storytelling has often been described as "word-of-mouth." Eventually, many of these early stories were written down, and you can still read them today. We call these stories **folktales**. The word folktale literally means "story of the people."

All folktales have several things in common. First, folktales begin orally. They may later be written down, but their roots are in the voices of the people. Second, folktales are based on the history, traditions, and values of the people who started them. In other words, they are a part of the people's **culture**. Third, folktales often involve exaggerated or fictional elements, along with some truth. This is because stories tend to be **expanded** with each telling. Finally, folktales usually share some kind of wisdom. This wisdom often takes the form of a life lesson, an explanation of a natural happening, or the preserved memory of a historical event or a person.

Folktales can be separated into four categories:

→ legends
→ myths
→ tall tales
→ fables

These categories are very similar, but there are distinct differences.

Legends are tales from long ago that first spread by word of mouth. Usually, legends are focused upon real historical events and individuals who become well-known for their deeds. Over time, these individuals became heroes, and their adventures became accepted as true. Many heroes of legend are adventurous thrill-seekers, great warriors, fearless leaders, and bold explorers. The heroes of legends usually represent the values that are important to the culture of a particular group of people. An example of a legendary hero is Davy Crockett.

Myths are stories that usually feature gods as a means to explain some belief or natural occurrence, such as the origins or beginning of stars and volcanoes. Before science explained these things, myths were the only explanation people had—so they believed them. An example of a mythical character is King Midas.

Tall tales are humorous stories that use extremely far-fetched exaggeration. They are based on the life of real persons who do impossible things. Tall tales are similar to legends and myths, but they always have elements that are not believable, like the stories of Paul Bunyan. Tall tales are usually local in nature, so characters often speak in a local dialect. Dialect is a nonstandard language used in a certain area.

Fables are imaginary stories, usually with animals or objects that talk and act like humans. Fables are designed to teach a life-lesson or moral. The animals in fables often talk and act just like humans. An example of a fable is "The Country Mouse and the City Mouse."

FOLKTALES

★ Come from oral tradition
★ Are part of the culture of the people who started them
★ Involve exaggerated or fictional elements
★ Share wisdom

Legends:

★ Based on real people made into heroes who have believable adventures
★ Exploits are accepted as true, but are not verifiable
★ Display important cultural values, such as bravery and honesty

Myths:

★ Use supernatural beings as a means to explain natural events or beliefs

Fables:

★ Use animals that talk and act like humans
★ Have moral or a life-lesson

Tall Tales:

★ Characters who do impossible feats
★ Use exaggeration
★ Use local dialect

Folktales are often short and very fun to read. Now that you know about different kinds of folktales, it is time to discover some of the most popular tales that have been passed down from generation to generation! By reading, understanding, and appreciating them, you help keep the tradition of storytelling alive.

Go to the library and select one of the folktales in each category below or choose your own folktales. Read your selections independently. Then, choose an activity listed for each type of folktale.

Legends:

★ *Johnny Appleseed*   ★ *Davy Crockett*   ★ *Robin Hood*

Legends Activities:

1. What characteristics of a legend can you identify in your selection? Cite examples from the text.

2. In a small group, retell a legend you have read. What is the theme?

3. What is your favorite legend? Explain the parts you like best.

4. Draw an illustration to go with your favorite legend.

5. Make up a legend of your own.

6. Think of a family story that has always been told among your relatives. Using the features of a legend you have learned, adapt your family story so that it sounds like a legend.

Read legends from the authors listed below. Also, find and read other books about legends.

Johnny Appleseed
by Steven Kellogg

The Adventures of Robin Hood (Puffin Classics)
by Roger Lancelyn Green and John Boyne

One-Hundred-and-One African-American Read-Aloud Stories
by Susan Kantor

Big Book of Favorite Legends
by Tommie DePaola

Tall Tales:

★ *Paul Bunyan*   ★ *Thunder Rose*

Tall Tales Activities:

1. What characteristics of a tall tale can you identify in your selection? Cite examples from the text.

2. In a small group, retell a tall tale you have read. What is the theme?

3. Read a tall tale from another culture or country. Compare and contrast its themes and topics with a similar American tall tale.

4. Write a summary of your favorite tall tale.

5. Draw an illustration to go with your favorite tall tale.

6. Find and read a tall tale with illustrations. Using specific details from the text, describe the characters, settings, or events from the story that are featured in the illustrations. Then, explain to your classmates how the illustrations relate to those characters, settings, or events.

7. Make up a tall tale of your own.
   Use exaggeration and dialect to enhance it.

Read tall tales from the authors listed below. Also, find and read other books about tall tales.

American Tall Tales by Mary Pope Osborne and Michael McCurdy

Paul Bunyan by Steven Kellogg

Thunder Rose by Jerdine Nolen and Kadir Nelson

Myths:

★ *From Greek:* Zeus, god of sky and thunder, Hercules

★ *From Norse:* Thor, God of Thunder and Strength

★ *From Native American:* Origin of the Buffalo (Cheyenne)

Myth Activities:

1. What characteristics of a myth can you identify in your selection? Cite examples from the text.

2. In a small group, retell a myth you have read. What is the theme?

3. What hardships or evil did the hero have to overcome in this myth?

4. What is the lesson taught in this myth? What parts of the story helped you understand this lesson?

5. Find and read a myth with illustrations. Using specific details from the text, describe the characters, settings, or events from the story that are featured in the illustrations. Then, explain to your classmates how the illustrations relate to those characters, settings, or events.

6. Make up a myth of your own. Use supernatural characters as a means to explain natural events or beliefs.

7. Think about a video of your favorite myth, such as Thor. Discuss how the video is like or different from the comic book.

Student Note:

The *theme* is the overall lesson about life that a story reveals.

Read myths from the authors listed below. Also, find and read other books about myths.

Tales of the Greek Heroes (Puffin Classics) by Roger Lancelyn Green and Rick Riordan

Fables:

- ★ *The Lion and the Mouse*
- ★ *The North Wind and the Sun*
- ★ *The Three Little Pigs*
- ★ *The City Mouse and the Country Mouse*

Fables Activities:

1. What characteristics of a fable can you identify in your selection? Cite examples from the text.

2. In a small group, retell a fable you have read. What is the theme?

3. Rewrite your favorite fable.

4. Draw an illustration to go with your favorite fable.

5. Find and read a fable with illustrations. Using specific details from the text, describe the characters, settings, or events from the story that are featured in the illustrations. Then, explain to your classmates how the illustrations relate to those characters, settings, or events.

6. What lesson do you think the author is trying to teach you in this fable? Which parts of the story helped explain the lesson?

7. Think of an important lesson that you have learned through experience. Write a fable that helps your readers learn this lesson, using your favorite animals for characters.

Read fables from the authors listed below. Also, find and read other books about fables.

Aesop's Fables by Anna Milbourne, Gillian Doherty and Linda Edwards

The Rainstick, A Fable by Sandra Chisholm Robinson

The Giant Book of Bedtime Stories: Classic Nursery Rhymes, Bible Stories, Fables, Parables, and Stories by William Roetzheim

Comprehension Strategy: Interpreting Visuals

One of the most efficient ways of presenting information is by using visuals, such as charts, graphs, tables, pictures, and digital animation. These and other kinds of visuals are helpful because you can interpret the information quickly and easily. They also allow you to interpret information in any order—whereas standard text can only be interpreted from one word or sentence to the next. For example, you could read the diagram on page 99 in this lesson about the types of folktales from top to bottom or from bottom to top, depending on the type of information you need. Finally, visual information often shows you how the information is related. For example, it is clear from the diagram that legends, myths, tall tales, and fables are four types of folktales, just from the way they are organized in the visual. In pairs or small groups, discuss a type of text you have read that featured visuals, such as charts, graphs, tables, pictures, etc. that helped you find information quickly or showed you how information was related.

Using Illustrations to Contribute to the Meaning of a Story

Sometimes, an illustration contributes to the meaning and mood of a story. For example, the illustration below demonstrates what happened in a specific part of the story, "The Three Little Pigs."

• It shows the wolf blowing down a little pig's house.

• It shows wooden pieces and sticks; therefore the house was built of wood and sticks.

• The second pig's house was built of wood, so this was the second pig's house.

• It shows that the first and second pigs were in the house made of wood.

• It uses facial expressions to emphasize that the wolf is mean and the pigs are frightened.

• It creates a mood of danger for the two little pigs.

Using a folktale or other story of your choice, explain how specific parts of an illustration contribute to a setting, a character, a certain mood, or the meaning of the story.

Understanding Theme

Every piece of literature has a *theme*. The **theme** of a story or poem is *the message or lesson that the author wants you to learn about life or human nature*. When stories seem similar, it is because they share a common theme. When you understand the theme of a story, you understand the entire story and its characters and their actions better.

Sometimes an author will tell you the theme of a story at the end, like Aesop does in his fables. However, the themes of most stories are not stated directly. You have to *infer*, or figure them out. For example, in the story *The Tale of Despereaux* by Kate DiCamillo, the author does not tell the theme directly, but you can infer that the theme is *"being different doesn't make you bad; it makes you unique."*

What part of the story helped you *infer* the theme?

When Despereaux discovers how different he is from other mice, he feels terrible because he doesn't feel like he belongs—neither a mouse nor a human—but he fights for what is right and ends up becoming a hero.

When you search for a story's theme, decide what the characters learned about life. This will help you determine the theme. Sometimes, a theme is stated in just one or two words that carry an overall message *(friendship, trust, loyalty, truth, keeping a promise)*. Other times, a theme is stated in a complete sentence. Most people will not express themes the same way, but the general idea will be similar.

The Difference Between Topic and Theme

Understanding the difference between a topic and a theme is simple. The topic of a story is basically what it is actually about. A story's theme is the overall message or lesson about life that the author wants the reader to get from the story. Study the example in the T-Chart to help you understand topic and theme.

Book: Charlotte's Web by E.B. White

TOPIC	THEME
A girl befriends a special pig.	A true friend is willing to make sacrifices.

Drama

Major Forms of Literature

Literature is a form of art that uses words to express feelings or ideas. There are three major forms of literature: **prose**, **poetry**, and **drama**.

→ **Prose** is the most common form of literature. Prose is arranged in *sentences* and *paragraphs*, and longer works may be arranged in chapters or whole books. Prose includes stories, essays, articles, and fiction and nonfiction books.

→ **Poetry** is a form of literature in which words are arranged as much for their sounds as for their meanings. Works of poetry—called **poems**—are arranged in *lines* and *stanzas*. Poems are usually shorter than prose works, but not always—some poems are book-length or even longer.

→ **Drama** is a form of literature that is written specifically to be presented by actors on a stage. Dramatic works—typically called **plays**—are usually arranged in *scenes* and *acts*. Plays are usually performed by a group of actors for an audience.

Main Elements of a Play

In some ways, a play is very similar to a fictional story told in prose. The narrative elements are all there—the main idea, setting, characters, plot, and ending. The main difference between a play and a prose story is HOW the story is told.

The person who writes a play is called a **playwright**. A play is written in a special format that is called a **script**. The script is mostly dialogue, and there is very little description. The script is like an instruction manual, telling the actors what to say and what to do. Important actions called **stage directions**, such as a character's entrance or exit, are listed in the script so that the actors know what to do.

More specific details about actions and movement are determined by the **director**, who tells the actors where to stand, when to move, and what to do while they speak their lines. Each **actor** represents a particular character in the story. Together, all the actors in a play are known as the play's **cast**.

A play is separated into a number of **acts**—usually between one and five. Each act is divided into **scenes**, and each scene usually takes place in its own particular setting.

The actors perform on a raised platform called the **stage**, which is usually decorated with sets to resemble the scenes in the story. The actors wear **costumes** appropriate to their characters, as well as special **make-up**. Any items the actors pick up or handle on the stage are called **props**. The people who build the sets, make the costumes, put on actors' make-up, and gather the props are called the play's **crew**.

When all these elements come together, the result can be an exciting experience for the cast, the crew, and the audience.

Two Main Categories of Drama: Comedies and Tragedies

Since drama's beginnings in ancient Greece, most plays have fallen into one of two main categories, or genres: comedies and tragedies.

A **comedy** is a play with a happy ending. Comedies often feature satire (poking fun at the problems in society), love stories, and plenty of humor. Despite numerous setbacks and misunderstandings, most of the characters in a comedy end up in a better position than where they were at the beginning. Comedies are very popular because they entertain audiences and make them laugh—and everyone likes to laugh. "Laughter is the best medicine," as the old saying goes.

A **tragedy** is a play with an unhappy ending. Tragedies usually involve a **tragic hero**—a main character who falls from a position of authority to a sad state at the end. The tragic hero often falls because of a **tragic flaw**—some trait or characteristic in his or her personality, such as pride or envy. You may wonder why anyone would want to read or watch a sad story, but tragedies serve a very important purpose. Reading or watching a sad story can help you face the sad things in your own life and help you feel better about them.

Discussion Questions:

1. Have you seen a live play—one with live actors on stage in front of you?

2. Was it a comedy or a tragedy? What did you enjoy most about the play?

3. Did you notice the change in scenes? How were the scenes different?

4. Who were your favorite characters?

5. In what ways were the characters believable?

6. Did they wear costumes? How did the actors' costumes contribute to the overall theme of the play?

7. How did the scenery and stage settings support the overall message of the play?

8. Did the play seem real?

Performing a Play

The Ants and the Grasshoppers

Scene 1

One half of the stage is set with two or three chaise lounges and a large umbrella for shade. Two small side tables have tall glasses of iced tea on them, arranged between the lounges. The other half of the stage is littered with small yellow pillows to represent grain. There is a cave-like set that serves as the ants' larder for food. A large green flat sheet serves as the backdrop of the scene.

Four ants are busily gathering the grain while two or three grasshoppers are resting on the chaise lounges, drinking iced tea and soaking up the sun. The four ants stand in a line on their side of the stage. Four "grain" pillows are on the floor, one in front of each character.

Ant 1: *(Sings as he picks up one grain pillow and places it on his head, balancing it with his hands.)* This is the way we pick the grain... *(Remains on stage until all helper ants finish the verse.)*

Ant 2: *(Sings as he picks up one grain pillow and places it on his head, balancing it with his hands.)* ...pick the grain... *(Stands next to the first ant and remains on stage until the last helper ant finishes the verse.)*

Ant 3: *(Sings as he picks up one grain pillow and places it on his head, balancing it with his hands.)* ...pick the grain... *(Stands next to the first two ants and remains on stage.)*

Ant 4: *(Sings as he picks up one grain pillow and places it on his head, balancing it with his hands.)* This is the way we pick the grain... *(Stands next to the first three ants and remains on stage.)*

Ants 1-4: *(Sing the last line all together.)* So early in the summer!

*(The second group of four ants enter the scene. They do exactly as the first four ants, singing the second verse. Ants in the second group carry the grain on their heads **as** they enter the stage.)*

Ant 5: *(Sings as he stacks one grain pillow in the larder.)* This is the way we store our grain... *(Remains on stage until all helper ants finish the verse.)*

Ant 6: *(Sings as he stacks the grain pillow in the larder.)* ...store our grain... *(Stands next to the first ant and remains on stage until the last helper ant finishes the verse.)*

Ant 7: *(Sings as he stacks the grain pillow in the larder.)* ...store our grain... *(Stands next to the first two ants and remains on stage until the helper ants finish the verse.)*

Ant 8: *(Sings as he stacks the grain pillow in the larder.)* This is the way we store our grain... *(Stands next to the first three ants and remains on stage.)*

Ants 1-8: *(Stack their grain pillows with those of the second group of ants and then all ants sing together.)* So early in the summer!

Ants 1-8: *(Sing all together)* This is the way we work all day, work all night, all week long. This is the way we plan ahead to make it through the winter!

The grasshoppers have been lazily lounging and listening to the ants. Now, it is their turn to speak their minds.

Grasshopper 1: You poor saps—spending all of your time working

and gathering night and day. You worry too much. Don't worry...

be happy!

Here's just a simple song that I'll sing to you.

Learn it because you might want to sing it, too.

Don't worry...be happy!

You work all day, and you work all night,

But you could be sitting here in the bright sunlight.

Don't worry...be happy!

Grasshopper 2: Yeah. You silly ants! Why waste your time with all this huffing and puffing. Why not just sit back and relax. It won't be winter for a long time from now!

Grasshoppers 1 and 2: *(Sing together)*

Here's just a simple song that we will sing to you.

Learn it because you might want to sing it, too.

Don't worry...be happy!

You think that winter is on its way,

But wouldn't it be fun to just sleep all day?

Don't worry...be happy!

Grasshopper 3: That's all right. Just go on and do what you do, and we will just keep on doing what we like to do, like sitting in the sun, drinking iced tea, and having fun!

Grasshoppers 1-3: *(Sing all together)*

You silly ants haven't got a clue;

Life's too short when work is all you do!

Don't worry...be happy!

You work all day, and you work all night!

But you could be sitting here in the bright sunlight,

Don't worry...be happy!

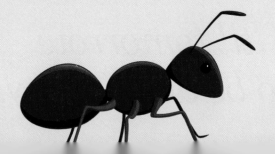

Scene 2

Scene two begins with a white flat sheet in the background to represent winter. The grasshoppers are all bundled up in winter clothes, knees knocking and teeth chattering. They are huddled together and are very cold. One grasshopper holds a sign up that says "Will work for food!" Other grasshoppers are holding out empty paper plates and acting starved.

The ants' side of the stage looks very much like the stage in Scene 1. The ants are relaxing in lounge chairs. They are sipping hot tea. There is a mock fireplace with a cozy fire.

One grasshopper knocks on an imaginary door that serves as the entrance to the ants' side of the stage. One ant hears the knock, goes to the imaginary door and opens it.

Ant: Why Grasshopper, what can I do for you on this fine winter day? *(The ant speaks with an air of "I told you so!")*

Grasshopper: Please, my friends and I are so hungry and cold. We remembered what a kind, hard-working lot you ants are. Could you please give us some food and a warm room?

Ants: *(Together)* We're sorry, Grasshopper, but we only have enough to feed ourselves through the long winter. Maybe you should eat the food you stored up for yourselves last summer.

Grasshopper: But, we didn't store any— *(At that moment, the grasshopper realized how right the ants were to have worked so hard last summer, and how wrong the grasshoppers had been by being so lazy and just having fun all summer long.)*

Grasshopper: Thank you anyway. Next summer, we will store up food for ourselves so that we won't starve in the winter.

All Characters: The moral of the story of the Grasshoppers and the Ants is...

Never put off 'til tomorrow what needs to be done today!

Quick Reference

Table of Contents

Jingles

Un-Quigley, Un-Quigley,
What are you going to do?
You've got a frown on your face,
And you're singing the blues!
You're not organized, Quigley;
You are not prepared.
You're not listening, and your mind's not there.
You don't have plans, and you don't have goals.
Your homework's unfinished,
And you've been told.
You need to get your act together
'Cause you don't have a clue.
You've got the Study Skills Blues!

O-Quigley, O-Quigley,
Now, you see what to do.
You've got a smile on your face,
And you're lookin' cool!
You're so organized, Quigley;
You are so prepared.
You're listening carefully,
And your mind is there.
You've got plans, and you've got goals.
Your homework is finished;
You don't have to be told.
You've got your act together, Quigley,
'Cause you followed the clues.
And you're **NOT** singing the Study Skills Blues!

Jingle 2   The Sentence Jingle

A sentence, sentence, sentence
Is complete, complete, complete
When five simple rules
It meets, meets, meets.

It has a subject, subject, subject
And a verb, verb, verb.
And it makes sense, sense, sense
With every word, word, word.

Add a capital letter
And a punctuation mark.
And now our sentence has all its parts!

But REMEMBER—
Subject and **verb** and **complete sense**,
With a **capital letter**
And an **end mark**, too.
Our sentence is complete,
And now we're through!

Jingle 3   The Noun Jingle

This is a noun jingle,
My friend,
A noun jingle, my friend.
You can shake it
To the left,
And shake it to the right.
Find yourself a noun,
And then recite:

A noun names a person.
A noun names a thing.
A noun names a person,
Place, or thing,
And sometimes an idea.
Person, place, thing, idea!
Person, place, thing, idea!

So, shake it to the left,
And shake it to the right.
Find yourself a noun,
And feel just right!

Jingle 4   The Verb Jingle

A verb, a verb.
What is a verb?
Haven't you heard?
There are two kinds of verbs:
The **action verb**
And the **linking verb**.

The action verb shows
A state of action,
Like *stand* and *sit*
And *smile*.
The action verb
Is always in motion
Because it tells
What the subject does.
*We **stand**!*
*We **sit**!*
*We **smile**!*

The linking verb shows
A state of being,
Like *am*, *is*, *are*, *was*,
And *were*,
Looks, *becomes*, *grows*,
And *feels*.
The linking verb shows
No action
Because it tells
What the subject is.
*He **is** a clown.*
*He **looks** funny.*

Jingle 5 The Adverb Jingle

An adverb modifies a verb, adjective, or another adverb.
An adverb asks, "HOW? WHEN? WHERE?"
To find an adverb: **Go,** *(snap)* **Ask,** *(snap)* **Get.** *(snap)*
But where do I **go**? *To a verb, adjective, or another adverb.*
What do I **ask**? *HOW? WHEN? WHERE?*
What do I **get**? An adverb, man. Cool!

Jingle 6 The Adjective Jingle

An adjective modifies a noun or a pronoun.
An adjective asks, "WHAT KIND?"
An adjective asks, "WHICH ONE?"
An adjective asks, "HOW MANY?"
To identify an adjective: **Go!** *(stomp, stomp)* **Ask!** *(clap, clap)* **Get!** *(snap)*
Where do I **go**? *(stomp, stomp)* *To a noun or a pronoun.*
What do I **ask**? *(clap, clap)* WHAT KIND? WHICH ONE? or HOW MANY?
What do I **get**? *(snap, snap)* An adjective!

Jingle 7 The Article Adjective Jingle

We are the article adjectives,
Teeny, tiny adjectives.
A, AN, THE — A, AN, THE

We are called article adjectives and noun markers.
We are memorized and used every day.
So, if you spot us, you can mark us
With a capital **A**.

We are the article adjectives,
Teeny, tiny adjectives.
A, AN, THE — A, AN, THE

Jingle 8 — The Preposition Jingle

A prep, prep, preposition
Is an extra-special word
That connects a

Noun, noun, noun
Or a pro, pro, pronoun
To the rest of the sentence.

Jingle 9 — The Object of the Preposition Jingle

An object of the preposition
Is a NOUN or PRONOUN.
An object of the preposition
Is a NOUN or PRONOUN

After the prep, prep, prep
After the prep, prep, prep
After the prep, prep, prep
That answers **WHAT** or **WHOM**.

Jingle 10 — The Prepositional Phrase Jingle

I've been working with prepositions
'Til I can work no more.
They're connecting their objects
To the rest of the sentence before.

When I put them all together,
The prep and its noun or pro,
I get a prepositional phrase
That could cause my mind to blow!

Jingle 11 — The Preposition Flow Jingle

1. Preposition, Preposition,
   Starting with an **A**:
   **aboard, about, above,
   across, after, against,
   along, among, around, as, at!**

2. Preposition, Preposition,
   Starting with a **B**:
   **before, behind, below,
   beneath, beside, between,
   beyond, but,** and **by!**

3. Preposition, Preposition,
   Starting with a **D**:
   **despite, down, during
   despite, down, during!**

4. Oh, Preposition,
   Please, don't go away.
   Go to the middle of the alphabet,
   And see just what we say.
   E and **F** and **I** and **L**
   And **N** and **O** and **P**:
   **except, for, from, in, inside,
   into, like, near, of, off, on, out,
   outside, over, past!**

5. Preposition, Preposition,
   Almost through.
   Start with **S** and
   end with **W**:
   **since, through,
   throughout, to, toward,
   under, underneath,
   until, up, upon,
   with, within, without!**

6. Preposition, Preposition,
   Easy as can be.

   We just recited
   All **fifty-one**
   of these!

Aw, listen, comrades,
And you shall hear
About transition words
That make your writing
Smooth and clear.

Transition words
Are connecting words.
You add them to the beginning
Of sentences and paragraphs
To keep your ideas spinning
And give your writing flow.

These words can clarify,
Summarize, or emphasize,
Compare or contrast,
Inform or show time.
Learn them now,
And your writing will shine!

Transition, Transition,
For words that **SHOW TIME:**
first, second, third,
before, during, after,
next, then, and *finally.*

Transition, Transition,
For words that **INFORM:**
for example, for instance,
in addition, as well, also,
next, another, along with,
And *besides.*

Transition, Transition,
For words that **CONTRAST:**
although, even though,
but, yet, still,
otherwise, however,
And *on the other hand.*

Transition, Transition,
For words that **COMPARE:**
as, also, like, and *likewise.*

Transition, Transition,
For words that **CLARIFY:**
for example, for instance,
And *in other words.*

Transition, Transition,
For words that **EMPHASIZE:**
truly, again, for this reason,
And *in fact.*

Transition, Transition,
For words that **SUMMARIZE:**
therefore, in conclusion,
in summary, and *finally,*
to sum it up, all in all,
as a result, and *last.*

TRANSITION
WORD

Jingle 13   The Pronoun Jingle

These little pronouns,
Hangin' around,
Can take the place
Of any of the nouns.

With a smile and a nod
And a twinkle of the eye,
Give those pronouns
A big high five! Yeah!

Jingle 14   The Subject Pronoun Jingle

There are seven
Subject pronouns
That are easy as can be.
SUBJECT PRONOUNS!

I and **We**,
He and **She**,
It and **They** and **You**.
Those are the subject pronouns!

Jingle 15   The Possessive Pronoun Jingle

There are seven
Possessive pronouns
That are easy as can be.
POSSESSIVE PRONOUNS!

My and **Our**,
His and **Her**,
Its and **Their** and **Your**.
Those are possessive pronouns!

Jingle 16   The Conjunction Sound-Off Jingle

Conjunctions are a part of speech.

Conjunctions are a part of speech.

They join words or sentences; it's quite a feat!

They join words or sentences; it's quite a feat!

Sound off! Conjunctions!   **Sound off! AND, OR, BUT!**

There are many conjunctions, but three stand out.

There are many conjunctions, but three stand out.

Put your hands together and give a shout!

Put your hands together and give a shout!

Sound off! Conjunctions!   **Sound off! AND, OR, BUT!**

     Sound off! Conjunctions!   **Sound off! AND, OR, BUT!**

Jingle 17 — The **23** Helping Verbs of the Mean, Lean, Verb Machine Jingle

These twenty-three helping verbs
Will be on my test.
I've gotta remember them
So I can do my best.
I'll start out with eight
And finish with fifteen.
Just call me the mean,
Lean, verb machine.

There are the eight **be** verbs
That are easy as can be.
    am, is, are   was and **were**
    am, is, are   was and **were**
    am, is, are   was and **were**
    be, being, and **been**

All together now, the eight **be** verbs:
am, is, are   was and **were**
    be, being, and **been**
am, is, are   was and **were**
    be, being, and **been**
am, is, are   was and **were**
    be, being, and **been**

There are twenty-three helping verbs,
And I've recited eight.
That leaves fifteen more
That I must relate.
Knowing all these verbs
Will save my grade.
The mean, lean, verb machine
Is here to stay.

    has, have, and **had   do, does,** and **did**
    has, have, and **had   do, does,** and **did**
      might, must, and **may**
      might, must, and **may**
    can and **could   would** and **should**
    can and **could   would** and **should**
      shall and **will   shall** and **will**
    has, have, and **had   do, does,** and **did**
      might, must, and **may**
    can and **could, would** and **should**
      shall and **will**

In record time, I did this drill.
I'm the mean, lean, verb machine — STILL!

Jingle 18 — The Interjection Jingle

Oh, Interjection, Interjection, Interjection, who are you?
    I'm a part of speech through and through.

Well, Interjection, Interjection, Interjection, what do you do?
    I show strong or mild emotion; need a review?

Oh, Interjection, Interjection, I still don't have a clue.
    I show strong emotion, like Wow! Great! or Yahoo!
    I show mild emotion, like Oh, Yes, Fine, or Toodle-doo.

Well, Interjection, Interjection, you really know how to groove!
    That's because I'm a part of speech through and through!

Jingle 19 — The Possessive Noun Jingle

A possessive noun
Just can't be beat.
It shows ownership,
And that is neat.
Add an apostrophe
To show possession.

This is a great ownership lesson.
Adjective is its part of speech.
Ask **WHOSE** to find it
As you speak.
Whose house? Tommy's house.
Possessive Noun Adjective!

Jingle 20 — The Eight Parts of Speech Jingle

Want to know how to write?
Use the eight parts of speech.
They're dynamite!

Nouns, **V**erbs, and **P**ronouns.
They rule!
They're called the **NVP's**, and they're really cool!
The **Double A's** are on the move.
Adjectives and **A**dverbs help you to groove.
Next come the **PIC's**, and then we're done.
They're **P**reposition, **I**nterjection, and **C**onjunction!

All together now.
The eight parts of speech, abbreviations, please.
NVP—AA—and**—PIC!**

Jingle 21 The Direct Object Jingle

A **direct object** is a NOUN
Or a PRO,
Is a noun or a pro,
Is a noun or a pro.
A **direct object**
Completes the meaning,
Completes the meaning
Of the sentence.

A **direct object** follows the verb,
Follows the *verb-transitive*.

To find a direct object,
Ask **WHAT** or **WHOM**
Ask **WHAT** or **WHOM**
After the verb.

Jingle 22 The Object Pronoun Jingle

There are seven
Object pronouns
That are easy as can be.
OBJECT PRONOUNS!

Me and **Us**,
Him and **Her**,
It and **Them** and **You**.
Those are the object pronouns!

Indirect, oh, indirect, oh, indirect object.
Give me that indirect, oh, indirect, oh, indirect object.

An indirect object is a NOUN or a PRONOUN
That receives what the direct, the direct object names.
An indirect object is found between the verb, **verb-transitive**,
And the direct object.
> To find the indirect object,　　(sha-bop)
> Ask **TO WHOM** or **FOR WHOM**　(sha-bop)
> After the direct object.　　(sha-bop)

An indirect, indirect, indirect, indirect, yeah!
An indirect object!
> *Just give me that indirect, oh, indirect, oh, indirect object.*
> *Give me that indirect, oh, indirect, oh, indirect object.*
> *Give me that object, oh, indirect, oh, indirect object.*
An **INDIRECT OBJECT!**

Jingle 24 — The Predicate Noun Jingle

A predicate, predicate noun
  Is a special, special noun
    In the predicate, predicate, predicate
      That means the **same as the subject**,
        The simple, simple subject.

    A predicate, predicate noun
      Follows after a linking verb.

To locate a predicate noun,
  Ask **WHAT** or **WHO** after the verb and verify the answer.
      Verify that the noun in the predicate means
      the same thing as the subject,
        The simple, simple subject.

Nouns will give you a run for your money.
They do so many jobs
That it's not even funny.

A noun — person, place, thing, or idea —
Is very appealing.
But it's the noun job *(noun job)*
That is so revealing.

To find the nouns in a sentence,
Go to their jobs *(go to their jobs)*.

Nouns can do objective jobs *(objective jobs)*.
They're the **IO** *(IO)*, **DO** *(DO)*, and **OP** jobs *(OP jobs)*.

And nouns can do subjective jobs *(subjective jobs)*.
They're the **SN** *(SN)* and **PrN** jobs *(PrN jobs)*.
Jobs. Jobs. Noun Jobs! Yeah!

A predicate, predicate, predicate adjective
Is a special, special adjective
In the predicate, predicate, predicate
That modifies, modifies, **modifies**
The simple, simple **subject**.

A predicate, predicate, predicate adjective
Follows after a linking verb.
To find a predicate adjective,
Ask **WHAT KIND** of subject
And verify the answer.

Verify that the adjective in the predicate
Modifies, modifies, modifies
The simple, simple subject.

The BE Verb Jingle
These are the BE verbs,
Mighty, mighty BE verbs!
am, is, are---**was** and **were**
be, **being**, and **been**

The mighty, mighty BE verbs
Can be **Linking Verbs**;
They link the subject and the predicate words.
They show no action; they're **state-of-being** verbs.

The mighty, mighty BE verbs
Can be **Helping Verbs**;
They help main verbs and determine the tense.
They're part of verb phrases and help them make sense.

The mighty, mighty BE verbs
Are useful verbs to know;
Learn your Mighty Be verbs now
And watch your knowledge grow!

These are the BE verbs,
Mighty, mighty BE verbs!
am, is, are---**was** and **were**
be, **being**, and **been**

Writing Process
References

Step 1: Prewriting

Step 1 is prewriting. In the first part of prewriting, you gather and group your ideas and thoughts for writing. In the second part of prewriting, you use a **graphic organizer** to help you organize your ideas on paper in a visual format. Some types of graphic organizers are clusters, Venn diagrams, outlines, and prewriting maps. As you do Step 1, use the prewriting checklist below.

Prewriting Checklist

 1. Know your purpose.
How do you want your writing to affect your reader?

➡ Knowing your purpose will help you decide which **genre**, or type of writing, you want to use.

Writing Genre:	Purpose
Descriptive:	to describe
Narrative:	to tell a story
Expository:	to explain or inform
Persuasive:	to persuade or convince
Creative:	to entertain
Comparison:	to compare

 2. Know your audience.
Who will be your primary reader?

➡ Knowing your audience will help you with certain word choice decisions, and it will also affect your voice. For example, you might describe an apple as "crimson" for your teacher, but "red" for your younger brother.

3. Choose your topic.
What can you write about?

➡ Brainstorm for ideas to make a list of possible topics. Consider each possible topic and the main points you could develop for each one. Pick the topic that you think you could best develop.

 ## 4. Narrow your topic.
What do you want to say about your topic?

➡ Once you've chosen a topic, you must decide if you need to narrow it. A narrowed topic is easier to develop because it is focused on one idea. A good way to narrow your topic is to write your topic in a complete sentence.

 ## 5. Gather your details.
How can you develop your topic?

➡ Brainstorm or research for supporting details to develop your main points. Use your own experience, ask other people, or look for additional information in books or other sources. Remember to use only details that support your topic.

 ## 6. Organize your details.
What is the best way to present your information?

➡ Think about the best way to arrange your main points and supporting details. Keep your audience and purpose in mind as you organize. Use a graphic organizer to help you organize your information.

Step 2: Rough Draft

Step 2 is writing a rough draft. Your first writing attempt is called a rough draft. You will use the ideas on your prewriting map to write your rough draft. Every good writer knows that the rough draft is never the best draft, so don't worry about mistakes. You will make improvements later.

To write a rough draft, use the following checklist.

Rough Draft Checklist

☑ **1. Write with a pencil on notebook paper.**

☑ **2. Record this information on the left side of your paper.**

➡ **Name:** (your name)
Date: (today's date)
WA: (Writing Assignment number)
Purpose: (to describe, to tell a story, to inform, etc.)
Genre: (descriptive, narrative, expository, etc.)
Audience: (classmates, teacher, parents, friend, etc.)
Topic: (the topic of your writing)

☑ **3. Skip the next line.**

☑ **4. Format your rough draft.**

➡ Skip every other line and use extra wide margins as you write.

➡ Indent the first line of every paragraph.

☑ **5. Use these writing traits as you write your rough draft.**

 Ideas

1. Write the ideas from your prewriting map in complete sentences.
2. Add interesting details to support main points.

Organization

3. Develop an engaging introduction, a powerful body, and a strong conclusion.

4. Have a clear topic sentence for each paragraph.

5. Arrange sentences and paragraphs in a logical order, using transition words to link ideas, opinions, reasons, or events.

Word Choice

6. Use precise nouns and verbs to engage the reader's imagination.

7. Use vivid adjectives and adverbs to create strong mental pictures.

8. Use prepositional phrases to add more detail and description.

Voice

9. Use word choices to express ideas in different ways.

10. Use similes, metaphors, or personification to add contrast and interest.

Sentence Fluency

11. Use a variety of simple, compound, and complex sentences.

12. Vary sentence length by making some long and some short.

13. Use different sentence patterns to give your writing variety.

Conventions

14. Follow the rules of capitalization and punctuation.

15. Use correct spelling, homonyms, plural forms, and subject-verb agreement.

 6. Think of a title after you finish writing your rough draft.

➡ Skip two lines below the last line of your rough draft and write your title.

➡ See Reference 63 on page Q22 for more about writing a title.

 7. Put your rough draft and prewriting map in your Rough Draft folder.

Writing an Effective Title

Most finished pieces of writing have a title at the beginning.

1. Use your title to grab your reader's attention and make them want to read more.

2. Write a title that is related to your topic.
   Unrelated titles are misleading, confusing, and frustrating for readers who expect one thing and get another from the piece of writing.

3. Show off your creativity.
   The title is a great place to get creative. Think of several possible titles and pick the one you like most.

4. Capitalize the first, last, and any important words in the title.
   Do not capitalize *a*, *an*, *the*, *and*, *but*, *or*, *of*, *on*, *in*, or other short prepositions unless they are the first or last word of the title.

5. Write the title last.
   The best time to think of a title is after you've finished your rough draft. Read your rough draft to get title ideas. Here are some titles that Quigley considered after he had written his rough draft:

   ➥ **My Favorite Pet**

   ➥ **My Dog**

   ➥ **Lady of the House**

   ➥ **Lady, My Basset Hound**

   Write the title at the end of your rough draft.

6. Write the title at the beginning of your final paper.
   The title should be placed in the center of the top line on the final paper.

Step 3: Revising

Step 3 is revising the rough draft. Revising means to find ways to improve word choices and sentences in your rough draft. Read through your rough draft several times. First, read it silently. Then, read it aloud to yourself. Finally, read it aloud to others. Reading your rough draft out loud will help you find "rough spots" that could use improvement. Use the checklist below to revise and improve your rough draft.

Revising Checklist

 Use these writing traits as you revise your rough draft.

 ### Ideas

    1. Are there any important or interesting ideas or details that could be added?

 ### Organization

    2. Is there a clear *introduction*, *body*, and *conclusion*? Do you need to make any improvements?

    3. Does each paragraph have a topic sentence?

    4. Are there sentences that should be deleted because they do not support your topic?

    5. Are the sentences and paragraphs in a logical order? Should they be rearranged?

    6. Does your writing reflect its *purpose*, *genre*, and *audience*?

 ### Word Choices

    7. Can you add or replace any weak words with stronger word choices?

    8. Are there any repeated or unclear words that should be deleted?

CONTINUED ON NEXT PAGE

Voice

9. Do your word choices make your writing sound unique?

10. Can you add figurative language (similes, metaphors, personification)?

Sentence Fluency

11. Are the sentences varied in length and type?

12. Do you need to combine or shorten any sentences?

13. Do you need to add or change transistion words?

☑ **Write your revisions in the blank spaces of your rough draft.**

☑ **Draw a line through words or sentences that you want to delete or replace.**

Step 4: Editing

Step 4 is editing the rough draft. Editing is correcting mistakes in spelling, grammar, usage, capitalization, and punctuation. Scan your newly revised rough draft several times, checking each paragraph, sentence, and word for convention mistakes. Use the editing checklist to edit your rough draft.

Editing Checklist

☑ **Use this writing trait as you edit your rough draft.**

Conventions

1. Is the first line of every paragraph indented?

2. Does every sentence begin with a capital letter and end with the proper end mark?

3. Have you followed all the rules for capitalization?

4. Have you followed all the rules for punctuation?

5. Are there any misspelled words or homonym mistakes?

6. Are there any misspelled contractions, possessives, or plural forms?

7. Are there any usage mistakes (a/an choices, subject-verb agreement, etc.)?

8. Have you punctuated the different types of sentences correctly? Are there any fragments?

 When you find an editing mistake, circle it and write the correction above it.

 Put the revised and edited rough draft back in your Rough Draft folder.

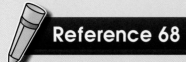

Revising & Editing Schedule

1 **Individual Revision:** Read your rough draft silently. Then, use the revision questions in Reference 64 to revise your rough draft.

2 **Individual Editing:** Now, go to the editing questions in Reference 66. Read your rough draft silently again, using the editing questions to edit your rough draft. Check thoroughly for errors.

3 **Partner Revision:** Get with your writing partner. Read each rough draft aloud. For each paper, ask the revision questions in Reference 64. Each partner should write revisions on his or her own paper.

4 **Partner Editing:** Using the editing questions in Reference 66, check each rough draft thoroughly for errors. Each partner should write corrections on his or her own paper.

5 **Peer Evaluation:** Your peers are your classmates. Join a peer evaluation group and take turns reading each paper aloud to the group. When another member of your group is reading, listen quietly and carefully. When each person is finished, politely offer helpful suggestions. Only the author of each paper can decide whether to make changes suggested by the group.

Step 5: Final Paper

Step 5 is writing a final paper. A final paper is a corrected copy of your rough draft. It should always be clean and neat, with no editing or revision marks on it. Use the checklist below to write a final paper.

Checklist for Writing a Final Paper

☑ 1. **Neatly write with a pencil on notebook paper.**

☑ 2. **Write the title at the center of the top line.**

☑ 3. **Write the word "by" just under the title, followed by your name.**

☑ 4. **Skip one line below your name and begin writing your paper.**
   ➡ Make sure you indent each paragraph.
   ➡ Single-space your paper; do not skip lines as you write.
   ➡ Use wide margins on both sides.

☑ 5. **Use the Student Rubric to make a final check of your paper.**

☑ 6. **Put your prewriting map, rough draft, and the final paper together.**
   ➡ Put your prewriting map on the bottom.
   ➡ Put your rough draft in the middle.
   ➡ Put your final paper on top.
   ➡ Staple them all together.

☑ 7. **Put the stapled papers in your Final Paper folder.**

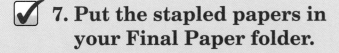

Final Paper

Step 6: Publishing

Step 6 is publishing. The publishing step is your chance to share your writing with others. To get started, follow these steps:

Publishing Checklist

☑ **1. Rewrite your graded paper in ink or type it on a computer.**

➡ Be sure to correct any mistakes. You never want to share papers that have any marked errors, notes from your teacher, or grades on them.

☑ **2. Give your teacher your stapled papers.**

➡ Your teacher will put them into your Writing Portfolio.

➡ Your papers should include the rubrics, your graded final paper, your revised and edited rough draft, and your prewriting map.

☑ **3. There are many ways to publish your work.**

➡ The directions for your writing assignment will include ideas for publishing your paper.

Reference 85

Guidelines for an Oral Presentation

Speaker Presentation

1. Have your paper ready to read when it is your turn.

2. Tell the title of your writing selection.

3. Tell the purpose and type of writing used.

4. Stand with your feet flat on the floor and your shoulders straight. Do not shift your weight as you stand.

5. Hold your paper about chin high to help project your voice to your audience.

6. Read in a clear voice that can be heard so your audience does not have to strain to hear.

7. Make sure you do not read too fast.

8. Change your voice tone for different characters or for different parts of the writing selection.

Audience Response

1. Look at the speaker.

2. Turn your body toward the speaker.

3. Listen attentively. Do not let your thoughts wander.

4. Do not distract the speaker or other listeners.

5. Show interest in what the speaker is saying.

6. Silently summarize what the speaker is saying. Take notes if necessary.

7. Ask questions about anything that is not clear.

8. Show appreciation by clapping after the speaker has finished.

clap, clap, clap
clap, clap, clap

Resource
Tools

Abbreviations Used in Shurley English

The following list provides a quick reference of the most commonly used abbreviations in Shurley English.

Abbreviation	Description
N	Noun
SN	Subject Noun
CSN	Compound Subject Noun
Pro	Pronoun
SP	Subject Pronoun
CSP	Compound Subject Pronoun
V	Verb
HV	Helping Verb
CV	Compound Verb
V-t	Verb-transitive
CV-t	Compound Verb-transitive
LV	Linking Verb
CLV	Compound Linking Verb
A	Article Adjective
Adj	Adjective
CAdj	Compound Adjective
Adv	Adverb
CAdv	Compound Adverb
P	Preposition
OP	Object of the Preposition
COP	Compound Object of the Preposition
PPA	Possessive Pronoun Adjective
PNA	Possessive Noun Adjective
C	Conjunction

Abbreviation	Description
I	Interjection
DO	Direct Object
CDO	Compound Direct Object
IO	Indirect Object
CIO	Compound Indirect Object
PrN	Predicate Noun
CPrN	Compound Predicate Noun
PrP	Predicate Pronoun
CPrP	Compound Predicate Pronoun
PA	Predicate Adjective
CPA	Compound Predicate Adjective

Sentences	
D	Declarative Sentence
E	Exclamatory Sentence
Int	Interrogative Sentence
Imp	Imperative Sentence
S	Simple Sentence
F	Fragment
SCS	Simple Sentence Compound Subject
SCV	Simple Sentence Compound Verb
CD	Compound Sentence
CX	Complex Sentence

Level 4 Patterns	
SN V P1	Subject Noun Verb Pattern 1
SN V-t DO P2	Subject Noun Verb-transitive Direct Object Pattern 2
SN V-t IO DO P3	Subject Noun Verb-transitive Indirect Object Direct Object Pattern 3
SN LV PrN P4	Subject Noun Linking Verb Predicate Noun Pattern 4
SN LV PA P5	Subject Noun Linking Verb Predicate Adjective Pattern 5

Capitalization Rules

Always capitalize...

1. the first word of a sentence, a direct quotation, an entry in an outline, or the greeting and closing of a letter.

   (We asked, "Are we there yet?"
   A. Otters and their homes
   Dear Meg,)

2. the pronoun I.

   (She and I love apple pie.)

Capitalize the names, nicknames, titles, initials, and abbreviations that name...

3. people, pets, and family names when used in place of or with the person's name.

   (James, Big Jim, Mom, Mr. J. R. Smith, Fluffy, Grandpa, Cousin Jeff)

   Note: Do not capitalize family names when a possessive noun or pronoun is used with it: *My mom, Kim's mom, Jim's father, His aunt,* etc.

4. days, months, and holidays.

   (Monday, October, Oct., Labor Day, Christmas)

5. places on a map (roads, waterways, cities, countries, continents, etc.) and objects in space (stars, planets, moons, space stations, constellations, etc.).

   (Maple Street, Dallas, Texas, TX, France, the West, Atlantic Ocean, Mars)

6. schools, specific classes, languages and proper adjectives, businesses, organizations, buildings, products, and ships.

   (Tom Landry Middle School, Language Arts, Spanish, Walmart, Boy Scouts, Sears Tower, Coca-Cola®, Titanic)

   Note: Only specific classes are capitalized, not general subjects: Elementary Astronomy, science, Mathematics II, math.)

7. historical events or periods, laws, conflicts, awards, monuments, and documents.

   (World War II, Statue of Liberty, Bill of Rights, Middle Ages, Civil War, Medal of Honor, etc.)

Capitalize the first, last, and important words in...

8. the titles of published or produced works, such as books, essays, poems, songs, movies, television shows, newspapers, magazines, paintings, and sculptures.

   (*The Call of the Wild, Starry Night, The New York Times, Avatar: The Last Airbender*)

   Note: Conjunctions, articles, and prepositions with fewer than five letters are not capitalized unless they are the first or last words.

Punctuation Rules

The End of a Sentence

1. Put a **period**, a **question mark**, or an **exclamation point** at the end of a sentence.

   • Use a **period** (.) for the end punctuation of a sentence that makes a statement. (James is very tall.)

   • Use a **question mark** (?) for the end punctuation of a sentence that asks a question. (Are you coming to my birthday party?)

   • Use an **exclamation point** (!) for the end punctuation of a sentence that expresses strong feeling. (We won the lottery!)

   • Use a **period** (.) for the end punctuation of a sentence that gives a command or makes a request. (Close the door.)

Clarifying Information

2. Put a **comma** (,) between words in a series. (I like apples, oranges, and bananas.)

3. Put **commas** between the words in a date:

   • Between the day and the month. (Friday, July 23)

   • Between the day and the year. (July 23, 2013)

   • Between the year and the rest of the sentence. (Our wedding is Saturday, April 24, 2013, at our church.)

Note: When just the month and the year appear in a sentence, no comma is required. (*We leave in May 2014 for our first vacation.*)

Contractions, Possessive Nouns, Abbreviations

4. Use an **apostrophe** in contractions (isn't) and possessive nouns (Mom's) and use a **period** (.) at the end of most abbreviations. (Dr. Feb. Mr.)

Letters and Addresses

5. Put a **comma** in the greeting and closing of letters:

   • After the name in the greeting. (Dear Charles,)

   • After the word(s) used in the closing. (Sincerely, Josh)

6. Put a **comma** between locations in an address:

   • Between the city and the state or country. (I live in Dallas, Texas.)

   • Between the state or country and the rest of the sentence. (Bart lives in Omaha, Nebraska, with his parents.)

Quotations

7. Use **quotation marks** before and after the exact words of a speaker.

   (Jay said, "I am hungry!")

CONTINUED ON NEXT PAGE

- Use a **comma** to set off the explanatory words that tell who is speaking.
  (Fred said**,** "I'm here.")

- Use a **comma** at the end of a quotation if the sentence continues, unless the quotation is a question or an exclamation.
  ("I'm here**,**" Fred said.)

- Use a new paragraph to indicate a change of speaker.

- When a speaker's speech is longer than one paragraph, use quotation marks at the beginning of each paragraph and at the end of the last paragraph of that speaker's speech.

- Use **single quotation marks** to enclose a quotation within a quotation.
  ("My bear says **'**I love you**'** four different ways," said little Amy.)

8. Put **quotation marks** before and after the exact words from a book, story, or poem.

   (The author describes Jim as **"**a tall, thin man with a friendly grin**."**)

Sentences

9. Put a **comma** *before* the coordinating conjunction in a compound sentence and *after* an introductory clause in a complex sentence.

   COMPOUND: Don played golf**,** and I played tennis.

   COMPLEX: After Trey entered the game**,** his team scored a goal.

10. Put a **comma** after an adverb or prepositional phrase before the subject of an inverted word-order sentence.

    (On Tuesday**,** we went to the movies.)

Titles of Works

11. *Italicize* or <u>underline</u> the titles and subtitles of full-length published works, such as books, movies, long plays, long poems, newspapers.

    (*The Giver* is a book written by Lois Lowry.)
    (<u>The Giver</u> is a book written by Lois Lowry.)

12. Put **quotation marks** around the titles of shorter published works and parts of long works, such as short stories, most poems, songs, one-act plays, chapters in a book, or newspaper articles.

    ("The Red-Headed League" is my favorite Sherlock Holmes mystery.)

Separating Extra Words from the Sentence

13. Use **commas** to set off interrupting words, such as appositives, nouns of direct address, tag questions, and introductory words.

    - An **appositive** is extra information given after a noun.
      (Sue**, my friend,** is an artist.)

    - A noun of direct address is the person spoken to.
      (**Aunt Jan,** will you visit us?)

    - A tag question is a short question at the end of a statement.
      (It is pretty**, isn't it?**)

    - Introductory words include *yes*, *no*, *well*, and others.
      (**Well,** I'm not sure.)

14. Use **parentheses (( ))** or **dashes (—)** to separate parenthetical information (*information that is useful but not necessary*) from the rest of the sentence.

    (Jake Jones — the tall boy in my class who sits in the corner desk — ate three hot dogs at lunch!)

Coordinate Adjectives

15. Use **commas** between adjectives that describe the same characteristic of the same noun, or adjectives in a series that are out of the usual order.

    (The music box played a beautiful, cheerful melody.)

Breaks, Pauses, and Omissions

16. Use **dashes (—)** or **ellipses (...)** in dialogue to indicate that a character has suddenly stopped speaking or let his words trail off without completing his thought.

    (Daniel could only say, "Hello? Is anyone—" before the phone went dead.

    ("Now, what do we have here..." the detective muttered.)

17. Use **ellipses** to replace omitted words in a direct quotation from a source.
    (According to the old nursery rhyme, "...the little dog laughed... and the dish ran away with the spoon.")

Other Punctuation Rules

18. Use a **hyphen (-)** to connect or divide words in the following ways:

    - to combine two words into a single adjective.
      (generous-hearted man)

- to write out numbers and fractions.
  (twenty-three, three-fifths)
- to add certain prefixes and suffixes.
  (all-knowing, ex-governor, self-serve,
  president-elect)
- to divide a word at the end of a line when
  typing on a typewriter.
  (com-
  pound)

19. Use a **colon** (**:**) to connect or divide words
    in the following ways:

- to separate hours and minutes.
  (8:45 a.m. and 9:00 p.m.)
- to introduce a listing of items after a
  complete sentence.
  (Dad bought four items at the hardware
  store: hammers, nails, wood, and paint.)

- to introduce a long statement, quotation,
  or question.
  (John Adams stated: "A desire to be ob-
  served, considered, esteemed, praised,
  beloved, and admired by his fellows is one
  of the earliest as well as the keenest dispo-
  sitions discovered in the heart of man.")

20. Use a **semicolon** (**;**) when a comma is not
    enough or would be confusing:

- to join independent clauses in a compound
  sentence without a conjunction.
  (We need food; therefore, I will go to the store.)
  (I liked this movie; I want to see it again.)
- to separate items in a series when the items
  include other commas.
  (During our business trip, we traveled to
  Dallas, Texas; Denver, Colorado; and
  Columbus, Ohio.)

About Prefixes and Suffixes

Prefixes

A **prefix** is a word part added to the beginning of a base word to change its meaning. Prefixes have meanings of their own.
If you know the meanings of the prefix part and the base word, you can usually figure out the meaning of the new word
that is made from combining the two parts. Some common prefixes are listed below to help you learn their meanings.

Prefix	Meaning	Examples
bi	two, twice	bicycle
dis, non, un	not, opposite of, without	distrust; nonfat; unhappy
im, in	not, in, into	impatient; independent
inter	between, among	interstate; interact
mis	wrong, wrongly, badly	misbehave; mistake
post	after	posttest
pre	before	pretest
re	again, back	repay; return
sub	beneath, under	submarine; subway

submarine

→ under   → sea

CONTINUED ON NEXT PAGE ▶

Suffixes

A suffix is a word part added to the end of a base word to change its meaning. Suffixes have meanings of their own, too. If you know the meanings of the suffix part and the base word, you can usually figure out the meaning of the new word that is made from the two parts. Some common suffixes are listed below to help you learn their meanings.

Suffix	Meaning	Examples
able	able to (use)	usable
er	one who (teaches)	teacher
ful	full of (joy)	joyful
ize	to make (final)	finalize
less	without (a home)	homeless
ly	in the manner of (quiet)	quietly
tion	the result of (inventing)	invention
ward	moving (up)	upward

✓ Suffix Spelling Check

The following spelling rules will help when adding suffixes to words. Since there are several exceptions to these rules, always check the dictionary if you are in doubt about the spelling of a word.

1. To add a suffix to a word that ends in a **silent -e**, *drop the final -e* if the suffix begins with a **vowel**.
   desire / desirable   approve / approval   drive / driving   **Exception:** noticeable

2. To add a suffix to a word that ends in **a silent -e**, *keep the final -e* if the suffix begins with a **consonant**.
   care / careful   state / statement   advance / advancement   **Exception:** true / truly

3. To add a suffix to a word ending in a **consonant plus -y**, *change the -y to i* unless the suffix begins with i-.
   fly / flier / flying   dry / drier / drying   study / studied / studying

4. To add a suffix to a word ending in a **vowel plus -y**, *do not change the -y to i*.
   play / played   pay / payment

5. To add a suffix to a short word that ends with one vowel and one consonant, *double* the final consonant.
   sit / sitting   drop / dropper   big / bigger   **Exception:** job / jobless

Listening and Speaking
Following Written Directions

It is important that you learn to follow written directions. Sometimes, you must read directions several times in order to understand what to do. Written directions are used for many reasons. Some of the ways you will follow written directions include following recipes, filling out forms, taking tests, and following "how to" instructions.

Directions to go from the post office to the Wagon Wheel Restaurant

To get to the Wagon Wheel Restaurant, first, turn right out of the post-office parking lot and head north on Main Street. Then, go ten blocks to the second stoplight. At the stoplight, turn right on Pine Street, heading east. Next, go six blocks and cross the Willow Street Bridge. Immediately past the bridge, the Wagon Wheel Restaurant will be the brown building on the left, with a large wagon wheel on its sign.

HANDS-ON ACTIVITIES

1. **Writing Connection:** Create a set of written directions for a student partner to follow. Observe as the partner follows your written directions. At the end of this activity, you and your partner will evaluate how easy the directions were to follow and how correctly the partner followed them. Analyze what went wrong if mistakes were made.

2. **Listening/Writing Connection:** Create different versions of "Simon Says" and see if your instructions for each version are clear and complete.

3. **Science Connection:** In small groups, find an interesting science experiment in a science book. Read through the experiment. Predict the outcome of the experiment. Then, discuss how the results would be different if the instructions were not followed. What conclusion can you draw about the importance of following the instructions for the experiment? Write directions for an experiment of your own.

Listening and Speaking
Following Oral Directions

Oral directions are spoken directions. You must listen carefully in order to follow spoken directions. To find out how well you listen and follow oral directions, select a partner and take turns doing the activity below. Compare each of your pictures after both of you have completed the activity. Was it easier or harder for the first reader to follow the directions? Why? Do you prefer oral directions or written directions? Report the findings to your teacher.

Student Instructions
Oral Activity: Read these directions orally to your partner.

1. Today, you will follow oral directions to draw a picture. I will read each step two times. You will have a short working time between each step.

2. Get a sheet of notebook paper and crayons (including yellow and orange) or markers.

3. Draw a large circle near the bottom of your paper.

4. Draw a medium-sized circle resting on top of the large circle.

5. Draw a smaller circle resting on top of the medium-sized circle.

6. Draw a face inside the small circle. Make a carrot nose, a mouth, and eyes.

7. Draw a hat, scarf, and boots on your snowman. You choose the colors.

8. Draw a bright yellow sun in the right, top corner of your page.

9. Draw background scenery for your snow scene.

Listening and Speaking
Interviews

You conduct an interview when you ask a knowledgeable person a series of questions in order to get information about a particular subject. The information that is gathered from an interview is most often used for reports or articles. Family interviews can be used to document and preserve events rooted in family history. Community interviews serve the same purpose as they preserve the history of local events.

The type of interview you are conducting will determine the questions you ask. However, it is helpful to have a few general guidelines to help you conduct a successful interview. Use the suggestions below to help you plan an interview.

Guidelines for Conducting Interviews

1. Call the person you want to interview, explain the purpose of the interview, and make an appointment. Be courteous and be on time for the interview.

2. Write down the questions that you will ask during the interview. Make sure the questions are designed to get the information you need. Avoid asking yes-no questions because they do not give you enough information. The *who, what, when, where, why,* and *how* questions are always good to ask because they provide plenty of details. (**EXAMPLES:** How do you feel about…, What do you think about…, Why did you…, What are the results of…, When do you expect…, What motivated you to…, etc.) Make sure your questions stay on the subject and are in good taste.

3. Take notes or use a tape recorder. If you take notes, leave plenty of space to write the answer to each question. If you use a tape recorder, ask permission first.

4. Make sure your notes accurately reflect what the person said. If you quote a person, be sure to place the exact words in quotation marks. If you are in doubt about any answers, repeat them to the person being interviewed to make sure your information is correct. This is especially important when recording dates or numbers.

5. Thank the person for the interview. Follow up with a thank-you note expressing your appreciation for his time.

6. Write the article as soon as possible after the interview while the details are fresh in your mind.

7. If possible, give a copy of the article to the person you interviewed as a courtesy before it is published.

HANDS-ON ACTIVITIES

Social Studies Connection: Create a list of people you would like to interview. It could be a fire fighter, police officer, nurse, teacher, principal, business person, grandparent, or another person you admire. Get permission to set up an interview. You might use some of the sample questions below.

1. What is your occupation?

2. How did you choose this profession?

3. What training was required for your job?

4. What do you like best about your job?

5. Where were you born and where did you grow up?

6. What is your best memory of growing up?

7. What do you remember about your school experiences?

8. What would you say to young people?

Literature Connection: Create a list of questions for an imaginary interview with an author of your choice from your favorite book. Make sure the topic of the interview is interesting and in good taste. Share your interview questions with family and friends.

Listening and Speaking
Video Presentations

Making video presentations is a fun way to publish any writing, including tall tales, poetry, and book reviews. Some general guidelines that will help video presentations go smoothly are listed below.

Student Guidelines for Making Video Presentations

1. Check the posted schedule so you will know when it is your turn to present.

2. Stay seated until the current presenter has finished and the video camera is no longer recording.

3. When it is your turn, go to the designated area. Make all preparations necessary for your presentation before the camera begins recording.

4. When you are ready, look at the camera operator and wait for the signal to begin.

5. Introduce yourself and your presentation. Be sure to say your first and last name. Here are two examples.

   - **Say, "Hello, my name is (*your first and last name*). The title of my story is (*the title of your story*)."**
   - **Say, "(*the title of your story*) by (*your first and last name*)."**

6. Read clearly, slowly, and loudly enough for everyone to hear and for the equipment to record your voice. Read with expression. Do not be afraid to raise your voice and read with feeling. Even though you are reading from your paper, make an effort to look directly into the camera from time to time.

7. Do not make fast movements. If you move, give the camera operator time to follow you. If you make a mistake, correct it and keep going. Most people do not notice minor mistakes if the speaker recovers quickly and smoothly. It takes practice to become a calm and fluent speaker.

8. After you have finished, look at the camera operator and wait for the signal that the camera is no longer recording.

9. You are part of the audience when you are not presenting. The camera may also zoom over the audience from time to time. As a member of the audience, you must be as quiet as possible because the recording equipment will pick up classroom sounds and movements.

Teacher Guidelines for Pre-Filming

1. Set the equipment up and test it before the presentations begin.

2. Make sure a responsible adult is present to help with setting up the presentation area.

3. Rope or tape an area around the recording equipment and the person operating the camera. Only authorized persons should be in this area!

4. Tape down any cords or loose wires around the equipment so no one will trip over them.

5. Make sure you have an extra blank tape, dvd, or flashcard on hand in case something happens to the first one.

6. Place tape marks on the floor where you want the presenters to stand while they give their presentations.

7. If possible, do a test run. Film the area where the students will be presenting. Is the lighting good? Is there a glare from the sunlight or indoor lights? Is the background appropriate? Do you have plenty of space for the presenter?

8. Be relaxed so you can encourage and reassure your students. Presentations in front of a camera will provide students with invaluable experience and will develop poise and confidence.

9. Have a prior schedule posted so everyone will know when it is his/her turn to present.

SCENE: Tall Tale   TAKE: 3   DIRECTOR: Quigley

Guidelines for Evaluating Video Presentations

At the top of a sheet of paper, write the date and title of your presentation. Next, choose the evaluation prompt according to the way you made your presentation. For example, if you portrayed a character, use the evaluation section under Character Portrayal. For each number, write your answers and comments in complete sentences. Try to be as objective as possible. This self-evaluation will help you improve your next video presentation.

Character Portrayal

1. Explain why you made the choice to do a character portrayal.

2. Which character did you choose to portray? Explain how you made your choice.

3. How did you look? (Describe your hair, face, costume or outfit, and shoes.)

4. Did you use any other props? If so, what were they? Did they add to your presentation? Did they distract from it?

5. Were you aware of nonverbal cues in your presentation? Did you hold your paper so that your face could be seen? Did you look at the audience from time to time? Did you use facial expressions and body gestures effectively? Did you move around or did you stand still?

6. Did you speak clearly and loudly enough to be heard? Did you use inflections in your voice to make the characters come alive?

7. How could you enhance your presentation? What would you change and what would you not change?

8. How would you evaluate your presentation? What were the strong points, and what areas needed improvement?

Illustration

1. Explain why you made the choice to use illustrations for your presentation.

2. How did you illustrate your story? Did you use paint, markers, chalk, crayons, pencils, or other media? Were your illustrations easy for the audience to see? Did you use them effectively?

3. Did you use any other props? If so, what were they? Did they add to your presentation? Did they distract from it?

4. Were you aware of nonverbal cues in your presentation? Did you hold your paper so that your face could be seen? Did you look at the audience from time to time? Did you use facial expressions and body gestures effectively? Did you move around or did you stand still?

5. Did you speak clearly and loudly enough to be heard? Did you use inflections in your voice to make the characters come alive?

6. How could you enhance your presentation? What would you change and what would you not change?

7. How would you evaluate your presentation? What were the strong points and what areas needed improvement?

Reading Dramatization

1. Explain why you made the choice to do a dramatic reading of your story.

2. Were you aware of nonverbal cues in your presentation? Did you hold your paper so that your face could be seen? Did you look at the audience from time to time? Did you use facial expressions and body gestures effectively? Did you move around or did you stand still?

3. Did you speak clearly and loudly enough to be heard? Did you use inflections in your voice to make the characters come alive?

4. How could you enhance your presentation? What would you change and what would you not change?

5. How would you evaluate your presentation? What were the strong points and what areas needed improvement?

Invitations

With all the commercial cards available today, the art of writing personal, unique, and individual invitations is almost obsolete. However, learning to write invitations is an important skill. An invitation should follow the same form as a friendly letter: heading, greeting, body, closing, and signature.

Before you begin writing an invitation, it helps to make an outline that includes specific information (what, who, where, when) in any logical order. Study the example of the outline and the invitation below.

An invitation will sometimes contain an RSVP. This is an acronym for a French expression that means "please respond," and a reply is needed. If a phone number is included, reply by phone. Otherwise, a written reply is expected.

Invitation Outline

1. What . . . . Tell what the event or special occasion is. . . . . A surprise birthday party
2. Who . . . . Tell whom the event is for. . . . . For Terrence Jones
3. Where . . . . Tell where the event will take place. At 330 Richland Drive
4. When . . . . Tell the date and time of the event. . . . . On Saturday, June 3, at 3:00
5. Whipped Cream . . . . A polite statement written to make the person feel welcome. . . . . . I hope you can come!

Sample Invitation

> 330 Richland Drive
> Roswell, New Mexico 88203
> May 15, 2013
>
> Dear Joseph,
>
> You are invited to a surprise birthday party for Terrence Jones. The party will be at 3:00 on Saturday, June 3, at our house at 330 Richland Drive. We will serve hot dogs and swim in the pool. I hope you can come!
>
> Your friend,
> Carl Williams

✓ Check Your Understanding

Why do you send an invitation?

HANDS-ON ACTIVITIES

1. **Writing Connection:** Pretend you are giving a party or other event. First, make an invitation outline. Then, write, revise, edit, and illustrate an invitation for your event. (Ideas: costume or theme party, food-tasting party, sports party, book-club meeting, science/history/math/Spanish-club meeting, movie party, etc.)

2. **Literature Connection:** Create an invitation to ask your friends to join a book club or participate in a book swapping event.

3. **Art Connection:** Create an invitation to encourage your parents, relatives, and friends to visit an art exhibit you are sponsoring.

Study Skills
Test-Taking

Preparing for Tests

1. Keep up with daily work to help you understand the material.
2. Pay attention during the class review. The teacher will usually highlight important information to study.
3. Ask questions about things you do not understand before the test.
4. Find out what testing format will be used (essay, true/false, multiple choice, fill-in-the-blank, etc.).
5. Begin studying several days before the test so you do not have to cram.
6. Use notes, worksheets, and review sheets to help you. Reread your notes and look over references.
7. Create acronyms to memorize a series of items, using the first letters of each word.
8. If your teacher permits, record lectures and/or notes. You can play them back as many times as necessary to help you learn the information.
9. Have a study-buddy. Find a classmate who takes their studies as seriously as you do. You can design a sample test for each other. Or, you can have oral reviews of the content to be covered on the next test.
10. You can design a lecture on the material to be covered on the next test. Then, you can "teach" a couple of your peers. Remember, you know it if you can teach it.

Taking the Test

1. Stay calm and do your best.
2. Read all directions carefully before you begin marking answers. Identify key words in the directions.
3. Go through your test and answer the ones you are sure about first.
4. Pace yourself. If you do not know an answer right away, come back to it later.
5. Utilize all your test time. Double-check your answers after you have finished.
6. Know how the test is scored. If you are penalized for wrong answers, answer only questions you are sure you know. If no points are deducted for wrong answers, make sure you've answered all the questions.

Test-taking Tips for True-False Tests

1. Read true-false questions carefully.
2. If a statement is **always** true, mark true. If it is only true sometimes, mark false.
3. Watch for tricky phrases such as: *it seems, I think, always, never,* and *maybe*.

Test-taking Tips for Fill-in-the-Blank Tests

1. Read and reread each question carefully.
2. If an answer bank is provided, check off answers as you use them.
3. Do not scratch answers out because you may need to read them again later.
4. Copy answers in the blanks correctly. Pay attention to correct spelling.
5. Write or print all answers as neatly as possible. Make sure each answer is legible.
6. If an answer bank is not provided, make sure you know whether to study for spelling as well as facts.

Test-taking Tips for Multiple-Choice Tests

1. Read and reread each question and any sample sentence or paragraph carefully.
2. Read all the answer choices carefully before choosing an answer.
3. Eliminate choices you know are wrong.
4. If more than one answer on a multiple choice test looks correct, mark the one that makes the strongest impression.
5. Write or print all letters as neatly as possible. Make sure each answer is legible.
6. If the test requires shading ovals, make sure each oval is filled in fully.

Test-taking Tips for Essay Tests

1. Read and reread each question or writing prompt carefully. Understand what kind of response is expected from the question or writing prompt.
2. Think about your purpose and audience.
3. Plan how you will organize your writing by jotting down ideas on a separate piece of paper. Use your favorite style of graphic organizer to organize your ideas.
4. Make sure the main idea is stated clearly in the topic sentence.
5. Use only details that support each of your main points.
6. If you have time, write a rough draft on another sheet of paper so you can revise and edit it.
7. Write the final essay as neatly as possible. Make sure every word is legible.
8. Reread the essay. Check one last time for correct punctuation, capitalization, and spelling.

Study Skills
Handwriting Tips

There are two different kinds of handwriting: **manuscript** and **cursive**. When you first learn to write the letters of the alphabet, you print them in manuscript form. **Manuscript writing** means that each letter in a word is written separately. Sometimes, manuscript writing is called printing. After you have learned and practiced manuscript writing, you are taught cursive writing. **Cursive writing** means that you connect the letters within a word.

Whether you use manuscript or cursive writing, you should make your writing legible. **Legible** means writing that is neat and easy to read. Form your letters correctly to prevent sloppy handwriting. Sloppy handwriting not only creates a negative impression, it often prevents clear communication.

Tips to Make Your Writing Legible

1. Make all similar letters uniform in height.
2. Use the correct slant and keep slant uniform.
3. Space letters and words correctly.
4. Connect the letters correctly.
5. Recognize unacceptable standards and redo the paper.

Other Handwriting Tips

1. **Use good writing posture.** Sit up straight with your feet flat on the floor. Your wrists should rest on the desk, but they should not support the weight of your body. Don't slouch.
2. **Hold your pencil correctly.** Place your pencil between the tip of your thumb and your index finger. The pencil will rest on your middle finger. Grip pencil at the end of the painted wood, right above where the sharpened part begins.
3. **Position your paper correctly.** Place your paper in front of you, slightly slanted, and parallel with your writing arm.
4. **Anchor your paper so it doesn't slide.** If you are right-handed, put your left hand lightly on the top left corner of the paper to keep it from moving. If you are left-handed, use your right hand on the top right corner. Make sure your hand stays flat and relaxed.
5. **Continue to check your writing posture and your paper placement.** As you near the bottom of your paper, slide your paper up so your arms don't hang off your desk. Your elbows should always remain under your shoulders.

HANDS-ON ACTIVITY

In order to evaluate your writing posture, have someone video you as you are writing an essay.
As you view the video, check how well you accomplished each of the areas under "Other Handwriting Tips."

1. Did you use good writing posture?
2. Did you hold your pencil correctly?
3. Did you position your paper correctly?
4. Did you anchor your paper?
5. Did you continue to check your writing posture and your paper placement?
6. Did you see any areas that needed improvement?
7. Did this evaluation help you make improvements?

Study Skills
Guide for Cursive Handwriting Standards

In the samples below, the small **x** shows you where to start, and the arrows guide your starting direction.

Group 1 Letters: a, c, e, i, m, n, o, r, s, u, v, w, x
- All characters rest on the baseline and have an x-height that stops at the waist line.

a   c   e   i   m   n   o

n   s   u   v   w   x

Group 2 Letters: b, h, k, l
- All characters rest on the baseline and have a tall thin loop that ascends to the cap line.

b   h   k   l

Group 3 Letters: d, t
- Both characters rest on the baseline and have a single line that ascends to the cap line.

d   t

Group 4 Letters: g, j, q, y, z
- All characters rest on the baseline, have an x-height that stops at the waist line, and have a looping tail.

g   j   q   y   z

Group 5 Letters: f, p
- **f**—The character has a tall thin loop that ascends to the cap line, descends below the baseline, and has a looping tail.
- **p**—The character rests on the baseline, has an x-height that stops at the waist line, and has a single-line tail that descends below the baseline.

f   p

Capital Letters: A, B, C, D, E, F, G, H, I, J, K, L, M, N, O, P, Q, R, S, T, U, V, W, X, Y, Z
- All characters rest on the baseline and ascend to the cap line.
- The letters **J, Y, Z** have looping tails that descend below the baseline.
- Care should be taken to connect to lower case letters correctly.

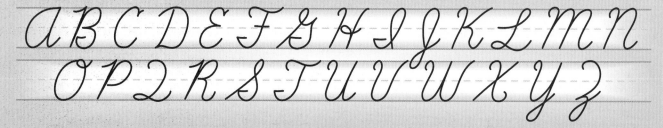

Study Skills
The Dictionary / Thesaurus

Sometimes, studying involves looking words up in a dictionary. You may need to see if you have spelled a word correctly, or you may want to check a word's meaning. A **dictionary** gives correct spellings, pronunciations, meanings, usage, and history of words.

A **thesaurus** is a type of dictionary that contains synonyms and antonyms for different words. Most writers use a thesaurus to find synonyms and antonyms that will make their writing clear and appealing.

Alphabetical order is important to know because words in a dictionary and a thesaurus are arranged in alphabetical order. There are two rules that help you put words in alphabetical order.

Rule 1: If the first letters of the words are different, use only the first letters to put the words in alphabetical order.

Rule 2: If the first letters of the words are the same, use the second letters to put the words in alphabetical order. If the second letters are the same, use the third letters to put the words in alphabetical order.

Guide words are the two words listed at the top of each dictionary page. Guide words tell the first and last words on the page. If the word you are looking up can be put alphabetically between the two guide words, then the word is located on that page. As you look up a word in the dictionary, you will use the first letter of the word to find the section you need. After you have found that section in the dictionary, you can use *guide words* to keep you from looking at every entry word on every page.

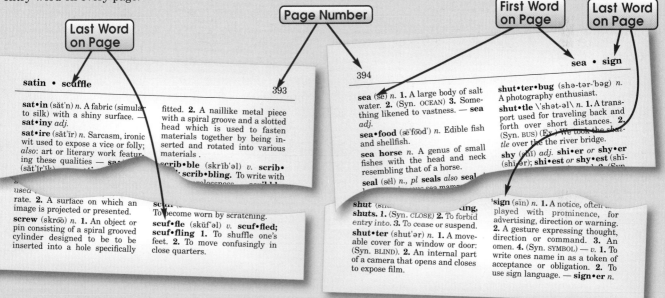

Entry words in a dictionary are the words in boldfaced type that are listed in alphabetical order and defined. A dictionary provides specific information about an entry word. It gives the...

- **pronunciation** – how to pronounce a word. It is usually in parentheses.
- **part of speech** – small *n.* for noun, small *v.* for verb, *adj.* for adjective, etc.
- **meanings** – numbered definitions of the word according to its parts of speech.
- **examples** – sentences that use the entry word to explain a meaning. Shown as (Ex.)
- **synonyms** – words that have similar meanings to the entry word. Shown as (Syn.)
- **origins** – tracing a word back to its original language source. Shown as [1350–1400 ME]. The date tells when the word was first used in its present form, and the initials tell the language origin. (ME stands for Middle English, Gr stands for Greek, Fr stands for French, L stands for Latin, Sp stands for Spanish, G stands for German, OE stands for Old English, etc.)

Some entries are slang words. The dictionary identifies slang words as nonstandard or informal. Slang words are not suitable for formal writing or speaking but may be used in casual speech.

CONTINUED ON NEXT PAGE

Sample Entry Word

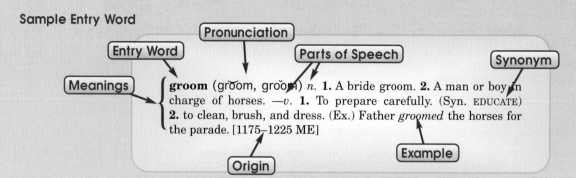

groom (groom, groom) *n.* **1.** A bride groom. **2.** A man or boy in charge of horses. —*v.* **1.** To prepare carefully. (Syn. EDUCATE) **2.** to clean, brush, and dress. (Ex.) Father *groomed* the horses for the parade. [1175–1225 ME]

Entry Word · Pronunciation · Parts of Speech · Synonym · Meanings · Origin · Example

✓ Check Your Understanding

1. How are words listed in a dictionary?

2. What are guide words in a dictionary?

3. What kind of information does the dictionary give for each entry word?

Study Skills
The Library

When you visit a library, you need to know how the books are arranged.
Most libraries have three main sections for books: fiction, nonfiction, and reference.

Fiction Section

Fiction books contain stories about people, places, or things that are not true even though the writer, or author, may use ideas based on real people or events. Fiction books are arranged on the shelves in alphabetical order according to the authors' last names

Nonfiction Section

Nonfiction books contain information and stories that are true. You can find a nonfiction book on just about any subject. Nonfiction books are grouped together in numerical order, according to a call number. A call number is the number found on the spine of all nonfiction books.

Reference Section

The Reference Section is designed to help you find information on many topics. The Reference Section contains many different kinds of reference books and materials. Some of these references are listed below.

1. **Dictionary.** The dictionary gives the definition, spelling, and pronunciation of words and tells briefly about famous people and places. Words in a dictionary are listed in alphabetical order.

2. **Thesaurus.** The thesaurus is actually a dictionary of synonyms and antonyms. Words in a thesaurus are listed in alphabetical order.

3. **Encyclopedia.** The encyclopedia gives concise, factual information about persons, places, and events of world-wide interest. Topics are arranged in alphabetical order in books called volumes. Each volume has a letter or letters on the spine that indicates the range of topics in that volume.

4. **Atlas.** The atlas is primarily a book of maps, but it often contains facts about oceans, lakes, mountains, areas, population, products, and climates in every part of the world.

5. **Almanac.** An almanac is a book that is published once a year and contains brief, up-to-date, factual information on important people, places, events, and a variety of other topics.

6. **Periodical.** Periodicals are magazines. The *Readers' Guide to Periodical Literature* is an index of magazine articles. It is a monthly booklet that lists the titles of articles, stories, and poems published in all leading magazines. These titles are listed under topics that are arranged alphabetically.

✓ Check Your Understanding

1. What are the three main book sections in the library?

2. How are fiction books arranged in the library?

3. How are nonfiction books arranged in the library?

4. What is a call number?

HANDS-ON ACTIVITIES

1. **Literature Connection:** Look up the Newberry and Caldecott award winners. Make a list of the Newberry and Caldecott books you have read and the ones you would like to read.

2. **Drama Connection:** Choose a scene from your favorite book or play and act it out with several of your classmates.

Study Skills
Parts of a Book

Do you know the parts of a nonfiction book? Actually, a book can be divided into three sections: **the front**, **the body**, and **the back**. Knowing the parts of a book will help you make full use of the special features that are frequently found in nonfiction books. The *front* includes these parts: **title page**, **copyright page**, **preface**, and **table of contents**. The *body* is the main section, or **text**, of the book. The *back* includes these parts: **appendix**, **glossary**, **bibliography**, and **index**.
(***Note:** For a more detailed description of the parts of a book, see Chapter 7 on pages 333–334.*)

✓ Check Your Understanding

1. What parts of a book are located in the front?

2. What parts of a book are located in the back?

3. What is the text of a book called?

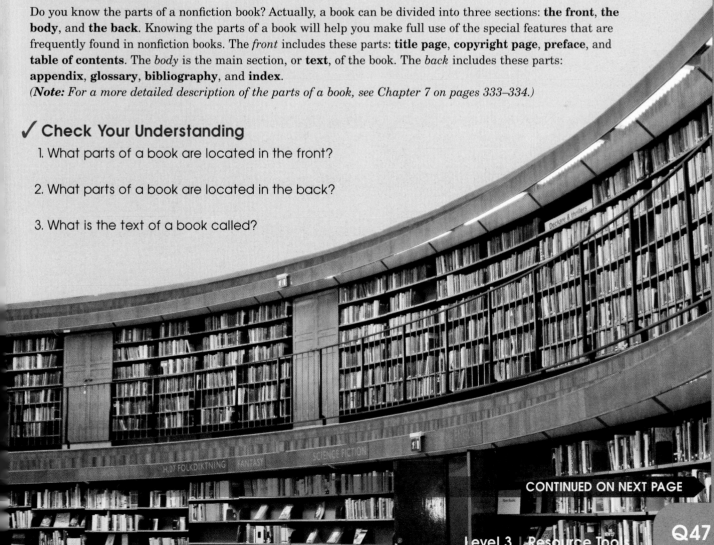

CONTINUED ON NEXT PAGE ▶

HANDS-ON ACTIVITY

1. Use the parts of a book listed on the previous page to complete the puzzle.
2. Use your vocabulary words, science words, social studies words, or spelling words to make your own crossword puzzle or a word-search puzzle.

Parts of a Book

Across:

1. is a list of sources used by the author
4. tells the title, author, and publisher (2 words)
7. tells beginning page numbers of units or chapters (3 words)
9. gives exact page numbers for a particular topic

Down:

2. is the main section of a book that contains the text
3. tells the reason the book was written
5. contains meanings of important words in a book
6. tells the copyright date and ISBN (2 words)
8. contains extra materials, such as maps and charts

Study Skills
The Table of Contents

Make your study time count by learning to use the shortcuts already available in a book. When you are looking for general information in a book, you can use a table of contents to help you find information quickly. A table of contents tells you four things.

1. What the book is about.
2. How many chapters are in a book.
3. The title of each chapter.
4. The first page of each chapter.

The main heading is *Contents*. The title of the first chapter is "*Selecting a Breed.*" By reading over the rest of the chapter titles, you can tell that this book is about cats.

Contents

The chapter numbers are the numbers on the left under the heading *Chapter*. There are eight chapters in the book. The beginning page numbers are the numbers on the right under the heading *Page*. The page number listed to the right of each title tells the **first** page of the chapter. Chapter 1 begins on page 2. To find the last page of Chapter 1, go to the page where Chapter 2 begins and back up one page number. Chapter 2 begins on page 5. Back up one number, and you will be on page 4. So, Chapter 1 ends on page 4.

✓ Check Your Understanding

1. A table of contents tells you what four things?

2. What is the title of the chapter that would tell you what to feed your hamster?

3. What is the number of the chapter?

4. On which page does Chapter 4 begin?

5. On which page does Chapter 4 end?

HANDS-ON ACTIVITIES

1. Make your own table of contents. Choose a topic that you know well enough to create titles for your chapters. You could also look up information about a topic you are interested in. List the chapter titles in a logical order. Give each title a chapter number and beginning page number. Think of three questions to ask about your table of contents. Exchange papers with a partner. Answer the questions and evaluate what you have learned about the table of contents.

2. Choose a nonfiction book that has a table of contents. Before you study the book's table of contents, make up an original table of contents, using the information you think will be in the book. Compare your table of contents to the one in the book. Analyze the similarities and differences. Evaluate why a table of contents is important in finding information about a book.

Study Skills

The Index

Do you know why an index of a book is important and how to use it? When you are looking for information about a specific topic in a book, you can use the index to help you find the information quickly. The index is located in the back of the book. It has an alphabetical listing of specific topics and tells on which page that information can be found. It is similar to the table of contents, but it is much more detailed. There are three main reasons to use an index:

1. When you want to find an answer quickly.
2. When you want to know the answer to a specific question.
3. When you want to know more about a subject.

There are **six features of an index** that you should know:

1. An index is located at the back of the book.
2. An index lists information alphabetically.
3. When an index lists key ideas in a book, they are called topics.
4. When an index lists specific information under a topic, it is called a subtopic.
5. The numbers following topics and subtopics tell on which pages the information is found.
6. Punctuation of page numbers appears in subtopics.
   - When you see a **dash** between numbers, say "**through**." (8–11 *means page 8 through page 11*)
   - When you see a **comma** between numbers, say "**and**." (8–11, 28 *means page 8 through page 11 and page 28*)
   - When you see a **semicolon**, it means stop. Go no further for pages on this subtopic.

Sample Index

Index

B

Behavior, 9–11, 27

H

Health issues,
  choosing a vet, 19–21, 27;
  first aid for, 17;
  sickness, 17–18, 23;
  special problems, 18–20;
  vaccine, 17

S

Special needs of older cats, 26
Sickness, *see* Health issues.
Supplies, 5–8, 16

The index topic under the letter *H* is *Health issues*. Notice that *Health* is the only word that is capitalized and the subtopics under it are indented. Each subtopic tells about the main topic *Health issues*.

Page numbers are listed after each subtopic. The page numbers listed after the subtopic *choosing a vet* are *19–21, 27*. The **dash** between the 19 and 21 is read as *19 through 21*. The **comma** between 21 and 27 is read as *and*. Together, it would mean that information about choosing a vet in health issues is found on pages 19 through 21 and on page 27.

✓ Check Your Understanding

How is information in an index listed?

HANDS-ON ACTIVITY

Choose two or three nonfiction books with indexes. Compare how the indexes are alike and how they are different. Exchange ideas with a partner. Write a paragraph to evaluate what you have learned about the value of the index.

Resource Tool: STUDY SKILLS

Reading Maps, Charts, and Graphs

Maps

Being able to read a map is an art unto itself. The more detailed the map, the greater the skill needed to interpret it. Virtually all maps have a legend for interpreting them. The legend includes such things as a distance scale, a set of symbols, and a collection of demographic information. The distance scale enables one to approximate the number of miles between two points. In addition to the distance scale, there is a set of symbols, which shows, among other things, types of roads, rest areas, medical facilities, historic markers, and airports. Finally, the demographic information contains the names of capital cities, populations, and land areas. A weather map has a legend that includes precipitation, highs and lows, fronts, and temperatures. Map information will vary, depending on the purpose of the map.

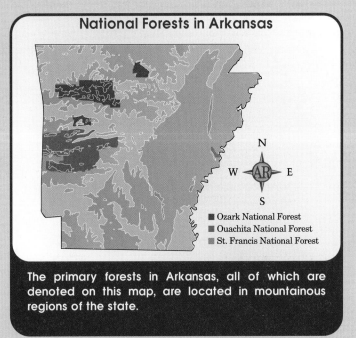

National Forests in Arkansas

N W E S

■ Ozark National Forest
■ Ouachita National Forest
■ St. Francis National Forest

The primary forests in Arkansas, all of which are denoted on this map, are located in mountainous regions of the state.

Task: 1. Which of the national forests covers the smallest area?

2. How many national forests are located in Arkansas?

3. Which national forest is located in the eastern part of the state?

4. Which national forest is located in the northern part of the state?

Oak Trees in the Ohio Valley

Red Oak

Pin Oak

Black Oak

White Oak

Bur Oak

🌳 =100 trees

There are several kinds of oak trees found in the Ohio Valley.

Charts

There are many different types of charts. Among others, there are meteorological charts (having to do with weather), navigational charts (having to do with air and/or ocean travel), and general information charts (having to do with facts and figures about some particular subject matter). Information in charts is usually easy to read and to understand because the facts and figures are arranged in columns and headings. Some charts contain directions for interpreting them. Other less technical charts are designed in such a way that interpreting them is self-explanatory.

Task: 1. How many trees are represented by one symbol?

2. How many red oak trees are found in the Ohio Valley?

3. Which kind of oak tree is found the most in the Ohio Valley?

4. Which kind of oak tree is found the least?

Graphs

Graphs reveal a wealth of information without making it necessary to read a series of paragraphs. A graph compares facts and figures in an easy-to-read format that can be read at a glance. Usually, a graph is accompanied by a legend that enables the reader to interpret it. Ordinarily, the purpose of a bar graph is to make a comparison between something past and present whereas the purpose of a pie graph is to show and compare the component parts that make up a whole. Sometimes, as in the case of a line graph, the intent is to show progression over a period of time.

Line Graph
Task: 1. In which two consecutive years did the amount of snowfall remain the same?

2. How much less was the snowfall in 2005 from the snowfall of 1997?

3. What winter showed the greatest increase in snowfall from the winter before?

4. How much snowfall was recorded in 2005?

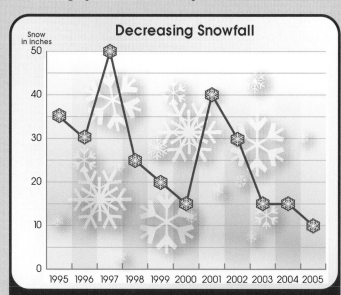

A little town on the shores of Lake Erie has had hard winters every year. In the past ten years, however, the little town has experienced a decrease in its yearly snowfall totals.

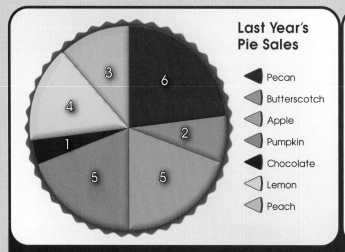

Miss Helen is in charge of the bakery at the fall festival this year. She will use last year's pie-sales' record as a guide for planning this year's event.

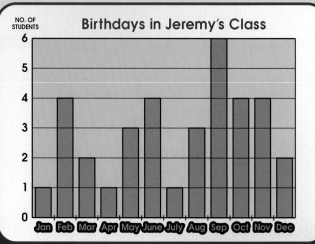

In Jeremy's class, birth dates span the calendar, from January to December. The graph above shows the number of birth dates per month for all 35 students.

Pie Graph
Task: 1. Which types of pies were equally popular?

2. How many butterscotch pies will be needed, based on last year's sales?

3. What kind of pie was sold most?

4. What kind of pie was sold least?

Bar Graph
Task: 1. During which month(s) are there two birth dates in Jeremy's class?

2. Which month has the most birthdays?

3. How many students have birthdays during the summer months of June, July, and August?

HANDS-ON ACTIVITIES

1. **Math, Science, and Social Studies Connections:** Look at the local and national weather report in a newspaper or on the Internet. Find and cut out examples of a weather map, a bar graph, a line graph, and a chart. Mount these examples on poster board. Identify them by labeling each kind, and, then, write one or two sentences explaining each one. Compare the local information to national information. Discuss how the local and national maps, graphs, and charts are alike and how they are different. Exchange ideas with a partner. Evaluate what you have learned about the value of maps, graphs, and charts.

2. **Spelling and Reading Connections:** For spelling, make a graph that list your grades and the number of minutes you studied. See if there is a connection between your grades and your study time. For reading, make a chart to show the books that you read during the year. You may use the following suggestions to design your chart:

   A. List the title of each book.

   B. List the type of book.

   C. List the number of pages in each book.

   D. List the time that it took to read each book (days or hours)

   E. List whether you would recommend the book.

You can put the map, graph, or chart that you make on construction paper or poster board. Make sure you organize and label the information so that it is easy to read. Exchange your chart and graph with a partner. Evaluate what you have learned about graphs and charts.

Technology

On-line Searches

Using the Internet for obtaining information is quick and effective. Many search engines exist on the Internet, and which one to use is a personal choice. For example, assume you want more information about the doctor who was killed at the Alamo in the Texas Revolution. First, you need keywords for the search engine to use. In this case, "Texas" and "Alamo doctor" may be good first choices. Too many words limit the results; too few words result in too many "hits." Use quotation marks around any phrase that you want used as a group and not as independent words.

Go to your favorite search engine website on the Internet and enter your keywords in the appropriate line. Click "Search" or hit the "Enter" key. A list of websites, usually with the most appropriate ones first, will appear on your screen. Click on any website link that seems to meet your needs. A new page will appear from that website. If this is not the information you need, click the "Back" option on the tool bar to return to the search results and try a different site.

If you decide to use the information, you may choose to print it in order to retain a hard copy of the information. This printout will usually have the web address in case you wish to return to the site at a later time for more information. One website will usually link, or connect, to other websites that have additional information. It is very easy to get distracted by irrelevant information, so remain focused on the topic.

Once you have found all the information you need from one website, return to the search result page and try additional websites. You may need to refine your search criteria. If you use the information in a report, make sure you document your source. If you use someone else's work without giving them appropriate credit, it is called plagiarism. Plagiarism is not only unethical, but it is illegal as well.

Be aware that all information on the Internet is not necessarily true. You should take the responsibility of verifying whether the information you obtain is valid before using it.

Privacy and the Internet

Since the Internet connects you to people all over the world, you must protect your privacy. Because you do not know who you can trust, safety rules are important.

1. All computers connected to the Internet should have a good software program for virus protection installed. It should be upgraded regularly.

2. Never enter ANY personal information about yourself or your family on ANY website. This includes names, addresses, phone numbers, and social security numbers.

3. Never agree to a personal meeting with anyone you meet on the computer. All safety rules designed to protect you from strangers apply when using the Internet.

4. Never go to websites that you know you should not see or that you are forbidden to use. If in doubt, don't go there.

5. Keep your parents informed. Tell your parents, guardian, or another responsible adult if something on the Internet makes you uncomfortable. Make sure a responsible adult has your password so that he/she can help keep you safe. Do not give your password to anyone else.

6. Never use a web camera without permission.

7. Go to www.cybercrime.gov/rules for additional tips on how to use the Internet safely.

Internet Terms

Internet users must have a working knowledge of the terminology and commands used in searching the web or using e-mail. A list of common terms relating to the Internet is provided below.

address book	a list of e-mail addresses and other important information most frequently used by an individual
browser	an application to view web pages such as Google, Internet Explorer, etc.
chat room	a place for an interactive conversation through the Internet by using the keyboard
cookies	software technology that collects (gathers) information of all users that visit a particular website
download	a process used to copy a file from the Internet to a user's computer
DSL	Digital Subscriber Line; a fast method of connection to the Internet
dial-up	a slower method to connect to the Internet
e-mail (mail)	electronic mail messages sent through the Internet
e-mail address	an electronic mail address for an individual computer user
forward mail	a process to send a copy of an e-mail message to another computer user
home page	the web page that appears when a web browser is started
IP address	a number assigned to a user's computer by a web server for the purpose of tracking the user's use or habits of what sites are visited
Internet	a world-wide collection of computers networked together
junk mail	unwanted e-mail (also called SPAM)
instant messaging	real-time, person-to-person interaction through the Internet
modem	a computer accessory that enables a computer to connect to other computers, such as the Internet, through a connection, using a standard telephone line or cable wire
news groups	an Internet group of users sharing an interest in a common topic
password	a series of unique characters that must be entered to access some websites, personal or company accounts, some files or directories
search engine	an application used to find appropriate websites by entering in "keywords" of a subject
send	button (or option) that sends an e-mail into the Internet
SPAM	unwanted junk e-mail messages sent in large quantities
surfing	exploring the Internet
upload	a process of sending a file to another user's computer
virus	a disguised program that inserts itself into programs of other computers to perform a malicious action such as destroying data or an entire hard drive
www	World Wide Web; refers to the network of computers that make up the Internet
web address	characters keyed in a web browser to get to a particular website
web cam	an electronic camera device used to send images over the Internet

E-mail

E-mail, or electronic mail, is a great way to communicate with people you know. However, e-mail is different than regular mail. Always ask a parent's permission before using e-mail. The following guidelines will help you use e-mail correctly.

1. Type a message title in the Subject line.

2. Keep your e-mail paragraphs short and to the point.

3. Try not to use special type fonts because some computers may not display them properly.

4. Put space between paragraphs by skipping a line.

5. Use correct spelling, capitalization, and punctuation.

6. Do not open or reply to an e-mail from anyone you do not know.

7. Tell an adult immediately if you get an e-mail that scares or upsets you.

Technology

Word Processing Terms

Computer users must have a working knowledge of the terminology and commands used in word processing. These commands can be executed from a menu on the screen or by typing a series of keys on the keyboard.

close	a command that allows you to exit a document
copy	a command that puts a selected (highlighted) object or text into a computer's memory for pasting into another location
cut	a command that removes highlighted text and places it into a storage area for later use
delete	a key or a command that removes highlighted text (Deleted text is not saved for later use.)
find	a command that locates specified letters, words, or phrases in a document
font	a menu item that allows you to choose a typestyle (Times New Roman, Courier, etc.)
new	a command that creates a new document
open	a command that brings up and displays a document from existing files
page break	a command that ends a page wherever you want it to end and creates a new page
paste	a command that allows copied or cut text to be inserted at a different location in the current document or in another document
print	a command that produces a printout (hardcopy) of the current document
exit/quit	a command that exits/quits the current application
return	an "enter" key that sends the cursor to the next line
save	a command that keeps all changes in a document for later use
select	a command to highlight chosen text
shift	a key that allows capital letters to be typed (It is also used for various other commands.)
spelling	a command that checks the spelling of the words in a document
tab	a command or key that moves the cursor to the right at specified intervals

Computer Terms

Whether you use a computer at home or at school, you will need to have a working knowledge of the most commonly used technology terms. Becoming familiar with computer terms and what they mean will be helpful as you learn more about computers. The definitions for the technology and computer terms below will guide you as you gain knowledge of how computers work.

Computer Files to Organize Writing

Think of your computer as a file cabinet that organizes and stores your writing in electronic folders. The number of folders you can create is almost unlimited. You can create separate folders for every type of writing that you do: stories, poems, reports, letters, and unfinished pieces. You can put these writing folders on your hard drive or copy your files onto other electronic storage devices. It is easy for you to add new documents or files throughout the year.

CD-ROM	a portable storage medium for computers (It consists of a plastic-like, round disk upon which data or music has been burned by a laser. CD-ROM's typically hold approximately 700 megabytes of data.)
CPU	Central Processing Unit; the main brain of a computer system that contains the electrical parts that interpret and execute the commands necessary for data processing
cursor	a square or bar, blinking on a computer screen that tells where you are typing or where the next command will be performed
data	pieces of information before they are formatted and organized into usable facts
disk drive	a computer component for storing and accessing data (The term "disk drive" is sometimes used to refer to a hard drive.)
document	an electronic file typically associated with a word-processing program
DVD	Digital Video Disc (A single DVD is typically used to hold a full-length motion picture.)
font	a style of letters and numbers used by word-processors on computers
hard copy	any electronic computer data file that has been printed on paper
hard disk drive	an internal computer component for storing and accessing large amounts of data
hardware	any part of a computer, or its accessories, that is physical, such as the keyboard, mouse, monitor, CPU, and printer
keyboard	the part of the computer system that is used to type letters, numbers, or symbols
menu	a list of options or commands shown on a monitor screen that is available to a user and allows the user to execute any command of choice
monitor	that part of a computer system that displays information on a screen and allows the user to interact with the system
mouse	a small input device used to position a cursor on a document and execute commands
printer	a computer accessory that prints hard copies of electronic documents
software	programs that tell computers what tasks to accomplish, also referred to as Applications (Software programs are nonphysical components of a computer system and are written by human programmers.)

Shurley English Pronunciation Key

Short Vowels: a = /ă/, u = /ŭ/, i = /ĭ/, o = /ŏ/, e = /ĕ/, y = /ĭ/

Long Vowels: a = /ā/, u = /ū/, i = /ī/, o = /ō/, e = /ē/, y = /ī/

3rd Uncommon Vowels: a = /ŏ/, u = /o͝o/, o = /o͞o/

Schwa: /uh/

Consonants:	
b = /b/	boy
c = /k/; /s/	cat; dice
d, ed₂ = /d/	dog; begged
f = /f/; /v/	fan; of
g = /g/; /j/	good; age
h = /h/	hat
j = /j/	jet
k, ck, ch₂ = /k/	kitten; pick, school
l = /l/	lip
m = /m/	man
n, kn, gn = /n/	not, know, gnat
p = /p/	pan
qu = /kw/;/k/	quit; quiche, masquerade
r = /r/	red
s, s₂ = /s/; /z/	sit; days
t, ed₃ = /t/	top, topped
v, f₃ = /v/	vet, of
w = /w/	well, was
x = /ks/	six
y (as a consonant) = /y/	yak
z = /z/	zip

Consonant Digraphs:	
ch = /ch/; /k/; /sh/	chop; school; machine
ph = /f/	phone
sh = /sh/	ship
th, th₂ = /th/	cloth; clothes
wh = /wh/ (breathy)	whip

Special Endings: -ar = /ar/ — star

EXCEPTION: *At the end of some multi-syllable words,*

-ar = /er/	dollar, grammar
-ur, -ir, -er, -ear = /er/	Burt, bird, herds, earth
-ing = /ēng/	thing
-le = /ul/	people
-ly = /lē/	quickly
-or = /or/	fort

EXCEPTION: *When the letter "w" precedes "or,"*

-or =/er/	worm, world

At the end of some words,

-or = /er/	doctor, collector, donor

-sion = /shun/; /zhun/	vision

-tion	nation
-cian } /shun/	Grecian
-tian	Martian

CONTINUED ON NEXT PAGE ▶

**Vowel Combinations
for Long A:**   ai ⎫   wait
                 aigh⎪   straight
                 ay ⎪   stay
                 ea ⎬ /ā/   break
                 ei ⎪   rein
                 ey ⎪   obey
                 a_ + e⎭   case

**Vowel Combinations
for Long U:**   ew ⎫   few
                 ue ⎬ /ū/   blue
                 ui ⎭   suit

**Vowel Combinations
for Long I:**   -y ⎫   fly
                 ie ⎪   pie
                 igh⎬ /ī/   sigh
                 i_ + e⎭   kite

**Vowel Combinations
for Long O:**   oa ⎫   toad
                 oe ⎪   toe
                 oo ⎪   door
                 ou ⎬ /ō/   shoulder
                 ough⎪   dough
                 ow ⎪   blow
                 o_ + e⎭   poke

**Vowel Combinations
for Long E:**   ea ⎫   fear
                 ee ⎪   keep
                 ei ⎪   receive
                 ey ⎬ /ē/   key
                 ie ⎪   chief
                 e_ + e⎭   here

The "AW" Sound: au ⎫   autumn
                      ough⎬ /aw/   ought
                      aw ⎭   saw

The "OW" Sound: ou ⎫   cloud
                      ough⎬ /ow/   drought
                      ow ⎭   brown

The "OY" Sound: oi ⎬ /oy/   coil
                      oy ⎭   toy

The "OO" Sound: oo = /o͞o/; /o͝o/   moon; book

Glossary

A

Abbreviation: the shortened form of a word.

Acrostic poem: a type of poem that spells a word using the first letter of each line.

Act: the largest division of a play; most plays have one to five acts.

Action verb: a verb that shows a state of action and tells what the subject does. (*Sara **runs** home.*)

Adage: a traditional saying that expresses a common experience or observation.
(*A bird in the hand is worth two in the bush.*)

Adjective: a word that describes, or modifies, a noun or pronoun; one of the eight parts of speech.
(***That black*** *dog jumped on the bed.*)

Adverb: a word that describes, or modifies, a verb, adjective, or another adverb; one of the eight parts of speech. (*The employees worked **quickly**.*)

Advertisements: the business of convincing people to buy certain products; using pictures and words to persuade people to buy things.

Affix: a group of letters added to a word to alter its meaning or part of speech; suffixes and prefixes are two types of affixes.

Alliteration: the repetition of consonant sounds at the beginning of words; used mostly in poetry.
(***F****ive **f**ine **f**eathered **f**owls*)

Allusion: a reference to a person, place, thing, or event from mythology, history, or literature.
(*I knew this argument would be my **Waterloo**. I searched for my missing shoe like **Ahab and his whale**.*)

Analogy: a kind of reasoning based on comparing one pair of words with another pair of words that are related in the same way.
(*glove : hand :: sock : foot*) (*purpose or use relationship*)

Antecedent: the noun to which a pronoun refers.
(*The **cat** devoured **its** food.*)

Antonyms: words that have opposite meanings.
(*hot, cold*)

Apostrophe: a punctuation mark (') used in contractions and possessive nouns. (*Harvey **doesn't** work on Saturday. **Mary's** car was parked in the street.*)

Appendix: the part of a book that contains extra information, such as maps and charts.

Appositive: a word, phrase, or title used directly after a noun to rename it. (*Sally, **my best friend**, helped me with the decorations.*)

Arabic numerals: the symbols used in English to indicate one, two, three, and so on; normal numbers. (***1, 2, 3**, etc.*)

Argumentative/persuasive writing: a type of writing in which the author's purpose is to convince someone to agree with his/her opinion.

Article Adjectives: specific adjectives (*a, an, the*) that come before a noun. (***A*** *bee stung me. I ate **an** orange at lunch. **The** paper was not delivered on time.*)

Assonance: the repetition of vowel sounds within words; used mostly in poetry. (*l**o**w m**oa**n*)

Audience: a group of people or a person who reads, listens, or watches something.

Autobiography: non-fiction writing in which the author tells about his own life.

Auxiliary verb: another name for a helping verb. *See* helping verb.

B

Base word: the core or root of a word to which affixes are added to form a new word.
(*un– + **cook** + –ed = uncooked*)

Bibliography: the part of a book that lists the sources used by the author as references.

Biography: a non-fiction writing in which the author tells about another person's life.

Blog: an online journal or forum, allowing a person to publish his or her thoughts and opinions on the Internet; shortened from weblog (*web + log*).

Body of a book: the part of a book that contains the text.

Bold: printed letters that appear thicker than usual, **like this example**; bold print is sometimes used to indicate emphasis on a word or phrase.

Book review: a written opinion of a book that includes a summary of what the book is about and reasons the reviewer likes or dislikes the book.

Brainstorm: to develop, broaden, or elaborate ideas by discussion.

Business letter: a formal letter that makes a request, applies for a job, orders something, or gives an opinion.

C

Capitalization: the use of capital letters in certain grammatical situations, such as a proper noun or the beginning of a sentence.

Case: the position of nouns and pronouns in a sentence that shows whether they are used as subjects (*nominative or subjective case*), objects (*objective case*), or possessive words (*possessive case*).

Cause and effect: an organizational strategy that is used to explain why things happen.

Chapter: the largest division of a prose story, especially in book form.

Citation: formal acknowledgment of information gained from an outside source; lack of proper citation is plagiarism.

Classifying: naming and labeling each word in a sentence to identify its job.

Clause: a group of words that has a subject and a verb. There are two kinds of clauses, independent and dependent.

Collaboration: working together in groups to produce and publish writing projects.

Collective noun: a noun used to name a group of specific things. (*a **flock** of birds, a **band** of gorillas, a **skulk** of foxes*)

Colon: a punctuation mark (:) used to separate a sentence from a list of words, hours from minutes, or words in an analogy.

Comma: a punctuation mark (,) used to separate items in a series, appositives, cities from states, dates, compound sentences, and complex sentences; also used in other grammatical situations.

Comma splice: a punctuation error in which two independent clauses are joined by a comma only. (*The doorbell rang**,** Jane answered the door.*)

Common noun: a noun referring to any person, place, or thing rather than to a specific person, place, or thing. (*desk, boys, playground*)

Comparative form: the form of an adjective or adverb that compares two people, places, things, or actions. To make comparative forms, add *-er* or *more* to the simple form. (*slower, **more** generous*)

Comparison-contrast writing: a type of writing in which the author's purpose is to tell how things are alike and how they are different.

Complete predicate: the main verb and all the words that modify the verb in a sentence. (*That red car <u>raced down our street</u>.*)

Complete subject: the subject noun or pronoun and all the words that modify it. (*<u>That red car</u> raced down our street.*)

Complex sentence: a sentence made by joining two clauses together: an independent clause and a subordinate clause. (*The alarm activates **when the store is closed**.*)

Compound sentence: a sentence containing two independent clauses and no dependent clauses. (*The girls rode the motorcycles**, and** the boys rode the four-wheelers.*)

Compound subject: two or more subjects in a sentence that are joined by the words **and**, **or**, or **but**. (***Michael** and **Judy** worked on a project in science class.*)

Compound verb: two or more verbs that are joined by the words **and**, **or**, or **but**. (*Michelle **sang** and **danced** in the talent contest.*)

Compound word: a word composed of two base words. (*heart + break = **heartbreak**, cow + boy = **cowboy***)

Comprehension: understanding; the ability to understand information that is read or heard.

Concise: written as simply and clearly as possible; short and to-the-point.

Conjunction: a word used to connect other words, phrases, clauses, or sentences. The three most common conjunctions are **and**, **or**, and **but**; one of the eight parts of speech. (*Sally **and** David played the violin in the recital.*)

Connective adverb: an adverb used to show the relationship between two clauses in a compound sentence; requires the use of a semicolon; also known as a conjunctive adverb. (*I was hungry this morning; **unfortunately**, we were out of cereal.*)

Consonant: any letter that is not a vowel. (***b, c, d, f, g, h, j, k, l, m, n, p, q, r, s, t, v, w, x, y, z***)

Context clue: words, phrases, sentences, and any information that comes before or after a word to help a reader understand the meaning of that word or phrase.

Contraction: a word formed by combining two words and adding an apostrophe to replace the letter or letters that have been left out. (*did not / **didn't***)

Glossary

Conventions: the commonly understood and followed rules for writing and speaking standard English, including capitalization, punctuation, and spelling rules; one of the writing traits.

Coordinate conjunction: a word that connects words, phrases, or sentences of equal importance. The three most common coordinate conjunctions are *and*, *or*, *but*. (*The weather was sunny, **but** the wind made it cool.*)

Copyright page: the part of a book that contains the copyright date and ISBN.

Correlative conjunctions: a pair of conjunctions that work like a coordinate conjunction. (***Either** we win this game, **or** we lose the championship.*)

Couplet: a poem or part of a poem that consists of two rhyming lines.

Creative writing: a type of writing in which the author's purpose is to entertain through stories, poems, plays, etc.

Cross-reference: a note in an information source that points readers to another source for more information.

D

Dead language: an ancient language that is no longer spoken.

Declarative sentence: a sentence that makes a statement and ends with a period. (*I went to work with my dad.*)

Deductive reasoning: a type of reasoning that makes specific predictions based on accepted generalizations. (*Jamie loves chocolate, so she will probably like this chocolate candy bar.*)

Definite article: the word *the* is a definite article because it refers to a specific or particular person, place, or thing. The word *the* can be used with singular or plural nouns. (***the** dog, **the** dogs*)

Degree of comparison (irregular): making a *word change* to an adjective or adverb so that it shows a comparison to something else. (*bad, worse, worst / good, better, best / little, less, least*)

Degree of comparison (regular): adding *–er*, *–est*, *more*, or *most* to an adjective or adverb so that it shows a comparison to something else. (*big, bigger, biggest / beautiful, more beautiful, most beautiful*)

Dependent clause: a group of words that has a subject and a verb but does not express a complete thought; also known as a subordinate clause.

Descriptive writing: a type of writing in which the author's purpose is to describe.

Details: information related to the main topic or topic sentence.

Dewey decimal system: a number system used to organize nonfiction books in a library.

Dialect: a nonstandard language used in a certain area.

Dialogue: the exact words spoken by a character in a story or play.

Diamante: a diamond-shaped poem about opposite concepts.

Dictionary: a book that gives information about words, such as spelling, meaning, pronunciation, syllabication, etymology, and parts of speech.

Direct object: a noun or pronoun that receives the action of the verb in a sentence. A direct object tells what or whom after the verb. (*Amy took her **books** to the library.*)

Direct quotation: the exact words someone has spoken. Quotation marks are used before and after a direct quotation. (*Mom said, **"Clean your room before dinner."***)

Double negative: incorrect use of two negative words in a sentence. Only one negative word can be used to express a negative. (*The plumber **can't** find **nothing** wrong with our sink.*)

Draft: writing that needs to go through the revising and editing stages.

Drama: a form of literature that is presented by actors on a stage; works of drama are called *plays*, which can be divided into *acts* and *scenes*.

E

Editing: the fourth step in the writing process. Editing involves checking and correcting mistakes in spelling, grammar, usage, capitalization, and punctuation.

Elaboration: giving enough details about a topic so that others can understand and picture what an author wants to say.

Glossary

End mark flow: the part of the Question and Answer Flow that identifies the kind of sentence being classified.

Essay: a written discussion of one idea that is made up of several paragraphs.

Etymology: the history of a specific word, including its previous forms and the ancient language from which it originated.

Exclamation point: a punctuation mark (**!**) used at the end of an exclamatory sentence.

Exclamatory sentence: a sentence that expresses strong feeling and ends with an exclamation point. (*My car is on fire!*)

Expository writing: a type of writing in which the author's purpose is to explain or inform.

F

Fable: a type of folktale about talking animals that ends with a life-lesson or moral.

Fact: a specific statement that can be looked up, measured, counted, or otherwise proven. (*John is six feet tall.*)

Fairy tale: a form of traditional literature or folktale that contains some or all of the following common elements: fantasy, a wretch, a prize, a trial, a villain, supernatural help, repetition, and a happy ending.

Fiction: stories about people, places, or things that are not true even though the author may use ideas based on real people or events.

Figurative language: another name for figure of speech.

Figure of speech: a poetic device, sometimes called *figurative language*, that uses words to create images by comparing one thing to another. Three figures of speech are simile, metaphor, and personification.

Final paper: the fifth step in the writing process. A final paper is a corrected copy of the rough draft.

First-hand account: when an author writes about an event that he/she has personally experienced.

First-person point of view: the writer writes as though he is personally involved in what is happening. The writer uses the personal pronouns *I, we, me, us, my, our, mine*, and *ours*. (***We** will leave for **our** vacation.*)

First principal part: the primary form of a verb, used to indicate the simple present or simple future tense; in the present tense, it can have an –*s* ending to indicate a singular subject. (***walk** / **walks**, will **walk***)

Folktale: a traditional story passed down orally from one generation to the next generation. A folktale is "a story of the people."

Formal language: word choices that set a respectful tone; used with adults, large groups, presentations, and in writing for school or work.

Forum: an online discussion place, allowing a person to publish his or her thoughts on a particular topic and interact with others on the Internet.

Fourth principal part: the fourth form of a verb, used to indicate the progressive tenses; formed with a *be* helping verb (*am, is, are, was,* or *were*) and an –*ing* ending. (***is walking***)

Fragment: an incomplete sentence. A fragment is missing one or more of the core parts: subject, verb, or complete thought. (*After the game.*)

Friendly letter: an informal letter that shares personal thoughts and feelings with a friend or relative.

Future perfect tense: the tense of a verb whose action will have already taken place in the future, represented by the verb's third principal part. (*The cars **will have raced**. The children **will have run**.*)

Future progressive tense: the tense of a verb whose action will still be taking place in the future, represented by the verb's fourth principal part. (*The cars **will be racing**. The children **will be running**.*)

Future tense: the tense of a verb whose action takes place in the future, represented by the verb's first principal part and the helping verb *will*; also known as simple future tense. (*The cars **will race**. The children **will run**.*)

G

Genre: a category that identifies what type of writing a piece of literature is. (*essays, poems, short stories, plays, etc.*)

Gerund: a noun formed from a verb with its –*ing* ending. (***Reading** is my favorite hobby.*)

Glossary: the part of a book that contains meanings of important words used in the book.

Glossary

Grammar: the study of the eight parts of speech and how they are used in the construction of sentences.

Graphic organizer: a prewriting tool that helps you organize your ideas on paper in a visual format.

Greek: the language of ancient Greece; one of the ancient languages that contributed many words to modern English.

Guide words: words listed at the top of each dictionary page that tell the first and last words on the page.

H

Helping verb: a verb or verbs that combine with a main verb to tell more about an action. Helping verbs are also called auxiliary verbs. (*He **is** helping his sister with her homework.*)

Homographs: words that are spelled alike but have different meanings and/or different pronunciations. (*You have the **right** answer. Turn into the **right** lane.*) (*He will **lead** us to a safe place. The metal pipe contained **lead**.*)

Homonyms: words that sound alike but have different meanings and spellings. Homonyms can be a combination of homographs and homophones.

Homophones: words that sound alike but have different meanings and spellings. (*write, right*)

How-to/process writing: a type of writing that gives directions to explain the process and steps for doing something.

Hyperbole: exaggeration for effect.

Hyphen: a punctuation mark used to form some compound words and adjectives. It is also used to connect syllables of a word that has been divided at the end of a line.

Hyphenated adjective: a single adjective formed from two separate words connected by a hyphen. (*I broke a **stained-glass** window. Jessie has **blue-green** eyes.*)

I

Ideas: a writer's thoughts about a particular topic, one of the writing traits.

Idiom: a word or phrase that has a commonly accepted non-literal meaning that differs from its literal meaning. (*The red car **flew** through the intersection. It's **raining cats and dogs** outside.*)

Imperative sentence: a sentence that gives a command and has an understood subject. (*Wash the dishes.*)

Indefinite articles: the words *a/an* are indefinite articles because they indicate persons, places, or things that are "not" specific, meaning one of several. The *a/an* articles are used in front of singular nouns. (***a** dog, **an** ugly dog*)

Indefinite pronoun: does not refer to a specific or definite person, place, or thing. (*anybody, everyone, everything, several*)

Independent clause: a group of words that has a subject and a verb and expresses a complete thought. It can stand alone as a sentence.

Index: the part of a book that lists topics in alphabetical order and provides exact page numbers for each topic.

Indirect object: a noun or pronoun that receives what the direct object names. An indirect object tells to whom or for whom after the direct object. (*I gave **you** the invitation.*)

Inductive reasoning: a type of reasoning that makes broad generalizations based on specific evidence. (*Jamie has a pink cell phone, pink rain boots, and a pink hat, so she must really like the color pink.*)

Inference: a conclusion formed through reasoning and evidence.

Informal language: word choices that set a casual tone; used with friends, small groups, and in writing stories and friendly letters.

Interjection: a word or short phrase that expresses strong or mild feeling; one of the eight parts of speech. (*No! Oh my! Wow! No way! Great!*)

Internet: an international network of computers.

Interrogative sentence: a sentence that asks a question and ends with a question mark. (*Will you go with me?*)

Interview: meeting with another person to ask questions about a topic; a way of gathering firsthand information from another person.

Intransitive verb: an action verb in a sentence that does not have a direct object to receive the action. (*He **laughed**.*)

Inverted word order: an adverb, prepositional phrase, or helping verb that modifies the predicate but is located at the beginning of a sentence. (*Today, we / fed Daisy. During the play, Jan / sang a song. Did he / write that song?*)

Irregular verb: a verb that forms the past tense by having a vowel change or by not changing at all. (*I **know** his name. I **knew** his name. Today, I **let** my dog eat a treat. Yesterday, I **let** my dog eat a treat.*)

Italics: printed letters that appear to lean to the right, *like this example*; italics are used to indicate the titles and subtitles of full-length published works in typed texts, and can also be used to indicate emphasis on a word or phrase.

J

Jargon: the language of a special group or profession.

Jingles: short, rhythmic songs or chants that are used to teach grammar definitions and functions.

Journal: a written record of personal thoughts and feelings.

K

Kinds of sentences: sentences that make a statement (declarative), ask a question (interrogative), give a command (imperative), or show strong feeling (exclamatory).

Kinesthetic: a learning style that incorporates the use of movement and rhythm.

L

Latin: the language of ancient Rome; one of the ancient languages that contributed many words to modern English. *See* dead language *and* etymology.

Lecture: an explanatory speech on a given topic or subject; an oral presentation that is instructional in nature.

Legend: a type of folktale based on real historical events or people whose accomplishments or importance has grown to epic heights after centuries of retelling.

Line: one row of words in a poem; several lines may make a stanza.

Linking verb: a verb that connects the subject of a sentence with a word in the predicate that renames or describes the subject. (*That man **is** a clown. That dress **was** beautiful.*)

Literature: a form of art that uses words to express feelings or ideas; the three forms of literature are prose, poetry, and drama.

Loaded words: a propaganda technique that uses specific opinion words to create pleasant or unpleasant feelings.

Logic: a rational system of organized thinking, or reasoning.

M

Main idea: the most important idea in a paragraph or an essay.

Main verb: the most important verb in the predicate that tells what the action is.

Mass media: channels of communication intended to reach large groups of people, such as newspapers, radio, television, billboards, magazines, books, websites, and movies.

Medium: a channel of communication, such as radio broadcasts or a bulletin board; singular form of media.

Metaphor: a figure of speech that compares things by stating that one thing is something else. Metaphors use linking verbs such as *am, is, are, was,* and *were.* (*The **fog was a curtain** during the morning hours.*)

Meter: the pattern of stressed and unstressed syllables in a poem.

Modal auxiliary verbs: certain helping verbs that give extra information about a main verb by indicating particular conditions like ability, permission, intention, possibility, etc. Modal verbs include *might, must, may, can, could, would, should, will,* and *shall.*

Modify: to describe another word. Adjectives and adverbs are words that describe, or modify, other words in a sentence.

Mover and shaker sentence: a sentence in which words are moved around to shake it up and create sentence variety.

Myth: a type of folktale that uses the actions of immortal characters to explain natural phenomena.

N

Narrative writing: a type of writing in which the author's purpose is to tell a story.

Natural word order: a sentence with all the subject parts located before the verb and the predicate parts located after the verb. (*We / went to the school play yesterday.*)

Negative: a word that means "no." Contractions with "not" are also negatives.

Nominative: another name for a predicate noun or a predicate pronoun.

Nonfiction: information and stories that are true. Autobiographies, biographies, and reference books are nonfiction.

Noun: a word that names a person, place, thing, or idea and tells *who* or *what*; one of the eight parts of speech. (*Mother, Alaska, desk, freedom*)

Noun chart: a chart that identifies each noun in a sentence and tells whether it is singular, plural, common, or proper.

Noun check: an oral check to identify each noun and its job in a sentence.

Noun job: the job or function of a noun in a sentence (SN, OP, DO, IO, PrN).

Nuance: a subtle difference in the meaning of two words; shades of meaning.

O

Object of the preposition: the noun or pronoun after a preposition in a sentence. (*She rode down the **elevator** with her **friend**.*)

Object pronoun: a pronoun that functions as an object of the preposition, a direct object, or an indirect object in a sentence. (Common object pronouns: *me, us, him, her, it, them, you*.) (*He gave **me** the ball. He went with **us** to town.*)

Objective case: pronouns that are used as objects of prepositions, direct objects, or indirect objects in a sentence. (*me, us, him, her, it, them, you*)

Old English: the language of ancient Britain; one of the ancient languages that contributed many words to modern English. *See* dead language *and* etymology.

Onomatopoeia: "sound words," or words that imitate the sounds they describe. (*buzz, meow, zoom*)

Opinion: a personal belief, judgment, or feeling held by one or more persons that cannot be checked or proven. (*John is a considerate young man.*)

Organization: using structure and order to arrange ideas, paragraphs, and essays; one of the writing traits.

Original and revised sentence: writing an original sentence using grammar labels; revising the original sentence by using specific revision strategies.

Outline: a method of organizing information into different levels of categories and sub-categories.

P

Paragraph: a group of sentences that is written about one particular subject, or topic.

Parallel form: the wording of topics, subtopics, and details within sections of an outline so that they begin in the same way: as nouns, verbs, noun phrases, verb phrases, or prepositional phrases.

Paraphrase: putting another person's ideas or information in your own words.

Part of speech: one of eight categories of words that have different functions within a sentence. The eight parts of speech are *noun, verb, adverb, adjective, pronoun, preposition, conjunction,* and *interjection*.

Past perfect tense: the tense of a verb whose action had already taken place in the past, represented by the verb's third principal part. (*The cars **had raced**. The children **had run**.*)

Past progressive tense: the tense of a verb whose action was still taking place in the past, represented by the verb's fourth principal part. (*The cars **were racing**. The children **were running**.*)

Past tense: the tense of a verb whose action takes place in the past, represented by the verb's second principal part; also known as simple past tense. (*The cars **raced**. The children **ran**.*)

Pattern of a sentence: the order of the core parts. (SN V, SN V-t DO, SN V-t IO, SN LV PrN, SN LV PA)

Perfect tense: the tense of a verb whose action has already taken place in the present, past, or future; represented by the verb's third principal part (present perfect, past perfect, and future perfect).

Period: a punctuation mark (.) used at the end of a declarative or imperative sentence to signify the end of a complete thought. A period is also used at the end of abbreviations, initials, and after Roman numerals, Arabic numbers, and letters of the alphabet in an outline.

Glossary

Personal essay: a short, well-organized piece of expository writing on a topic from the author's own experience.

Personal narrative: a story or narrative written from a first-person point of view.

Personal pronoun: pronouns like *I*, *we*, *me*, *he*, *she*, *it*, *they*, and *you* that refer either to a person, people, or things.

Personification: a figure of speech used to compare things by giving human qualities to something non-human. (*The door **eyed** the visitor with **contempt** and refused to open.*)

Persuasive/argumentative writing: a type of writing in which the author's purpose is to convince someone to agree with his/her opinion.

Plagiarism: the use of another person's ideas and information without proper citation; a form of academic dishonesty equal to cheating on a test.

Plot: the events that take place in a story; most plots include conflict, rising action, climax, falling action, and resolution.

Plural noun: more than one person, place, thing, or idea. (*cats, glasses, children, women*)

Poetry: a form of literature in which words are carefully arranged for both meaning and sound; works of poetry are called poems, which can be divided into stanzas and lines.

Point of view: the writer's use of personal pronouns to show who is telling a story. First-person point of view uses the pronouns: *I*, *we*, *me*, *us*, *my*, *our*, *mine*, and *ours*. Second-person point of view uses the pronouns: *you*, *your*, and *yours*. Third-person point of view uses the pronouns: *he*, *his*, *him*, *she*, *her*, *hers*, *it*, *its*, *they*, *their*, *theirs*, and *them*.

Portfolio: a folder for each student that contains selected writing pieces that serve as his/her writing record for that school year.

Possessive case: pronouns that are used to show ownership in a sentence. (*my, our, his, her, its, their, your*)

Possessive noun: the name of a person, place, or thing that owns something. The possessive noun will have either an apostrophe before the *s* (*'s*) or an apostrophe after the *s* (*s'*). The apostrophe shows ownership. (*Kim's car*)

Possessive pronoun: a pronoun that shows ownership and takes the place of a possessive noun. (Common possessive pronouns: *my*, *our*, *his*, *her*, *its*, *their*, *your*.)

Posttest: a test that is given at the end of a course of study to determine how much a student has learned and how far he/she has progressed.

Predicate: the part of the sentence that tells what the subject is or does.

Predicate adjective: an adjective in the predicate of a sentence that modifies the simple subject. It tells what kind of subject. (*Her new dress is absolutely **gorgeous**!*)

Predicate nominative: another name for a predicate noun or a predicate pronoun.

Predicate noun: a noun located in the predicate of a sentence that means the same thing as the simple subject. (*Dad is an excellent **carpenter**.*)

Predicate pronoun: a pronoun located in the predicate of a sentence that means the same thing as the simple subject. (*My friend is **she**.*)

Preface: the part of a book that tells the reason the book was written.

Prefix: a word part added to the beginning of a base word to change its meaning. (***bi**monthly, **inter**state, **un**happy*)

Preposition: a word that shows how a noun or pronoun is related to other words in the sentence; one of the eight parts of speech. (*The little boy walked **beside** his mother.*) (*The Preposition Flow Jingle gives a list of common prepositions.*)

Prepositional phrase: a group of words made up of a preposition, the object of the preposition, and any words between them. (*The little boy walked **beside his mother**.*)

Present perfect tense: the tense of a verb whose action has already taken place in the present, represented by the verb's Third Principal Part. (*The cars **have raced**. The children **have run**.*)

Present progressive tense: the tense of a verb whose action is still taking place in the present, represented by the verb's Fourth Principal Part. (*The cars **are racing**. The children **are running**.*)

Glossary

Present tense: the tense of a verb whose action takes place in the present, represented by the verb's First Principal Part; also known as Simple Present Tense. (*The cars race. The children run.*)

Presentations: a form of publishing during which students present their works in front of an audience.

Pretest: a test that is given at the beginning of a course of study to determine how much a student knows before instruction begins.

Prewriting: the first step in the writing process. The stage of planning and organizing writing ideas.

Principal parts: the forms a verb can take to indicate its verb tense; every verb has four Principal Parts.

Progressive verb tenses: the tense of a verb whose action is still taking place in the present, past, or future; represented by the verb's Fourth Principal Part (present progressive, past progressive, and future progressive).

Pronoun: a word that can take the place of a person, place, thing, or idea in a sentence; one of the eight parts of speech.

Pronoun antecedent: the noun that the pronoun replaces.

Pronoun cases: the different forms that a pronoun can take to match its use in a sentence; the cases are **subjective** (*I, we, he, she, it, they, you*), **objective** (*me, us, him, her, it, them, you*), and **possessive** (*my, our, his, her, its, their, your*).

Proofreading: part of the fourth step in the writing process. Proofreading involves checking sentences or paragraphs for mistakes in spelling, grammar, usage, capitalization, and punctuation.

Propaganda: an organized effort to spread ideas or information in an attempt to change the opinions and actions of a group of people. Propaganda usually contains some accurate facts along with exaggerations and untruths.

Proper adjective: an adjective that is formed from a proper noun. Proper adjectives are always capitalized no matter where they are located in the sentence. (***Mexican*** *food,* ***English*** *language,* ***French*** *bread,* ***Japanese*** *maple*)

Proper noun: a noun that names a specific, or particular, person, place, or thing. Proper nouns are always capitalized no matter where they are located in the sentence.
(***Charles*** *is my dad. We are moving to* ***Peru***.)

Prose: the most common form of literature, written in complete sentences; works of prose are called stories, essays, articles, or books, and and can often be divided into chapters and paragraphs.

Proverb: a traditional saying that gives advice or wisdom. (*Don't count your chickens before they hatch.*)

Publishing: the sixth step in the writing process. Publishing is sharing the final copy of a written work with others.

Punctuation: the practice of using conventional marks (periods, commas, etc.) to make the meaning clear.

Purpose of writing: the author's reason for writing. The purpose determines the organization of a piece of writing.

Q

Quantitative note-taking: recording information in tables, graphs, charts, and outlines in order to organize a lot of facts.

Quatrain: a poem or part of a poem that consists of four lines, at least two of which rhyme.

Question and Answer Flow: an oral set of questions and answers used to find the function of each word in a sentence.

Question mark: a punctuation mark (**?**) used at the end of an interrogative sentence.

Quotations: the exact words spoken by someone. Quotation marks (" ") are used to indicate a direct quotation. Quotations are also called dialogue in narrative writing.

R

Reasoning: the use of organized thinking skills to answer a question, solve a problem, or draw a conclusion based on available information.

Reference books: books, like encyclopedias and dictionaries, that contain factual information about specific topics.

Reflection: to reflect means to think carefully about something. These thoughts and feelings can be recorded on paper.

Reflexive pronoun: a special type of pronoun used to refer back to the subject.
(*He scared* ***himself***. *We saw* ***ourselves***.)

Regular verb: a verb that is made past tense by adding an *–ed* ending. (*want, wanted*)

Relative adverb: an adverb used to introduce a subordinate clause. The most common relative adverbs are ***where, when,*** and ***why.***

Relative pronoun: a pronoun used to introduce a subordinate clause. The most common relative pronouns are ***that, who, whom, whose,*** and ***which.***

Repetition: saying or doing something again and again.

Research report: writing a report following these steps: investigate a topic, take notes from different sources, cite the sources, make an outline, write a rough draft, revise and edit the rough draft, write a final report, and publish the report.

Revised sentence: a sentence in which changes and improvements have been made using revision strategies.

Revision: the third step in the writing process. Revising is the process of improving the content and meaning of a sentence, paragraph, or essay.

Rhyme: the sound-alike quality of words, regardless of their spellings (*do/few, made/paid*). Rhyme may be of two types: end rhymes and internal rhymes. Rhyme is often used in poetry.

Roman numerals: the symbols used in Latin to indicate one, two, three, and so on; used in outlines to number the main points, and in plays to designate the act number. (***I, II, III, IV, V, VI, VII, VIII, IX, X, XI, XII,*** etc.)

Rough draft: the second step in the writing process. A rough draft is the first writing attempt before it is revised or edited.

Rubric: a checklist used to evaluate a specific kind of writing.

Run-on sentence: a grammatical error that occurs when two or more sentences are written continuously without the required punctuation.

S

Scene: a division of a play which usually takes place in a single setting; one or more scenes together make an act.

Second-hand account: when an author writes about an event that someone else has experienced.

Second-person point of view: used in giving directions. The writer uses the pronouns *you, your,* or *yours* almost exclusively to name the person or thing being addressed. (***You** may leave now.*)

Second principal part: the second form of a verb, used to indicate the simple past tense; formed with an *–ed* ending for regular verbs or a spelling change for irregular verbs. (***walked, ran***)

Semicolon: a punctuation mark (**;**) used to join two independent clauses in a compound sentence.

Sensory details: details that explain how a character, place, or thing looks, feels, smells, tastes, or sounds. Sensory details help readers form a picture of the different elements of a story.

Sentence: a group of words that has a subject and a verb and expresses a complete thought. A sentence must begin with a capital letter and have a period, question mark, or exclamation point at the end.

Sentence fluency: using various types of sentences and transition words to make writing sound smooth and polished; one of the writing traits.

Setting: the time and location for the events of a story.

Short story: a story or narrative written from a third-person point of view that can be read in one sitting.

Simile: a figure of speech that compares things, using the words *like* or *as*. (*Jeff is **as** tall **as** a giraffe. My brother jumps **like** a frog.*)

Simple form: the form of an adjective or adverb that is used when no comparison is made. (*pretty, fast, good*)

Simple predicate: another name for the verb in a sentence. (*Our soccer team **played** well yesterday.*)

Simple sentence: a sentence that has three core parts: a *subject*, a *verb*, and a *complete thought*.

Simple subject: another name for the subject noun or subject pronoun in a sentence. (*Our soccer **team** played well.*)

Simple verb tenses: the tense of a verb whose action takes place in the present, past, or future; represented by the verb's First Principal Part (simple present tense, simple future tense) and Second Principal Part (simple past tense).

Singular noun: only one person, place, thing, or idea. (*cat, glass, child, woman*)

Slang: informal language used in everyday conversation. It is not considered appropriate in formal writing. (*dude, cool*)

Glossary

Source: what a person uses to find information, such as the encyclopedia, nonfiction books, magazines, interviews, and the Internet.

Stanza: divisions of a poem.

Story: a form of expressive writing that has these characteristics: *main idea, setting, characters, plot,* and *ending.*

Story elements: the five necessary characteristics of every story: *main idea, setting, characters, plot,* and *ending.*

Subject noun: a person, place, thing, or idea that tells who or what a sentence is about.

Subject pronoun: a pronoun that tells who or what a sentence is about. (Common subject pronouns: *I, we, he, she, it, they, you.*)

Subject-verb agreement: matching the singular and plural forms of present-tense subjects and verbs. If the subject is singular, the verb form must be singular. If the subject is plural, the verb form must be plural.

Subjective case: pronouns that are used as the subject or predicate pronoun in a sentence. (*I, we, he, she, it, they, you*)

Subordinate clause: a clause having a subject and a verb but not expressing a complete thought. (*When the bell rang for class.*)

Subordinate conjunction: a connecting word that introduces a subordinate clause. (*after, before, since, etc.*)

Suffix: a word part added to the end of a base word that changes its meaning. (*careless, advancement, joyful, huggable.*)

Summary: a short explanation of a piece of writing or a speech that includes the main idea and only the most important facts.

Superlative form: an adjective or adverb that compares three or more people, places, or things. To make the superlative form, add *–est* or *most* to the simple form. (*fastest, most nervous*)

Syllable: an individual chunk of sound containing one vowel sound; spoken words are made of one or more syllables. (*Syl-la-ble has three syllables.*)

Synonyms: words that have similar, or almost the same, meanings. (*reply, answer*)

T

Table of contents: the part of a book that contains the titles of units and chapters.

Tall tale: a type of folktale that tells a humorous, exaggerated story, stretching a believable situation into an unbelievable tale. Local dialect is often used.

Technology: using science to produce practical, technical, mechanical, and computerized inventions that solve problems and improve life.

Tense: the quality of a verb that shows when the action of the verb takes place; a verb's tense is determined by which of its four principal parts is used.

Thank-you note: a short letter that thanks another person for doing something.

Theme: the central idea of a piece of literature; what the author wants to say about the subject of a story or poem. (*The theme of "The Itsy-Bitsy Spider" is the **importance of perseverance**, or "If at first you don't succeed, try and try again."*)

Thesaurus: a book of synonyms and antonyms

Thesis statement: a statement in an essay that tells the reader what to expect from the rest of the essay; a "roadmap" to reading the essay, which should include the topic of the essay and the main points that will be addressed.

Third-person point of view: the writer writes as though he is watching the events take place. The writer uses the pronouns *he, his, him, she, her, hers, it, its, they, their, theirs,* and *them.* (***He** bought **his** new car today.*)

Third principal part: the third form of a verb, used to indicate the perfect tenses; formed with a specific helping verb (*have, has,* or *had*) and an *–ed* ending or spelling change. (***has walked***)

Title page: the part of a book that tells the title, publisher, and city of publication.

Topic: a word or group of words that tells what something is about.

Topic sentence: a sentence that states the main idea of a paragraph or essay.

Traits of effective writing: characteristics of successful writing: *ideas, organization, word choice, voice, sentence fluency,* and *conventions.*

Transition word: a word or phrase used at the beginning of a sentence or a paragraph to show how ideas are connected. *(The Transition Words Jingle gives a list of common transition words.)*

Transitive verb: a verb that transfers action to a direct object in a sentence.

Triplet: a poem or part of a poem that consists of three rhyming lines.

U

Underlining: a horizontal line drawn underneath handwritten titles of full-length published works (books, magazines, newspapers, movies), works of art, ships, etc.

Understood subject pronoun: a sentence that gives a command or request without naming the subject. The subject is unwritten and unspoken and is always the pronoun you.
([You] Sit down. [You] Give me your report.)

V

Verb: a word in a sentence that expresses action (*see* action verb) or a state of being (*see* linking verb); one of the eight parts of speech.

Visual aid: a chart, graph, illustration, slideshow, or other object designed to help a reader or audience comprehend the information in a piece of writing or a presentation.

Visualization: using the author's descriptions to create a mental image of the characters, settings, and action of a story as you read; sensory adjectives and adverbs, specific nouns, and strong verbs can help you.

Vocabulary: words an individual person knows, understands, and uses in speaking and writing.

Voice: the individual way writers express themselves; one of the writing traits.

Vowel: any letter that is not a consonant.
(*a, e, i, o, u*, and sometimes *y*)

W

World Wide Web: a network of computers that makes up the Internet.

Word choice: selecting appropriate words to make a writing piece unique; one of the writing traits.

Word study: using context, prefixes, suffixes, synonyms, antonyms, meaning, etc. to expand knowledge of particular words in sentences.

Works-cited: recording the author and publishing details of a source used in a research report.

Writing conference: a meeting between the teacher and student to discuss his/her writing.

Writing process: the steps it takes to plan, write, rewrite and publish a final paper. Steps in the writing process include prewriting, writing a rough draft, revising, editing, writing a final paper, and publishing.

Writing prompts: different kinds of writing assignments given to students.

Writing toolbox: a skill lesson in the writing chapters designed to give students tools to improve usage skills for speaking and writing.

Writing traits: ideas, organization, word choice, voice, sentence fluency, conventions.

I3

I 5

Source Citations

Chapter 1:
Henley, Scott. "How An Injured Tortoise Rolls Now." *Shots NPR's Health Blog*. © 2011 National Public Radio. 22 July 2011. http://www.npr.org/blogs/health/2011/07/22/138604044/heres-how-an-injured-tortoise-rolls?ft=1&f=1001

Chapter 3:
"Photosynthesis." *Britannica Elementary Encyclopaedia*. Britannica Ultimate Reference Suite 2004 CD ROM.

Chapter 5:
"Hippopotamus." *www.nationalgeographic.com*. © 1996–2010. National Geographic Society. 21 May 2010. http://animals.nationalgeographic.com/animals/mammals/hippopotamus.html

Chapter 7:
"Sylvan Goldman." *www.ideafinder.com*. © 1997–2007 The Great Idea Finder. 13 July, 2010. <http://www.ideafinder.com/history/inventors/goldman.htm>

Chapter 9:
"Comet." *Encyclopædia Britannica 2004 Ultimate Reference Suite* CD-ROM. Pearson Software.

Chapter 17:
Hadley, Debbie. "How to tell the Difference Between a Butterfly and a Moth." *www.insects.about.com*. © 2012 about.com. 9 Oct, 2012 <http://insects.about.com/od/learningaboutinsects/a/butterflyormoth.htm>

"Large Sea Animals." Projects by Students for Students. *Thinkquest.org*. Oracle Think Quest Education Foundation. 9 Oct 2012. <http://library.thinkquest.org/J003292>

"Butterflyfish." *NationalGeographic.com*. © 1996–2012 National Geographic Society. 9 Oct 2012.http://animals.nationalgeographic.com/animals/fish/butterflyfish/

Hoyt, Erich. "Fins: Do All Whales Have Them?" *ASK Archive 2001*. 8 Oct 2012. <http://whale.wheelock.edu/archives/ask01/0146.html>

"Blowhole." ©1997–2010. *EnchantedLearning.com*. 31 Oct 2012. http://www.enchantedlearning.com/subjects/whales/anatomy/Blowhole.shtml

Iggulden, Conn and Hal. *The Dangerous Book for Boys*. New York: HarperCollins Publishers, 2007.

Photo/Image Credits

Abbreviations: (t) top, (b) bottom, (c) center, (l) left, (r) right

Front Cover: (cr), Gorilla, Todd Poling, www.flickr.com

Back Cover: (bl), Baby Gorilla, Hjalmar Gislason, www.flickr.com

Chapter 1: 1 (bl), Third-Grade Girl, Varina and Jay Patel/Think Stock; 2 (tl), Nurse Jumping Happily, Maridav/ThinkStock; 3 (cl), Football Receiver, Photodisc/ThinkStock; 3 (tl), Parachuter, Dusan Bartolovic/ThinkStock; 3 (tr), Parachuter Landing, Rebecca Brockie/ThinkStock; 3 (br), Space Shuttle Launch, Stockbyte/ThinkStock; 3 (bc),Vacation Pictures, Anna Khomulo/ThinkStock; 7 (c), Girl Writing on Desk, iStockphoto/ThinkStock; 8 (c), Blog (RSS) Symbol, Spectral Design/ThinkStock; 8 (c), Blog Finger, Fatih Donmez/ThinkStock; 8 (c), Student using Laptop, Cemarkbild/ThinkStock; 9 (bl), Chihuahua, Dan Century, Absolut Vision Stock Photo; 9 (r), Giraffe, Jon Mountjoy, AbsolutVision Stock Photo; 0 (tr), Chess Pieces, Alena Osipava/ThinkStock; 15 (b), Cup, AbsolutVision Stock Photo; 15 (bl), Rain, AbsolutVision Stock Photo; 15 (bl), Train, Bruce Fingerhood, www.flickr.com; 15 (cl), Umbrella (orange), AbsolutVision Stock Photo; 16 (bl), Bird on Foot, AbsolutVision Stock Photo; 17 (cr), Blue Ribbon, Absolut Vision Stock Photo; 17 (r), Worker in Vest, U.S. Army Corps of Engineers Europe District; 17 (tr), Up-Down Arrows, Donovan Graen/SIM; 18 (b), Dinner Plate, AbsolutVision Stock Photo; 19 (br), Clock, AbsolutVision Stock Photo; 22 (b), Crate, Absolut Vision Stock Photo; 22 (cl), Worker with Dolley, AbsolutVision Stock Photo; 22 (cr), Forklift, AbsolutVision Stock Photo; 22 (t), Cargo Ship, AbsolutVision Stock Photo; 25 (b), Whale, Absolut Vision Stock Photo; 26 (br), Gas Pump Nozzle, AbsolutVision Stock Photo; 29 (br), Rope-Frayed Knot, Donovan Graen/SIM; 29 (c), No Rope Allowed, Donovan Graen/SIM; 29 (cl), Rope-Tying Up, Donovan Graen/SIM; 29 (tr), Rope-Enter Hotel, Donovan Graen/SIM; 35 (b), Veterinarian with Girls & Puppy, AbsolutVision Stock Photo; 39 (br), Get Creative Turtle, Donovan Graen/SIM

Chapter 2: 43 (b,r,tr,cr), Finger Pointing, AbsolutVision Stock Photo; 45 (c), Dog Howling, AbsolutVision Stock Photo; 49 (br), Dog, AbsolutVision Stock Photo; 50 (c), Girl Playing with Blocks, AbsolutVision Stock Photo; 52 (cr), Grasshopper, AbsolutVision Stock Photo; 61 (tr), Basketball, AbsolutVision Stock Photo; 63 (c), Phone (Rotary), AbsolutVision Stock Photo; 63 (cl), Phone (Cordless), AbsolutVision Stock Photo; 63 (cr), Puppy and Phone, AbsolutVision Stock Photo; 63 (cr), Phone (Business), Absolut Vision Stock Photo; 63 (cr), Phone (Office), Donovan Graen/SIM; 63 (tr), Phone (Antique), AbsolutVision Stock Photo; 65 (bc), Angel, AbsolutVision Stock Photo; 65 (bc), Devil, AbsolutVision Stock Photo; 65 (br), Thumbs Up, AbsolutVision Stock Photo; 69 (br), Duck, Ed Kohler, AbsolutVision Stock Photo; 73 (cr), Horse Head, Marilyn Peddle, www.flickr.com; 77 (b), Mouse (Rodent), AbsolutVision Stock Photo; 77 (r), Elephant, Christopher Schmidt, www.flickr.com; 83 (c), Panther (Jaguar), C. Burnett, Wikipedia; 86 (c), Polite Ladies Having Lemonade, AbsolutVision Stock Photo; 90 (cr), Clown, AbsolutVision Stock Photo; 93 (c), Hummingbird, Paul Sapiano, www.flickr.com; 94 (t), Deer (Buck), Dan Davison, www.flickr.com; 95 (c), Tools Mounted, Absolut Vision Stock Photo; 103 (br), Dragster, AbsolutVision Stock Photo; 104 (br), Man Walking Up Stairs, AbsolutVision Stock Photo; 105 (cr), Cell Phone, AbsolutVision Stock Photo; 106 (b), Hotrod, AbsolutVision Stock Photo

Chapter 3: 110 (bl), Horses Racing, AbsolutVision Stock Photo; 111 (bc), Bread Basket, AbsolutVision Stock Photo; 111 (bl), Bandana Pattern, Márcio Silveira, www.flickr.com; 111 (bl), Bread (Plait), AbsolutVision Stock Photo; 111 (br), Bread (Roll), Absolut Vision Stock Photo; 111 (br), Rooster, Michael Pick, www.flickr.com; 111 (tr), Bread (Loaf), AbsolutVision Stock Photo; 113 (br), Siren, KAZ Vorpal, www.flickr.com; 115 (br), Abbr Examples, Donovan Graen/SIM; 119 (r), Grand Canyon, Paul

Fundenburg, www.flickr.com; 120 (b), Fire, AbsolutVision Stock Photo; 121 (l), Football Player, AbsolutVision Stock Photo; 122 (b), Football, Ron Almog, www.flickr.com; 129 (b), Ant 4, Mick Talbot, www.flickr.com; 129 (b), Ant, Mick Talbot, www.flickr.com; 129 (r), Ant 2, Mick Talbot, www.flickr.com; 129 (r), Ant 3, Mick Talbot, www.flickr.com; 129 (br), Chocolate Donut, AbsolutVision Stock Photo; 131 (c), Subway Train, AbsolutVision Stock Photo; 134 (b), Flower Field, Tony Hisgett, www.flickr.com; 142 (b), Chickens Eating Corn, Jo Naylor, www.flickr.com; 142 (b), Ear of Corn, AbsolutVision Stock Photo; 142 (bl), Sun, AbsolutVision Stock Photo; 142 (br), Chicken Dish, Elvert Barnes, www.flickr.com

Chapter 4: 148 (br), Light Bulb, AbsolutVision Stock Photo; 155 (b), Bookworm, AbsolutVision Stock Photo; 156 (c), Suitcases, AbsolutVision Stock Photo; 164 (bl), Basketball, AbsolutVision Stock Photo; 165 (bl), Airplane-P52, AbsolutVision Stock Photo; 165 (br), Sunflower, Dwight Sipler, www.flickr.com; 166 (bl), Worker (Busy Beaver), AbsolutVision Stock Photo, (modified) Donovan Graen/SIM; 167 (b), Football, AbsolutVision Stock Photo; 167 (r), Peyton's Heart, Donovan Graen/SIM; 168 (c), Guarded Mountain Town, AbsolutVision Stock Photo, (modified) Donovan Graen/SIM; 172 (br), Sea Shells, AbsolutVision Stock Photo; 173 (b), Beach Scene, AbsolutVision Stock Photo; 182 (br), hand writing report, Ron Chapple Stock/ThinkStock; 184 (br), Dog "Bobby", AbsolutVision Stock Photo; 187 (b), Dog "Bobby", Absolut Vision Stock Photo

Chapter 5: 212 (b), Asian Dragon & Phoenix, AbsolutVision Stock Photo; 212 (bl), Asian Lady Eating Noodles, AbsolutVision Stock Photo; 212 (br), Meal (Asian), AbsolutVision Stock Photo; 219 (b), Pumpkin Patch, Kam Abbott, www.flickr.com; 223 (b), Kitten with Toy, William Warby, www.flickr.com; 228 (tr), Dog Pack, Carterse, www.flickr.com; 230 (br), Heart of Courage, Donovan Graen/SIM; 231 (b), Tomato (macro), Ajith Kumar, www.flickr.com; 231 (r), Tomatoes, AbsolutVision Stock Photo; 232 (b), Dolphins, Daniel H. Parks, www.flickr.com; 237 (c), Gorilla, Sam Pullara, www.flickr.com; 242 (b), Hippos, Geoff Gallice, www.flickr.com; 242 (tr), Hippopotamus, AbsolutVision Stock Photo; 247 (r), Stack of Books, AbsolutVision Stock Photo

Chapter 6: 256 (c), Frost Gum pack, Donovan Graen/SIM; 257 (b), Frost Gum logo, Donovan Graen/SIM; 257 (l), Skier Skiing, AbsolutVision Stock Photo; 257 (r), Skier (adolescent), Absolut Vision Stock Photo; 257 (r), Skiing Medal, AbsolutVision Stock Photo; 271 (br), Man Devouring Sandwich, AbsolutVision Stock Photo

Chapter 7: 289 (c), Man Listening, AbsolutVision Stock Photo; 289 (r), Lady Kneeling, AbsolutVision Stock Photo; 290 (r), Kids in Park, Zherun, www.flickr.com; 292 (b), Speed Boat, Tony Hisgett, www.flickr.com; 295 (r), Cowboy Boots, cuttlefish, www.flickr.com; 296 (b), Shelves of Boots, Lin Pernille Photography; 303 (b), Dolphins, Ryan Mcdonald, www.flickr.com; 306 (br), Bug-Eyed Nikki, Donovan Graen/SIM; 306 (cr), Spider, Keith Kissel, www.flickr.com; 309 (br), Children Swimming, AbsolutVision Stock Photo; 311 (br), Thomas Edison, Library of Congress; 311 (r), Edisions Patent of Light Bulb, National Archives; 313 (c), Cornucopia 09, Art Explosion/Nova Development Corporation; 328 (tr), First Thanksgiving, Art Explosion/Nova Development Corporation; 330 (r), Tarantula, Dallas Krentzel, www.flickr.com

Chapter 8: 352 (bl), Puppies Nudging Door, Matt Webb Zahn, www.flickr.com; 353 (br), Man's Comical Walk, AbsolutVision Stock Photo

Chapter 9: 361 (br), Jogger on Track, AbsolutVision Stock Photo; 363 (c), Dog Sleeping on Couch, Mazaletel, www.flickr.com; 364 (r), House, AbsolutVision Stock Photo; 368 (b), Lil Girl using Laptop, AbsolutVision Stock Photo; 372 (b), Toni with Flat Tire; 373 (bl), Elf, Donovan Graen/SIM; 389 (r), Rodin's Thinker,

Vladimir Liverts/ThinkStock; 395 (b), Caveman Valentine, (modified) Donovan Graen/SIM, Art Explosion/Nova Development Corporation; 401 (br), Woman with Glasses, AbsolutVision Stock Photo; 401 (c), Eye Chart, AbsolutVision Stock Photo; 405 (r), Comet (Unspecified), NASA; 406 (bl), Edmund Halley, WikiMedia; 406 (br), Halley's Comet, NASA; 408 (br), Goldfish, Jason Clapp, www.flickr.com; 409 (br), Orange-Eye Bkgrnd, AbsolutVision Stock Photo; 409 (b), Coral, AbsolutVision Stock Photo

Chapter 10: 424 (b), HD Television, AbsolutVision Stock Photo; 427 (cr), Robosauras Rex, (modified) Donovan Graen/SIM, Art Explosion/Nova Development Corporation; 429 (bl), Girl Glaring, AbsolutVision Stock Photo; 429 (br), Boy Sticking Tongue Out, AbsolutVision Stock Photo

Chapter 11: 436 (bl), Interjection Parrot, Donovan Graen/SIM; 439 (r), Gecko, Donovan Graen/SIM; 442 (bl), Cat Toy, Ross Berteig, www.flickr.com; 442 (br), Kitten, AbsolutVision Stock Photo; 466 (tr), Toddler Bear, AbsolutVision Stock Photo; 470 (bl), Rhonda Running, Donovan Graen/SIM; 471 (br), Bus Backside, Donovan Graen/SIM; 472 (tr), Little Miss Muffet & Spider

Chapter 12: 473 (b), Girl with Hands Held Up Deciding, Zoonar RF ThinkStock; 474 (r), Old Woman Baking Cake, Thomas Lammeyer ThinkStock; 478 (tr), Bald Eagle Flying, ThinkStock; 487 (b), Cat Pawing at Dog, ThinkStock; 487 (b), Long Grass Border, ThinkStock; 491 (b) Group of Excited Kids, iStockphoto; 494 (c), Person Diving Into Pool, ThinkStock; 495 (br), Toothbrush with Toothpaste, ThinkStock; 504 (b), Woman Painting Wall, Think Stock; 508 (br), Man Freezing, ThinkStock; 518 (b), Band Silhouette, ThinkStock; 521 (r), Steak on a Fork, ThinkStock; 522 (b), Ship Storm, ThinkStock; 529 (br), Small Dog Barking, Eric Issel/ThinkStock; 534 (br), Diamond Ring, Norman Chan/Think Stock; 537 (b), House, ThinkStock

Chapter 13: 545 (br), Abstract Background, AbsolutVision Stock Photo; 545 (br), Scared Woman with Popcorn, Ariwasabi/Think Stock; 548 (bl), Boys Whispering, iStockphoto; 555 (bl) Ladder with Dummy Climbing, Hemera; 563 (b), Sports Equipment, iStockphoto; 571 (b), Team with Trophy, ThinkStock

Chapter 14: 578 (br), Girl Eating Cookie, Comstock Images/Think Stock; 580 (bl), Girl Looking At Puppy, Getty Images/iStockphoto/ ThinkStock; 581 (br), Blueberry Pie, JeffreyW, www.flickr.com; 582 (br), White Horse Rampant, Maria Itina/ThinkStock; 585 (bc), Wild Horses, Jeanne Hatch/ThinkStock; 589 (br), Toolbox of Tools, Maksym Yemelynov/ThinkStock; 592 (bc). Skydiver, Joggie Botma/ ThinkStock; 593 (c) Boy and Father in Field, Margaryta Vakhterova/ThinkStock; 603 (b) Hot Dogs, Mike Flippo/Think Stock; 606 (b) Pug Puppy Sleeping with Alarm Clock, Vitaly Titov/ ThinkStock; 609 (bc) Identical Twins, Getty Images/ThinkStock; 610 (b) Under Water, Nastco/ThinkStock; 610 (bl) Single Goldfish, Stockbyte/ThinkStock; 610 (br) Goldfish School, Eric Isselee/ ThinkStock; 611 (br), Donkey Front, Eric Isselee/ThinkStock; 616 (tr), Butterfly, Green, AbsolutVision Stock Photo; 616 (cr), Moth, AbsolutVision Stock Photo; 617 (b), School Buses, Anton Novikov/ ThinkStock; 622 (br) Baby Orangutan, Eric Isselee/ThinkStock; 624 (BR) Girl Reading Book, Svetlana Ivanova/ThinkStock

Chapter 15: 635 (br), Firefighter, Photodisc/ThinkStock; 638 (bl), Roses Corner, Anna Khomulo/ThinkStock; 639 (br), Big Ben, stockbyte/ThinkStock; 642 (br), Little Boy Kicking Soccer Ball, Jacek Chabraszewski/ThinkStock; 648 (bl), Detective Following Footprints, Uros Petrovic/ThinkStock; 649 (br), Thief with Flashlight, Milan Vasicek/ThinkStock; 652 (cr), Horse Drawing, Andreas Meyer/ThinkStock; 658 (b), Grand Canyon, Medioimages Photodisc/ThinkStock; 669 (bl), Public Bus, Craig Jewell/Think Stock; 671 (b), Kid Looking at Homework, Catalin Petolea/Think Stock; 676 (b), Boy Pulling Dog in Wagon, Photodisc/ThinkStock

Chapter 16: 681 (r), Flamingo, Eric Issel/ThinkStock; 682 (cr), Blueberries, Morninegarage/ThinkStock; 686 (b), Rose Bush, Yury Kisialiou/ThinkStock; 693 (br), Girl Eating Huge Sandwich, iStockphoto; 697 (br), Trees in Winter at Park, Mister Twister/ThinkStock; 699 (b), Shopping in Supermarket (illustration), Dorling Kindersley/ThinkStock; 700 (b), Businesspeople, Photodisc/ThinkStock; 707 (br), Trojan Horse Drawing, Think Stock; 708 (br), Lake Shack, Bernhard Richter/ThinkStock; 713 (cr), Guy with Big Head, Photodisc/ThinkStock; 713 (tr), Rainbow Trout, Alexander Raths/ThinkStock; 714 (br), Dog with Popcorn and Drink, Damedeeso/ThinkStock; 719 (br), Little Girl in Toy Car, ThinkStock; 721 (c), Boxing Ring, Alexander Shirokov/Think Stock; 721 (cl), Gold Ring, Zentilia/ThinkStock; 721 (cr), Old Red School Phone, Simon Ingate/ThinkStock; 722 (b), Books on Shelf, Joanne Ingate/ThinkStock; 726 (b), Boy Writing on Paper, Wavebreakmedia Ltd/ThinkStock

Chapter 17: 740 (b), 2 Cats 2 Dogs, Eric Issel/ThinkStock; 749 (c), Sundial, Dorling Kindersley/ThinkStock; 750 (bl) School Supplies Border, Jennifer Barrow/ThinkStock

Chapter 18: 757 (tr), Scroll and Quill, Alexeyzet/ThinkStock; 758 (c), Child Writing (illustration), Davi Sales Batista/ThinkStock; 763 (r), Rock Climber, Greg Epperson/ThinkStock; 767 (b), Orchestra Conductor, James Steidl/ThinkStock; 771 (tr), Toolbox, ThinkStock; 776 (bl), Orange, Red Apple, Green Apple, Angelo Angeles/ThinkStock; 777 (b), Apple/Orange Scales, Raymond Gregory/ThinkStock; 778 (bc), Rubber Duckies in a Circle, Amanda Rohde/ThinkStock; 780 (br), Vanilla Chocolate Ice Cream Cones, Thomas Perkins/ThinkStock

Chapter 19: 791 (br), Eastern Glass Lizard, Nicolas Ray, Wikipedia Commons; 791 (c), Lizard Silhouettes, ThinkStock; 791 (cl), Animal Silhouettes, ThinkStock; 791 (b), Reptile Silhouettes, ThinkStock; 793 (c), Glass Lizard, VinceFL, www.flickr.com; 800 (b), Colored Index Cards, Victoria Short/ThinkStock; 802 (bl), Glass Lizard, vinceFL, www.flickr.com; 811 (c), Glass Lizard, BSC Photography, www.flickr.com; 812–813 (b), Pencil Background, Karen Roach/ThinkStock; 818 (b), Glass Lizard, Hunter Desportes, www.flickr.com; 821 (c), Glass Lizard, Ryan Somma, www.flickr.com; 828 (b), Girl on Computer (Thumbs Up), Jacek Chabraszewski/ThinkStock; 833 (b), Group of Young Adults (Thumbs Up), Andreas Rodriguez/ThinkStock

Chapter 20: 836 (b), Children Writing, Jupiter Images/ThinkStock

Study Skills Section: U2 (tr), Quigley–Formal Bow, Donovan Graen/SIM; U4 (br), Getting Organized-L3, Donovan Graen/SIM; U12 (tr), Apple, AbsolutVision; U14 (b), Calendar, Andreanna Moya; U15 (tr), Key-Antique, AbsolutVision; U16 (bl), Girl Holding Folders, Sergiy Bykhunenko/ThinkStock; U16 (tl), Alarm Clock, AbsolutVision; U17 (bl), Do Your Homework, Donovan Graen/SIM; U17 (tr), House Puzzle, AbsolutVision

Letter Writing Section: U22 (cr), Pen, AbsolutVision; U23 (br), Quigley Stamp, Donovan Graen/SIM; U25 (br), Mailbox, Absolut Vision; U26 (bl) Thank-You Card Background 1, Donovan Graen/SIM; U26 (br), Thank-You Card Background 2, Donovan Graen/SIM; U33 (bl), Pen, AbsolutVision; U35 (b), Man Writing Business Letter, HansKim/ThinkStock; U40 (bl), Statue of Liberty, Donovan Graen/SIM; U41 (br), horse running, Kseniya Abramova/Think Stock; U45 (bl), music box, Ryan McVay/ThinkStock

Poetry Section: U49 (cr), Scroll and Quill, Alexeyzet/ThinkStock; U50–U51, Tree on Hill Background, iStockphoto/ThinkStock; U53 (b), Ink Splatters, AbsolutVision; U58–U59, Leaves Blowing, iStockphoto/ThinkStock; U59 (c), Cat Relaxing, Stockbyte/Think Stock; U60 (bl), Ink Pen, AbsolutVision; U60–U61, Poetry Background, AbsolutVision; U63 (cr), Photo of Robert Louis Stevenson (Wikipedia,org); U65 (b), Rainbow Spots, Hemera/Think Stock; U67 (tr), Granny Baking Cookies, Photodisc/ThinkStock

Analyzing Literature Section: U70 (b), Fox and Hen, digital vision/ThinkStock; U70, Green Pasture Background, Olaf Bender/Think Stock; U71 (br), Fox Standing, Eric Issel/ThinkStock; U71 (br), Kettle Over Fire, Yuriy Chaban/ThinkStock; U74 (bl), Dragon cartoon illustration, Yael Weiss/ThinkStock; U77 (bl), Red Hen, istockphoto/ThinkStock; U80 (br), Cyclops, dedMazay/Think Stock; U83, Swan on Lake Background, Design Pics/ThinkStock; U85 (br), Asian Girl with Magnifying Glass, Sze Fei Wong/Think Stock

Analyzing Informational Text Section: U89 (br), Smart Kid Reading, Leah-Anne Thompson/ThinkStock; U90 (br), Puzzle Pieces, ssstep/ThinkStock; U91 (bc), Brain with Gears, Volodymyr Grinko/ThinkStock; U93 (br), book stack, koya79/ThinkStock; with Gears, Volodymyr Grinko/ThinkStock

Folktales Section: U96 (br), Lady Eating Sub Sandwich, iStockphoto/ThinkStock; U97 (br), Parakeets, Khmel/ThinkStock; U97 (cl), Girls Jumping, Photodisc/ThinkStock; U97 (tr), Chicken Counter, John Takai/ThinkStock; U100 (br), Coonskin Cap, iStockphoto; U101 (b), Paul Bunyan Illustration, liquidlibrary/ThinkStock; U102 (r), Zeus Statue, Hemera/ThinkStock; U103 (bc), Lion, iStockphoto/ThhinkStock; U103 (br), Mouse, iStockphoto/ThinkStock; U104 (br), Three Little Pigs, Anton Brand/ThinkStock

Drama Section: U108 (b), Poetry Background, AbsolutVision; U110 (cr), Comedy & Tragedy Masks, Art Explosion/Nova Development Corporation; U113 (b), Bugs, Suomuurain/Think Stock

Jingles Section: Q2 (tl), Quigley (Thumbs Down), Donovan Graen/SIM; Q2 (br), Quigley (Thumbs Up), Donovan Graen/SIM

Resource Tools Section: Q35 (br), Submarine, Kevin King; Q38 (tr), Quigley Interviewing Doctor, illustration, Donovan Graen/SIM; Q39 (br), Film Strip and Clapper Board, illustration, Donovan Graen/SIM; Q46 (br), Reference Books, illustration, Donovan Graen/SIM; Q47 (b), Library, Samantha Marx; Q49 (b), Thai Cat, ThinkStock; Q51–Q2, Maps, Charts, and Graphs, (data) Dr. Robert Wilson, (illustrations) Donovan Graen/SIM

Writing Process Section: Q24 (bc), Pencils, AbsolutVision Stock Photo; Q28 (bc), Pencil, Q29 (br), Boy with Thumbs Up, Absolut Vision Stock Photo; Q29 (tl), Hand with Mic, AbsolutVision Stock Photo; Q29 (br), Hands Clapping, AbsolutVision Stock Photo

Authors

Brenda Shurley, Author
Ruth Wetsell, Author
David Lutz, Coauthor
Ashley Shackleford, Coauthor

Administration

Brenda Shurley
Billy Shurley, Jr.
Kim Shurley
Keith Covington
Teresa Reid
Jani Turkia

Consulting and Editing

Dr. MaryJo Thomas
Jamie Geneva
Ardean Coffman

Jamie Causey, Kimberly Crady, Cindy Goeden, Scott Keathley,
Cassie Kemp-Speaks, JoAnn Lafferty, Leah Lockwood,
Teressa Logan, Jill Meyer, Teresa Reid, Carolann Scott,
Andrea Turkia, Dana Wilcox, Carolyn Winkler

Graphics

Donovan Graen
Jeremy Reagan
Byron Taylor

Technology

Jani Turkia
Markus Turkia
Duke Boyne
Ted Siems
Jerry Coffman

Audio

Jamie Geneva
David Lutz

Memoriam

In loving memory of our dear Leah Lockwood: beloved wife,
mother, friend, and co-worker.
Leah was a ray of sunshine around everyone she met. Her
dedication, sweet nature, and willingness to help others will
always be an inspiration to all of us. Sweet memories cling to
her name as she is remembered by each and every one of us.

"What you leave behind is not
 what is engraved in stone monuments,
 but what is woven into the lives of others."
         – Pericles

"It is not length of life,
 but depth of life."
         – Ralph Waldo Emerson